Advances in Intergroup Con

D1757465

Intergroup contact remains one of the most effective means to reduce prejudice and conflict between groups. The past decade has witnessed a dramatic resurgence of interest in this time-tested phenomenon, with researchers now focusing on understanding when, why, and for whom contact does (and does not) work.

This new volume focuses on one of the hottest topics in the social sciences: prejudice. Covering not only basic principles but cutting-edge findings and theoretical directions, key questions surrounding this subject are addressed, such as:

- how perceptions of other groups lead to anxiety and avoidance;
- how cross-group contact influences the development of prejudice in children;
- whether highly-prejudiced people benefit from contact;
- how status and power influence the effectiveness of contact.

In addition to exploring methodological challenges facing contact researchers, attention is devoted to prejudice interventions that are rooted in our understanding of contact effects. These range from zero-acquaintance contact to intimate cross-group friendships, and even involve simulated contact experiences.

This volume draws together world-renowned experts in prejudice and intergroup contact to provide a long-awaited update on the state of affairs in intergroup contact research. As well as synthesizing and integrating the key topics, it also provides possible new directions for future research. Given the prominence of contact as a powerful prejudice-reduction tool, this book is a must-read for students and scholars of social psychology and sociology, as well as policy-makers and practitioners.

Gordon Hodson is Professor of Psychology at Brock University (Canada), where he is Director of the Brock Lab of Intergroup Relations (BLIP). He is currently an Associate Editor at the *Journal of Experimental Social Psychology*. His research interests involve prejudice and discrimination, with an emphasis on individual differences (e.g. ideology), emotions (e.g., disgust, empathy), and intergroup contact.

Miles Hewstone is Professor of Social Psychology and a Fellow of New College, Oxford University (UK). He has written two books and edited over twenty volumes, publishing on attribution theory, social cognition, stereotyping, and intergroup relations. He is the recipient of numerous awards, and has been elected to the British Academy (National Academy for Arts and Social Sciences).

Advances in Intergroup Contact

Edited by
Gordon Hodson and Miles Hewstone

Ψ Psychology Press
Taylor & Francis Group
LONDON AND NEW YORK

First published 2013
by Psychology Press
27 Church Road, Hove, East Sussex BN3 2FA

Simultaneously published in the USA and Canada
by Psychology Press
711 Third Avenue, New York, NY 10017

Psychology Press is an imprint of the Taylor & Francis Group, an informa business

British Library Cataloguing in Publication Data
A catalogue record for this book is available from the British Library

Library of Congress Cataloging-in-Publication Data
A catalog record has been requested for this book

ISBN13: 978–1–84872–054–1 (hbk)
ISBN13: 978–1–84872–114–2 (pbk)
ISBN13: 978–0–20309–546–1 (ebk)

Typeset in Times New Roman
by Swales & Willis Ltd, Exeter, Devon

Printed and bound by CPI Group (UK) Ltd, Croydon, CR0 4YY

To Myrtle, for your love and compassion, and to Holly, for your boundless patience and support. (GH)

To the memory of Ed Cairns (1945–2012), a wonderful research colleague who opened the doors of Northern Ireland to me. (MH)

Finally, to the memory of Brian Mullen (1955–2006), a truly unique scholar, mentor, and friend. (GH & MH)

Contents

Illustrations

Figures

Tables

x *Illustrations*

Contributors

Frances Aboud (McGill University). Department of Psychology McGill University 1205 Dr Penfield Avenue Montreal, QC Canada H3A 1B1.

Ananthi Al Ramiah (Yale–NUS College) University Hall, Lee Kong Chian Wing, UHL # 03–01, 21 Lower Kent Ridge Road, Singapore 119077.

Arthur Aron (Stony Brook University). Department of Psychology, Stony Brook University, Stony Brook, NY 11794–2500, United States.

Oliver Christ (University of Marburg). Department of Psychology, Section for Psychological Methods, University of Marburg, Gutenbergstraße 18, 35032 Marburg, Germany.

Joseph Comeau (Simon Fraser University). Department of Psychology, Simon Fraser University, 8888 University Drive, Burnaby, BC V5A 1S6, Canada

Kimberly Costello (Brock University). Department of Psychology, Brock University, St. Catharines, Ontario, Canada L2S 3A1.

Richard Crisp (University of Kent). Centre for the Study of Group Processes, University of Kent, School of Psychology, University of Kent, Canterbury, CT2 7NP, United Kingdom.

Kristin Davies (York College of The City University of New York). Department of Behavioral Sciences, York College of The City University of New York, 94–20 Guy R. Brewer Boulevard, Jamaica, NY 11451, United States.

John Dovidio (Yale University). Department of Psychology, Yale University, Box 208205 New Haven, CT 06520–8205, United States.

Diala Hawi (University of Massachusetts Amherst). Department of Psychology University of Massachusetts Amherst, Tobin Hall, 135 Hicks Way, Amherst, MA 01003, United States.

Miles Hewstone (University of Oxford). Department of Experimental Psychology, University of Oxford, South Parks Road, Oxford, OX1 3UD, United Kingdom.

Gordon Hodson (Brock University). Department of Psychology, Brock University, St. Catharines, Ontario, Canada L2S 3A1.

Simon Lolliot (University of Oxford). Department of Experimental Psychology, University of Oxford, South Parks Road, Oxford, OX1 3UD, United Kingdom.

Cara MacInnis (Brock University). Department of Psychology, Brock University, St. Catharines, Ontario, Canada L2S 3A1.

Tamar Saguy (Yale University). Department of Psychology, Yale University, Box 208205 New Haven, CT 06520–8205, United States.

Katharina Schmid (University of Oxford). Department of Experimental Psychology, University of Oxford, South Parks Road, Oxford, OX1 3UD, United Kingdom.

Christia Spears Brown (University of Kentucky). Department of Psychology 207-E Kastle Hall University of Kentucky Lexington, KY 40506–0044.

Hermann Swart (Stellenbosch University). Department of Psychology, Stellenbosch University, Private Bag X1, Matieland, 7602, South Africa.

Nicole Tausch (University of St. Andrews). University of St. Andrews (School of Psychology). St Mary's Quad, South Street, St Andrews, KY16 9JP, Scotland.

Linda Tropp (University of Massachusetts Amherst). Department of Psychology University of Massachusetts Amherst, Tobin Hall, 135 Hicks Way, Amherst, MA 01003, United States.

Rhiannon Turner (University of Leeds). Institute for Psychological Sciences, University of Leeds University of Leeds, Leeds, LS2 9JT, United Kingdom.

Ulrich Wagner (University of Marburg). Department of Psychology, Section for Psychological Methods, University of Marburg, Gutenbergstraße 18, 35032 Marburg, Germany.

Tessa West (New York University). New York University 6 Washington Place New York, NY 10003, United States.

Stephen Wright (Simon Fraser University). Department of Psychology, Simon Fraser University, 8888 University Drive, Burnaby, BC V5A 1S6, Canada.

Jacquie Vorauer (University of Manitoba). Department of Psychology, P431 Duff Roblin Building, University of Manitoba, Winnipeg, MB, Canada R3T 2N2.

Preface

The seed for this project, like many good ideas, took root over a cup of tea in the Senior Common Room of New College, Oxford. We found ourselves deeply engrossed in a conversation concerning the staggering advances made in intergroup contact research in recent years. But we also lamented the fact that an up-to-date account of these advances had not been published since Hewstone and Brown's edited volume in 1986, the last attempt to bring together a group of international contact experts. We found ourselves wishing that someone would pull together such a volume, only to realize that we were well-positioned (and strongly motivated) to do so ourselves. In some ways, however, we approached this project from different trajectories. The relative neophyte (GH) to the contact field came with a strong grounding in research on personality and ideology, whereas the more established partner (MH) had evolved more directly from the social identity and self-categorization perspectives. Whereas some consider these theoretical emphases diametrically opposed, we immediately recognized the fruit to be borne from merging our interests and passions.

Whereas the Hewstone-Brown volume in 1986 primarily sought to emphasize the many different contexts in which ideas concerning intergroup contact were relevant and had been investigated (e.g., Israel, Northern Ireland, or South Africa), the goal of the present volume is to highlight the theoretical and empirical ferment that characterizes this field today. We approached a broad range of scholars within the discipline of psychology, representing different theoretical perspectives, but all at the cutting edge of the new wave of contact research. We were fortunate enough to reach this goal (and then some). The work you will find in these pages truly represents, in our opinion, an up-to-the date synthesis of our understanding of the so-called "Contact Hypothesis" (undeniably now promoted to the rank of "theory"). Framed by introductory and conclusion chapters by the editors, each chapter presents a unique vantage point. But the themes addressed interlink across chapters; consequently, we sought to highlight these themes in the final chapter in the volume. These ten themes represent some of the key issues that are being studied in the field today, and that will likely remain a focus for some years to come: mediators of contact (intergroup anxiety, threat, empathy and perspective taking); norms surrounding contact; the efficacy of cross-group friendships; the role of group status; processes of attitude generalization; individual differences as predictors and moderators of contact effects; advances in methodology and statistics that have opened up yet more possibilities for future research in this fascinating field; and alternatives to direct contact. Last but not least, the editors of this volume are well aware that contact is not a panacea for prejudice or intergroup conflict, but it is beyond all doubt a demonstrably effective means of improving intergroup relations.

In our minds, such a volume could not have come at a more pressing or critical time in human history. As we argue in the introductory and epilogue chapters, the world is experiencing levels of immigration and intergroup contact at levels never before witnessed (or dreamed possible). Our day-to-day lives and economies are tightly interwoven, for better or for worse, in ways that stress old alliances and forge new ones. As we close out the first decade of the new millennium, we are faced with tremendous challenges that will undoubtedly affect us all as a species, ranging from the collapse of the global economy (and economic alliances, such as the EU), to the collapse of our biosphere and irreversible climate change (and its ensuing "climate refugees"). Never before has intergroup contact been so relevant, not only in terms of understanding our current world, but also in shaping our collective future.

Unfortunately, this urgent need to understand and explain intergroup contact experiences has knocked at the door at the same time that major research funding agencies in countries such as the US, UK, and Canada are implementing deep cuts to the funding of *basic* social science research (in favor of industry-relevant research, much of which ironically feeds the insatiable appetite for consumer-products that contribute to many of our present challenges). One of our explicit goals, therefore, is to provide educators, governments, and policy-makers with a volume that addresses the critical importance of intergroup contact in managing positive intergroup relations. As the work in this volume attests, intergroup contact plays a critical, even fundamental, role in generating attitudes toward other social groups and boosting the willingness to cooperate rather than fight.

Of course this book would not have been possible without the help of many people. First and foremost we would like to thank the contributors to the volume, without whom the project would have been literally impossible. Thanks also to Psychology Press, particularly Sharla Plant, who was both patient and helpful. Gordon would like to thank Holly for her patience and support, and Mike Ashton, Carolyn Hafer, and Michael Busseri for their intellectual support and curiosity. Miles would like to thank Rachel New, for bringing her perennial organizational skills to this project. We are also extremely grateful to the Social Sciences and Humanities Research Council of Canada (Gordon Hodson, grant 410–2007–2133) and the Leverhulme Trust, UK (Miles Hewstone) for funding during the time at which we worked on this volume.

Reference

Hewstone, M., & Brown, R. J. (1986). (Eds.). *Contact and conflict in intergroup encounters*. Oxford, UK: Basil Blackwell.

Part I
Introduction

1   Introduction

Advances in intergroup contact

Gordon Hodson and Miles Hewstone

The notion that intergroup contact can improve intergroup relations is a deceptively simple idea with strong intuitive appeal. Indeed, this basic notion became a fundamental cornerstone of twentieth-century policymaking, at least in principle, as the world's economies and interests became increasingly intertwined and co-dependent. Explicit contact goals are now formally enshrined in our most important international agreements. For instance, in the wake of World War II the newly-formed UNESCO constitution famously declared that:

> since wars begin in the minds of men, it is in the minds of men that the defences of peace must be constructed; that ignorance of each other's ways and lives has been a common cause, throughout the history of mankind, of that suspicion and mistrust between peoples of the world through which their differences have all too often broken into war.
>
> (Besterman, 1951, p. 113)

This assertion firmly entrenched the importance of *psychology* in building and maintaining peace between nations, emphasizing ignorance and anxiety as root causes of intergroup conflict. Perhaps less widely-known, however, is UNESCO's assertion that the success of strategies for sustained peace would hinge on psychological solutions centering on intergroup contact. That is, peace would not be possible through formalized structural negotiations between nation states alone, but rather would depend on "the intellectual and moral solidarity of mankind," making appeals to both reason and social harmony. With this in mind, states that were signatories to UNESCO formally recognized the importance of education, not only in terms of science and ideas, but *of each other*. To this end, the Constitution stipulated that member states:

> are agreed and determined to develop and increase the means of communication between their peoples and to employ these means for the purposes of mutual understanding and a truer and more perfect knowledge of each other's lives.
>
> (Besterman, 1951, p. 114)

What lies at the heart of this international agreement, born from the ashes of an unprecedented global conflict, is the recognized need for groups to experience *contact and communication* with one another to establish mutual appreciation and ease intergroup tension. Consistent with these propositions, we recognize that intergroup contact is at its core a psychological process, the symbolic assembly and union of representatives from different social groups. Being inherently psychological, positive contact experiences between individual members of different groups, either direct or indirect (i.e., via friends or media), carry the promise of *generalizing* outcomes to the group-level. In other words, positive contact between group representatives exerts profound influence at higher levels of abstraction and categorization, influencing attitudes toward the *groups* to which the encounter participants belong.

But we are not solely concerned with contact between nations. Indeed, this same post-war period also bore witness to remarkable social changes *within* societies, such as the end of apartheid in South Africa, educational and military desegregation between races in America, and relative peace in Northern Ireland after 40 years of The Troubles. Many of these (largely) resolved conflicts were the direct result of formalized and often legally enforced imperatives for increased contact, directly rooted in empirically-based recommendations by empiricists (see Cook, 1957). Although well-intentioned, these policies were not, however, generally implemented in ways that maximized the benefits of contact (see Cook, 1979; Stephan, 2008). Rather, the historical and empirical record makes clear that contact does not universally improve relations, but can also exacerbate problems and intensify strife. The simple premise that contact improves intergroup attitudes is therefore not as straightforward as it would at first appear. Put simply, contact is no panacea for prejudice (see Hewstone, 2003).

For this reason the empirical scientific evidence has become crucial in understanding whether and how contact works, in addition to mapping out its boundary conditions. Fortunately, this literature is now rather sizeable. Relative to other topics on intergroup relations, interest in contact peaked in the 1950s and 1960s before evidencing decreased share in the market-place of ideas (i.e., psychology journals) through the 1970s to 1990s (Brown & Hewstone, 2005). The last edited volume on this topic, drawing together international scholars to reflect on the contact literature, is now 25 years old (see Hewstone & Brown, 1986a). Since that time an undeniably large body of research has accrued that speaks to the benefits of intergroup contact, advancing the field not only theoretically but also in terms of methodology and application. In recent years, intergroup contact has recaptured the passions of psychologists at a truly impressive rate. As of December 2011, literature searches for the terms "intergroup contact" or the "contact hypothesis" as keywords in psychology journals revealed over 675 papers, with two-thirds of these papers published since 2000 (see publication trends in Figure 1.1). As is evident from these trends, intergroup contact is a rapidly expanding field. The present volume brings together leading researchers in the field to provide a much-needed update on the latest psychological advances in understanding contact as a prejudice-reduction strategy. Before turning to these recent advances, however,

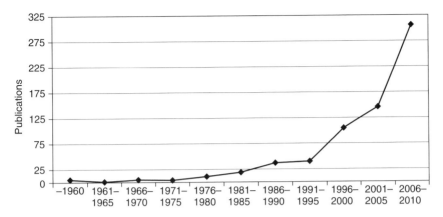

Figure 1.1 Psychology publications with "intergroup contact" or "contact hypothesis" as keywords

we first outline the fundamental ideas outlined in what theorists originally termed the "Contact Hypothesis."

Intergroup contact theory

Serious interest in the empirical study of the effects of contact on outgroup attitudes began to take root in the 1940s through the early 1960s. Early work by sociologist Robin Williams (1947, 1964) and social psychologist Stuart Cook (1957) was well-established at the time, but arguably the most influential voice came from social psychologist Gordon Allport's (1954) seminal book *The Nature of Prejudice*, in which he devoted an entire chapter to contact. Analysis and synthesis of this body of work has been covered in depth elsewhere (see Amir, 1969; Brown & Hewstone, 2005; Hewstone & Brown, 1986b; Kenworthy, Turner, Hewstone, & Voci, 2005; Pettigrew, 1998; Pettigrew & Tropp, 2005, 2006, 2011) and does not represent the goal of the present volume. From the start, Allport's stated reservations about the ability of contact to reduce prejudice (see Hodson, Costello, & MacInnis, this volume) led him to propose four key conditions required to improve the likelihood of positive contact outcomes. These "optimal conditions," as they have come to be known, emphasize primarily the structural features of the contact setting.

First, contact is optimized when it involves members of different groups who have relatively *equal status* in terms of power, influence, or social prestige in the contact context. This condition is, of course, difficult to satisfy, and groups of equal status can themselves become competitive in order to serve needs for distinct identities (e.g., Tajfel & Turner, 1979). Even the future prospect of equal group status can be perceived as threatening in contact settings (see Saguy, Tropp, & Hawi, this volume). Low-status Whites, for instance, may reject racial integration with low-status Blacks in the interest of maintaining a relatively more dominant position in the overall social hierarchy (Cook, 1957). Second, groups are encouraged to pursue *common or shared goals*. According to Allport (1954), "Only the type of contact that leads people to *do* things together is likely to result in changed attitudes" [italics in original] (p. 276). To illustrate this point, Allport suggested that athletic teams comprised of members from different racial groups should work toward a common goal (i.e., winning a game) that has nothing to do with race per se. He also reviewed research showing lower prejudice toward Blacks among Whites serving in mixed-race military units. Contemporary research confirms this intergroup contact effect among US soldiers recently serving in Afghanistan and Iraq: heterosexual military personnel who formed bonds with homosexual squadmates were particularly likely to oppose the ban on open homosexuality in the military (Moradi & Miller, 2010). Third, *cooperation* (vs. competition) between groups is considered ideal. (Although groups can have divergent or distinct goals that *can* be mutually satisfied via cooperation, common goals and cooperation are generally correlated positively, with the benefits of contact most fully realized when these factors are congruent with one another – the pursuit of common goals through intergroup cooperation.) Fourth, *socialized* or *institutionalized support* for positive intergroup relations is posited to enhance both the likelihood of contact and the potential for positive outcomes. Institutional support can range from informal or implied social norms in support of contact to rules that are explicitly sanctioned or enforced by authorities to promote intergroup engagement.

Over time, researchers understandably elaborated the optimal conditions for contact. Somewhat ironically, this led to a decreased interest in the theory as the number of preferential pre-conditions became unmanageable and increasingly difficult to satisfy (Pettigrew, 1986; Stephan, 1987). Fortunately, interest in the theory surged again by the late 1990s and early 2000s (see Figure 1.1). Undoubtedly a key factor in this renewed enthusiasm was Pettigrew's (1998) very influential and highly-cited paper, in which he revised and reformulated the Contact Hypothesis, breathing new life into the idea of contact as a means to reduce prejudice. In his analysis Pettigrew emphasized several factors of change induced by contact, including the opportunity to learn about the outgroup, and willingness to undertake a re-think of one's own group, its attributes, values, and so on (i.e., ingroup reappraisal).

Recent meta-analytic summaries confirm the proposition that ignorance is reduced via contact, but the knock-on effects on attitudes are quite small relative to mediating factors such as reduced anxiety (Pettigrew & Tropp, 2008). Although some research provides evidence of ingroup reappraisal following contact (e.g., Verkuyten, Thijs, & Bekhuis, 2010), Eller and Abrams (2004) found that ingroup reappraisal failed to materialize as an outcome in a longitudinal investigation. However, appraisals here were operationalized as ingroup identification and pride, yet ingroup appraisals can take other forms. Indeed, one of the benefits of cross-group friendships, especially indirect friendships through one's ingroup friends, concerns the promotion of positive ingroup contact norms (Wright, Aron, McLaughlin-Volpe, & Ropp, 1997; Pettigrew, Christ, Wagner, & Stellmacher,

2007; see Davies, Wright, Aron, & Comeau, this volume). Such norm development, we argue, can involve reappraisals of the ingroup. To the extent that this is the case, ingroup reappraisals do result from intergroup contact, in the form of positive contact norm development. Lolliot, Schmid, Hewstone, Ramiah, Tausch and Swart, this volume, discuss this issue, and propose a role for ingroup reappraisal in "secondary transfer" effects of contact, whereby contact with members of one group reduces prejudices toward members of another (unrelated) group.

In considering how contact works, Pettigrew (1998) particularly emphasized the importance of *affective ties* derived through contact. Meta-analyses again bear out these predictions, with increased empathy and decreased anxiety largely explaining contact effects on attitudes (see Pettigrew & Tropp, 2008) relative to cognitive factors (see Tropp & Pettigrew, 2005a; see also summary tables in Hodson, Hewstone, & Swart, this volume). Arguably, Pettigrew's reformulation re-kindled an earlier emphasis on affect, intimacy, and cross-group friendship through contact (see Cook, 1957). This should come as no surprise. After all, cross-group friendships optimally characterize desirable, positive, and intimate contact that occurs repeatedly through time and across situations. Through an emphasis on intimate contact and friendship, this reinterpretation of the Contact Hypothesis has reinvigorated interest in the potential of intergroup contact, and has generated impressive results (see meta-analysis by Davies, Tropp, Aron, Pettigrew, & Wright, 2011).

Finally, Pettigrew (1998) provided a theoretical model integrating several cognitive strategies known to improve intergroup relations. Specifically, he argued that initial contact is optimized when group representatives interact as individuals (through *decategorization*, de-emphasizing group memberships). However, once contact is established, salient group memberships are enhanced (through *salient identities*, or sometimes *dual-group identities*), with psychological union realized at the final step through shared social identity (*recategorization* as a common ingroup). Prior to this explicit theoretical synthesis these various theoretical camps appeared to be working at cross-purposes. However, by integrating these seemingly divergent psychological processes into a formalized contact model that incorporated a temporal component, Pettigrew's line of thinking provided fertile theoretical ground for researchers, linking these cognitive approaches not only to contact but also to each other. Although this reformulation has received solid support in one study (Eller & Abrams, 2004), further research is sorely needed, particularly studies that test all of the components specified in the full model.

After a half a century of research, the field is now well-positioned to examine the impact of intergroup contact on attitudes both in the laboratory and the world more globally. In a comprehensive meta-analytic study, integrating and statistically quantifying results from empirical research from over 500 studies, Pettigrew and Tropp (2006) provided a clear and convincing case for the benefits of contact on intergroup attitudes. Overall, increased contact predicted less prejudice toward the contact group. The effect size (mean $r = -.21$) was small-to-medium by conventional standards (e.g., Cohen, 1988) and very reliable ($p < .0001$). To practitioners outside of the social sciences, this effect might appear unimpressively small. However, this contact-attitude association represents an effect size that is actually very common in psychology, a discipline explaining processes that are often extraordinarily complex and multifaceted.

To put this finding in context, consider first an extensive meta-analysis covering 100 years of psychology research more generally, that reveals that many important and meaningful effects in personality (mean $r = .19$) or social psychology (mean $r = .22$) fall in this range (Richard, Bond, & Stokes-Zoota, 2003). As Al Ramiah and Hewstone (2011) have noted, the size of the contact meta-analytic effect is comparable to that for the relation between condom use and sexually-transmitted HIV (Weller, 1993), or between passive smoking and the incidence of lung cancer at work (Wells, 1998). More to the point, however, is the fact that even small effects can have large outcomes (see Rosenthal, 1990, on the small but very meaningful effects of aspirin on reducing heart attacks). The substantial impact of small effects is particularly evidenced in social systems, such as those that promote intergroup bias. For instance, even the smallest degree of intergroup bias (e.g., 1 percent), situated in the context of a complex social system, can result in substantial group-based discrimination that is both meaningful and self-perpetuating over time (Martell, Lane, & Emrich, 1996). In sum, the fact that contact reduces intergroup prejudice, and that this effect is of similar magnitude to many of the most important psychological effects and interventions isolated by psychologists over the past century, is a theoretically important and practically significant finding.

But the potential benefits of intergroup contact become even more promising when contact unfolds under optimal contact conditions: the positive effects of contact on attitudes are significantly enhanced (mean $r = .29$) under Allport's "optimal" contact conditions (Pettigrew & Tropp, 2006). That is, *although increased contact itself is associated with reduced prejudice, the effect is magnified significantly under conditions characterizing equal status, cooperation, common goals, and institutional support.* As some of the chapters in the present volume note (e.g., Hodson, Costello et al., this volume; Lolliot et al., this volume), Pettigrew and Tropp's (2006) meta-analysis also confirmed empirically that contact with one group generalizes to positive attitudes toward other, unrelated groups (see also Tausch, Hewstone, Kenworthy, Psaltis, Schmid, Popan et al., 2010). Contact was also found to be effective across a range of intergroup contact settings (e.g., based on sexual orientation or race), and empirical designs (experimental, correlational, longitudinal). Subsequent meta-analyses have identified two important qualifiers, which have themselves provided rich ground for researchers. Specifically, contact works better for majority (or dominant) than minority (or subjugated) groups (Tropp & Pettigrew, 2005b), and works more effectively through affective (e.g., reducing anxiety, building empathy) than cognitive (Pettigrew & Tropp, 2008; Tropp & Pettigrew, 2005a) processes.

In recent years, there has clearly amassed an incredible amount of diverse research not only supporting the benefits of intergroup contact, but explaining why contact is beneficial, and pointing out its boundary conditions. As Pettigrew and Tropp (2005, p. 271) point out:

Allport's formulation specified neither the processes involved in intergroup contact's effects nor how these effects generalize to other situations, the entire outgroup, and other outgroups not involved in the contact (Pettigrew, 1998). Indeed, these omissions explain why he called it a "hypothesis" and not a "theory."

Because the limitations in the original formulation have now been overcome, it is more appropriate to speak of *intergroup contact theory*, rather than a mere hypothesis (Hewstone & Swart, 2011). The present volume brings some of the latest new findings to the fore.

Advances in intergroup contact

As shown in Figure 1.1, the contact literature field has grown remarkably, even since the publication of the highly-cited Pettigrew and Tropp meta-analysis in 2006. One might reasonably ask, "Why the sudden surge in interest?" We suspect that there are historical, cultural, and science-related answers to this question. One possibility is simply that "the timing is right." The formal and legal desegregation of Blacks and Whites in the US was viewed by most psychologists and sociologists as a "ready-made laboratory" (Cook, 1957, p. 6) for the examination of contact in the real world. Several generations have now lived through this experience or similar experiences in other settings. Recent popular books have reviewed the success of racial desegregation in the US (e.g., Adams, Biernat, Branscombe, Crandall, & Wrightsman, 2008), and journals have devoted special issues to race relations in post-apartheid South Africa (e.g., Finchilescu & Tredoux, 2010), or to extended and indirect contact (Eller, Hewstone, & Dovidio, 2011). With the benefit of a rich historical tapestry, a comprehensive analysis of the success of contact has become an imperative. The results, unfortunately, are somewhat mixed. However, many researchers feel that contact, as an idea, has rarely been afforded the opportunity to unfurl its full potential. For instance, Cook (1979) and Stephan (2008) ultimately concluded that, despite the promise of prejudice reduction, contact was not given a fair try in the desegregated US, failing to meet or even approximate the preconditions specified by Allport (1954) and other advocates of contact. Yet intergroup contact has also claimed clear successes. For instance, contact in Northern Ireland has proven quite successful despite the overwhelming political and religious obstacles (Hewstone, 2009). It should therefore come as no surprise that contact researchers and social commentators have turned their attentions to contemplating such "natural experiments" in contact that have unfolded in the post-World War II era.

But this "timing is right" explanation alone seems unsatisfactory, placing an overly strong emphasis on history and its judges. We argue that intergroup contact research is presently so pressing and attention-grabbing as a direct result of contemporary and future global conditions. That is, immigration and its associated intergroup contact represents one of the most serious and pressing concerns for academics and policymakers in the twenty-first century. Whereas much of the empirical contact research of the previous century focused on interaction and integration *within societies* (e.g., in Northern Ireland, in South Africa, in the US), or *between subcultures within societies* (e.g., between heterosexuals and homosexuals; between men and women in the workplace), policymakers and social scientists have increasingly focused their attention on the new millennium, where interaction and integration *between ethnic and national cultures* represents a unique and universal challenge. We are presently witnessing human migration patterns unprecedented in our collective history as a species. Figures by the UN suggest that as many as 214 million people are classified as migrants, up 37 percent over 20 years, with growth up 80 percent in North America alone (DeParle, 2010). With the prospect of rapidly disappearing finite natural resources such as oil and water, and increased drought and disease brought on by global warming and other man-made influences, migration will increase ever more rapidly, creating so-called "climate refugees." Unfortunately, these future conditions are almost guaranteed to fall short of Allport's (1954) optimal contact conditions. As a species, we nervously peer down the road toward the largest scale natural experiment of its kind. Understanding how, when, why, and for whom contact works therefore represents an urgent *practical* concern for policymakers and governments. It is small wonder that leading academics in the social sciences are converging on a recognition of intergroup contact as one of the most serious social and political concerns we face.

It is likely, therefore, that the recent surge of interest in contact theory is borne by the inherent promise in the concept, the simple idea that contact *can* improve intergroup attitudes and relations, an idea now corroborated by an impressive array of findings (see Pettigrew & Tropp, 2006, 2011). Despite some clear challenges and vocalized concerns (e.g., Dixon, Durrheim, & Tredoux, 2005), contact has an impressive track record. Put simply, contact works (or at minimum, it *can*). This particular finding must be placed in context against a backdrop of other psychological interventions to reduce prejudice and improve intergroup relations that have failed. For instance, presenting an immigrant group as valuable to the host society has previously produced no attitude benefit (Meeus, Duriez, Vanbeselaere, Phalet, & Kuppens, 2009, Study 1). Similarly, attempts by an outgroup to induce a common (shared) identity have failed (Rutchick & Ecclestone, 2010), and attempts to induce multiculturalism have ironically increased the strength of and reliance on stereotypes and categorization (Wolsko, Park, Judd, & Wittenbrink, 2000). (For additional examples see Aboud & Spears Brown, this volume; Vorauer, this volume).

Even more problematic is the general concern that *prejudiced persons* can be particularly resistant to prejudice interventions of any kind. For instance, whereas value-confrontation procedures that highlight inconsistencies between cherished values and one's prejudicial attitudes have proven effective at improving intergroup attitudes among people in general (Rokeach, 1973; see also Grube, Mayton, & Ball-Rokeach, 1994), such interventions have frequently failed among authoritarians (Altemeyer, 1996) and prejudiced people generally (see also Monteith & Walters, 1998). Moreover, interventions can *backfire* among prejudiced people,

further entrenching their biases and divisiveness. Consider an educational curriculum, aimed at promoting tolerance for cultural diversity in schools, that in
fact made authoritarians increasingly intolerant (Avery, Bird, Johnstone, Sullivan, & Thalhammer, 1992). Likewise, efforts to target the zero-sum beliefs (e.g.,
immigrants take jobs from the host group) among socially dominant individuals
(those people endorsing intergroup hierarchy and inequality) have been met with
increased opposition to immigrants (Esses, Dovidio, Jackson, & Armstrong, 2001).
In contrast, contact actually works well among those individuals otherwise prone
to anti-outgroup biases, as reviewed by Hodson, Costello et al. (this volume) (see
also Hodson, 2008, 2011, in press; Hodson, Harry, & Mitchell, 2009). Unlike the
majority of other interventions, criticized for being insufficiently evaluated (see
Stephan & Stephan, 2004; Stephan, Renfro, & Stephan, 2004), contact research
has a long history and impressive record of empirical confirmation, comprising
hundreds of studies testifying to its efficacy and highlighting its underlying psychological processes. It is only natural, therefore, that the field is currently excited
about intergroup contact as a prejudice-reduction strategy. The present volume
provides a synthesis of recent efforts by leading researchers to understand the
contact process and its implications.

Contributions to this volume

Part II of this volume outlines potential barriers to successful intergroup contact.
Vorauer (this volume) introduces the notion that *evaluative concerns* play a fundamental role in intergroup dynamics. In short, we are concerned about how outgroup members perceive our ingroup and ourselves as a member of that group.
Contrary to the lay perception that people are relatively uninterested in their outgroups, Vorauer convincingly demonstrates that people are hungry for information
about "how they see us" (*meta-stereotypes*). In fact, she argues, humans devote
considerable energy to this cause during intergroup contact. As her comprehensive review demonstrates, these evaluative concerns can paradoxically encourage withdrawal from contact, can interfere with contact goals during interactions,
can be cognitively draining, and can interfere with generalization of positive attitudes from one's outgroup partner to the outgroup at large. Evaluative concerns,
therefore, are fundamental factors to consider in contact settings. Vorauer also
discusses some intriguing counter-intuitive findings on the effects of perspective-
taking and empathy; those planning interventions utilizing these methods would
be well-advised to consult this body of research. Based on a review of the evidence, the author provides recommendations with regard to when multiculturalism and diversity make for suitable intervention goals, and when anti-racism and
color-blindness (seeing people as people, not group members) are more appropriate (see also Aboud & Spears Brown, this volume).

   Another potential obstacle to establishing contact and translating contact
encounters into positive outcomes can be individual differences in prejudice-prone
tendencies. Evidence for this possibility, however, has been slow in coming. Hodson, Costello et al. (this volume) focus on two key themes historically reflected

in the contact literature: (a) individual differences, as constructs, are *irrelevant* (i.e., are not informative); or (b) individual differences, as processes, are *obstacles* (i.e., prejudiced people do not benefit from contact and may become increasingly prejudiced as a result of contact). Through both a review of existing data and the presentation of new findings, the authors consider the empirical merit of these two positions. Although person-variables have long been ignored in the contact field, particularly as moderators of contact effects (i.e., factors that qualify the effects of contact), evidence suggests that their consideration is long overdue. First of all, person variables such as authoritarianism and social dominance orientation predict intergroup attitudes beyond contact variables. More importantly, however, the authors then directly consider the effects of contact *among* the highly prejudiced. As noted above, many prejudice interventions fail, particularly among those with strong prejudicial proclivities. However, the review by Hodson and colleagues suggests that contact, in fact, works well (even best) among prejudiced persons, operating via many of the mediators through which contact generally exerts influence on attitudes. This long-overlooked question considerably strengthens the case that contact "works," suggesting that contact effects may have been seriously underestimated in studies that have collapsed across individual differences between people. New analyses in this chapter also rule out between-person differences in how contact is construed. That is, it is possible that contact differentially impacts those low versus high in prejudice-prone tendencies because what constitutes "a lot of contact" or "convivial contact" differs between these types of people. These new analyses address this possibility, revealing that *within* individuals increased contact with a particular group is associated with more favorable attitudes toward that particular group relative to other groups, regardless of one's prejudice-relevant proclivities. The benefits of contact among prejudiced individuals, therefore, appear to be more than mere methodological artefacts. The authors conclude with policy recommendations for more widely implementing well-structured contact interventions.

Lolliot and colleagues (this volume) tackle a topic that has remained a pressing concern for decades but, until recently, has received little rigorous empirical attention: *secondary transfer effects*. Specifically, these authors provide up-to-date evidence on whether contact with one group (i.e., the primary group) affects biases toward another group uninvolved with the contact encounter (i.e., the secondary group). Included in their discussion is a consideration of *how* such generalization might occur, and whether this effect differs from basic attitude generalization outside of intergroup contexts. Crucially, the authors consider the *mechanisms* through which contact can exert a secondary transfer effect. For instance, does contact result in "deprovincialization," opening interactants to experiences beyond their own ingroup experiences? Moreover, does contact lead to an appreciation of multiculturalism and a reappraisal of the primacy of one's ingroup, and, if so, can this explain why contact often demonstrates secondary transfer effects? Lolliot and colleagues also propose several intriguing models detailing the role that outgroup empathy (feelings of warmth and compassion) might play in facilitating secondary transfer effects. Finally, the authors explore potential moderators of secondary transfer effects, including the perceived similarity between the secondary and primary group, and prejudice-prone individual differences. Overall, the chapter provides a compelling case for the power of contact, not only to affect attitudes toward the contact group but toward a range of outgroups. This earmarks contact as a particularly powerful and practical prejudice intervention tool that is of unique value in our increasingly diverse societies that often comprise multiple different outgroups, according to criteria of nationality, religion, ethnicity, sexual orientation, and so on.

Of course, structural features of the contact setting are also extremely influential in determining contact outcomes. Saguy, Tropp, and Hawi (this volume) center their discussion on the role of status and power, one of Allport's (1954) key contact conditions. The particular contribution of their analysis lies in the recognition that advantaged and disadvantaged groups hold markedly different motivations in contact settings with regard to the status quo, with the former preferring hierarchy maintenance and the latter generally preferring change (but not always). Saguy and colleagues draw attention to a feature all too often missing from the contact literature: the *content* of the discussion or intergroup interaction: that is, what groups actually communicate about, and the functions these group positions serve. As the authors note, advantaged group members prefer contact topics that emphasize intergroup commonality, to the extent that such focus detracts from structural features that otherwise suggest unfairness and need for social change. Disadvantaged group members, on the other hand, prefer contact opportunities that involve an analysis and consideration of the (unfair) power imbalance characterizing the intergroup context. This long overdue analysis suggests that people are acutely aware of the functional and strategic value of contact discussion points. As evidence, the authors demonstrate that content preferences become entrenched and acted upon when structural features are unstable (vs. stable) and thus susceptible to change. Ultimately, Saguy and colleagues not only demonstrate differences in motivations for contact discussion topics between majority and minority groups, but explore the potential pitfalls of implementing common or shared intergroup representations (i.e., "we are alike"). Such perceptions, particularly in the absence of direct discussions of power differentials and need for change, can ironically promote the status quo, even among disadvantaged groups, who come to admire the advantaged group and lose motivation for collective social change. For the benefit of society as a whole, contact clearly needs to be more than simply pleasant. For true social change, contact must also address (and potentially redress) social inequality.

The next set of chapters, in Part III, generally discuss contact-based solutions to the problems of intergroup hostility and dislike. In the US, many culturally and scientifically important contact experiences have most directly affected and involved youth, as when the 1954 *Brown vs. Board of Education* decision led to desegregation of races in education settings (schools). It is no surprise, therefore, that researchers recognize the enormous potential for contact-based interventions among children. In their comprehensive review, Aboud and Spears Brown (this volume) argue that intergroup contact among young children is critical if stereotypes and prejudice are to be reduced. They note that children are exposed not only to direct outgroup contact, but indirect contact (via friends and media), and are often exposed to negative encounters (e.g., intergroup bullying). The implications for modern social life and contact in the twenty-first century are clear. Aboud and Spears Brown stress the particular importance of ingroup norms (see also Davies, Wright, Aron & Comeau, this volume) in guiding children's avoidance decisions (e.g., which group member to play with), noting that children sometimes demonstrate a preference for ingroup members who express bias (vs. non-bias). We concur with the authors' call for more research on group norms, particularly in the development of negative contact tendencies. Aboud and Spears Brown propose several useful and practical solutions. In particular, the authors consider media outlets (television, books) powerful conduits for improving intergroup contact where contact is not possible or has not yet occurred. Yet the authors also note some very sensible caveats. For one, perspective-taking and empathy have boundary conditions in contact settings (see also Vorauer, this volume). More importantly, they draw attention to the social-cognitive limitations in young children, calling for contact-based interventions to be explicit, concrete, and to the point, in order for their potential power to be unfolded among developing minds. Perhaps most importantly of all, Aboud and Spears Brown discuss the importance of teaching children the actual skills for intervening when contact encounters go awry and begin to deteriorate. Ultimately, their review offers tremendous hope for the implementation of contact strategies among children.

The importance of intergroup friendship as a positive conduit for intergroup contact among adults is particularly highlighted by Davies et al. (this volume). These authors outline the importance of friendships in general, including the many positive outcomes for the self and others. Importantly, the authors demonstrate how cross-group friendships, both direct and also vicarious (through the friendships of one's fellow ingroup members), predicts more favorable attitudes toward the outgroup as a whole. In doing so the authors emphasize the importance of contact-attitude mediators, such as the reduction of intergroup anxiety, but draw particular attention to the amount of time spent with the friend and the potential for self-disclosure. In short, Davies and colleagues focus on the *intimacy* that defines a friendship bond in an intergroup contact setting, demonstrating the importance of psychological closeness with an outgroup friend, to the point of increasing the sense of self-other overlap. Central to their thesis is the notion that perceived group norms are fundamental to understanding the intergroup friendship process – they consider such norms as both mediators (i.e., explanations of) and moderators (i.e., qualifiers of) contact-attitude effects. Interestingly, they focus not only on ingroup norms ("*we* are positive toward cross-group friendships"), but also on perceived outgroup norms ("*they* are positive toward cross-group friendships"). This consideration of the "other's" perception is repeatedly proving critical to understanding contact effects (see Vorauer, this volume). In sum, the authors provide a convincing argument for the importance of friendship as a powerful means to introduce positive contact norms in a way that reduces prejudice and conflict.

In this vein, West and Dovidio (this volume) draw on many psychological principles to map out the processes involved in such cross-group friendship development. In particular, the authors examine interpersonal (dyadic) interactions that occur when representatives of different groups engage in face-to-face contact. The great value of their approach is that the authors consider sustained interactions over time, providing some of the first empirical insights into the *formation* of cross-group friendships. This line of research is long overdue and contributes considerably to our understanding of the difficulties and challenges that await practitioners. However, their review also offers promise concerning how alliances can be developed across group boundaries. Like Vorauer (this volume), the authors emphasize the importance of outgroup perceptions in the role of making attributions (and misattributions). Importantly, West and Dovidio demonstrate the importance of non-verbal behavioral cues expressed during interactions, and the ability of outgroup members to read (and mis-read) these cues, which seriously influences the outcomes of contact. Their review reminds us not to be overly optimistic about contact, because one's admirable intentions to avoid being prejudiced are difficult to sustain over time, and become increasingly apparent to outgroup representatives over prolonged exposure. Most prior research has arguably failed to identify these processes adequately. Overall, these authors introduce compelling new statistical procedures that allow researchers to identify the influence of each interaction partner on the other in a dynamic manner. It turns out that interaction partners are actually very sensitive and adept at reading anxiety in contact settings, and that this social reading in turn impacts their own contact behavior. On a positive note, the authors highlight the importance of common or shared group perceptions; those who naturally perceive intergroup similarities and commonality are better able to weather the storm of intergroup tension and remain on positive terms despite the ups and downs experienced in any relationship. This is a promising finding considering that common ingroup representations (i.e., *we are part of a common group*) are readily manipulated and induced in laboratory and field settings (see Gaertner & Dovidio, 2000, for a review).

In Chapter 6, Crisp and Turner offer the reader a bold new idea that provides insights into where the future of contact research might lead. Specifically, these authors provide evidence that *imagining* contact, as a mental simulation, can improve intergroup attitudes. This approach is particularly in keeping with the UN declaration that peace must be won in the human mind. Impressively, Crisp and Turner have demonstrated that imagined contact reduces anxiety, stereotyping, and prejudice, while also increasing behavioral intentions to engage in real contact. Importantly, the authors propose imagined contact not as a substitute or alternative to contact; as contact researchers themselves, they are only too aware of the benefits of face-to-face contact. Rather, they consider imagined contact as a pre-contact tool, a strategy for bringing participants to the encounter in ways that can maximize the chances of success. The contribution by this line of research is tremendous in scope and potential, addressing two problems that have continued to plague contact researchers: (1) what if there are no suitable opportunities for contact, and (2) how do we mentally prepare people in advance for intergroup contact? Their analysis suggests that simulated contact promotes more favorable intergroup attitudes (both implicit and explicit) via many of the same psychological variables accounting for the effects of "real" face-to-face contact (e.g., anxiety reduction). These findings speak to the very psychological nature of intergroup contact, consistent with our earlier contention that contact represents an inherently psychological process.

Finally, Part IV addresses methodological issues relevant to contact researchers and practitioners, providing insights into future directions for the field. Christ and Wagner (Chapter 10) provide a solid synthesis of the methodologies commonly employed in the field (and their inherent weaknesses), before offering expert opinion about where the field can improve its approach to addressing these important questions. First the authors address several problems that have troubled the field for a long time, such as a strong reliance on self-report measures, concerns about the causal influence of contact on attitudes and not the converse, and problems associated with the fact that prejudiced persons avoid contact (see also Hodson, Costello et al., this volume). Christ and Wagner discuss methodologies that are commonly used, such as experimental randomization and non-recursive correlational models, reviewing the strengths and weaknesses of each. They then consider more recent approaches, such as propensity scoring (matching individuals on covariates), sensitivity analysis, and selection models. Not surprisingly, the authors are favorably disposed toward longitudinal studies, particularly of the cross-lagged variety that employ appropriate statistical controls. These methods are particularly useful for examining the causal inferences implied by contact theory (i.e., contact causes improved attitudes over time). Perhaps most importantly, Christ and Wagner propose latent-growth curve models and multi-level structural equation modeling as strong candidates for examining the questions we *really* need to address: person-level change nested within quantifiable structural features of the context. The implications for the field are clear. As a discipline, we finally possess the statistical tools and sophistication to address contract theory *in situ* (i.e., the psychological effects of contact within a larger sociological and cultural context, in all its real-world complexity).

In closing the book, Hodson, Hewstone, and Swart (this volume) provide a synthesis of the advances forwarded by these leading scholars in the field. Contact Theory has a strong history and has passed the test of time. Like all theoretical approaches, however, refinements have been encouraged, sought, and implemented. Contact Theory, like all scientific ideas, is clearly a work in progress, and one that will face many future challenges. To date, however, the evidence clearly indicates that intergroup contact is a viable prejudice-reduction strategy that is well-equipped to deal with the intergroup challenges that face us in the twenty-first century. Hodson and colleagues offer their insights into what we have learned, where the field is now, and where we are likely to find ourselves in the future.

Acknowledgments

Gordon Hodson was supported by Social Sciences and Humanities Research Council of Canada grant (410–2007–2133).

Miles Hewstone's contribution to this chapter was funded, in part, by a grant on 'Ethno-religious diversity and trust in residential and educational settings' from the Leverhulme Trust, UK.

References

Adams, G., Biernat, M., Branscombe, N. R., Crandall, C. S., & Wrightsman, L. (2008). *Commemorating Brown: The social psychology of racism and discrimination.* Washington, DC: American Psychological Association.

Allport, G. W. (1954). *The nature of prejudice.* Reading, MA: Addison-Wesley.

Al Ramiah, A., & Hewstone, M. (2011). Intergroup difference and harmony: The role of intergroup contact. In P. Singh, P. Bain, C. M. Leong, G. Mistra, and Y. Ohtsubo (Eds.), *Individual, group and cultural processes in changing societies. Progress in Asian Social Psychology* (Series 8, pp. 3–22). Delhi: University Press.

Altemeyer, B. (1996). *The authoritarian specter.* Cambridge, MA: Harvard University Press.

Amir, Y. (1969). Contact hypothesis in ethnic relations. *Psychological Bulletin, 71,* 319–342.

Avery, P. G., Bird, K., Johnstone, S., Sullivan, J. L., & Thalhammer, K. (1992). Exploring political tolerance with adolescents. *Theory and Research in Social Education, 20,* 386–420.

Besterman, T. (1951). *UNESCO: Peace in the minds of men.* London: Methuen & Co. Ltd.

Brown, R., & Hewstone, M. (2005). An integrative theory of intergroup contact. In M. Zanna (Ed.), *Advances in Experimental Social Psychology* (Vol. 37, pp. 255–343). San Diego, CA: Academic Press.

Cohen, J. (1988). *Statistical power analysis for the behavioral sciences.* Hillsdale, NJ: Erlbaum.

Cook, S. W. (1957). Desegregation: A psychological analysis. *American Psychologist, 12,* 1–13.

Cook, S. W. (1979). Social science and school desegregation: Did we mislead the Supreme Court? *Personality and Social Psychology Bulletin, 5,* 420–437.

Davies, K., Tropp, L. R., Aron, A., Pettigrew, T. F., & Wright, S. C. (2011). Cross-group friendships and intergroup attitudes: A meta-analytic review. *Personality and Social Psychology Review, 15,* 322–351.

DeParle, J. (2010, June 26). Global migration. A world ever more on the move. *The New York Times.* Retrieved from: http://www.nytimes.com/2010/06/27/weekinreview/27deparle.html?_r=2&ref=world

Dixon, J., Durrheim, K., & Tredoux, C. (2005). Beyond the optimal contact strategy: A reality check for the contact hypothesis. *American Psychologist, 60,* 697–711.

Eller, A., & Abrams, D. (2004). Come together: Longitudinal comparisons of Pettigrew's reformulated intergroup contact model and the Common Ingroup Identity Model in Anglo-French and Mexican-American contexts. *European Journal of Social Psychology, 34,* 229–256.

Eller, A., Hewstone, M., & Dovidio, J. F. (2011). Prejudice reduction through extended and other forms of indirect contact. Special issue: *Group Processes and Intergroup Relations, 14*(2).

Esses, V. M., Dovidio, J. F., Jackson, L. M., & Armstrong, T. L. (2001). The immigration dilemma: The role of perceived group competition, ethnic prejudice, and national identity. *Journal of Social Issues, 57,* 389–412.

Finchilescu, G., & Tredoux, C. (2010). Intergroup relations in post apartheid South Africa: Change, and obstacles to come. Special issue: *Journal of Social Issues, 66(2)*.

Gaertner, S., & Dovidio, J. (2000). *Reducing intergroup bias: The common ingroup identity model*. New York: Psychology Press.

Grube, J. W., Mayton, D. M., & Ball-Rokeach, S. J. (1994). Inducing change in values, attitudes, and behaviors: Belief system theory and the method of value self-confrontation. *Journal of Social Issues, 50*, 153–173.

Hewstone, M. (2003). Intergroup contact: Panacea for prejudice? *The Psychologist, 16*, 352–355.

Hewstone, M. (2009). Living apart, living together? The role of intergroup contact in social integration. *Proceedings of the British Academy, 162*, 243–300.

Hewstone, M., & Brown, R. J. (1986a). (Eds.). *Contact and conflict in intergroup encounters*. Oxford, UK: Basil Blackwell.

Hewstone, M., & Brown, R. J. (1986b). Contact is not enough: An intergroup perspective on the "Contact Hypothesis." In M. Hewstone, & R. J. Brown (Eds.), *Contact and conflict in intergroup encounters* (pp. 1–44). Oxford, UK: Basil Blackwell.

Hewstone, M., & Swart, H. (2011). Fifty-odd years of inter-group contact: From hypothesis to integrated theory. *British Journal of Social Psychology, 50*, 374–386.

Hodson, G. (2008). Interracial prison contact: The pros for (socially dominant) cons. *British Journal of Social Psychology, 47*, 325–351.

Hodson, G. (2011). Do ideologically intolerant people benefit from intergroup contact? *Current Directions in Psychological Science, 20*, 154–159.

Hodson, G. (in press). Authoritarian contact: From "tight circles" to cross-group friendships. In F. Funke, T. Petzel, J. C. Cohrs, & J. Duckitt (Eds.), *Perspectives on authoritarianism*. Weisbaden, Germany: VS-Verlag.

Hodson, G., Harry, H., & Mitchell, A. (2009). Independent benefits of contact and friendship on attitudes toward homosexuals among authoritarians and highly identified heterosexuals. *European Journal of Social Psychology, 39*, 509–525.

Kenworthy, J. K., Turner, R. N., Hewstone, M., & Voci, A. (2005). Intergroup contact: When does it work and why? In J. Dovidio, P. Glick. & L. Rudman (Eds.), *Reflecting on the nature of prejudice* (pp. 278–292). Malden, MA: Blackwell.

Martell, R. F., Lane, D. M., & Emrich, C. (1996). Male-female differences: A computer simulation. *American Psychologist, 51*, 157–158.

Meeus, J., Duriez, B., Vanbeselaere, N., Phalet, K., & Kuppens, P. (2009). Examining dispositional and situational effects on outgroup attitudes. *European Journal of Personality, 23*, 307–328.

Monteith, M. J., & Walters, G. L. (1998). Egalitarianism, moral obligation, and prejudice-related personal standards. *Personality and Social Psychology Bulletin, 24*, 186–199.

Moradi, B., & Miller, L. (2010). Attitudes of Iraq and Afghanistan war veterans toward gay and lesbian service members. *Armed Forces & Society, 36*, 397–419.

Pettigrew, T. F. (1986). The intergroup contact hypothesis re-considered. In M. Hewstone & R. Brown (Eds.), *Contact and conflict in intergroup encounters* (pp. 169–195). New York: Blackwell.

Pettigrew, T. F. (1998). Intergroup contact theory. *Annual Review of Psychology, 49*, 65–85.

Pettigrew, T. F., Christ, O., Wagner, U., & Stellmacher, J. (2007). Direct and indirect intergroup contact effects on prejudice: A normative interpretation. *International Journal of Intercultural Relations, 31*, 411–425.

Pettigrew, T. F., & Tropp, L. R. (2005). Allport's intergroup contact hypothesis: Its history and influence. In J. F. Dovidio, P. Glick, & L. Rudman (Eds.), *On the nature of prejudice: Fifty years after Allport* (pp. 262–277). Malden, MA: Blackwell.

Pettigrew, T. F., & Tropp, L. R. (2006). A meta-analytic test of intergroup contact theory. *Journal of Personality and Social Psychology, 90*, 751–783.

Pettigrew, T. F., & Tropp, L. R. (2008). How does intergroup contact reduce prejudice? Meta-analytic tests of three mediators. *European Journal of Social Psychology, 38*, 922–934.

Pettigrew, T. F., & Tropp, L. R. (2011). *When groups meet: The dynamics of intergroup contact*. Philadelphia, PA: Psychology Press.

Richard, F. D., Bond, C. F. Jr., & Stokes-Zoota, J. J. (2003). One hundred years of social psychology quantitatively described. *Review of General Psychology, 7*, 331–363.

Rokeach, M. (1973). *The nature of human values*. New York: The Free Press.

Rosenthal, R. (1990). How are we doing in soft psychology? *American Psychologist, 45*, 775–777.

Rutchick, A. M., & Ecclestone, C. P. (2010). Ironic effects of invoking common ingroup identity. *Basic and Applied Social Psychology, 32*, 109–117.

Stephan, C. W., Renfro, L., & Stephan, W. G. (2004). The evaluation of multicultural education programs: techniques and a meta-analysis. In W. G. Stephan, & W. P. Vogt (Eds.), *Education programs for improving intergroup relations: Theory, research and practice* (pp. 227–242). New York: Teachers College Press.

Stephan, W. G. (1987). The contact hypothesis in intergroup relations. In C. Hendrick (Ed.), *Group processes and intergroup relations: Review of personality and social psychology* (Vol. 9, pp. 13–40). New York: Academic Press.

Stephan, W. G. (2008). Brown and intergroup relations: Reclaiming a lost opportunity. In G. Adams, M. Biernat, N. R. Branscombe, C. S. Crandall, & L. Wrightsman (Eds.), *Commemorating Brown: The social psychology of racism and discrimination* (pp. 63–78). Washington, DC, US: American Psychological Association.

Stephan, W. G., & Stephan, C. W. (2001). *Improving intergroup relations*. Thousand Oaks, CA: Sage.

Tajfel, H., & Turner, J. C. (1979). An integrative theory of intergroup conflict. In W. G. Austin, & S. Worchel (Eds.), *The social psychology of intergroup relations* (pp. 33–47). Monterey, CA: Brooks/Cole Publishing Company.

Tausch, N., Hewstone, M., Kenworthy, J. B., Psaltis, C., Schmid, K., Popan, J. R., Cairns, E., & Hughes, J. (2010). Secondary transfer effects of intergroup contact: Alternative accounts and underlying processes. *Journal of Personality and Social Psychology, 99*, 282–302.

Tropp, L. R., & Pettigrew, T. F. (2005a). Differential relationships between intergroup contact and affective and cognitive dimensions of prejudice. *Personality and Social Psychology Bulletin, 31*, 1145–1158.

Tropp, L. R., & Pettigrew, T. F. (2005b). Relationships between intergroup contact and prejudice among minority and majority status groups. *Psychological Science, 16*, 951–957.

Verkuyten, M., Thijs, J., & Bekhuis, H. (2010). Intergroup contact and ingroup reappraisal: Examining the deprovincialization thesis. *Social Psychology Quarterly, 73*, 398–416.

Weller, S. C. (1993). A meta-analysis of condom effectiveness in reducing sexually transmitted HIV. *Social Science and Medicine, 36*, 1635–1644.

Wells, A. J. (1998). Lung cancer from passive smoking at work. *American Journal of Public Health, 88*, 1025–1029.

Williams, R. M. Jr. (1947). *The reduction of intergroup tensions*. New York: Social Science Research Council.

Williams, R. M, Jr. (1964). *Strangers next door: Ethnic relations in American communities*. Englewood Cliffs, NJ: Prentice-Hall.

Wolsko, C., Park, B., Judd, C. M., & Wittenbrink, B. (2000). Framing interethnic ideology: Effects of multicultural and color-blind perspectives on judgments of groups and individuals. *Journal of Personality and Social Psychology, 78*, 635–634.

Wright, S. C., Aron, A., McLaughlin-Volpe, T., & Ropp, S. A. (1997). The extended contact effect: Knowledge of cross-group friendships and prejudice. *Journal of Personality and Social Psychology, 73*, 73–90.

Part II

Potential obstacles to positive intergroup contact and directions for circumvention

2 Getting past the self

Understanding and removing evaluative concerns as an obstacle to positive intergroup contact effects

Jacquie D. Vorauer

In recent years the positive effects of contact between members of different groups on intergroup attitudes have become increasingly clear. In particular, there is now substantial empirical evidence indicating that intergroup contact is typically beneficial, usually leaving individuals with more favorable feelings toward and beliefs about outgroups than they initially possessed (see, e.g., Hodson & Hewstone, this volume; Pettigrew & Tropp, 2006; Van Laar, Levin, Sinclair, & Sidanius, 2005). Moreover, it appears that the conditions identified by Allport (1954) as key to the prejudice-reducing effect of intergroup contact, such as common goals and institutional support, are not essential and thus should be considered to be facilitating rather than necessary features of the contact situation.

Nonetheless, it is also true that the benefits of contact are not always realized. Sometimes interactions with outgroup members are awkward, full of tension and miscommunication, and ultimately propel individuals farther away from rather than closer to the outgroup. Indeed, individuals may flee intergroup contact situations at their earliest opportunity. In other cases, exchanges with outgroup members are positive in nature yet do not result in a more favorable stance toward other members of the outgroup.

What, then, are the forces that derail intergroup contact experiences, such that the opportunity to develop cross-group friendships and acquire positive information about outgroup members is lost? Pinpointing these obstacles has been identified as one of the most pressing objectives of contemporary research on the effects of intergroup contact (see Pettigrew & Tropp, 2006). In the present chapter, I examine the role that evaluative concerns can play in reducing the likelihood of intergroup contact, tarnishing the quality of intergroup interaction, and blocking generalization from exchanges with outgroup members that are pleasant and successful.

In focusing on evaluative concerns, I build on extensive research and theory in the broader social psychological literature indicating that the need for acceptance by others plays a fundamental role in guiding social experience (Baumeister & Leary, 1995). Extending these ideas to the domain of intergroup relations, I argue that individuals' concerns about how they themselves are evaluated are of paramount importance to their thoughts, feelings, and behaviors during exchanges with outgroup members. Indeed, the data even suggest that people sometimes care *more* about an outgroup member's than an ingroup member's impression of them. Considering the role played by evaluative concerns leads to some counter-intuitive predictions and findings regarding many common strategies for improving intergroup relations. For example, encouraging empathy with outgroup members or promoting anti-racism can sometimes backfire and do more harm than good. Understanding the influence of evaluative concerns also points to some potential solutions.

Information search model

Evaluative concerns reflect a desire to know another person's evaluation of oneself and involve some level of conscious preoccupation with getting an answer to the question of how one is viewed. According to the Information Search Model (Vorauer, 2006), these concerns stem from and serve the larger goal of predicting and controlling how one is treated by others, and are activated when: 1) another person's evaluation is *important* because it is judged to be diagnostic of one's social standing and probable outcomes and 2) there is *uncertainty* about the nature of that evaluation. That is, people need to both care what an outgroup member thinks of them and be uncertain about this in order to experience evaluative concern.

At first blush it may seem likely that individuals will typically dismiss outgroup members' opinions as unimportant. However, in the (extremely common) case where the ingroup and outgroup are of unequal status, the distinct social position of each group gives each group its own (perceived) domain of special expertise. In particular, individuals may often consider an outgroup member's opinion to be important because they believe that the outgroup possesses special competence-relevant expertise or moral authority. Specifically, when members of lower status groups accept the social system as fair and legitimate, they may view members of higher status groups as "competence experts" by virtue of higher status group members having the skills and characteristics necessary for success in society (see, e.g., Schmader, Major, Eccleston, & McCoy, 2001). This prediction is rather straightforward, in that those who are seen as being "ahead," and *deserving* to be ahead, should also be seen as valuable sources of information.

Less obviously, those who are seen as being "behind," but *not deserving* their inferior position, should also be seen as valuable sources of information – but in a different domain. Members of disadvantaged groups who are perceived as victims of current or past mistreatment may seem to be the only ones who can truly inform higher status group members about whether own their actions and inclinations are fair and good. In essence, when members of higher status groups perceive their own group to be enjoying unfair advantage, they may view members of lower status groups as the "morality experts." Those who are perceived as targets of discrimination may be considered the best judges of who is accountable or forgiven for group-based transgressions. This prediction is consistent with research indicating that individuals use the reactions of minority group members to decide whether specific remarks are offensive or reflect prejudice (Crosby, Monin, & Richardson, 2008).

As suggested by the foregoing examples, whether and in what domain individuals perceive an outgroup to have special expertise – and, thus, opinions that are especially valuable for self-evaluation – are predicted to depend on the status of the outgroup relative to the ingroup and the perceived legitimacy of the group status difference. Members of lower status groups are predicted to have a further general tendency to attach pragmatic importance to the opinions held by members of the higher status group. Knowing the evaluations of higher-power others is useful for predicting and controlling social outcomes regardless of whether those evaluations are taken to heart.

Although evaluative concerns plague many different types of social interaction, such concerns should be especially likely to arise in intergroup exchanges because of the high levels of uncertainty that outgroup members typically induce. In particular, lack of familiarity with an outgroup or the perception of differences between the ingroup and an outgroup can lead individuals to wonder whether an outgroup member will interpret their behavior the same way that they do. These basic antecedents of evaluative concerns according to the Information Search Model are summarized in Figure 2.1.

Recent research supports many of the Information Search Model's key predictions regarding the antecedents of evaluative concerns. In particular, across a series of four studies Vorauer and Sakamoto (2008) found that members of a lower status group (i.e., First Nations or Chinese Canadians) cared more about how a member of a higher status group (i.e., White Canadians) viewed them the more that they perceived the group status difference as legitimate. In contrast, members of the higher status group cared more about how a member of a lower status group viewed them the more that they perceived the group status difference as illegitimate. Moreover, whereas lower status group members focused on how competent they were believed to be, higher status group members focused on

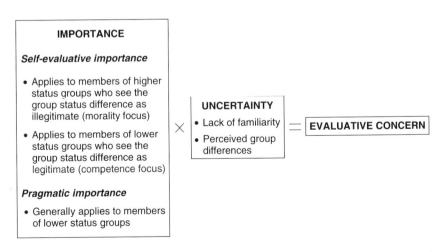

Figure 2.1 Basic antecedents of evaluative concern according to the Information Search Model (simplified from Vorauer, 2006)

whether they were considered to be "a good person." These findings are consistent with recent research by Bergsieker, Shelton, and Richeson (2010) examining interactions between Black and White Americans and between Latino and White Americans. Bergsieker et al.'s findings indicated that whereas minority group members seek to be respected and viewed as competent during intergroup interaction, majority group members' main goal is to be liked and viewed as moral. Other recent research confirms the Information Search Model's prediction that individuals tend to be more uncertain about how they are viewed by outgroup members as compared to ingroup members (Sakamoto & Vorauer, 2010).

Once evaluative concerns are activated, they set in motion a chain of reactions that are likely to interfere with positive intergroup contact effects through a variety mechanisms. First, I consider how such concerns can detract from the quality of intergroup exchanges by triggering egocentric biases, behavior disruption, and resource depletion, and ultimately foster a desire to avoid such exchanges altogether. Next, I discuss how the egocentrism fostered by evaluative concerns can interfere with drawing the other-focused inferences that are necessary to generalization from positive contact experiences. Finally, I examine the effectiveness of different strategies for reducing evaluative concerns.

Evaluative concerns and reduced quality and likelihood of intergroup contact

According to the Information Search Model, individuals experiencing evaluative concerns during intergroup interaction should, because of their interest in figuring out their outgroup interaction partner's impression of them, be vigilant for information in the interaction that might possibly provide some insight into how they are viewed. Individuals experiencing evaluative concerns should also activate pre-existing knowledge structures that are potentially relevant to an outgroup member's evaluation. These cognitive processes may ultimately make positive intergroup contact less likely. The basic consequences of evaluative concerns according to the Information Search Model are summarized in Figure 2.2.

Scrutinizing the interaction

First consider individuals' search for information within the interaction. This search is expected to involve scrutinizing their own actions and remarks in an effort to imagine how they will be perceived by the outgroup member. Individuals experiencing evaluative concerns may also attend closely to the outgroup member's comments and behaviors, ready to detect clues about the impression that he or she is forming of them. The end result of the energy that individuals devote to interpreting behavior and their motivation to learn how they are viewed is that they will perceive much of what they see as being somehow indicative of how they are evaluated. In particular, they will be likely to exhibit: (a) a *self-as-targeting* bias, whereby they take an outgroup member's behavior more personally than is warranted (e.g., "He looked away; he must want to get away from me"), as well

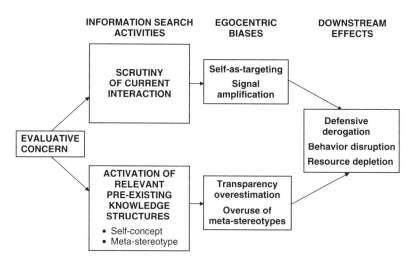

Figure 2.2 Basic consequences of evaluative concern according to the Information Search Model (simplified from Vorauer, 2006)

as (b) a *signal amplification* bias, whereby they exaggerate the implications of their own behavior for an outgroup member's impression of them (e.g., "I smiled a lot, so that will clearly tell him that I want to be friends"). Notably, the behavior disruption triggered by evaluative concerns (Vorauer & Turpie, 2004) likely contributes to the signal amplification bias by reducing the clarity of individuals' actual communications just when they are most inclined to see it as full of meaning. That is, individuals' intense analysis of what their behavior might convey to an outgroup member (e.g., "Maybe he'll think I'm trying hard because I want to show I'm not prejudiced") can lead them away from acting in line with their inner feelings and attitudes, and toward less natural actions and remarks that are more ambiguous and thus more difficult to read.

Several studies have confirmed that egocentric biases such as self-as-targeting and signal amplification are indeed elevated under conditions that foster evaluative concerns. Consider, for example, one recent investigation involving face-to-face interactions between White and Chinese Canadians (Vorauer & Sakamoto, 2008, Study 4). In this study, individuals' experience of evaluative concerns and associated propensity to exhibit egocentric biases were expected to follow the pattern predicted by the Information Search Model. That is, members of the higher status group should be more invested in an outgroup member's opinions with decreasing perceived legitimacy of the group status difference, because outgroup members are seen as better judges of moral goodness. Members of the lower status group, on the other hand, should be more invested in an outgroup member's opinions with increasing perceived legitimacy of the group status difference, because outgroup members will be seen as better judges of the competencies necessary for success in society.

In line with predictions, the individuals who exhibited the greatest egocentric bias were those who were the most likely to be concerned with evaluation. Specifically, members of the higher status group (White Canadians) who perceived the group status difference as relatively unfair exaggerated the signals that their behavior communicated to their interaction partner about their own moral goodness; members of the lower status group (Chinese Canadians) who perceived the group status difference as relatively fair exaggerated the extent to which their interaction partner's behavior communicated judgments of their competence. In another study involving interactions between White and Chinese Canadians (Vorauer & Sakamoto, 2006), White Canadians who were liable to be experiencing evaluative concerns because they had limited prior intergroup contact experience (and were thus uncertain about how they were viewed) exaggerated the friendship interest that their own behavior communicated to their outgroup interaction partner.

Activation of pre-existing knowledge structures

The Information Search Model also predicts that evaluative concerns will prompt activation of pre-existing knowledge structures of potential relevance to an outgroup member's evaluation, such as individuals' self-concept and meta-stereotypes regarding how the outgroup views the ingroup. When these knowledge structures are accessible they should lead individuals to "fill in the gaps" in the evidence that is available to them in an egocentrically biased manner. Specifically, greater salience of self-knowledge should be associated with greater likelihood of *transparency overestimation*, whereby individuals exaggerate another person's ability to detect their traits, emotional states, and inclinations (e.g., "I'm sure it's obvious to her that I am uncomfortable"): they expect the other person to view their traits and states the same way that they do. Further, once meta-stereotypes regarding how the outgroup generally views the ingroup are activated, these meta-stereotypes should guide individuals' metaperceptions regarding how they personally are viewed by an outgroup interaction partner (e.g., "She must think I'm racist") – regardless of whether that outgroup member actually holds or uses the stereotypes.

There is some complexity in that self-concepts and meta-stereotypes can point to similar or different conclusions. But the end result is always that individuals form ideas about an outgroup member's view of them that are driven by their own personal knowledge structures, knowledge structures that are very unlikely to be similarly available or salient to the outgroup member. Further, it may seem strange that individuals look within, to their own self-concept, when they want to learn about an outgroup member's impression of them. Yet self-knowledge about traits and inner states can at least *seem* to provide answers when other cues are hard to come by, as they often are.

Numerous studies have confirmed the Information Search Model's predictions regarding transparency overestimation and meta-stereotype-driven metaperceptions. For example, White Canadians were shown to exaggerate the transparency of their interest in friendship to a greater extent when interacting with an Aboriginal rather than a White Canadian, presumably because of the greater uncertainty and evaluative concern experienced in the intergroup case (Vorauer, 2005). In the aforementioned study involving interactions between White and Chinese Canadians (Vorauer & Sakamoto, 2008, Study 4), those individuals who were most likely to be concerned with evaluation (i.e., White Canadians who perceived the group status difference as relatively illegitimate and Chinese Canadians who perceived the group status difference as relatively legitimate) exhibited the greatest transparency overestimation. Moreover, each group's transparency overestimation was only evident in the domain in which the outgroup was perceived to have special expertise. That is, Chinese Canadians exaggerated the transparency of their competence (high or low), whereas White Canadians exaggerated the transparency of their moral goodness (high or low).

Other investigations involving exchanges between White and Aboriginal Canadians have demonstrated that White Canadians expect to be viewed in light of Aboriginal Canadians' (ostensible) stereotype of White Canadians, which includes traits such as *prejudiced, closed-minded,* and *cruel* (Vorauer, Hunter, Main, & Roy, 2000; Vorauer, Main, & O'Connell, 1998). However, White Canadians' meta-stereotype-driven metaperceptions are not corroborated by an Aboriginal partner's actual impressions and are thus inaccurate and unwarranted (Vorauer & Kumhyr, 2001).

Reduced positive intergroup contact

All of these biases triggered by evaluative concerns, whether they involve self-as-targeting, signal amplification, transparency overestimation, or the unwarranted use of meta-stereotypes, can have negative implications for the dynamics of intergroup exchanges. For example, self-as-targeting or reliance on meta-stereotypes can lead individuals to erroneously perceive criticism or negative evaluations from an outgroup interaction partner who in fact has friendly inclinations. Individuals may then respond in a defensive manner that induces hostility or discomfort in the outgroup member. When signal amplification or transparency overestimation leads individuals to exaggerate the clarity of their own overtures toward friendship, they may be disappointed with the apparent lack of reciprocation by the outgroup member, perceiving rejection where none exists. Ultimately, individuals may engage in defensive derogation, whereby they decide that they were not that interested in friendship with the outgroup member after all. That is, individuals may respond to perceived rejection by the outgroup member in kind, by rejecting the outgroup member ("I don't like you either"). Indeed, a recent study involving exchanges between White and Chinese Canadians illustrates precisely this chain of reactions (Vorauer & Sakamoto, 2006). The behavior disruption triggered by evaluative concerns (Vorauer & Turpie, 2004; see also Shelton, Richeson, Salvatore, & Trawalter, 2005) can have more direct negative implications, rendering individuals' actions and remarks difficult to read and potentially misleading.

Another negative consequence of evaluative concerns is cognitive resource depletion. Research by Richeson and Shelton (2003) suggested that the self-regulation involved in engaging in intergroup interaction uses up executive resources, such that performance on subsequent tasks involving those same resources is compromised. Specifically, White individuals interacted with either a White or Black partner and then completed the Stroop color-naming task, which requires inhibition of inappropriate responses. Participants performed worse on the Stroop task following intergroup interaction than they did after an intragroup exchange. Interestingly, this pattern was only evident for higher-prejudice individuals, who presumably had to work harder to suppress potentially inappropriate behavior when interacting with an outgroup member. Parallel results have since been obtained with Black individuals as participants (Richeson, Trawalter, & Shelton, 2005). Further research probing exactly why depletion occurs has clarified that concerns about appearing prejudiced are critical for White individuals: depletion after an intergroup exchange was greater when these concerns were heightened via false negative feedback about prejudice and reduced when these concerns were minimized via the provision of a script to follow during the exchange (Richeson & Trawalter, 2005).

Presumably, feelings of exhaustion stemming from being concerned about evaluation during intergroup exchanges can lead to a disinclination to enter such interactions in the future: individuals who are concerned with evaluation by outgroup members may anticipate the taxing nature of intergroup interactions and avoid them for that reason. Indeed, evaluative concerns may generally render individuals disinclined to fully engage with outgroup members – or to even approach them at all – during opportunities for intergroup contact. Along these lines, research suggests that worries about being rejected (Shelton & Richeson, 2005) or perceived as prejudiced (Devine, Evett, & Vasquez-Suson, 1996; Norton, Mason, Vandello, Biga, & Dyer, 2010) directly foster avoidance of intergroup interaction.

Evaluative concerns and reduced generalization from positive contact experiences

A further important consequence of the egocentrism involved in evaluative concern is that it may lead individuals to link the events and behaviors that occur in the context of intergroup interaction to something about themselves rather than to something about the outgroup member. This is not necessarily problematic when an intergroup exchange goes poorly (e.g., "it was all my fault"), but is likely to pose a significant obstacle to generalization from contact experiences that are positive in nature. In particular, negative beliefs and feelings about outgroup members may not be mitigated by favorable experiences if individuals are too preoccupied with assessing their own standing with the outgroup to draw other-focused inferences during intergroup contact. Consistent with this possibility, in a recent study in which White Canadians interacted with an ostensible Aboriginal Canadian partner, those who were prompted to think about the outgroup's perspective on their ingroup evidenced less prejudice reduction than did those who were not (Vorauer & Sasaki, 2009). These results suggest that considering how they themselves might be evaluated by the outgroup interaction partner undercut individuals' propensity to engage in the other-focused generalization processes that are critical to the beneficial attitudinal effects of positive intergroup contact experiences. That is, individuals experienced the exchange as "all about them" and did not take away any new ideas about outgroup members.

Notably, evaluative concerns may disrupt generalization both by diverting individuals' attention away from outgroup interaction partners and by prompting self-inferences that interfere with other-inferences. For example, individuals who are preoccupied with their own evaluation during an intergroup exchange may fail to notice positive behaviors and qualities exhibited by an outgroup interaction partner, or may interpret a successful intergroup exchange as reflecting their own (not their partner's) open-mindedness. Findings from recent research examining the locus of the inferences that lower- and higher-prejudice individuals draw from intergroup contact experiences are consistent with this latter possibility (Vorauer, 2008). In one study that was presented to participants as examining "speed dating with respect to friendship," lower- and higher-prejudice individuals engaged in an initial controlled exchange with an outgroup member (a First Nations Canadian) who either responded positively or negatively to them. Participants' feelings about ingroup worthiness were then assessed with Luhtanen and Crocker's (1992) private collective self-esteem scale. Participants were also asked to indicate their liking for another member of the same outgroup (First Nations Canadians) and their expectations regarding his or her probable liking for them.

Results revealed that for lower-prejudice individuals, who are apt to be more concerned with evaluation by virtue of perceiving group status differences as illegitimate, the initial intergroup exchange affected feelings about ingroup worthiness: private collective self-esteem was higher when the initial exchange went well rather than poorly. Lower-prejudice individuals' reactions to a subsequently encountered outgroup member were not affected, however. Higher-prejudice individuals, who were less likely to be concerned with evaluation, demonstrated the opposite pattern, drawing other- rather than self-inferences from the initial intergroup exchange. These individuals' private collective self-esteem was not affected by the initial exchange, but their reactions to the next outgroup member were. That is, higher-prejudice individuals generalized from the initial intergroup contact experience, whereas lower-prejudice individuals did not. Lower-prejudice individuals' failure to generalize from one outgroup member to other outgroup members might be considered appropriate or even admirable, in that it is consistent with the idea that one should respond to outgroup members in terms of individual characteristics instead of category memberships. Yet, lower-prejudice individuals' reluctance to generalize, which appeared to be tied to their concerns about their own evaluation, may limit the extent to which they benefit from positive intergroup contact experiences.

Strategies for reducing evaluative concerns

In view of the multiple pathways through which evaluative concerns can pose an obstacle to positive contact effects, any means of reducing such concerns would seem to have considerable potential for improving intergroup relations. In particular, minimizing evaluative concerns should both pave the way for more positive intergroup interaction experiences and enhance individuals' readiness to draw inferences about the outgroup from those experiences. How, then, might evaluative concerns be minimized?

Intergroup contact

Perhaps the first possibility that comes to mind, particularly in an analysis of intergroup contact effects, is that contact with outgroup members might itself reduce these concerns. Consistent with this idea, several lines of research suggest that intergroup contact, especially in the form of intergroup friendship, reduces anxiety and threat experienced in intergroup interaction and is also connected to more positive outcome expectancies regarding exchanges with outgroup members (e.g., Blair, Park, & Bachelor, 2003; Blascovich, Mendes, Hunter, Lickel, & Kowai-Bell, 2001; Dijker, 1987; Islam & Hewstone, 1993; Levin, van Laar, & Sidanius, 2003; Page-Gould, Mendoza-Denton, & Tropp, 2008; Paolini, Hewstone, Cairns, & Voci, 2004; Pettigrew & Tropp, 2008; Plant & Devine, 2003; Plant, 2004; Stephan, Boniecki, Ybarra, Bettencourt, Ervin, Jackson et al., 2002; Turner, Hewstone, Voci, & Vonofakou, 2008). However, these are relatively broad constructs that potentially involve outcomes other than concerns about evaluation by outgroup members, such as negative stereotypes about the outgroup, anticipated physical violence, irritation, or discomfort, or feelings of self-efficacy in controlling one's own prejudiced responses.

Nonetheless, there is good reason to suspect that evaluative concerns can sometimes be assuaged by intergroup contact. Specifically, exposure to outgroup members – whether positive or negative experiences are involved – should allow individuals to acquire information about how they are viewed by outgroup members. Individuals should then be less preoccupied with determining outgroup members' impressions of them in any given intergroup interaction as a function of being less uncertain (Vorauer, 2006; see also Vorauer & Sakamoto, 2006). The results of research that somewhat more directly addresses concerns about evaluation are consistent with this possibility. Shelton and Richeson (2005, Study 7) found that individuals anticipated being less worried about rejection in an ambiguous intergroup interaction scenario if they were told to imagine that their best friend was a friend of the outgroup members involved. That is, consistent with Wright, Aron, McLaughlin-Volpe, and Ropp's (1997) work on the extended-contact effect (see Davies, Wright, Aron, & Comeau, this volume), the knowledge that an ingroup member had a close relationship with an outgroup member reduced individuals' worries about negative evaluation by outgroup members.

One counter-intuitive implication of the prediction that intergroup contact reduces evaluative concerns is that these concerns may be less commonly experienced by members of minority than majority groups, by virtue of the fact that (almost by definition) minority group members are likely to have greater experience with intergroup interaction involving majority group members than vice versa: the majority group is the most frequently encountered group, not just in terms of superficial everyday interaction but also in terms of representation in the media. Because this experience should reduce minority group members' uncertainty, it should also reduce their preoccupation with determining how they are viewed during exchanges with the majority group. However, there is countervailing pressure in the other direction associated with minority group members' need to understand majority group members' evaluations for pragmatic reasons (see Vorauer, 2006).

Interestingly, another potential implication of minority group members' high contact experience with the majority is that their beliefs about how the ingroup is viewed by the majority may be relatively unlikely to change. A positive contact experience with one outgroup member is more likely to generalize, affecting perceptions and evaluations of the outgroup as a whole, if that outgroup member's ethnicity is salient (Brown & Hewstone, 2005; Ensari & Miller, 2002; Pettigrew & Tropp, 2006). Yet, all other things being equal, an outgroup member's ethnicity is more likely to be salient when it is novel and unfamiliar than when it is commonplace (Taylor & Fiske, 1978). Thus, the ethnicity of an interaction partner belonging to the majority group might not be particularly salient to minority group members during any given everyday intergroup exchange. Consistent with this possibility, the results of a recent study – conducted in a context in which White Canadians were the majority group and Chinese Canadians a minority – indicated that during intergroup exchanges White Canadians were more cognizant of their interaction partner's ethnicity than were Chinese Canadians (Sakamoto & Vorauer, 2011).

This differential salience of an interaction partner's ethnicity has implications for the readiness with which individuals' general beliefs about how their ingroup is viewed might be modified, suggesting that change might be more frequent for majority than minority group members. And indeed, recent research has revealed that intergroup contact effects on intergroup attitudes tend to be stronger for majority than for minority group members (Tropp & Pettigrew, 2005). However, there are a number of potential explanations for this general pattern, including the possibility that a history of devaluation leads minority group members to be cautious about drawing positive intergroup inferences (see Tropp & Pettigrew, 2005). Another study by Sakamoto and Vorauer (2011) specifically tested the differential salience account for greater malleability in majority (vs. minority) group members' meta-evaluations about how their ingroup is regarded. Consistent with the differential salience account, results revealed that although majority group members' beliefs about how their group was viewed were generally improved by positive intergroup contact, for minority group members' positive intergroup contact had a beneficial effect only when group membership salience was experimentally heightened.

Thus, majority group members' general beliefs about how their ingroup is viewed may be more malleable and unstable than minority group members' general beliefs about how their ingroup is viewed. Of course, beyond any such broad, group-level patterns, individual-level variation in previous contact experience should also play a role. That is, the beliefs of minority group members with relatively little previous intergroup contact experience should be more open to change, and the beliefs of majority group members with relatively more experience less so.

Limits to the benefits of intergroup contact

Even though contact undoubtedly exerts a positive influence under many circumstances it may not always be sufficient to reduce evaluative concerns. As it is not normative to provide explicit evaluative feedback during social interaction (Blumberg, 1972), individuals may not obtain clear information about how they are viewed from outgroup members during intergroup exchanges. Individuals may of course respond to this situation by being overly inclined to perceive subtle and ambiguous aspects of an outgroup member's behavior as providing clues as to how they are viewed. That is, they may exhibit a *self-as-targeting* bias. But because their readiness to perceive signals is liable to lead them to be rather indiscriminate (e.g., making a lot of both negative and positive cues), they may not end up with a coherent and satisfying sense of how the outgroup member views them.

Individuals who are concerned with evaluation will also likely exaggerate the clarity of their own communications to outgroup members, especially if uncertainty about how any overtures they might make will be received leads them to be tentative in their efforts. Such signal amplification can set off a chain of miscommunications that results in negative feelings and defensive distancing from outgroup members (Vorauer & Sakamoto, 2006). Thus, even though cross-group friendships should constitute a strong antidote by virtue of the clear positive feedback that is conveyed in the forming of such a bond, evaluative concerns may prevent such relationships from developing. Indeed, as mentioned previously, evaluative concerns are apt to reduce the likelihood of even minimal forms of intergroup contact.

In sum, then, although intergroup contact and friendships can serve to ease individuals' worries about evaluation, evaluative concerns are apt to reduce the likelihood of such experiences. As outlined previously, evaluative concerns may render positive intergroup contact experiences less likely and reduce generalization from such experiences. Indeed it would seem that the greater the need to reduce evaluative concerns (i.e., the higher they are), the less likely it is that they will be alleviated by intergroup contact and friendship. Thus it would clearly be helpful to identify other means of reducing these concerns. One especially promising and complementary strategy involves prompting individuals to adopt alternative, more other-focused, mindsets during intergroup interaction.

Empathy

At first blush it might appear that encouraging individuals to empathize with outgroup members could substantially improve intergroup interaction dynamics. After all, the salutary effects of empathy on general intergroup attitudes are well-established (e.g., Batson, Polycarpou, Harmon-Jones, Imhoff, Mitchener, Bednar et al., 1997; Stephan & Finlay, 1999), as are the multiple pathways through which these benefits are achieved. For example, taking the perspective of an outgroup member can foster stronger perceptions of injustice regarding the ingroup's treatment of the outgroup (Dovidio, ten Vergert, Stewart, Gaertner, Johnson, Esses et al., 2004), more situational attributions for negative outcomes experienced by an outgroup member (Vescio, Sechrist, & Paolucci, 2003), and cognitive merging of an outgroup member with the self (Dovidio et al., 2004), all of which can contribute to more positive attitudes toward the outgroup as a whole.

However, recent research indicates that adopting an empathic stance can have negative rather than positive effects during intergroup interaction. Trying to take an outgroup member's perspective in such contexts, where there is the potential for evaluation (which has not been the case in most previous studies), leads individuals to become preoccupied with how the outgroup member views them. Thus evaluative concerns are enhanced rather than reduced. One of the very first things that individuals are apt to see when they try to look through the eyes of an outgroup member who is an interaction partner is *themselves*. The desire to know what the outgroup member thinks of them will likely lead individuals to consider meta-stereotypes about how the outgroup views the ingroup in the hope of gaining some insight into how they are viewed (Frey & Tropp, 2006; Vorauer, 2006; Vorauer et al., 1998). Meta-stereotype activation can then disrupt behavior, trigger defensive derogation of the outgroup, and interfere with positive intergroup contact effects through a variety of mechanisms (Vorauer, Martens, & Sasaki, 2009; Vorauer & Sasaki, 2009).

The biased metaperceptions fostered by meta-stereotypes play an important role in generating these negative outcomes. Several previous studies focusing on White Canadians' beliefs about how they are viewed by Aboriginal Canadians have documented a "divergent metaperceptions" pattern. Lower-prejudice White Canadians expect an Aboriginal Canadian to contrast them with the meta-stereotype (which includes traits such as *prejudiced*, *closed-minded*, and *cruel*) and view them in a favorable light (e.g., as extremely open-minded). Higher-prejudice White Canadians instead expect to be assimilated to the meta-stereotype and viewed in a negative light (e.g., as extremely closed-minded). These divergent metaperceptions are thought to arise because, relative to higher-prejudice individuals, lower-prejudice individuals have self-concepts that are more inconsistent with the meta-stereotype and they do not identify with their ethnic ingroup as strongly as do higher-prejudice individuals (Vorauer et al., 1998, 2000; Vorauer & Kumhyr, 2001).

Recent research on the effects of perspective-taking suggests that these positive and negative metaperceptions are key to behavior disruption, whereby individuals' treatment of an outgroup member becomes incongruent with their intergroup attitudes. Specifically, these divergent metaperceptions affect the effort that individuals devote to managing their behavior during intergroup interaction. Lower-prejudice individuals "slack off" because they are confident that their positive attributes and inclinations are fully understood, whereas higher-prejudice individuals work hard to avoid being stereotyped (Vorauer et al., 2009). The end result is that warm and friendly intergroup behavior and prejudice are positively rather than negatively correlated.

For example, in one study (Vorauer et al., 2009, Study 4), pairs comprised of one White Canadian and one Aboriginal Canadian partner had a 15–minute face-to-face interaction in which they discussed topics such as positive and negative academic and social experiences, social issues, and family relationships. White pair members were randomly assigned to adopt either an observational (i.e., "be objective") or perspective-taking (i.e., "imagine how the other person feels") mindset during the exchange. In line with the idea that empathy triggers behavior disruption, results revealed that in the perspective-taking condition higher-prejudice White participants exhibited more intimacy-building behaviors and left their Aboriginal partner feeling happier than did lower-prejudice White participants. This pattern was not evident in the observational condition. That is, perspective-taking triggered behavior disruption, at least in part because it prompted higher-prejudice individuals to worry more about being stereotyped and exert greater self-regulatory effort than lower-prejudice individuals during the exchange.

The negative metaperceptions formed by higher-prejudice individuals also account for their propensity to engage in defensive derogation, whereby they negatively evaluate an outgroup member to undermine criticisms they perceive as having been directed toward them. In another recent study, White Canadians were led to adopt either an empathic or an objective stance when viewing a documentary about the abysmal living conditions of a group of Aboriginal Canadians; the film focused on the experiences of one Aboriginal woman in particular (Vorauer & Sasaki, 2009). Participants expected to discuss the documentary with an ostensible White or Aboriginal partner in the study after first exchanging some personal information with him or her. Both lower- and higher-prejudice individuals who were prompted to adopt an empathic stance in intergroup interaction evidenced meta-stereotype activation. This makes sense because for these individuals the outgroup's perspective was salient (by virtue of the mindset manipulation) and there was the potential for being personally evaluated by an outgroup member (by virtue of their interaction partner's ethnicity). However, only higher-prejudice individuals, who believed that their outgroup interaction partner would assimilate them to the stereotype of their group and view them in an unfavorable light, engaged in defensive derogation and reciprocated the negative evaluation that they imagined was being directed toward them. This effect was specific to the source of the ostensible negative appraisal, centering on the outgroup member who could derogate them personally (their interaction partner) rather than the one who could not (the outgroup member featured in the documentary). Mediation analyses confirmed that the effects obtained on individuals' evaluations of their interaction partner were mediated by their metaperceptions regarding how they themselves were evaluated. That is, higher-prejudice individuals evaluated their outgroup interaction partner negatively because they thought that their outgroup partner evaluated them negatively.

Notably, in line with previous findings, even though lower- and higher-prejudice individuals formed divergent metaperceptions about how the outgroup member would view them, lower- and higher-prejudice individuals activated the meta-stereotype to the same extent. Moreover, although the negativity of individuals' metaperceptions was key to whether they exhibited defensive derogation, meta-stereotype activation alone was sufficient to interfere with positive intergroup contact effects. Regardless of their level of prejudice, individuals who adopted an empathic stance in the context of an intergroup interaction exhibited greater meta-stereotype activation and less prejudice reduction than did those who maintained a more objective mindset. The results of mediation analyses were consistent with the idea that preoccupation with how one might be negatively evaluated undercuts the other-focused generalization processes that are necessary for prejudice reduction. Individuals were too focused on themselves to learn about the outgroup.

All of these negative effects attached to empathy strongly suggest that other-focused mindsets that do not invoke perspective-taking have better potential for short-circuiting evaluative concerns and paving the way for more positive and productive intergroup exchanges. In particular, prompting individuals to adopt the other-focused goal of learning about outgroup members may be especially beneficial.

Learning about outgroup members

Several lines of research have illuminated the potential benefits of trying to learn about others during social interaction in general and intergroup interaction in particular. For example, Leary, Kowalski, and Bergen (1988) found that individuals who were instructed to find out as much as possible about an interaction partner during mixed-sex interactions felt more confident and experienced the exchange more positively than did those who did not receive such instructions. Interestingly, their interaction partner enjoyed these same benefits. Along similar lines, Thompson (1991) demonstrated that instructing negotiators to seek information about the other party's interests leads to more mutually beneficial agreements. Saenz and Lord (1989; Lord & Saenz, 1985) found that instructing individuals with token status to adopt the role of evaluator in an interaction situation and form impressions of other people corrected the negative effects of token status on recall. Specifically, although having token status is usually associated with memory deficits with respect to comments made during group interaction, such deficits are not apparent when tokens adopt the role of evaluator.

In recent research explicitly examining both intraethnic and interethnic exchanges, the goal of forming an accurate impression of an interaction partner reduced individuals' own and their interaction partner's cognitive resource depletion and negative affect. Importantly, even though interethnic interaction was generally characterized by greater uneasiness and more negative metaperceptions than intraethnic interaction, impression formation instructions were equally beneficial across both types of exchange (Sasaki & Vorauer, 2010). The results of these various studies are all consistent with the idea that adopting an impression formation mindset essentially blocks evaluative concerns by diverting individuals away from a focus on how they themselves are viewed.

Salient intergroup ideology

How might individuals be broadly encouraged to adopt an orientation toward learning about and from outgroup members during intergroup interaction? Different intergroup ideologies that are regularly encountered in educational and work settings, at public events, and on the internet and television, appear to encourage this orientation to varying degrees. In particular, by virtue of its focus on appreciating differences between groups and recognizing how these groups can each make unique and valuable contributions to society, *multiculturalism* (e.g., *Celebrate Diversity*) suggests that individuals should seek to discover and appreciate novel and distinctive qualities of outgroup interaction partners. Thus this ideology would seem apt to prompt an especially other-focused and learning-oriented approach to intergroup exchanges. In contrast, by virtue of their explicit or implicit focus on avoiding reacting in any way to ethnic group membership, *anti-racism* (e.g., *Racism: Spot It and Stop It*) and *color-blindness* (e.g., *We Are All the Same Inside*) suggest that individuals should try to make sure that they treat outgroup interaction partners the same way that they would treat ingroup interaction partners. Thus these ideologies may prompt a self-control focus on ignoring social categories and preventing inappropriate behavior, particularly among members of dominant groups. However, because anti-racism and color-blindness both enforce a norm in which being treated on the basis of group membership is not tolerated, these ideologies might instead foster enhanced feelings of identity security in minority group members.

These predictions regarding the effects of multiculturalism and color-blindness were supported by the results of two studies involving either real face-to-face interactions between White and Aboriginal Canadians or ostensible interactions in which White and Aboriginal Canadians were led to believe that they were exchanging written messages with an outgroup interaction partner (Vorauer, Gagnon, & Sasaki, 2009). Right before the interaction, the experimenter advised participants that it would be helpful for them to first reflect on issues relevant to intergroup interaction, to make their views more accessible and better prepare them to answer the questions that they would be asked afterwards. This reflection involved reviewing written materials virtually identical to those used by Wolsko, Park, Judd, and Wittenbrink (2000; see also Richeson & Nussbaum, 2004). Specifically, participants assigned to the color-blind condition read a message emphasizing that "we must look beyond skin color and understand the person within," and that "at our core, we really are all the same." Participants assigned to the multicultural condition read a message emphasizing that "different cultural groups bring different perspectives to life," and that "each ethnic group within Canada can contribute in its own unique way."

Rendering multiculturalism salient in this way led both White and Aboriginal participants to adopt a more outward focus, as indexed by the length of the open-ended descriptions they provided of their interaction partner. Salient multiculturalism also led both White and Aboriginal participants to direct more positive remarks and questions to their interaction partner during the exchange. Mediation analyses suggested that the effect of multiculturalism on behavior was mediated by the enhanced other-focus it triggered.

The results of this research further indicated that rendering color-blindness salient led White participants to adopt a prevention orientation and express negative affect toward their Aboriginal partner. Mediation analyses confirmed that the negative effect of color-blindness on behavior was mediated by the prevention orientation it triggered. That is, being told to ignore group membership led individuals to focus on preventing negative outcomes, and this focus on prevention led them to express negative feelings.

Finally, Aboriginal participants who were exposed to the color-blind ideology reported enhanced feelings of identity safety (i.e., less anxiety and more positive beliefs about how White Canadians view Aboriginal Canadians) in the ostensible but not the real interaction paradigm. These distinct results across the two paradigms may reflect that in real interactions the direct positive effect of color-blindness on Aboriginal Canadians was countered by its aforementioned negative effect on their White interaction partner's behavior. In other research, Apfelbaum, Sommers, and Norton (2008) found that Whites who adopted a color-blind approach to intergroup interaction (by avoiding mentioning race) exhibited reduced nonverbal friendliness, an effect that was mediated by cognitive resource depletion.

Notably, although ideologies that encourage individuals to direct their attention outward and respond to an outgroup interaction partner's actions, remarks, and qualities may generally be more beneficial than those that prompt them to turn their attention in toward themselves, it seems likely that what individuals *see* matters just as much as where they *look*. Specifically, paying close attention and reacting to an outgroup member should only foster more positive behavior in the case of favorable perceptions: When an outgroup member is viewed unfavorably, enhanced attention to negative impressions may lead to more hostile rather than more friendly actions and remarks. Key predictions regarding how the effects of different intergroup ideologies on dominant group members' responses during intergroup interaction are moderated by the favorability of dominant group members' perceptions are summarized in Figure 2.3.

Along these lines, recent research has examined how individual differences in intergroup attitudes moderate the effects of salient ideology on behavior (Vorauer & Sasaki, 2010). In this research, higher-prejudice individuals, whose perceptions should be relatively negative, behaved less warmly toward an outgroup interaction partner when they were primed with multiculturalism prior to the exchange. In contrast, lower-prejudice individuals, whose perceptions should be relatively positive, behaved more warmly when they were primed with multiculturalism. Results further revealed that although multiculturalism generally enhanced individuals' sense of being different from their outgroup interaction partner as well as their perception of broader cultural differences, only higher-prejudice individuals were threatened by these perceived differences. Thus it appeared that multiculturalism essentially amplified the behavioral implications of *what individuals saw* when they looked at their outgroup interaction partner. That is, salient multiculturalism seemed to lead those who saw something negative and threatening when they

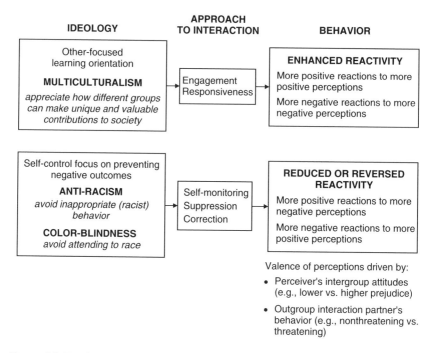

Figure 2.3 Key implications of intergroup ideologies for dominant group members' intergroup interaction behavior

looked outward (i.e., higher-prejudice individuals) to behave more negatively, and
those who saw something positive and interesting when they looked outward (i.e.,
lower-prejudice individuals) to behave more positively.

Directly complementary findings have been obtained for ideologies that
exacerbate rather than reduce self-focus and evaluative concerns, and thus are
liable to trigger inhibition, self-monitoring, and behavior disruption. These reactions should be most problematic when they interfere with positive inclinations.
Interfering with negative inclinations should instead have a beneficial effect on
outward behavior. And indeed, harmful effects of anti-racism are most clearly
evident when individuals are positively disposed toward an outgroup interaction
partner. For example, in the study by Vorauer and Sasaki (2010) examining how
individual differences in prejudice moderate the effects of salient intergroup ideology, rendering anti-racism salient had a negative effect on lower-prejudice individuals' behavior but tended to have positive implications for higher-prejudice
individuals' behavior.

Conceptually parallel results have been obtained in research examining how
the behavior of an outgroup interaction partner, rather than individual differences
in attitudes, moderates the effect of salient ideology. Vorauer and Sasaki (2011)
conducted three studies in which participants were exposed to different intergroup

ideologies prior to entering into an exchange with an outgroup member who either did or did not pose a threat. In one study, threat was operationalized in terms of rejection, with the manipulation centering on the level of interest the outgroup member expressed regarding an opportunity for more extensive interaction with participants. The other two studies followed the same basic paradigm but instead operationalized threat in terms of whether the outgroup member agreed or disagreed with participants on a series of social issues (e.g., euthanasia, abortion). Across all three studies, individuals for whom multiculturalism was made salient conveyed more hostility (e.g., made more negative other-directed comments) to a threatening outgroup member than did those not primed with multiculturalism. Further, as expected, any effects of anti-racism and color-blindness ran in the opposite direction to those of multiculturalism. Specifically, anti-racism triggered a "reverse reactivity" pattern involving more positive reactions to more negative behavior (and more negative reactions to more positive behavior) exhibited by an outgroup interaction partner.

These studies also systematically tested a comprehensive list of potential mediators of the effect of salient multiculturalism on hostile behavior during threatening interactions. Interestingly, the results clearly pointed to the enhanced learning orientation prompted by multiculturalism, assessed in terms of the frequency of words such as *learn, understand*, and *why* in open-ended thought-listings that participants completed immediately following the ideology manipulation, as the key mediator. In line with previous research documenting that deeper processing of social information is connected to higher-level (i.e., more abstract) construals that carry more meaning and importance than lower-level construals (e.g., Freitas, Gollwitzer, & Trope, 2004; Vallacher & Wegner, 1987), it seemed that when individuals worked to make sense of actions and remarks that threatened them in some way, their thoughts involved a higher level of abstraction that intensified their reactivity. That is, trying to learn and understand led to more abstract thought that prompted individuals to really engage with and attach importance to threatening behaviors exhibited by an outgroup interaction partner.

Interestingly, although this research also indicated that salient multiculturalism enhanced other-focus, as indexed by participants' recall for their interaction partner's versus their own comments during the exchange, other-focus did not mediate the effect of multiculturalism on hostile behavior. It seems quite possible that the less precise measure of other-focus used in Vorauer et al.'s (2009) studies, the length of individuals' descriptions of their interaction partner, reflected the influence of learning orientation in addition to other-focus. Alternatively, enhanced other-focus might be more important to the effects of multiculturalism in non-threatening exchanges, where individuals are less likely to pay much attention to an outgroup interaction partner's qualities and behavior than is the case in more threatening interactions.

In sum, then, a salient multicultural ideology appears to prompt a learning orientation that involves greater effort to understand an outgroup interaction partner's qualities, actions, and remarks. This increased effort to learn and understand results in enhanced reactivity, in the form of more positive reactions when perceptions of an outgroup partner are positive and more negative reactions when perceptions are negative. In contrast, a salient anti-racist or color-blind ideology appears to prompt inhibition, and, if anything, reduced reactivity to perceptions of an outgroup partner. This reduced (or even reversed) reactivity has negative implications when perceptions are positive and positive implications when perceptions are negative.

However, to fully understand the effects of the different intergroup ideologies across a variety of circumstances, it is important to consider consequences beyond the overall positivity of individuals' outward behavior toward outgroup members (see, e.g., Saguy, Tausch, Dovidio, & Pratto, 2009). For example, although encouragement to adopt an other-focused learning orientation could exacerbate negative behavior in the case of unfavorable perceptions, responsiveness to the outgroup member's actions and remarks – and, by extension, the outgroup member's ability to exert control over the course of the exchange – are preserved. It seems that salient multiculturalism prompts individuals to take outgroup members' actions and remarks more seriously. Thus, even when ideologies heighten hostile behavior toward outgroup interaction partners, there may be a silver lining in terms of heightened engagement and responsiveness to outgroup members' attributes and behavior.

Further potential benefits of the other-focused learning orientation invoked by multiculturalism include the coherence of individuals' private experience of intergroup interaction. Recent research suggests that ideologies that instead prompt a self-control focus on avoiding inappropriate behavior foster a range of negative internal experiences. For example, Vorauer and Sasaki (2010) found that in comparison to no salient ideology at all, salient anti-racism fostered greater evaluative concerns and behavior disruption, whereby individuals' outward behavior became disconnected from their inner attitudes. Consider also the reverse reactivity pattern that anti-racism fostered in Vorauer and Sasaki's (2011) investigations of threatening intergroup interactions. This pattern, which involved more positive reactions to more negative behavior (and more negative reactions to more positive behavior) exhibited by an outgroup interaction partner, suggests that salient anti-racism may have prompted over-zealous efforts to correct away from initial inclinations that seemed potentially inappropriate. Vorauer et al.'s (2009) studies documented that salient color-blind ideology prompts an orientation toward preventing negative outcomes in dominant group members, which has been shown in other research to result in cognitive resource depletion (Trawalter & Richeson, 2006).

It seems, then, that both anti-racism and color-blindness could foster a disorganized and exhausting experience of intergroup interaction that feels dictated by external pressures and which could foster a disinclination to enter into such exchanges in the future. The possibility that any apparent benefits might be short-lived is bolstered by Correll, Park, and Smith's (2008) recent finding that rebound effects occur for stereotype suppression prompted by salient color-blind ideology. Specifically, Correll et al. (2008) found that in high-conflict situations color-blindness initially resulted in less bias on a self-report explicit attitude measure than did multiculturalism. However, this pattern reversed 20 minutes later. Apparently color-blindness led participants to initially suppress negative attitudinal responses that eventually came to the surface in an even more extreme form. Similar suppression-rebound patterns have previously been documented for individuals who have been directly instructed to avoid thinking in terms of stereotypes (Macrae, Bodenhausen, Milne, & Jetten, 1994; see also Hodson & Dovidio, 2001; Monteith, Spicer, & Tooman, 1998).

Thus, a salient multicultural ideology would seem to be an effective antidote to many of the negative effects that evaluative concerns can have on the quality of intergroup interaction. In everyday non-conflictual exchanges it can trigger more positive other-directed behavior. More generally, regardless of the level of conflict or threat involved, rendering this ideology salient is liable to engender greater attention and responsiveness to outgroup members' actions and remarks. Importantly, multiculturalism fosters this responsiveness without the negative side effects on private experience associated with color-blindness or anti-racism.

In addition to improving the quality of intergroup contact experiences, the focus on learning about outgroup members prompted by multiculturalism may also facilitate generalization from positive contact experiences. Notably, Vorauer and Sasaki's (2011) recent research indicated that making multicultural ideology salient prompts a focus on groups as well as enhanced learning orientation and other-focus. Group-level thinking did not contribute to the effects of multiculturalism on hostile behavior. However, in line with the idea that greater salience of social categories leads to stronger contact effects (Brown & Hewstone, 2005), enhanced group-level thinking might contribute to generalization from positive contact experiences. Although such group-based inferences can be considered problematic on rational grounds and in the context of contemporary social norms (see, e.g., Henderson-King & Nisbett, 1996), the generalization processes involved here are critical to the positive effects of intergroup contact.

Overall, then, in conflictual intergroup contact situations where the top priority is minimizing the negativity of individuals' outward behavior, alternative ideologies to multiculturalism that enhance rather than reduce evaluative concerns, such as anti-racism and color-blindness, may be most beneficial. Here the inhibition prompted by evaluative concerns may limit hostility directed toward outgroup members. The self-focus involved in evaluative concerns may also limit generalization of negative feelings.

Otherwise, however, multiculturalism seems most helpful, both with respect to enhancing the quality of intergroup interaction and with respect to encouraging generalization from these experiences. To the extent that it is possible to heighten the prominence of multicultural ideology, then, it should be possible to maximize the likelihood that intergroup contact experiences will have positive implications for individuals' feelings about outgroup members and intergroup interaction more generally. Moreover, the negative effects of multiculturalism on higher-prejudice individuals' behavior might be mitigated by a shift away from focusing on differences between groups and toward emphasizing the benefits of learning about individual outgroup members. In particular, a salient learning- rather than difference-centered multicultural ideology might minimize higher-prejudice individuals' propensity to feel threatened by outgroup interaction partners, such that the benefits of this ideology extend to all parties involved in intergroup interaction regardless of the nature of their ingoing intergroup attitudes. An emphasis on learning and discovery might also be more effective in fostering a sense of identity security in minority group members, as reference to difference and uniqueness could activate concerns about being stereotyped that detract from their ability to focus on their interaction partner.

Conclusion

Evaluative concerns clearly constitute a significant obstacle to positive effects of intergroup contact, leading individuals to be hesitant to enter intergroup interaction situations, increasing the likelihood that these interactions will be awkward, tense, and characterized by miscommunication, and reducing individuals' propensity to generalize from pleasant and successful exchanges with individual outgroup members to the outgroup as a whole. Although greater experience interacting with outgroup members may mitigate these concerns to some extent, the effects of evaluative concerns themselves work against this process. Inducing a focus on learning about outgroup members during intergroup exchanges, perhaps by rendering some form of multicultural ideology salient, should minimize evaluative concerns and their negative consequences and thus pave the way for improved contact experiences.

References

Allport, G. W. (1954). *The nature of prejudice*. Reading, MA: Addison-Wesley.

Apfelbaum, E. P., Sommers, S. R., & Norton, N. I. (2008). Seeing race and seeming racist? Evaluating strategic colorblindness in social interaction. *Journal of Personality and Social Psychology, 95*, 918–932.

Batson, C. D., Polycarpou, M. P., Harmon-Jones, E., Imhoff, H. J., Mitchener, E. C., Bednar, L. L., Klein, T. R., & Highberger, L. (1997). Empathy and attitudes: Can feeling for a member of a stigmatized group improve feelings toward the group? *Journal of Personality and Social Psychology, 72*, 105–118.

Baumeister, R. F., & Leary, M. R. (1995). The need to belong: Desire for interpersonal attachments as a fundamental human motivation. *Psychological Bulletin, 117*, 497–529.

Bergsieker, H., Shelton, J. N., & Richeson, J. A. (2010). To be liked versus respected: Divergent goals in interracial interactions. *Journal of Personality and Social Psychology, 99*, 248–264.

Blair, I. V., Park, B., & Bachelor, J. (2003). Understanding intergroup anxiety: Are some people more anxious than others? *Group Processes and Intergroup Relations, 6* (2), 151–169.

Blascovich, J., Mendes, W. B., Hunter, S. B., Lickel, B., & Kowai-Bell, N. (2001). Perceiver threat in interactions with stigmatized others. *Journal of Personality and Social Psychology, 80*, 253–267.

Blumberg, H. H. (1972). Communication of interpersonal evaluations. *Journal of Personality and Social Psychology, 23*, 157–162.

Brown, R., & Hewstone, M. (2005). An integrative theory of intergroup contact. In M. Zanna (Ed.), *Advances in experimental social psychology* (Vol. 37, pp. 255–343). San Diego, CA: Academic Press.

Correll, J., Park, B., & Smith, J. A. (2008). Colorblind and multicultural prejudice reduction strategies in high-conflict situations. *Group Processes and Intergroup Relations, 11*, 471–491.

Crosby, J. R., Monin, B., & Richardson, D. (2008). Where do we look during potentially offensive behavior? *Psychological Science, 19*, 226–228.

Devine, P. G., Evett, S. R., & Vasquez-Suson, K. A. (1996). Exploring the interpersonal dynamics of intergroup contact. In E. T. Higgins, & R. M. Sorrentino (Eds.), *Handbook of motivation and cognition: Vol. 3. The interpersonal context* (pp. 423–464). New York, NY: Guilford Press.

Dijker, A. J. M. (1987). Emotional reactions to ethnic minorities. *European Journal of Social Psychology, 17*, 305–325.

Dovidio, J. F., ten Vergert, M., Stewart, T. L., Gaertner, S. L., Johnson, J. D., Esses, V. M., Riek, B. M., & Pearson, A. R. (2004). Perspective and prejudice: Antecedents and mediating mechanisms. *Personality and Social Psychology Bulletin, 30*, 1537–1549.

Ensari, N., & Miller, N. (2002). The out-group must not be so bad after all: The effects of disclosure, typicality, and salience on interethnic bias. *Journal of Personality and Social Psychology, 83*, 313–329.

Freitas, A. L., Gollwitzer, P., & Trope, Y. (2004). The influence of abstract and concrete mindsets on anticipating and guiding others' self-regulatory efforts. *Journal of Experimental Social Psychology, 40*, 739–752.

Frey, F. E., & Tropp, L. R. (2006). Being seen as individuals versus as group members: Extending research on metaperception to intergroup contexts. *Personality and Social Psychology Review, 10*, 265–280.

Henderson-King, E. I., & Nisbett, R. E. (1996). Anti-Black prejudice as a function of exposure to the negative behavior of a single Black person. *Journal of Personality and Social Psychology, 71*, 654–664.

Hodson, G., & Dovidio, J. F. (2001). Racial prejudice as a moderator of stereotype rebound: A conceptual replication. *Representative Research in Social Psychology, 25*, 1–8.

Islam, M. R., & Hewstone, M. (1993). Dimensions of contact as predictors of intergroup anxiety, perceived out-group variability, and out-group attitude: An integrative model. *Personality and Social Psychology Bulletin, 19*, 700–710.

Leary, M. R., Kowalski, R. M., & Bergen, D. J. (1988). Interpersonal information acquisition and confidence in first encounters. *Personality and Social Psychology Bulletin, 14*, 68–77.

Levin, S., van Laar, C. Y., & Sidanius, J. H. (2003). The effects of ingroup and outgroup friendships on ethnic attitudes in college: A longitudinal study. *Group Processes and Intergroup Relations, 6*, 76–92.

Lord, C. G., & Saenz, D. S. (1985). Memory deficits and memory surfeits: Differential cognitive consequences of tokenism for tokens and observers. *Journal of Personality and Social Psychology, 49*, 918–926.

Luhtanen, R., & Crocker, J. (1992). A collective self-esteem scale: Self-evaluation of one's social identity. *Personality and Social Psychology Bulletin, 18*, 302–318.

Macrae, C. N., Bodenhausen, G. V., Milne, A. B., & Jetten, J. (1994). Out of mind but back in sight: Stereotypes on the rebound. *Journal of Personality and Social Psychology, 67*, 808–817.

Monteith, M. J., Spicer, C. V., & Tooman, G. D. (1998). Consequences of stereotype suppression: Stereotypes on AND not on the rebound. *Journal of Experimental Social Psychology, 34*, 355–377.

Norton, M., Mason, M., Vandello, J., Biga, A., & Dyer, R. (January, 2010). *Racial paralysis: The impact of color-blindness on interracial relations.* Presented at the annual meeting of the Society for Personality and Social Psychology, Las Vegas, Nevada.

Page-Gould, E., Mendoza-Denton, R., & Tropp, L. R. (2008). With a little help from my cross-group friend: Reducing anxiety in intergroup contexts through cross-group friendship. *Journal of Personality and Social Psychology, 95*, 1080–1094.

Paolini, S., Hewstone, M., Cairns, E., & Voci, A. (2004). Effects of direct and indirect cross-group friendships on judgments of Catholics and Protestants in Northern Ireland: The mediating role of an anxiety-reduction mechanism. *Personality and Social Psychology Bulletin, 30*, 770–786.

Pettigrew, T. F., & Tropp, L. R. (2006). A meta-analytic test of intergroup contact theory. *Journal of Personality and Social Psychology, 90*, 751–783.

Pettigrew, T. F., & Tropp, L. R. (2008). How does intergroup contact reduce prejudice? Meta-analytic tests of three mediators. *European Journal of Social Psychology, 38*, 922–934.

Plant, E. A. (2004). Responses to interracial interactions over time. *Personality and Social Psychology Bulletin, 30*, 1458–1471.

Plant, E. A., & Devine, P. G. (2003). The antecedents and implications of interracial anxiety. *Personality and Social Psychology Bulletin, 29*, 790–801.

Richeson, J. A., & Nussbaum, R. J. (2004). The impact of multiculturalism versus colorblindness on racial bias. *Journal of Experimental Social Psychology, 40*, 417–423.

Richeson, J. A., and Shelton, J. N. (2003). When prejudice does not pay: Effects of interracial contact on executive function. *Psychological Science, 14*, 287–290.

Richeson, J. A., & Trawalter, S. (2005). Why do interracial interactions impair executive functions? A resource depletion account. *Journal of Personality and Social Psychology, 88*(6), 934–947.

Richeson, J. A., Trawalter, S., & Shelton, J. N. (2005). African Americans' implicit racial attitudes and the depletion of executive function after interracial interactions. *Social Cognition, 23*, 336–352.

Saenz, D. S., & Lord, C. G. (1989) Reversing roles: A cognitive strategy for undoing memory deficits associated with token status. *Journal of Personality and Social Psychology, 56*, 698–708.

Saguy, T., Tausch, N., Dovidio, J. F., & Pratto, F. (2009). The irony of harmony: Intergroup contact can produce false expectations for equality. *Psychological Science, 20*, 114–121.

Sakamoto, Y., & Vorauer, J. D. (January, 2010). *What do they think of me? Evaluative uncertainty during intergroup interaction.* Presented at the annual meeting of the Society for Personality and Social Psychology, Las Vegas, Nevada.

Sakamoto, Y., & Vorauer, J. D. (2011). *Learning that one's group is liked: Group membership salience mediates differential responsiveness of majority and minority group members' meta-evaluations to intergroup contact.* Manuscript in preparation.

Sasaki, S. J., & Vorauer, J. D. (2010). Contagious resource depletion and anxiety? Spreading effects of evaluative concern and impression formation in dyadic social interaction. *Journal of Experimental Social Psychology, 46*, 1011–1016.

Schmader, T., Major, B., Eccleston, C. P., & McCoy, S. K. (2001). Devaluing domains in response to threatening intergroup comparisons: Perceived legitimacy and the status value asymmetry. *Journal of Personality and Social Psychology, 80*, 782–796.

Shelton, J. N., & Richeson, J. A. (2005). Intergroup contact and pluralistic ignorance. *Journal of Personality and Social Psychology, 88*, 91–107.

Shelton, J. N., Richeson, J. A., Salvatore, J., & Trawalter, S. (2005). Ironic effects of racial bias during interracial interactions. *Psychological Science, 16*, 397–402.

Stephan, W. G., Boniecki, K. A., Ybarra, O., Bettencourt, A., Ervin, K. S., Jackson, L. A., McNatt, P. S., & Renfro, C.L. (2002). The role of threats in the racial attitudes of blacks and whites. *Personality and Social Psychology Bulletin, 28*, 1242–1254.

Stephan, W. G., & Finlay, K. (1999). The role of empathy in improving intergroup relations. *Journal of Social Issues, 55*, 729–743.

Taylor, S. E., & Fiske, S. T. (1978). Salience, attention, and attribution: Top of the head phenomena. In L. Berkowitz (Ed.), *Advances in experimental social psychology, 11*, Academic Press: NY.

Thompson, L. L. (1991). Information exchange in negotiation. *Journal of Experimental Social Psychology, 42*, 406–412.

Trawalter, S., & Richeson, J. A. (2006). Regulatory focus and executive function after interracial interactions. *Journal of Experimental Social Psychology, 42*, 406–412.

Tropp, L. R., & Pettigrew, T. F. (2005). Relationships between intergroup contact and prejudice among minority and majority status groups. *Psychological Science, 16*, 951–957.

Turner, R. N., Hewstone, M., Voci, A., & Vonofakou, C. (2008). A test of the extended intergroup contact hypothesis: The mediating role of intergroup anxiety, perceived ingroup and outgroup norms, and inclusion of the outgroup in the self. *Journal of Personality and Social Psychology, 95*, 843–860.

Vallacher, R. R., & Wegner, D. M. (1987). What do people think they're doing? Action identification and human behavior. *Psychological Review, 94*, 3–15.

Van Laar, C., Levin, S., Sinclair, S., & Sidanius, J. (2005). The effect of university roommate contact on ethnic attitudes and behavior. *Journal of Experimental Social Psychology, 41*, 329–345.

Vescio, T. K., Sechrist, G. B., & Paolucci, M. P. (2003). Perspective taking and prejudice reduction: The mediational role of empathy arousal and situational attributions. *European Journal of Social Psychology, 33*(4), 455–472.

Vorauer, J. D. (2005). Miscommunications surrounding efforts to reach out across group boundaries. *Personality and Social Psychology Bulletin, 31*, 1653–1664.

Vorauer, J. D. (2006). An information search model of evaluative concerns in intergroup interaction. *Psychological Review, 113*, 862–886.

Vorauer, J. D. (2008). Unprejudiced and self-focused: When intergroup contact is experienced as being about the ingroup rather than the outgroup. *Journal of Experimental Social Psychology, 44*, 912–919.

Vorauer, J. D., Gagnon, A., & Sasaki, S. J. (2009). Salient intergroup ideology and intergroup interaction. *Psychological Science, 20*, 838–845.

Vorauer, J. D., Hunter, A. J., Main, K. J., & Roy, S. (2000). Meta-stereotype activation: Evidence from indirect measures for specific evaluative concerns experienced by members of dominant groups in intergroup interaction. *Journal of Personality and Social Psychology, 78*, 690–707.

Vorauer, J. D., & Kumhyr, S. (2001). Is this about you or me? Self- versus other directed thoughts and feelings in response to intergroup interaction. *Personality and Social Psychology Bulletin, 27*, 706–719.

Vorauer, J. D., Main, K. J., & O'Connell, G. B. (1998). How do individuals expect to be viewed by members of lower status groups? Content and implications of meta-stereotypes. *Journal of Personality and Social Psychology, 75*, 917–937.

Vorauer, J. D., Martens, V., & Sasaki, S. J. (2009). When trying to understand detracts from trying to behave: Effects of perspective-taking in intergroup interaction. *Journal of Personality and Social Psychology, 96*, 811–827.

Vorauer, J. D., & Sakamoto, Y. (2006). I thought we could be friends, but...Systematic miscommunication and defensive distancing as obstacles to cross-group friendship formation. *Psychological Science, 17*, 326–331.

Vorauer, J. D., & Sakamoto, Y. (2008). Who cares what the outgroup thinks? Testing an information search model of the importance individuals accord to an outgroup member's view of them during intergroup interaction. *Journal of Personality and Social Psychology, 95*, 1467–1480.

Vorauer, J. D., & Sasaki, S. J. (2009). Helpful only in the abstract? Ironic effects of empathy in intergroup interaction. *Psychological Science, 20*, 191–197.

Vorauer, J. D., & Sasaki, S. J. (2010). In need of liberation or constraint? How intergroup attitudes moderate the behavioral implications of intergroup ideologies. *Journal of Experimental Social Psychology, 46*, 133–138.

Vorauer, J. D., & Sasaki, S. J. (2011). In the best versus the worst of times: Effects of salient intergroup ideology in threatening intergroup interactions. *Journal of Personality and Social Psychology, 101*, 307–320.

Vorauer, J. D., & Turpie, C. (2004). Relation of prejudice to choking versus shining under pressure in intergroup interaction: The disruptive effects of vigilance. *Journal of Personality and Social Psychology, 87*, 384–399.

Wolsko, C., Park, B., Judd, C. M., & Wittenbrink, B. (2000). Framing interethnic ideology: Effects of multicultural and color-blind perspectives on judgments of groups and individuals. *Journal of Personality and Social Psychology, 78*, 635–654.

Wright, S. C., Aron, A., McLaughlin-Volpe, T., & Ropp, S. A. (1997). The extended contact effect: Knowledge of cross-group friendships and prejudice. *Journal of Personality and Social Psychology, 73*, 73–90.

3 Is intergroup contact beneficial among intolerant people?

Exploring individual differences in the benefits of contact on attitudes

Gordon Hodson, Kimberly Costello, and Cara C. MacInnis

Researchers have traditionally dismissed the relevance of individual differences in domains such as intergroup contact, or have expressed pessimism about contact as a means to reduce prejudice among highly prejudiced (HP) individuals. Consider some of the following prominent examples:

> *Certain personalities . . . will not be affected positively by interracial contact. Their inner insecurity and their personal disorder will not permit them to benefit from the contact with a group against whom they are prejudiced because they will always need a scapegoat.*
>
> (Amir, 1969, p. 335)

> *The social identity perspective . . . suggests that personality tends to become irrelevant to prejudice where social identity or group membership is salient.*
>
> (Reynolds et al., 2007, p. 519)

> *Contact, as a situational variable, cannot always overcome the personal variable in prejudice.*
>
> (Allport, 1954, p. 280)

> *The deeply prejudiced both avoid intergroup contact and resist positive effects from it.*
>
> (Pettigrew, 1998, p. 80)

> *Intergroup interactions are also doomed when the interactants are prejudiced against each other's groups.*
>
> (Nelson, 2006, p. 154)

If individual differences are indeed *irrelevant*, situational interventions would work with efficiency and efficacy across all individuals. Unfortunately this is not the case, and dismissing such variance as measurement error does not reflect the reality that some individuals (e.g., Hitler, Stalin) are arguably more prejudiced than others (e.g., Ghandi, Mandela), with most falling on a continuum somewhere between these extremes. If prejudice-relevant individual differences are considered *obstacles* to intergroup contact, the field might prematurely dismiss contact as an effective prejudice-reduction strategy targeting those most in need of intervention. As noted by Dhont and Van Hiel (2009, p. 176), "the idea that contact 'only works' among those who are already at a low level of prejudice precludes it from being adapted as a social engineering tool." A prejudice-reduction strategy is valuable, in part, to the extent that it improves intergroup attitudes among intolerant persons. As our review and analyses of new data will soon reveal, contact may not only improve intergroup attitudes among intolerant persons, but it may even work best among such individuals.

Surprisingly, the role of individual differences in contact settings has remained relatively unexamined until recently. In addressing this shortcoming, we consider the merits of two prominent perspectives in influencing the contact literature: (a) individual differences are *irrelevant*, a spill-over from some social psychological approaches toward prejudice more generally; and (b) individual differences are *obstacles* to prejudice reduction via intergroup contact. The prominence of these implicit propositions may explain the dearth of research available on person-based factors in contact settings. Our present review discusses past research and introduces new data, concluding that pessimism about the benefits of contact among HPs is unwarranted. Noting that contact does work among prejudiced people, we conclude by proposing directions for theory development and future research.

Contact hypothesis

Researchers and theorists have long argued for the benefits of intergroup contact on intergroup attitudes (Allport, 1954; Cook, 1960; Hewstone & Brown, 1986; Pettigrew, 1998; Williams, 1964). The *Contact Hypothesis* is the simple premise that increased contact among groups, especially congenial contact, improves outgroup attitudes (see also Hodson & Hewstone, Chapter 1). In support, a recent comprehensive meta-analysis by Pettigrew and Tropp (2006) reveals a consistent but small correlation between contact and favorable outgroup attitudes (approximately .20). As hypothesized, this relation strengthens under "optimal" contact conditions (e.g., equal group status, cooperation norms, common goals, institutional support). Less clear is the causal nature of contact-attitude relations: does contact reduce prejudice, or do tolerant people approach contact (and intolerant people avoid contact)? This question ultimately concerns *individual factors*, plaguing contact researchers for decades, in part from a failure to consider person variables. Although there remains little doubt that contact exerts causal influence on attitudes, as evidenced through sophisticated correlational analyses (Pettigrew, 1997), longitudinal studies (Binder et al., 2009; Van Laar, Levin, Sinclair, & Sidanius, 2005), and experiments (Ensari & Miller, 2002; Van Laar et al., 2005; Wilder & Thompson, 1980), the tricky problem of the "intolerant person avoiding contact" lingers. After all, demonstrating experimentally that X (contact) *can* cause Y (positive attitudes) does not preclude the possibility that Y can also cause X (Simonton, 1982; see also Costello & Hodson, 2011). Indeed, recent longitudinal evidence reveals an attitudes-to-contact effect of equal magnitude to its contact-to-attitudes counterpart (Binder et al., 2009). Such findings beg the question: do individuals who bring personal biases into contact settings benefit from these experiences, exhibiting more favorable intergroup attitudes than their contact-free counterparts?

Early contact theorists were not optimistic. Allport (1954) understood that contextual factors might be impeded or even "overcome" by person-factors (see introductory quotations), and others shared this view (e.g., Cook & Selltiz, 1955; Mussen, 1950). However, individual differences failed to feature prominently in theory development until Pettigrew's (1998) re-formulation put person factors relatively on par with situational determinants. Individual differences, he argued, are critical for two reasons: "prior attitudes and experiences influence *whether people seek or avoid* intergroup contact, and *what the effects of contact will be*" (Pettigrew, 1998, p. 77, emphases added). Although it is well-known that HPs avoid intergroup contact (e.g., Hodson, 2008; Hodson, Harry, & Mitchell, 2009; Jackson & Poulsen, 2005; Williams, 1964), the issue concerning the effects of contact is more complicated. Initially, little evidence was available to address the concern. Despite Pettigrew's (1998) highly-cited theoretical reformulation, the role of person-factors remains empirically unclear and a pressing concern. If contact is beneficial only among persons low in prejudice (LPs), contact is of limited value, lowering biases among those already favorable toward the outgroup. Even more worrying is the possibility that contact exacerbates prejudices among HPs, a concern we outline shortly.

In our analysis, two ideological orientations characterizing outgroup intolerance serve as our focal points.[1] *Right-wing authoritarians* (RWAs), (Altemeyer, 1996) cling to conventions and traditions, submit to authorities, and aggress against outgroups when sanctioned. Representative scale items include: "Our country desperately needs a mighty leader who will do what has to be done to destroy the radical new ways and sinfulness that are ruining us", and "There is no 'ONE right way' to live life; everybody has to create their *own* way (reversed)." Those higher in *social dominance orientation* (SDO), (Pratto, Sidanius, Stallworth, & Malle, 1994) endorse intergroup hierarchies and group inequality. Sample items include: "To get ahead in life, it is sometimes necessary to step on other groups," and "Group equality should be our ideal (reversed)." Because these variables represent particularly strong individual difference predictors of prejudice (Altemeyer, 1998; Hodson & Esses, 2005), identifying strategies to reduce prejudices held by such individuals is imperative. However, interventions have frequently met with failure. For example, a prejudice reduction value-confrontation technique challenging the common endorsement of individual (e.g., freedom) over collective (e.g., equality) values was ineffective among RWAs (Altemeyer, 1996). Educational exercises stressing equality and respect for others through case studies and role-playing have also backfired among authoritarians, worsening their outgroup attitudes (Avery, Bird, Johnstone, Sullivan, & Thalhammer, 1992). Likewise, challenging zero-sum competition beliefs held by SDOs has backfired (Esses, Dovidio, Jackson, & Armstrong, 2001).

Notably, these failed interventions all provoke or challenge dearly held ideological worldviews, one's "beliefs about the proper order of society and how it can be achieved" (Erikson & Tedin, 2003, p. 64). Idcologies are deeply rooted and psychologically meaningful, providing stability and enhancement of one's sense of prediction. Such beliefs are unlikely to be altered by short-term interventions, particularly when overtly seeking to generate change. Intergroup contact, in contrast, does not inherently provoke or antagonize one's worldviews (although, of course, it can). Rather, contact improves attitudes by reducing intergroup anxiety, boosting perspective-taking and empathy, and increasing outgroup knowledge (Pettigrew & Tropp, 2008), rendering outgroups less threatening. These findings suggest potential for contact benefits among HPs, because SDOs are higher in intergroup anxiety (Hodson, 2008), lower in empathy (Hodson, 2008; Pratto et al., 1994), lower in intergroup perspective-taking (Hodson, Choma, & Costello, 2009), and less inclusive in their intergroup representations (Costello & Hodson, 2010). Moreover, RWAs and SDOs perceive outgroups as threatening, partially explaining their negative attitudes (Hodson, Hogg, & MacInnis, 2009). Fortunately, intergroup contact operates on intergroup attitudes by attenuating factors that feed prejudice among people generally, suggesting the potential for positive contact effects among HPs. So why is the contact literature so mute about individual differences?

Proposition 1: Individual differences are irrelevant to addressing intergroup contact questions

A recurring theme in social psychology is that person factors do not meaningfully predict intergroup attitudes and/or should largely be ignored. An extreme version of this argument suggests that psychological processes brought into contact settings (e.g., beliefs, fears, cognitive styles, ideologies, personal goals/motives) are inconsequential. Few adopt this extreme position in earnest, but person factors are seriously minimized by some theorists adopting a social identity perspective. For instance, Reynolds, Turner, Haslam, and Ryan (2001, p. 433) argue that "it may be misleading and inappropriate to locate *explanations* of prejudice at the level of individual personality . . . . it is not possible to extrapolate directly from individual processes (i.e., personality) to shared collective intergroup behavior." At the same time, the SDO construct is criticized for being too pessimistic, fatalistic, and "bleak" by (supposedly) overemphasizing biology (Turner & Reynolds, 2003).[2] Interestingly, social identity theory has itself come under fire for being too bleak and over-emphasizing the relative inevitability of negative intergroup outcomes. Brown's (2002) two-pronged defence of social identity theory inadvertently defends empirical consideration of "bleak" individual differences: (a) it is better to know than deny psychological processes; (b) despite any apparently unavoidable negativity, "social psychologists have enough weapons in their armoury to combat any such 'inevitable' tendency toward in-group bias" (p. 196). We agree completely. Given the ubiquity of intergroup strife, we cannot reject theoretical approaches for reflecting negativity or we risk misrepresenting the very social problems we seek to solve.

Regardless of the reasons, "the individual" remains puzzlingly irrelevant in some theoretical camps (Hodson, 2009). This is problematic because social psychology ultimately seeks to understand how *individuals* participate in and react to group phenomena. Why would person factors influence interpersonal phenomena but become irrelevant in intergroup settings? Do human brains parse the social environment in this manner? Interactions with Brian (interpersonal) versus Brian the American (interpersonal *and* intergroup) will undoubtedly involve distinct processes. But are these processes so distinct as to involve entirely person-based factors in the former case but entirely social factors in the latter? Such a questionable conclusion would imply that we perceive targets only as individuals or group representatives, not both (either simultaneously or in rapid succession). Given that intergroup contact typically plays out over time, both person- and social-based factors undoubtedly contribute to outcomes.

More to the point, there is no sharp divide between individual and group behavior, but rather a *continuum* (Tajfel, 1978). Emphasizing social factors to the complete exclusion of person factors over-states an otherwise valid point that social contexts are important. As noted by Tajfel:

> if I take part in a race riot or strenuously and vocally support my local team during a football match, or demonstrate against the oppression of my group by another group, I interact with another group – as Sherif wrote – fully in terms of my group identification. However, the truism that marked individual differences will persist even in these situations is still valid.
>
> (1978, p. 402)

Although Tajfel stressed social factors in determining social outcomes, he recognized that social life is rarely so extreme as to negate individual differences. We agree. It makes little sense to posit a theoretical precipice (or line drawn in the sand) over which personal factors suddenly become irrelevant. Because group behavior originates within individuals, group life is influenced by person factors unless people are blank slates passively written upon by situations. In reality, links between social and person factors are flexible and reciprocal. Moreover, an analysis of both is necessary in order to grasp the complexity of social life. As reasoned by Kurt Lewin (1946), "[G]eneral laws and individual differences are merely two aspects of one problem; they are mutually dependent on each other and the study of the one cannot proceed without the study of the other." Intergroup contact, we argue, is no exception, to the extent that it involves individuals (as group representatives) interacting within an intergroup context.

Contemporary prejudice researchers are drawing explicit theoretical and empirical links between variables traditionally considered person versus situational. For instance, RWA and SDO are conceptualized as ideological constructs at the "interface between personality and social psychology" (Ekehammar, Akrami, Gylje, & Zakrisson, 2004, p. 465) rather than traditional "personality" variables. Duckitt (2005) places these ideological variables between broader personality variables and situational factors on the one hand, and prejudice on the other, with personality operating on outgroup attitudes via RWA and SDO (see Hodson, Hogg et al., 2009; Sibley & Duckitt, 2008). These synergies recognize that persons react to and influence intergroup contexts.

These theoretical developments are recent however, with individual differences remaining largely absent from contact research. Pettigrew and Tropp's (2006) meta-analysis reviewed over 500 studies, with only age and sex examined frequently enough to serve as testable moderators.[3] Even when examined, the treatment of individual differences frequently reveals little about if or how HPs benefit from contact. Many consider person variables *independently* from contact variables (Sagiv & Schwartz, 1995; Stephan & Rosenfield, 1978; Williams, 1964). For instance, Miller, Smith, and Mackie (2004) found that among White participants, attitudes toward Blacks were predicted by both SDO and contact, through emotional reactions. Others consider contact as a mediator, with low Openness and low Agreeableness predicting outgroup attitudes through lower contact (Jackson & Poulsen, 2005), or with lower abstract reasoning predicting increased prejudice through heightened RWA and decreased contact (Hodson & Busseri, 2012). Others negate person factors, removing individual differences from contact-attitude relations as statistical noise (e.g., Liebkind, Haaramo, & Jasinskaja-Lahti, 2000). In elaborate experimental and longitudinal studies, Van Laar and colleagues "removed much of the variance in prejudice associated with individual variability, including pre-existing differences in attitudes and behaviors, demographic factors, and previous contact experiences" (Van Laar, Levin, & Sidanius, 2008, p. 133). These strategies suited their research question (*does contact impact attitudes?*), and we ourselves employ such techniques in some upcoming analyses. However, analyses that statistically control person factors preclude consideration of positive contact effects *among* HPs, a point we revisit later.

First we consider the proposition that person-factors are irrelevant in predicting intergroup attitudes. For the present chapter, we collected a dataset (111 women, 38 men, 3 unspecified) at a Canadian university (mean age = 19.43, *SD* = 3.67). Most self-identified as White/Caucasian (91 percent), with members of target groups excluded from pertinent analyses. Participants indicated attitudes toward homosexuals, professors, immigrants, depressed people, the obese, AIDS patients, the homeless, and illegal drug users (1 = *strongly dislike*, 7 = *strongly like*). Degree and quality of contact with each group was assessed on 7-point scales. The 16-item SDO scale (Pratto et al., 1994) and a shortened 12-item RWA scale (from Altemeyer, 1996) were administered. Political conservatism was assessed by 3 items reflecting conservatism generally, toward social issues, and economics (Skitka, Mullen, Griffin, Hutchinson, & Chamberlin, 2002).

Regression analyses tested the relative contributions of situation (contact) and person (ideology) variables to intergroup attitudes (see Table 3.1). In Model A, contact variables were entered at Step 1, with person variables entered at Step 2. Model B tested the reverse order. Several findings are noteworthy. First, in Model A Step 1, contact quality consistently predicted attitudes across outgroup targets, and contact quantity uniquely predicted in 50 percent of cases. At Step 2, person variables as a block significantly improved prediction of intergroup attitudes beyond contact variables in virtually every case. This finding is impressive considering that contact variables and attitude measures share method-variance by tapping the same target (e.g., contact with X and attitudes toward X), whereas the individual difference measures are largely non-group specific. In Model B, person variables (especially SDO) predicted attitudes toward groups at Step 1.

Table 3.1 Relative contributions of person and situation variables on intergroup attitudes

	Favorable attitudes toward target								
	Homo	Prof	Immt	Depress	Obese	AIDS	Homeless	Drug	Mean
Model A									
Step 1									
Contact quantity	.14*	.22**	.02	.08	.04	.06	.18*	.19*	
Contact quality	.65***	.53***	.60***	.49***	.53***	.65***	.46***	.40***	
R^2	.54***	.37***	.36***	.27***	.30***	.44***	.32***	.30***	.36
Step 2									
SDO	−.17*	−.12	−.17*	−.13	−.15‡	−.13‡	−.15‡	−.13	
RWA	−.19*	.11	−.16	−.15	.00	−.04	−.01	−.19*	
Conservatism	−.04	−.23**	−.04	.01	−.06	−.13	−.10	.03	
R^2	.61***	.43***	.43***	.31***	.33***	.49***	.36***	.36***	.42
ΔR^2	.07***	.06*	.07***	.05*	.03	.05*	.04*	.06*	.05
Model B									
Step 1									
SDO	−.27***	−.20*	−.28***	−.20*	−.20*	−.25**	−.25**	−.06	
RWA	−.36***	.11	−.26**	−.22*	−.06	−.21*	−.03	−.40***	
Conservatism	−.14	−.24*	−.01	.07	−.09	−.09	−.10	.04	
R^2	.38***	.09**	.20***	.10**	.08**	.19***	.10**	.16***	.16
Step 2									
Contact quantity	.16*	.22**	.03	.12	.03	.07	.20**	.18*	
Contact quality	.47***	.50***	.50***	.43***	.50***	.57***	.40***	.34***	
R^2	.61***	.43***	.43***	.31***	.33***	.49***	.36***	.36***	.42
ΔR^2	.23***	.34***	.23***	.22***	.25***	.30***	.26***	.19***	.25

Note. Homo = homosexual, Prof = professor, Immt = immigrant, Depress = depressed people, Drug = drug user. Analyses exclude target members. Standardized betas reported. ‡ $p \le .06$; * $p < .05$; ** $p < .01$; *** $p < .001$.

At Step 2, contact variables predicted attitudes beyond person-variables. Intriguingly, contact quantity uniquely predicted attitudes toward four target groups, even after removing individual avoidance tendencies. Mere contact promotes positive attitudes beyond personal biases. Overall, both person and contact variables are important in predicting intergroup attitudes.

Again statistically controlling person factors, our present dataset addresses another pressing contact question: do contact-attitude benefits involving one group *generalize* to attitudes toward uninvolved groups? Pettigrew (2009, p. 56) summarizes this problem succinctly:

> Do primary contact effects typically generalize to other, non-contacted outgroups? Or does the secondary transfer effect largely reflect the nonrecursive phenomenon whereby more tolerant people engage in more intergroup contact generally *and* harbor less prejudice against a wide variety of outgroups?

Questions concerning the influence of person-variables, therefore, underlie basic questions about contact generalization.

Pettigrew and Tropp (2006) found evidence for this "rarely considered form of generalization" (p. 759; see also Lolliot et al., Chapter 4). Using large-scale survey datasets, contact effects generalized to uninvolved groups (Pettigrew, 1997, 2009). In these studies, individual differences are controlled statistically, leading to conclusions that generalization occurs *despite* individual differences in education, age, sex, or even conservatism (Ha, 2008 [cited in Pettigrew, 2009]; Pettigrew, 1997). These rich and representative datasets nonetheless lack the psychological or ideological variables that serve as our focus. An ideal test would control individual differences more proximal to prejudice, such as RWA and SDO. If contact with Group X predicts attitudes toward Group Y after controlling for conservatism, RWA, and SDO, we can assert with confidence that generalization effects are attributable to intergroup contact, not prejudice-relevant characteristics of individuals.

The analyses in Table 3.2 consider relations between contact (quantity/quality) and outgroup attitudes. These partial correlations statistically remove variance from RWA, SDO, and conservatism. First note the *specificity* regarding contact-attitude relations: congruent values in the diagonals (contact with X and attitudes toward X) are predominantly significant and larger than incongruent cases (contact with X and attitudes toward Y). In some cases, specificity was exclusive. For instance, attitudes toward homosexuals were only predicted by increased contact with homosexuals (not other groups). In addition, increased contact with professors was only associated with favorable attitudes toward professors, not other outgroups.

However, *generalization* effects were also evident. For instance, favorable attitudes toward the homeless were also predicted by: (a) increased contact with homosexuals, immigrants, the depressed, the obese, and AIDS sufferers; (b) more positive contact with homosexuals, the depressed, the obese, AIDS sufferers, and illegal drug users. Increased contact with homosexuals also predicted more favorable attitudes toward the depressed, AIDS sufferers, and the homeless.[4] Consistent with Pettigrew (2009), generalization (or "secondary transfer") emerged for

Table 3.2 Partial correlations (controlling person-variables) between contact and attitudes

| | Favorable attitudes | | | | | | | | |
	Homosexuals	Professors	Immigrants	Depressed	Obese	AIDS	Homeless	Drug users	Generalized mean
CONTACT QUANTITY									
Homosexuals	**.36***	.14	.06	.31***	.11	.21*	.23**	-.02	.15
Professors	.07	**.31***	.07	-.05	.04	.04	.09	.13	.06
Immigrants	.00	.19*	**.13**	.08	.14	.13	.18*	.12	.12
Depressed	-.01	.02	-.04	**.26**	.18*	.11	.19*	.15‡	.09
Obese	-.01	-.01	-.07	.07	**.19***	.09	.21**	-.02	.04
AIDS	.05	.15‡	.01	.14	.23**	**.21**	.18*	.16*	.13
Homeless	.07	.12	.15*	.21*	.26***	.26***	**.38***	.13	.17
Drug users	-.03	.02	-.10	.30**	-.03	.14	.12	**.38***	.06
CONTACT QUALITY									
Homosexuals	**.57***	.26**	.20*	.31**	.13	.32***	.30**	.02	.22
Professors	.17*	**.55***	.14	.02	.06	.16*	.11	-.02	.09
Immigrants	.10	.05	**.50***	.11	.06	.03	.16	-.08	.06
Depressed	.12	.11	.02	**.47***	.28**	.33***	.29***	.21*	.19
Obese	.15*	.17*	.14	.10	**.51***	.24**	.37***	.02	.17
AIDS	.21**	.23**	.27**	.42***	.46***	**.60***	.45***	.19*	.32
Homeless	.13	.17*	.24**	.28**	.40***	.35***	**.50***	.17*	.25
Drug users	-.06	.11	-.14	.27**	-.03	.21**	.19*	**.45***	.08

Note. Person-variables (social dominance orientation, right-wing authoritarianism, conservatism) statistically removed from correlations. Values in diagonal boxes represent congruence between contact group and attitude toward that group. Analyses exclude target members. ‡ $p < .06$; * $p < .05$; ** $p < .01$; *** $p < .001$.

similar/related outgroups, here across marginalized/deviant outgroups (vs. high-status professors). By considering rather than ignoring person-variables (here controlling their influence) we have clarified a "pivotal" (Pettigrew, 1998) question about contact generalization to uninvolved outgroups: *secondary transfer occurs even after controlling strong personal tendencies toward intolerance.*

In conclusion, empirically ignoring individual differences can hinder efforts to understand basic contact effects. Person-variables independently predicted attitudes beyond contact variables (Table 3.1), complementing contact effects on intergroup bias while highlighting the predictive importance of contact. Examining (rather than ignoring) person-variables also clarified generalization effects on attitudes toward uninvolved outgroups (see Table 3.2) in ways highlighting the importance of intergroup contact. Next we consider the joint (vs. competing) influence of person and situation variables in contact settings.

Proposition 2: Individual differences are obstacles to intergroup contact

The proposition that individual differences are relevant but problematic to promoting positive intergroup attitudes is also well-established in the contact literature. As an eminent personality theorist, Allport (1954) not surprisingly contemplated individual factors in contact settings. His seminal chapter on contact, however, emphasized *negative* person factors. He concluded that "Prejudice (*unless deeply rooted in the character structure of the individual*) may be reduced by equal status contact between majority and minority groups in the pursuit of common goals [emphasis added] (p. 281)." Although little direct evidence of person-based resistance was then available, Allport observed that contact rarely succeeds uniformly across individuals. He drew heavily on Mussen's (1950) research on boys attending an interracial camp: half were uninfluenced by intergroup contact, one-quarter showed attitude improvements, but one-quarter demonstrated *increased* prejudice. Boys exhibiting increased prejudice following intergroup contact presented personalities characterized by aggression and dominance, fear of punishment, and parental antipathy (i.e., authoritarian qualities).

In his classic book on prejudice, Allport's (1954) contact chapter closed pessimistically: contact will fail "whenever the inner strain within the person is too tense, too insistent, to permit him to profit from the structure of the outer situation" (p. 281). This thinking influenced the field over the subsequent 50 years. However, this early pessimism was based on an outdated depiction of authoritarianism as a dysfunctional, maladjusted "personality syndrome" (Hodson, 2008, 2011, in press). The then-prevailing authoritarianism construct (Adorno, Frenkel-Brunswik, Levinson, & Sanford, 1950) was founded upon psychodynamic principles, such as displaced aggression, with a distinctly clinical and dysfunctional flavor. Although Allport's personal take on authoritarianism similarly highlighted fear and insecurity, he also introduced cognitive factors, ideological worldviews, and emphasized contextual factors. However Allport maintained an emphasis on maladjustment (Duckitt, 2005). Such operationalizations naturally fuelled pessimism about whether authoritarians were stable and cooperative enough to benefit from intergroup contact (Amir, 1969).

In contrast, modern operationalizations of authoritarianism (e.g., RWA) are not necessarily associated with psychological maladjustment (Altemeyer, 1996; Hodson, Hogg et al., 2009). Nevertheless, other factors set the stage for potentially negative responses to contact among HPs. For instance, the *intergroup* nature of contact is very salient for prejudiced individuals, and perceiving interactions as "intergroup" can increase intergroup anxiety and prejudice (Islam & Hewstone, 1993). Furthermore, authoritarians are lower in Openness to Experience (Ekehammar et al., 2004; Hodson, Hogg et al., 2009; Hodson & Sorrentino, 1999), therefore resisting novelty and change. Authoritarians associate in "tight circles" of similarly-prejudiced others (Altemeyer, 1996), resulting in heightened ethnocentricity and ingroup-focus (Duckitt, 2005). RWAs are generally threat-sensitive (Cohrs & Ibler, 2009), expressing prejudice because outgroups are considered threatening (Cohrs & Ibler, 2009; Duckitt, 2005; Hodson, Hogg et al., 2009). Invested in intergroup power, SDOs may seek dominance over outgroups in contact settings, exacerbating conflict. Troublingly, RWAs and SDOs consider prejudice inevitable and interventions futile (Hodson & Esses, 2005). These ideological orientations could therefore hinder positive contact effects. Although pessimism expressed by early contact theorists originated from outdated conceptualizations of authoritarianism, contemporary research nonetheless suggests sizeable obstacles for positive contact among HPs.

However, contact may yet improve intergroup attitudes among HPs. High RWAs consider themselves good and moral people (Altemeyer, 1994, 1996), self-reporting as interpersonally agreeable (Ekehammar et al., 2004; Sibley & Duckitt, 2008), or even more agreeable (Hodson, Hogg et al., 2009), than others generally. These good intentions may be harnessed upon overcoming natural tendencies to avoid the unfamiliar. Moreover, with RWAs and SDOs being sensitive to situational factors (Duckitt, 2005), it is important to target processes that otherwise exacerbate motivations to reduce danger/threat and act competitively. For instance, because SDOs reject immigrants posing symbolic or realistic threats (Costello & Hodson, 2011), interventions reducing perceptions of *outgroup threat* and *foreignness/difference* should attenuate their negative attitudes. Interventions can be tailored to specific personality-types, with intergroup contact well-positioned to serve this function. Contact exposes outgroup-relevant concerns and fears as exaggerated and unfounded (Stephan & Stephan, 2000), reducing anxiety while boosting empathy and outgroup knowledge (Pettigrew & Tropp, 2008). To the extent that intergroup contact reduces biases through mechanisms that do not challenge or provoke one's worldviews, but increase empathy and reduce anxiety/threat, contact can theoretically benefit HPs.

To our knowledge, this question was first addressed by Maoz's (2003) two-day structured dialogue exercise among Israeli and Palestinian youth (15–16 years). Maoz predicted that Jewish-Israeli "hawks" (tough-minded individuals defending ingroup interests) would be less motivated to engage in contact and would benefit less than self-identified "doves" (those preferring negotiation and cooperation), reflecting the aforementioned pessimism. Indeed, doves (vs. hawks) demonstrated more desire for contact and reported more positive contact goals on pre-contact measures, and increased encounter satisfaction, perceived outgroup knowledge gain, and openness toward the outgroup on post-contact measures. However, doves demonstrated no actual change in attitudes or orientations over time, whereas hawks showed significant improvements in Palestinian attitudes from pre- to post-contact encounter. This encouraging result was unanticipated by Maoz, who subsequently called for future research to replicate beneficial contact effects among hawkish adults.

Two conceptual considerations informed the next study we discuss, directly testing this possibility. First, HPs avoid outgroup contact when left to their own devices, making naturalistic studies of HP-contact challenging. Second, meta-analytic evidence (Pettigrew & Tropp, 2006) reveals stronger contact effects in relatively "closed" (e.g., workplace, schools) than "open" (e.g., travel) settings. Prisons therefore represent unique and socially important contact settings, with racial strife unfolding in highly constrained contexts placing limits on outgroup avoidance. However, *extremely* confined contact settings may exceed the normal boundary conditions that otherwise suggest stronger contact benefits in closed set-tings, worsening intergroup attitudes. Exploring these possibilities, Hodson (2008) tested Person x Situation interaction patterns in several UK prisons. Among White inmates higher in SDO, increased contact with Black inmates was hypothesized to be associated with less ingroup bias. Whites equivalently high in SDO but lacking intergroup contact were expected to exhibit relatively higher ingroup bias. Inmates lower in SDO were expected to be relatively uninfluenced by contact, demonstrat-ing less bias generally. In Study 1, high SDOs reported less intergroup contact and less perceived institutional support for positive contact, setting the stage for inter-group bias. However, significant Person (SDO) x Contact (quantity/quality) inter-actions emerged as expected direction: (a) inmates higher in SDO and reporting lit-tle contact demonstrated substantial bias, but (b) inmates similarly high in SDO but reporting increased contact demonstrated significantly reduced ingroup bias. This pattern held after controlling perceived prison norms favoring positive contact. A similar Person x Situation pattern was found for contact conditions: increased SDO was associated with decreased ingroup bias when supportive institutional contact norms were perceived, even after controlling for contact quantity. In all cases, rela-tions between contact and attitudes were non-significant among low SDOs.

Hodson (2008, Study 2) aimed to replicate and explain this effect in a larger prison. Whereas Study 1 inmates provided subjective reports of contact (e.g., *no contact at all* to *very much contact*), Study 2 inmates provided more objective indications (e.g., number of hours per week interacting). Perceived contact qual-ity (i.e., pleasant and cooperative) was also assessed. The results replicated Study 1: White inmates higher in SDO demonstrated less ingroup bias after engaging in more intergroup contact or experiencing more positive contact. As in Study 1, Person x Contact Quantity interactions remained significant after controlling for contact quality and *vice versa*. Overall, these studies indicate the importance of institutional norms, contact quantity and quality, in reducing biases among SDOs. Study 2 also revealed *why* contact was associated with decreased bias among

SDOs: increased and more positive contact was associated with increased out-group empathy that subsequently reduced bias.[5]

Hodson's (2008) prison studies provided consistent evidence that HPs experiencing contact exhibit less bias. Although non-experimental, these findings are informative when interpreted literally: "*those high in SDO who do experience optimal contact conditions exhibit significantly less in-group bias*, and *increased and positive contact conditions are related to decreased in-group bias in part through their relation to increased empathy* among these individuals" (Hodson, 2008, p. 345). But do these effects extend to RWA? Moreover, will contact benefits among HPs in prison extend to unconstrained "everyday" intergroup contact settings? That is, given more choice about engaging in contact, HPs might fail to benefit from contact through outgroup avoidance.

Shedding some light, Pettigrew (2008) analyzed German poll data. As expected, contact with immigrants was positively associated with more favorable attitudes. Unlike the prison studies, this association was evident among low and high HPs (here, RWAs). Nevertheless, the essential finding from Hodson (2008) was replicated using RWA as the person variable: HPs experiencing more contact demonstrated less outgroup bias, whereas HPs experiencing less contact demonstrated more outgroup bias. Benefits of contact among prejudiced individuals are not limited to confined intergroup settings ensuring intergroup contact.

Dhont and Van Hiel (2009) examined Person x Situation patterns in several community samples. These authors considered both RWA and SDO in interaction with quantity (Study 1) or quality (Study 2) of contact with immigrants in Belgium. Their results confirmed contact benefits among HPs. In Study 1, high RWAs experiencing more contact reported less prejudice, whereas low RWAs were less prejudiced regardless of contact (conceptually similar to Hodson, 2008). The SDO x Contact interaction was not significant but nonetheless supported the central proposition: among high SDOs increased contact was associated with significantly less prejudice. Among low SDOs, a marginally significant contact-attitude relation showed the same pattern, weakening the interaction (akin to Pettigrew, 2008). In Study 2, similar patterns were established: RWAs or SDOs experiencing more positive or less negative interactions with immigrants reported significantly less prejudice than like-minded counterparts experiencing less positive or more negative contact.

Countering doubts by earlier theorists (Allport, 1954; Cook & Selltiz, 1955; Williams, 1947), Dhont and Van Hiel (2009) confirmed the benefits of contact among HPs, replicating Maoz (2003), Hodson (2008), and Pettigrew (2008). However, their participants were adult neighbors of student researchers, potentially introducing undetectable biases in sampling or responding. Consistent with this concern, their samples were unrepresentatively well-educated (55–62 percent with postsecondary degrees). In addition, mediators were not considered, leaving it unclear why HPs in free-contact settings benefit from contact.

This question was addressed in a study on contact and friendship effects on attitudes toward homosexuals among heterosexuals higher in RWA or heterosexual identification (Hodson, Harry et al., 2009). Heterosexual university students in the

UK (M_{age} = 20 years) disclosed contact quantity and quality with homosexuals, in addition to information about direct and indirect friendships with homosexuals. Whereas direct friendships represent straightforward relationships extending across group boundaries, indirect friendships (or "extended-contact") involve ingroup friends with cross-group friendships (Wright, Aron, McLaughlin-Volpe, & Ropp, 1997; see Davies, Wright, Aron, & Comeau, this volume). It was then unknown whether either direct or indirect friendships would be effective among HPs. After all, prejudiced persons may avoid friendship-based contact even more than casual contact. However, given the intimate nature of friendships, and the positive friendship norms promoted by indirect friendships, cross-group relations may represent powerful prejudice-reduction means among HPs *once established or perceived.* Because contact and friendship work among HPs by greasing the wheels of successful interaction, rather than directly antagonizing ideological belief systems, contact/friendship among those higher in RWA or ingroup identification were expected to reduce outgroup prejudice through *reduced outgroup threat perceptions* and *increased inclusion of other with the self* (see Davies et al., this volume).

Hodson, Harry et al. (2009) found evidence of significant Person (RWA/identification) x Contact (quantity/quality/direct friendship/indirect friendship) interactions. Higher RWA was associated with significant decreases in anti-homosexual attitudes upon experiencing increased contact, more positive contact, more homosexual friends, or more heterosexual friends with homosexual friends. All RWA x Contact interactions remained significant even after statistically controlling for other contact/friendship variables or ingroup identification. Similar patterns were found considering identification as the person-variable: strong identifiers demonstrated less outgroup prejudice when experiencing more contact, positive contact, or either type of friendship. Interaction patterns held after controlling for RWA and the other contact variables. Two interactions were not statistically significant due to positive contact/friendship effects also found among low identifiers. In every test, HPs exhibited less outgroup prejudice when experiencing contact or friendship, but increased prejudice when contact or friendship were relatively absent. As predicted, contact and friendship among RWAs or high identifiers reduced prejudice through the proposed mediators: decreased outgroup threat perceptions and increased self-outgroup overlap. These encouraging results provide researchers and intervention strategists multiple methods to reduce prejudice among HPs. For instance, indirect friendship norms can be manipulated in laboratories, classrooms, and work environments.

Our present dataset provides additional evidence of contact benefits among HPs, but this time across several individual difference variables and multiple outgroups. Panel A of Table 3.3 reveals expected negative relations between ideology (SDO, RWA, conservatism) and favorable intergroup attitudes across various outgroups. These ideologues expressed negativity toward outgroups generally liked (e.g., professors) and disliked (e.g., the depressed) by the sample overall. Person x Contact interaction analyses revealed mostly non-significant interactions.[6] As with past studies reporting no Person x Situation interactions

(Dhont & Van Hiel, 2009, Study 1 for SDO; Hodson, Harry et al., 2009 for ingroup identification; Pettigrew, 2008), these failed interactions were explained by contact benefits among LPs *and* HPs. Encouragingly, persons higher in SDO, RWA, or conservatism (based on median-splits) benefitted from intergroup contact across multiple outgroups (Panel B, Table 3.3). Increased contact benefitted

Table 3.3 Relations between: (A) person variables and favorable intergroup attitudes (top panel); and (B) contact and favorable attitudes, as a function of person variables (bottom panel)

(A) Relations between individual differences and intergroup attitudes

	SDO	RWA	Conservatism
Intergroup attitudes			
Professors (+)	−.24**	−.10	−.24**
Immigrants (+)	−.37***	−.31***	−.23**
Homosexuals (+)	−.45***	−.54***	−.43***
Obese (+)	−.25**	−.17*	−.19*
AIDS inflicted (+)	−.37***	−.35***	−.28***
Homeless (0)	−.29***	−.18*	−.19*
Depressed (−)	−.25**	−.25**	−.13
Illicit drug users (−)	−.19*	−.35***	−.15

(B) Relations between contact and intergroup attitudes (as function of person variables)

	SDO		RWA		Conservatism	
	low	high	low	high	low	high
Contact quantity						
Professors	.34**	.35**	.33**	.42***	.21	.48***
Immigrants	.05	.20	.24*	.11	.12	.19
Homosexuals	.40***	.51***	.46***	.44***	.37**	.50***
Obese	.13	.21	.23*	.17	.15	.22*
AIDS inflicted	.24*	.24*	.28*	.12	.24*	.22*
Homeless	.37**	.37**	.37**	.44***	.32**	.46***
Depressed	.35**	.03	.39**	.07	.18	.25*
Illicit drug users	.36**	.44***	.45***	.27*	.46***	.31**
Mean	.28	.29	.34	.26	.26	.33
Contact quality						
Professors	.53***	.60***	.58***	.55***	.58***	.56***
Immigrants	.54***	.62***	.50***	.67***	.67***	.53***
Homosexuals	.74***	.64***	.70***	.62***	.69***	.68***
Obese	.52***	.52***	.39**	.68***	.53***	.52***
AIDS inflicted	.71***	.53***	.59***	.67***	.67***	.62***
Homeless	.61***	.35**	.60***	.47***	.51***	.59***
Depressed	.59***	.29*	.60***	.30*	.47***	.56***
Illicit drug users	.41***	.53***	.49***	.34**	.64***	.29*
Mean	.58	.51	.56	.54	.60	.54

Note. Target groups rank-ordered by positivity; valences reflect means significantly above scale midpoint (+), below midpoint (−), or at mid-point (0). Analyses exclude members of target groups (*N*s range 131–152). *$p \leq .05$, *$p < .01$, *$p < .001$.

high SDOs (for 63 percent of groups), RWAs (for 50 percent of groups), and conservatives (for 88 percent of groups). Results for contact quality are particularly encouraging: those high in SDO, RWA, or conservatism demonstrated more positive attitudes toward all outgroups when previous contact was considered pleasant and cooperative. These results illustrate HPs benefitting from increased contact and more pleasant contact across a range of outgroups, from those generally liked to those generally disliked. Contact among HPs therefore reduces prejudicial attitudes across various types of social groups, including those severely marginalized.

To conclude, the proposition that contact is problematic among prejudice-prone persons is not well-supported. Early pessimism about HPs not benefitting from contact appears unwarranted. Intolerant ideologues either benefitted from contact more than tolerant individuals (Dhont & Van Hiel, 2009; Hodson, 2008; Hodson, Harry et al., 2009; Maoz, 2003), or equivalently (present dataset; see also Pettigrew, 2008). In fact, *failing to find positive contact effects among HPs is clearly the exception, not the norm* (see also Hodson, 2011). When considering contact quality, HPs consistently demonstrated beneficial contact effects across studies. Although HPs bring negativity to intergroup interactions, their prejudicial attitudes are attenuated upon experiencing intergroup contact.

Impediments to theory development: construct operationalization

A complete understanding of the individual in contact settings is hindered by a lack of conceptual clarity. That is, many so-called "situational" variables actually involve elements of the person, and so-called "person" variables involve elements of the situation. Ideological variables (RWA, SDO) are becoming less problematic, explicitly being considered "hybrids" (Hodson, 2009) that psychologically link person-based and situation-based constructs (see Duckitt, 2005; Ekehammar et al., 2004; Hodson, Hogg et al., 2009). The case is less clear for other contact-relevant variables. Although this issue warrants more attention than space allows, we introduce these issues to spur future theory development.

"Situational" variables are not clearly situational

The contact literature traditionally considers many (if not most) contact variables as *situational*, especially contact quantity and quality (even in our research). However, the extent to which these variables are driven by person factors remains largely unknown. Responses to questions about the amount or quality of intergroup contact experienced are undoubtedly influenced by personal processes. Thus, when exploring institutional support for contact (e.g., Hodson, 2008, Study 1), responses should be recognized as *perceived* norms that may have little bearing on actual institutional support. Likewise, contact quality typically reflects *personal reactions* to contact as positive or negative, not objective assessments.

Being largely self-report, the contact literature primarily informs us about contact *perceptions*. This is not necessarily problematic; psychologists specialize in construals and mental representations, and these psychological processes may be more important and easily corrected than actual contact conditions. Our point is that failing to recognize personal filters of contact experiences perpetuates an under-emphasis of person-factors in contact settings.

A similar point applies to variables typically considered mediators of contact-attitude relations (e.g., intergroup anxiety, outgroup threat). As noted elsewhere (Hodson, 2008), measures of intergroup anxiety typically tap *general* unease about interacting with outgroup members as the sole ingroup representative. Even when tapping anxiety toward a specific outgroup it remains unclear whether we are assessing situational processes (as assumed) or personal ones. Scoring high in intergroup anxiety may inadvertently represent anxiety about interactions generally, including those with strangers or ingroup members. Similarly, outgroup threat perceptions can represent spillover from a generalized threat sensitivity not intergroup in nature. These constructs may therefore involve more "personal" elements than is commonly acknowledged, representing both personal and situational processes. At minimum it is important to keep in mind that some people are naturally higher in intergroup anxiety, and that intergroup anxiety can be evoked in context. Researchers are encouraged to carefully conceptualize and label constructs to avoid obscuring the role of individual and situation factors.

"Person" variables have situational origins and reactivity

Researchers emphasizing personal sources of prejudice are often misrepresented as arguing that *only* person factors are important. Although few presently adopt this position, early authoritarian-based approaches (Adorno et al., 1950) failed to specify roles for contextual factors, creating an early theoretical divide. Critics (e.g., Reynolds et al., 2001) have raised interesting concerns that have pressed contemporary researchers to clarify person-based theorizing in prejudice research. In modern theorizing, contexts such as contact settings are considered important in the development and expression of individual differences. Altemeyer (1994, 1996) argues that RWA originates from infrequent outgroup contact and excessive ingroup contact. Duckitt's (2005) Dual Process Model clearly stipulates roles for situational influences (e.g., dangerous or competitive contexts) in fuelling ideology (RWA, SDO). Rather than pitting explanations against each other, researchers bear fruit by adopting integrative approaches. For example, Gatto, Dambrun, Kerbrat, and de Oliveira (2010) tracked police officers during training, finding both selection (i.e., person) and socialization (i.e., situation) forces responsible for developing bias amongst police in their outgroup interactions. That is, police academies attract those higher in RWA, and socialization processes foster bias norms. Even more promisingly, personality can be considered a *process* operating by "if-then" rules directly in tune with one's intergroup-relevant environment (Devine, Rhodewalt, & Siemionko, 2008).

Oustanding issues and future directions

(Quasi)experimental and longitudinal research

Although most of the studies we reviewed are not experimental, they nonetheless shed light on causal factors in ways corroborating experimental evidence on contact-attitude effects (Ensari & Miller, 2002; Van Laar et al., 2005). That is, HPs reporting little or poor contact expressed heightened prejudice, but similarly ideological HPs experiencing contact or friendships expressed significantly less bias (present data; Dhont & Van Hiel, 2009; Hodson, 2008; Hodson, Harry et al., 2009; Pettigrew, 2008). Although the vast majority of contact research generally is self-report (Pettigrew & Tropp, 2006), suitably capturing real-life experiences (Hodson, 2008; Michela, 1990; Miller et al., 2004; Voci & Hewstone, 2003), multi-method convergence is required. Although Mussen's (1950) early quasi-experimental research on authoritarianism generated pessimistic conclusions, his sample was small and conceptualization of person-factors now outdated. Likewise, a quasi-experiment that randomly assigned adults taking ski lessons to minimal groups produced mixed results: authoritarians expressed more anti-outgroup bias following decreased contact, but infrequent outgroup contact also increased their anti-ingroup biases (Downing & Monaco, 1986). Like Mussen (1950), however, these results were based on an invalidated authoritarianism measure.

Although experimental research is encouraged, researchers are advised to approach this task cautiously (Hodson, 2008, in press). Intergroup interactions among HPs may work best when self-initiated or when contact exposure is relatively passive (vs. overtly orchestrated). Direct manipulations to coerce changes in values/beliefs can fall flat (Altemeyer, 1996) or backfire (Avery et al., 1992; Esses, Dovidio, Jackson, & Armstrong, 2001) among HPs. The power of contact lies in its ability to reduce anxiety, tension, perceived threat, and social distance between groups. Researchers overtly manipulating contact are advised to be cognizant of these processes to avoid inadvertently exacerbating intergroup conflict and hostility.

Longitudinal research in both children and adults is clearly needed. At present, only Maoz (2003) has demonstrated contact-based changes in attitudes among prejudice-prone individuals over time, but that was a short interval in a relatively safe, structured, and controlled context. Ideally, future longitudinal research will cover a longer and more "real-life" transition, while tracking the influence of mediators and moderators.

Increasing contact opportunities and receptivity

Because contact appears beneficial among HPs, our next challenge is to increase their contact opportunities. This task represents a considerable challenge given their natural proclivity to avoid contact (Altemeyer, 1996; Williams, 1964) and to feel threatened by outgroups (Hodson, Hogg et al, 2009; Stephan & Stephan, 2000). Problematically, fears that the outgroup knows one's personal prejudices significantly reduces willingness to engage in contact (MacInnis & Hodson, in press). Effort should therefore be devoted to strategies *laying the groundwork for positive contact*, initiating anxiety- and threat-reduction processes *prior to contact*. Imagined contact (Crisp & Turner, this volume) represents a promising avenue in this regard. Encouraging people to simply imagine positive contact, as a mental simulation, improves outgroup attitudes through the same variables mediating actual contact-attitude relations. Alternatively we can engage people in intergroup contact experiences in ways simulating an outgroup's contact experience, thus inducing intergroup perspective-taking. Hodson, Choma et al. (2009) employed a teaching strategy by Hillman and Martin (2002), where students imagine and discuss life after being stranded on an alien planet. In this "Alien-Nation" exercise participants experienced alienation as a minority group, akin to discrimination faced by homosexuals, without making homosexuality salient. Experimental (vs. control) participants showed heightened intergroup perspective-taking, which improved attitudes toward homosexuals through more inclusive intergroup representations ("we are all part of a common group") and elevated empathy. Impressively, this exercise worked despite individual differences in RWA, SDO, conservatism, and religious fundamentalism, although they disliked the exercise (see also Maoz, 2003). Like imagined contact, this method promotes engagement in intergroup-related activities while keeping threats that feed negative reactions to a minimum. More importantly, the activity's objectives are disguised: participants experience contact-relevant discrimination *as the outgroup*, facilitating an understanding of their ingroup's actual role in perpetuating prejudice and dominance. Contact simulations can reduce psychological defences, instigating perspective-taking and empathy and reducing threat before contact begins, enhancing the likelihood of actual contact and potential for positive outcomes.

Another means to increase contact involves disgust-sensitivity. Disgust is a natural reaction to contact with aversive stimuli, evoking withdrawal responses often coupled with a sense of superiority (Rozin, Haidt, & McCauley, 2000). Despite being perhaps the most relevant contact emotion, the influence of disgust is remarkably underexplored. Yet heightened interpersonal disgust-sensitivity predicts increased anti-immigrant prejudice, mediated by heightened RWA and SDO (Hodson & Costello, 2007). Follow-up experimental research exposed participants to disgust stimuli (Hodson & Schoonderbeek, in preparation). Unwillingness to engage in disgust-inducing (vs. matched control) tasks was correlated positively with SDO, RWA, and anti-foreigner prejudices. To the extent that HPs are disgust-sensitive, reducing their disgust sensitivity through systematic desensitization, rational emotive therapy, or evaluative conditioning may attenuate disgust-relevant reactions, facilitating intentions to engage in contact with "unsavoury others" (outgroups). Our laboratory is currently exploring this potential.

Potential contact effects on ideology

Might contact interventions reduce levels of RWA, SDO, and related ideological constructs? Given that contact reduces anti-outgroup attitudes among HPs, this looks promising at first glance. That is, feedback loops can be expected over prolonged exposure: after HPs lower their anti-outgroup prejudices, increased outgroup contact is more likely, promoting gradual changes in personal worldviews that de-emphasize intolerance and exclusion. Only longitudinal research can address this question adequately (Dhont & Van Hiel, 2009). It is important to keep in mind, however, that ideologies are influenced by more than intergroup contact, and that contact might differentially impact attitudes and ideological orientations. With regard to the first point, Altemeyer (1994, 1996) emphasizes the social learning of social attitudes and authoritarianism. Recent evidence also reveals heritable origins of RWA, SDO, and conservatism (Stößel, Kämpfe, & Riemann, 2006), and that lower childhood intelligence predicting increased right-wing ideology in adulthood (Hodson & Busseri, 2012). Reducing ideology via contact therefore represents a substantial challenge. On the second point, contact has previously improved Whites' *attitudes* toward Blacks without influencing *public policy attitudes* relevant to helping Blacks combat institutional racism (Jackman & Crane, 1986). Contact, therefore, may improve intergroup attitudes but leave ideologies and cultural worldviews justifying inequality intact. Recall that previous attempts to change ideologies and values have failed (e.g., Altemeyer, 1996; Avery et al., 1992; Esses et al., 2001). Researchers and policymakers are encouraged to concentrate energies on increasing contact opportunities among intolerant individuals, ensuring that contact interactions unfold in ways capitalizing on anxiety- and threat-reduction processes, rather than counting on contact to change ideological orientations in the short-run.

Cross-group friendships among HPs

Because cross-group friendships represent intimate and prolonged contact epitomizing positive contact (Pettigrew, 1998; Wright et al., 1997), future researchers can explore friendships among otherwise intolerant persons. Initial research suggests that such friendships are effective among HPs (Hodson, Harry et al., 2009). Encouragingly, negative associations between authoritarianism and outgroup friendship are surprisingly small (Pettigrew, Christ, Wagner, & Stellmacher, 2007) or non-significant (Hodson, Harry et al., 2009), and SDO-friendship correlations are non-significant (Pettigrew et al., 2007). Outgroup friendships among HPs are therefore possible. Research on how friendships *form* among such individuals is particularly needed. The timing of outgroup membership disclosure might be critical in contexts where outgroup membership is not immediately apparent (e.g., sexual/political orientation, internalized mental illness). It is possible, for instance, that friendship has benefitted RWAs and ingroup identifiers (see Hodson, Harry et al., 2009) because intimate bonds were formed prior to knowledge of outgroup membership (i.e., homosexuality). Similar relationship effects involving more salient outgroup friends remain unexplored.

Contact among LPs

Our review has focused primarily on HPs, with intergroup attitudes among LPs either positively affected or unaffected by contact[7]. To some extent, weak effects among LPs may represent ceiling effects. Even if true, this does not detract from the important finding that contact is beneficial among prejudiced individuals most in need of intervention (see also Hodson, 2011; Maoz, 2003). Note also that, in the present dataset, LPs demonstrated stronger contact benefits than HPs for contact involving extremely marginalized and disliked individuals (see Note 6), but this preliminary finding requires corroboration. Simple ceiling effects are unlikely to underlie such findings, and greater understanding about LP-reactions to contact is clearly needed.

One research direction offering promise concerns categorization tendencies. Contact effects among LPs fail to generalize to interactions with other members from that outgroup (Vorauer, 2008), potentially explaining their inconsistent reactions to contact in our review. Among LPs, decreased proclivity toward exclusive categorization in general contributes to more favorable outgroup attitudes, but in contact settings results in a failure to generalize from one contact setting to the next. In contrast, HPs generally exhibit negative outgroup attitudes as a result of heightened categorization tendencies, perceiving the context as relatively intergroup in nature and outgroup members as typical. Fortunately, categorizing contact partners as "typical" outgroup members can facilitate contact effects on attitudes (Brown & Hewstone, 2005). Therefore, heightened categorization tendencies naturally underpinning negative attitudes among HPs are presumably co-opted and put to good use in contact settings, where elevated categorization ensures that positive benefits from contact with group members generalize to the outgroup.

Individuals may also differentially construe the contact setting. For instance, individuals high (vs. low) in SDO may over- or under-estimate contact subjectively, or distort their memories to minimize (or exaggerate) contact. Recent evidence, however, speaks against simple construal as an explanation for contact effects. For instance, those higher (vs. lower) in SDO or RWA are no less confident about past outgroup contact occurring, and report equally vivid contact memories (Hodson & Crisp, 2010). It is possible, however, that individual differences influence how people respond to questions about contact in the present. As noted by Michela (1990), "different use of the response scale by different persons can occur" (p. 286), with research terms having different use and meaning across people. An example from the classic movie *Annie Hall* illustrates this potential effectively. In separate therapy sessions, a therapist asks how often a married couple engages in intercourse. The husband, played by Woody Allen, replies "*Hardly ever*, maybe three times a week," whereas his wife replies "*Constantly*, I'd say three times a week." What is construed as "a lot" or "a little" contact might meaningfully differ across individuals in contact settings also. To adjust for potential "calibration" problems, we returned to the present dataset, examining averaged *within-person* correlations between contact with various groups and attitudes toward those groups (for each person). In a within-person analysis, what constitutes little/substantial or negative/positive contact remains constant within the individual, in contrast to more traditional between or across-person correlations, where "a lot of contact" might have differential meaning across people.

The dataset was first transposed, with outgroups placed on individual rows and contact and attitudes ratings in separate columns (see Michela, 1990). After standardizing responses within individuals, within-person correlation "variables" can be created, following r-to-z' transformations to test for significance, and z'to-r transformations to adjust for potential non-normality. In our dataset, the average within-person correlation between contact quantity and attitudes (r = .30), and between contact quality and attitudes (r = .63), were each significant (ps < .001). Moreover, these values were of similar magnitude as our more typical, across-person correlations (rs = .30 and .57, respectively, ps < .001). These within-person analyses control between-person differences in how contact or attitudes are construed or interpreted, revealing, for the first time, evidence of stable and meaningful contact-attitude correlations *within* individuals. Within-person contact-attitude associations did not correlate with SDO or Conservatism (rs < .14, ns), and only correlated with RWA with regard to contact quantity-attitude correlations (r = .20, p = .018), such that those higher in RWA demonstrated stronger positive contact-attitude correlations. Overall, positive relations between contact and attitudes appear universal and largely uncorrelated with individual differences in prejudice-prone tendencies. Contact-attitude effects are not artefacts of response calibration differences between individuals.

Advances in understanding contact: the importance of individual differences

Our discussion has been framed around implicit propositions. Proposition 1 argues that individual differences are unimportant to the study of prejudice and contact. To the contrary, the consideration of person variables as covariates clarified fundamental questions about situational processes, such as generalization across outgroups (see Table 3.2). It becomes increasingly difficult to dismiss the consideration person factors as irrelevant to our understanding of contact-attitude relations. Moreover, main effects of person variables *beyond* situation variables (and *vice versa*) consistently emerge (Dhont & Van Hiel, 2009; Maoz, 2003; Hodson, 2008; Hodson, Harry et al., 2009; see also Table 3.1), demonstrating that each is important. Although existing contact theories have carefully mapped out situational factors involved in contact, future theoretical approaches need to capture the reality that people bring their goals, motives, fears, anxieties, ideologies, disgust sensitivities and various other psychological processes into interaction settings. These mental processes are not left in reserve for expression only in interpersonal interactions, but rather influence whether contact occurs and the outcomes (Pettigrew, 1998). People not only select themselves into and out of situations, but influence how contexts evolve (Gatto et al., 2010). Failure to incorporate person-variables into our contact theories leaves us ill-prepared to predict and control contact outcomes.

The second proposition, that individual differences are obstacles to positive contact effects, represents another strong tradition. HPs may fan the flames of hatred and competition during contact, but their personal intergroup prejudices are attenuated following contact. These effects may even generalize to related but uninvolved groups (see Note 4). As noted in our review, failure to find benefits from contact among HPs is the exception, not the rule. This was the case for mere contact, and especially true for positive contact.

Contrary to historical concerns, our review reveals benefits of contact among HPs. Such benefits have been demonstrated in (a) *different types of samples*, including prisons (Hodson, 2008), community samples (Dhont & Van Hiel, 2009; Pettigrew, 2008), and university populations (present data; Hodson, Harry et al., 2009); (b) *different age groups*, with participants in their mid-teens (Maoz, 2003), 20s (present data; Hodson, Harry et al., 2009), 30s (Hodson, 2008), or 40s (Dhont & Van Hiel, 2009); (c) *different outgroup targets*, including Blacks (Hodson, 2008), immigrants (Dhont & Van Hiel, 2009), Muslims (Pettigrew, 2008), Palestinians (Maoz, 2003) or homosexuals (present data; Hodson, Harry et al., 2009), whether liked or disliked overall (present data); (d) in *different regions*, including Britain (Hodson, 2008; Hodson, Harry et al., 2009), Belgium (Dhont & Van Hiel, 2009), Canada (present data), Germany (Pettigrew, 2008), and the Middle East (Maoz, 2003). In addition, the benefits of contact quantity were independent of contact quality (Hodson, 2008; Hodson, Harry et al., 2009), with each factor independent of direct and indirect friendships (Hodson, Harry et al., 2009). As this text goes to press, recent evidence has surfaced supporting the benefits of contact among high RWAs over time (i.e., longitudinally, see Asbrock, Christ, Duckitt, & Sibley, 2012)[8]. Recent evidence also reveals that contact likewise increases support for outgroup-benefitting public policy (e.g., gay rights) among HPs (Lewis, 2011).

The take-home message regarding contact among HPs is clear. Our within-subjects analyses indicate that commonly established between-subject correlations between contact and attitudes are not explained by between-subject differences in conceptualizing contact. Rather, these analyses corroborate the claim that HPs are no less likely to benefit from contact. If anything, those higher in RWA demonstrated stronger contact quantity and attitude associations. Traditional between-subjects approaches to data analysis also reveal promising results. Although sometimes simple contact main effects emerged (see Figure 3.1a), with contact predicting positive attitudes across individual differences (Pettigrew, 2008; present data), most often contact effects were more effective (or only effective) among HPs (Dhont & Van Hiel, 2009, Studies 1–2; Hodson, 2008, Studies 1–2; Hodson, Harry et al., 2009; Maoz, 2003). Such interaction patterns are represented in Figures 3.1b – c. In no known studies have contact effects backfired among HPs and soured their intergroup attitudes (conceptualized in Figure 3.1d). Rather, across all observed patterns in our review (Figures 3.1a–c), increased or more positive contact was associated with more favorable attitudes among prejudiced persons. Put another way, contact effects are generally stronger to the extent that contact is experienced by those higher in personal prejudices. Across within- and between-subject statistical methods, HPs in no studies demonstrated worsened attitudes with more contact. In contrast, consistent evidence points to contact benefits among HPs.

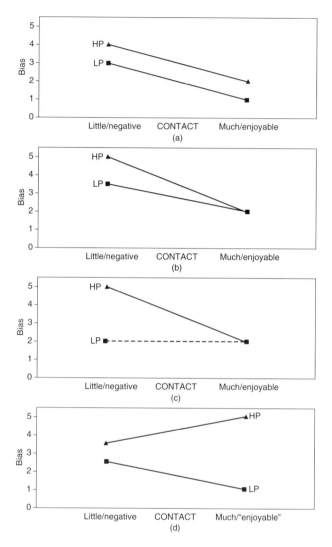

Figure 3.1 Potential outcomes of contact among individuals relatively high (HP) or low
(LP) in prejudice. Solid lines represent hypothesized significant slopes

The time is ripe for moving beyond the person versus situation debates that
have torn the prejudice field into competing camps. Neither theoretical side is
capable of capturing the complexity of intergroup relations on its own (Hodson,
2009). One response has been to posit distinct and equally important roles for person versus situation factors. In a widely cited paper, Verkuyten and Hagendoorn
(1998) found that person factors (RWA) predict prejudice when personal identity
is salient, but that situation factors (ingroup stereotypes) predict prejudice when

social categorization is salient. Although highlighting the importance of both person and situation factors, these results are typically taken as evidence supporting self-categorization theory, with individual factors supposedly irrelevant in salient social contexts (Turner & Reynolds, 2003). However, Heaven and St. Quintin (2003) failed to replicate these results, with RWA and SDO predicting prejudice under both personal and national identity conditions (see also Bergh, Akrami, & Ekehammar, 2010). Personality and ideology (SDO, RWA) have previously predicted prejudice in both control and experimental conditions manipulating either norms (Study 1) or threat (Study 2) (Akrami, Ekehammar, Bergh, Dahlstrand, & Malmsten, 2009). Similarly, Dru (2007) found that SDO and RWA predicted prejudicial attitudes not only under control conditions but also under situational manipulations relevant to each ideology (competition or value threat).

From our perspective, these latter results are unsurprising – these particular ideological individual differences are directly relevant to intergroup life. Although social categorization heightens the importance of social factors under salient social categorization conditions, the relevance of person factors will depend on the nature of the person variables under consideration. When social categorization is salient, person factors irrelevant to intergroup behavior (e.g., tidiness) will become increasingly less important in predicting intergroup outcomes, whereas those directly relevant to intergroup life (e.g., ideologies pertaining to cultural values or intergroup hierarchies) will remain important or become increasingly predictive (as in Reynolds, Turner, Haslam, Ryan, Bizumic, & Subasic (2007, Study 2). Rather than further entrenching theoretical camps by pushing person and situation factors into separate domains, we argue that person- and situation-based approaches must become more fully integrated, drawing on the strengths of each to capture intergroup contact as psychologically experienced by individuals. Person and situation processes can operate separately, in conjunction, or simultaneously at different levels of analysis. A recent example can elaborate the latter point. Among Canadians, disparaging intergroup humor served intergroup distinctiveness (social identity) motives at the group level, evidenced by preference for anti-American jokes, but social dominance motives directed toward a lower-status group at the individual level, with SDOs preferring anti-Mexican jokes (Hodson, Rush, & MacInnis, 2010). Multi-level analysis in the contact literature, despite being encouraged (Pettigrew & Tropp, 2006), has been slow to catch on (for recent developments, see Christ & Wagner, this volume).

There are several implications of our review. First, contact researchers may have historically *underestimated* contact benefits by ignoring individual differences. Relatively weaker contact effects among LPs, documented in several studies, weaken overall contact-attitude relations. In some instances contact-attitude relations represented large effects among high RWAs and strong ingroup identifiers, but only small or very small effects among LPs (e.g., Hodson, Harry et al., 2009). These findings conceptually correspond to those found at the national level, where contact effects are stronger in conflict-ridden areas such as South African and Northern Ireland, precisely because there is such room for improvement in these areas relative to more tolerant locales, where ceiling effects may dampen apparent contact benefits (Pettigrew, 2010). Therefore the finding that contact works as well (if not better) among HPs (vs. LPs) is an incentive to implement contact interventions more widely (see also Maoz, 2003). Considering person-factors within the contact domain has strengthened the case for contact as a critical prejudice-reduction intervention.

Second, Person x Situation interaction effects may have been underestimated in contact settings. Moderation tests, particularly among non-manipulated variables, are underpowered (McClelland & Judd, 1993). Contact may therefore be even more beneficial to HPs (vs. LPs) than our review suggests. However, our key question concerns whether or not contact works among prejudiced persons, and that answer is clear: HPs consistently benefit from intergroup contact, not only in "loose" community samples but in "confined" prison samples and contracted conflict zones. These findings single out contact as a practical prejudice intervention. In contrast, strategies based on compunction and inducements to constrain personal biases remain relatively untested outside of university settings, and are considered unlikely to succeed beyond the ivory tower (Henry, 2008). Unlike interventions confronting ideologies directly, contact is effective among HPs, similar to interventions stressing shared (vs. unshared) group memberships (Costello & Hodson, 2010; Esses et al., 2001) or outgroup perspective-taking (Hodson, Choma et al., 2009).

Whereas some argue that contact researchers are overly optimistic (Dixon, Durrheim, & Tredoux, 2005; Jackman & Crane, 1986), we reach a different conclusion. From the beginning contact researchers have been hesitant and cautious about the practicalities of intergroup contact, particularly among prejudiced persons (e.g., Allport, 1954; Williams, 1947). The field openly acknowledges that contact effects are relatively small (Pettigrew & Tropp, 2006), with contact no panacea for solving prejudice (Hewstone, 2003). Yet the accumulating weight of evidence clearly indicates that contact reduces negative outgroup attitudes, justifying an optimistic outlook. Our review suggests that contact works well, if not best, among intolerant people. With intergroup contact the exception rather than the norm, our next challenge is to uncover new methods to increase contact, combating natural tendencies to avoid and socially exclude outgroups among intolerant persons.

Notes

Supported by Social Sciences and Humanities Research Council of Canada grant (410–2007–2133).

1 These are continuous (vs. categorical) constructs. The terms "low" and "high" are merely writing conventions unless otherwise indicated.

2 This position misinterprets social dominance theory. Sidanius and Pratto (1999) stress "socialization experiences, situational contingencies, and temperament" as origins (p. 77), de-emphasizing temperament from lack of available data. Although SDO has genetic origins, most variance is explained by unique environmental factors (Stößel, Kämpfe, & Riemann, 2006).

3 Stronger contact effects emerged among younger (vs. older) participants and women (vs. men).

4 Related analyses considered generalization *among* HPs. For instance, does homosexual

contact among SDOs predict attitudes toward the depressed, controlling for RWA and conservatism? As with the sample overall, results were mixed. Increased or positive contact with homosexuals predicted more favourable attitudes toward the depressed among high RWAs, SDOs, and conservatives (*p*s < .05), demonstrating generalization. However, homosexual contact among HPs did not generalize to homeless attitudes. As with people generally, secondary transfer among HPs is less consistent than primary contact.

5 Analyses not reported in Hodson (2008, Study 2) are encouraging. Inmates low or high in SDO (based on median splits) did not differ in empathy for Black inmates under high or positive contact (*t*s < 1, *ns*). Among high SDOs, those experiencing contact reported significantly more empathy toward Blacks than those not experiencing contact (*p* < .05), and those experiencing positive contact reported significantly more empathy toward Blacks than those reporting negative contact (*p* <.01).

6 Only 4 of 48 2-way interactions were significant. These should be interpreted cautiously, potentially representing Type I error. Relative to high SDOs, low SDOs exhibited significantly stronger benefits of: (a) increased contact with depressed people; and (b) more positive contact with AIDS sufferers and the homeless. Relative to high RWAs, low RWAs showed stronger benefits from increased contact with drug users. Although contact among LPs (vs. HPs) generally produces weaker or equivalent contact-attitude effects in studies examining social groups such as homosexuals, immigrants, and Blacks, the converse might be true for "extremely" marginalized outgroup members characterized by low competence and low warmth (Harris & Fiske, 2006) (e.g., depressed people, AIDS patients, the homeless, illegal drug users). Heightened disgust sensitivity among HPs (see Hodson & Costello, 2007) may limit contact-benefits with such targets.

7 In contrast, recent evidence by Lewis (2011) reveals that LPs (vs. HPs) benefit more from contact with homosexuals. However, Lewis examined support for gay rights (i.e., public policy) rather than attitudes (i.e., liking vs. disliking of homosexuals). Future research more definitively parsing attitude from policy support variables is needed.

8 The results of Asbrock et al. (2012) should be interpreted with some caution because the contact measures demonstrated low reliability (approximately .55), only 2 or 3 items from the RWA or SDO scales were used (respectively), and because only the aggressive authoritarianism subscale was tapped (which overlaps the most with SDO, yet was statistically controlled in the RWA-relevant analyses). Although Asbrock and colleagues interpret their findings in terms of "differential effects" of contact among RWAs and SDOs, with high SDOs not responding to contact favorably, their findings actually support the tenet of the present chapter: contact failed to work among high SDOs (Study 1) or produced a weaker (but nonetheless significant) positive effect among highs than lows (Study 2). In each study, contact did not worsen attitudes among socially dominant persons.

References

Adorno, T. W., Frenkel-Brunswik, E., Levinson, D. J., & Sanford, R. N. (1950). *The authoritarian personality*. New York: Harper.

Akrami, N., Ekehammar, B., Bergh, R., Dahlstrand, E., & Malmsten, S. (2009). Prejudice: The person in the situation. *Journal of Research in Personality, 43*, 890–897.

Allport, G. W. (1954). *The nature of prejudice*. Reading, MA: Addison-Wesley.

Altemeyer, B. (1994). Reducing prejudice in right-wing authoritarians. In M. P. Zanna, & J. M. Olson (Eds.), *The Psychology of Prejudice: The Ontario Symposium* (Vol. 7, pp. 131–148). Hillsdale, NJ: Lawrence Erlbaum Associates.

Altemeyer, B. (1996). *The authoritarian specter*. Cambridge, MA: Harvard University Press.

Altemeyer, B. (1998). The other "authoritarian personality." In M. Zanna (Ed.), *Advances in Experimental Social Psychology, 30* (pp. 47–92). San Diego: Academic Press.

Amir, Y. (1969). Contact hypothesis in ethnic relations. *Psychological Bulletin, 71*, 319–342.

Asbrock, F., Christ, O., Duckitt, J., & Sibley, C. G. (2012). Differential effects of intergroup contact for authoritarians and social dominators: A dual process model perspective. *Personality and Social Psychology Bulletin, 38*, 477–490.

Avery, P. G., Bird, K., Johnstone, S., Sullivan, J. L., & Thalhammer, K. (1992). Exploring political tolerance with adolescents. *Theory and Research in Social Education, 20*, 386–420.

Bergh, R., Akrami, N., & Ekehammar, B. (2010). Social identity and prejudiced personality. *Personality and Individual Differences, 48*, 317–321.

Binder, J., Zagefka, H., Brown, R., Funke, F., Kessler, T., Mummendey, A., Maquil, A-M., Demoulin, S., & Leyens, J.-P. (2009). Does contact reduce prejudice or does prejudice reduce contact? A longitudinal test of the Contact Hypothesis amongst majority and minority groups in three European countries. *Journal of Personality and Social Psychology, 96*, 843–856.

Brown, R. (2002). Henry Tajfel's "Cognitive aspects of prejudice" and the psychology of bigotry. *British Journal of Social Psychology, 41*, 195–198.

Brown, R., & Hewstone, M. (2005). An integrative theory of intergroup contact. *Advances in Experimental Social Psychology, 37*, 255–343.

Cohrs, J. C., & Ibler, S. (2009). Authoritarianism, threat, and prejudice: An analysis of mediation and moderation. *Basic and Applied Social Psychology, 31*, 81–94.

Cook, S. W. (1960). The systematic analysis of socially significant events: A strategy for social research. *Journal of Social Issues, 18*, 66–84.

Cook, S. W., & Selltiz, C. (1955). Some factors which influence the attitudinal outcomes of personal contact. *International Social Science Bulletin, 7*, 51–58.

Costello, K., & Hodson, G. (2010). Exploring the roots of dehumanization: The role of animal-human similarity in promoting immigrant humanization. *Group Processes and Intergroup Relations, 13*, 3–22.

Costello, K., & Hodson, G. (2011). Social dominance-based threat reactions to immigrants in need of assistance. *European Journal of Social Psychology, 41*, 220–231.

Devine, P. G., Rhodewalt, F., & Siemionko, M. (2008). Personality and prejudice in interracial interactions. In F. Rhodewalt (Ed.), *Personality and social behavior* (pp. 223–249). New York: Psychology Press.

Dhont, K., & Van Hiel, A. (2009). We must not be enemies: Interracial contact and the reduction of prejudice among authoritarians. *Personality and Individual Differences, 46*, 172–177.

Dixon, J., Durrheim, K., & Tredoux, C. (2005). Beyond the optimal contact strategy: A reality check for the contact hypothesis. *American Psychologist, 60*, 697–711.

Downing, L. L., & Monaco, N. R. (1986). In-group/out-group bias as a function of differential contact and authoritarian personality. *The Journal of Social Psychology, 126*, 445–452.

Dru, V. (2007). Authoritarianism, social dominance orientation and prejudice: Effects of various self-categorization conditions. *Journal of Experimental Social Psychology, 43*, 877–883.

Duckitt, J. (2005). Personality and prejudice. In J. F. Dovidio, P. Glick, & L. A. Rudman (Eds.), *On the nature of prejudice: Fifty years after Allport* (pp. 395–412). Malden, MA, USA: Blackwell Publishing.

Ekehammar, B., Akrami, N., Gylje, M., & Zakrisson, I. (2004). What matters most to prejudice: Big five personality, social dominance orientation, or right-wing authoritarianism? *European Journal of Personality, 18*, 463–482.

Ensari, N., & Miller, N. (2002). The out-group must not be so bad after all: The effects of disclosure, typicality, and salience on intergroup bias. *Journal of Personality and Social Psychology, 83*, 313–329.

Erikson, R. S., & Tedin, K. L. (2003). *American Public Opinion* (6th ed). New York: Longman.

Esses, V. M., Dovidio, J. F., Jackson, L. M., & Armstrong, T. L. (2001). The immigration dilemma: The role of perceived group competition, ethnic prejudice, and national identity. *Journal of Social Issues, 57*, 389–412.

Gatto, J., Dambrun, M., Kerbrat, C., & de Oliveira, P. (2010). Prejudice in the police: On the processes underlying the effects of selection and group socialisation. *European Journal of Social Psychology, 40*, 252–269.

Harris, L. T., & Fiske, S. T. (2006). Dehumanizing the lowest of the low: Neuroimaging responses to extreme outgroups. *Psychological Science, 17*, 847–853.

Heaven, P. C. L., & St. Quintin, D. (2003). Personality factors predict racial prejudice. *Personality and Individual Differences, 34*, 625–634.

Henry, P. J. (2008). College sophomores in the laboratory redux: Influences of a narrow data base on social psychology's view of the nature of prejudice. *Psychological Inquiry, 19*, 49–71.

Hewstone, M. (2003). Intergroup contact: Panacea for prejudice? *The Psychologist, 16*, 352–355.

Hewstone, M., & Brown, R. J. (1986). Contact is not enough: An intergroup perspective on the "Contact Hypothesis." In M. Hewstone, & R. J. Brown (Eds.), *Contact and conflict in intergroup encounters* (pp. 1–44). Oxford, UK: Basil Blackwell.

Hillman, J., & Martin, R. A. (2002). Lessons about gay and lesbian lives: A spaceship exercise. *Teaching of Psychology, 29*, 308–311.

Hodson, G. (2008). Interracial prison contact: The pros for (socially dominant) cons. *British Journal of Social Psychology, 47*, 325–351.

Hodson, G. (2009). The puzzling person-situation schism in prejudice research. *Journal of Research in Personality, 43*, 247–248.

Hodson, G. (2011). Do ideologically intolerant people benefit from intergroup contact? *Current Directions in Psychological Science, 20*, 154–159.

Hodson, G. (in press). Authoritarian contact: From "tight circles" to cross-group friendships. In F. Funke, T. Petzel, J. C. Cohrs, & J. Duckitt (Eds.), *Perspectives on authoritarianism*. Weisbaden, Germany: VS-Verlag.

Hodson, G., & Busseri, M. A. (2012). Bright minds and dark attitudes: Lower cognitive ability predicts greater prejudice through right-wing ideology and low intergroup contact. *Psychological Science, 23*, 187–195.

Hodson, G., Choma, B. L., & Costello, K. (2009). Experiencing Alien-Nation: Effects of a simulation intervention on attitudes toward homosexuals. *Journal of Experimental Social Psychology, 45*, 974–978.

Hodson, G., & Costello, K. (2007). Interpersonal disgust, ideological orientations, and dehumanization as predictors of intergroup attitudes. *Psychological Science, 18*, 691–698.

Hodson, G., & Crisp, R. J. (2010). *Intergroup contact meta-cognitions*. Unpublished manuscript.

Hodson, G., & Esses, V. M. (2005). Lay perceptions of ethnic prejudice: Causes, solutions, and individual differences. *European Journal of Social Psychology, 35*, 329–344.

Hodson, G., Harry, H., & Mitchell, A. (2009). Independent benefits of contact and friendship on attitudes toward homosexuals among authoritarians and highly identified heterosexuals. *European Journal of Social Psychology, 35*, 509–525.

Hodson, G., Hogg, S. M., & MacInnis, C. C. (2009). The role of "dark personalities" (nar-
cissism, Machiavellianism, psychopathy), Big Five personality factors, and ideology in
explaining prejudice. *Journal of Research in Personality, 43*, 686–690.

Hodson, G., Rush, J., & MacInnis, C. C. (2010). A "joke is just a joke" (except when
it isn't): Cavalier humor beliefs facilitate the expression of group dominance motives.
Journal of Personality and Social Psychology, 99, 660–682.

Hodson, G., & Schoonderbeek, J. (2009). *Manipulated disgust and prejudice*. Manuscript
in preparation.

Hodson, G., & Sorrentino, R. M. (1999). Uncertainty orientation and the big five personality structure. *Journal of Research in Personality, 33*, 253–261.

Islam, M. R., & Hewstone, M. (1993). Dimensions of contact as predictors of intergroup
anxiety, perceived outgroup variability, and out-group attitude: An integrative model.
Personality and Social Psychology Bulletin, 19, 700–710.

Jackman, M. R., & Crane, M. (1986). "Some of my best friends are black . . . .": Interracial
friendship and Whites' racial attitudes. *Public Opinion Quarterly, 50*, 459–486.

Jackson, J. W., & Poulsen, J. R. (2005). Contact experiences mediate the relationship
between Five-Factor Model of personality traits and ethnic prejudice. *Journal of Applied
Social Psychology, 35*, 667–685.

Lewin, K. (1946). Behavior and development as a function of the total situation. In L. Car-
michael (Ed.), *Manual of Child Psychology* (pp. 791–802). New York: Wiley.

Lewis, G. B. (2011). The friends and family plan: Contact with gays and support for gay
rights. *The Policy Studies Journal, 39*, 217–238.

Liebkind, K., Haaramo, J., & Jasinskaja-Lahti, I. (2000). Effects of contact and personality
on intergroup attitudes of different professionals. *Journal of Community and Applied
Social Psychology, 10*, 171–181.

MacInnis, C. C., & Hodson, G. (in press). "Where the rubber hits the road" en route to
intergroup harmony: Examining contact intentions and contact behavior under meta-
stereotype threat. *British Journal of Social Psychology*.

Maoz, I. (2003). Peace-building with the hawks: Attitude change of Jewish-Israeli hawks
and doves following dialogue encounters with Palestinians. *International Journal of
Intercultural Relations, 27*, 701–714.

McClelland, G. H., & Judd, C. M. (1993). Statistical difficulties of detecting interactions
and moderator effects. *Psychological Bulletin, 114*, 376–390.

Michela, J. L. (1990). Within-person correlational design and analysis. In C. Hendrick, &
M. Clark (Eds.), *Research methods in personality and social psychology: Review of personality and social psychology* (Vol. 11, pp. 279–311). Thousand Oaks, CA: Sage.

Miller, D. A., Smith, E. R., & Mackie, D. M. (2004). Effects of intergroup contact and
political predispositions on prejudice: Role of intergroup emotions. *Group Processes
and Intergroup Relations, 7*, 221–237.

Mussen, P. H. (1950). Some personality and social factors related to changes in children's
attitudes toward Negroes. *Journal of Abnormal and Social Psychology, 45*, 423–411.

Nelson, T. D. (2006). *The psychology of prejudice*. (2nd ed). Boston: Pearson.

Pettigrew, T. F. (1997). Generalized intergroup contact effects on prejudice. *Personality
and Social Psychology Bulletin, 23*, 173–185.

Pettigrew, T. F. (1998). Intergroup contact theory. *Annual Review of Psychology, 49*,
65–85.

Pettigrew, T. F. (2008). Future directions for intergroup contact theory and research. *International Journal of Intercultural Relations, 32*, 187–199.

Pettigrew, T. F. (2009). Secondary transfer effect of contact: Do intergroup contact effects spread to noncontacted outgroups? *Social Psychology, 40*, 55–65.

Pettigrew, T. F. (2010). Commentary: South African contributions to the study of intergroup relations. *Journal of Social Issues, 66*, 417–430.

Pettigrew, T. F., Christ, O., Wagner, U., & Stellmacher, J. (2007). Direct and indirect intergroup contact effects on prejudice: A normative interpretation. *International Journal of Intercultural Relations, 31*, 411–425.

Pettigrew, T. F., & Tropp, L. R. (2006). A meta-analytic test of intergroup contact theory. *Journal of Personality and Social Psychology, 90*, 751–783.

Pettigrew, T. F., & Tropp, L. R. (2008). How does intergroup contact reduce prejudice? Meta-analytic tests of three mediators. *European Journal of Social Psychology, 38*, 922–934.

Pratto, F., Sidanius, J., Stallworth, L. M., & Malle, B. F. (1994). Social dominance orientation: A personality variable predicting social and political attitudes. *Journal of Personality and Social Psychology, 67*, 741–763.

Reynolds, K. J., Turner, J. C., Haslam, A., & Ryan, M. K. (2001). The role of personality and group factors in explaining prejudice. *Journal of Experimental Social Psychology, 37*, 427–434.

Reynolds, K. J., Turner, J. C., Haslam, A., Ryan, M. K., Bizumic, B., & Subasic, E. (2007). Does personality explain in-group identification and discrimination? Evidence from the minimal group paradigm. *British Journal of Social Psychology, 46*, 517–539.

Rozin, P., Haidt, J., & McCauley, C. (2000). Disgust. In M. Lewis, & J. Haviland (Eds.), *Handbook of emotions.* (2nd ed), (pp. 637–652). New York: Guilford Press.

Sagiv, L., & Schwartz, S. H. (1995). Value priorities and readiness for out-group social contact. *Journal of Personality and Social Psychology, 69*, 437–448.

Sibley, C. G., & Duckitt, J. (2008). Personality and prejudice: A meta-analysis and theoretical review. *Personality and Social Psychology Review, 12*, 248–279.

Simonton, D. K. (1982). One-way experimentation does not prove one-way causation. *American Psychologist, 37*, 1404–1406.

Skikta, L. J., Mullen, E., Griffin, T., Hutchinson, S., & Chamberlin, B. (2002). Dispositions, scripts, or motivated correction? Understanding ideological differences in explanations for social problems. *Journal of Personality and Social Psychology, 83*, 470–487.

Stephan, W. G., & Rosenfield, D. (1978). Effects of desegregation on racial attitudes. *Journal of Personality and Social Psychology, 36*, 795–804.

Stephan, W. G., & Stephan, C. W. (2000). An integrated threat theory of prejudice. In S. Oskamp (Ed.), *Reducing prejudice and discrimination. "The Claremont Symposium on Applied Social Psychology"* (pp. 23–45). Mahwah, NJ, US: Lawrence Erlbaum Associates, Inc.

Stößel, K., Kämpfe, N., & Riemann, R. (2006). The Jena twin registry and the Jena twin study of social attitudes (JeTSSA). *Twin Research and Human Genetics, 9*, 783–786.

Tajfel, H. (1978). Intergroup behaviour. I. Individualistic perspectives. In H. Tajfel & C. Fraser (Eds.), *Introducing social psychology* (pp. 401–422). Harmondsworth, UK: Penguin.

Turner, J. C., & Reynolds, K. J. (2003). Why social dominance theory has been falsified. *British Journal of Social Psychology, 42*, 199–206.

Van Laar, C., Levin, S., & Sidanius, J. (2008). Ingroup and outgroup contact: A longitudinal study of the effects of cross-ethnic friendships, dates, roommate relationships and participation in segregated organizations. In U. Wagner, L. Tropp, G. Finchilescu, and C. Tredoux (Eds.), *Improving intergroup relations: On the legacy of Thomas F. Pettigrew* (pp. 127–142). Oxford, UK: Blackwell.

Van Laar, C., Levin, S., Sinclair, S., & Sidanius, J. (2005). The effect of university roommate contact on ethnic attitudes and behavior. *Journal of Experimental Social Psychology, 41*, 329–345.

Verkuyten, M., & Hagendoorn, L. (1998). Prejudice and self-categorization: The variable role of authoritarianism and in-group stereotypes. *Personality & Social Psychology Bulletin, 24*, 99–110.

Voci, A., & Hewstone, M. (2003). Intergroup contact and prejudice toward immigrants in Italy: the mediational role of anxiety and the moderational role of group salience. *Group Processes and Intergroup Relations, 6*, 37–54.

Vorauer, J. (2008). Unprejudiced and self-focused: When intergroup contact is experienced as being about the ingroup rather than the outgroup. *Journal of Experimental Social Psychology, 44*, 912–919.

Wilder, D. A., & Thompson, J. E. (1980). Intergroup contact with independent manipulations on in-group and out-group interaction. *Journal of Personality and Social Psychology, 38*, 589–603.

Williams, R. M., Jr. (1947). *The reduction of intergroup tensions*. New York: Social Science Research Council.

Williams, R. M., Jr. (1964). *Strangers next door: Ethnic relations in American communities*. Englewood Cliffs, NJ: Prentice-Hall.

Wright, S. C., Aron, A., McLaughlin-Volpe, T., & Ropp, S. A. (1997). The extended contact effect: Knowledge of cross-group friendships and prejudice. *Journal of Personality and Social Psychology, 73*, 73–90.

4 Generalized effects of intergroup contact
The secondary transfer effect

Simon Lolliot, Katharina Schmid,
Miles Hewstone, Ananthi Al Ramiah,
Nicole Tausch, and Hermann Swart

Introduction

In chapter 5 of his seminal book, *The Nature of Prejudice*, Gordon Allport (1954) described a study performed in 1946 by E.L. Hartley in which college students were asked about their attitudes towards 35 nations and races. Hidden among the 35 nations were the Daniereans, Pireneans, and the Wallonians – three fictitious ethnic groups. What Hartley found was quite surprising: not only were attitudes to the 32 real groups highly correlated, but the correlations between the real and fictitious groups were also extremely high (around .80). Indeed, one of the more prejudiced participants remarked, "I don't know anything about [the fictitious groups]; therefore I would exclude them from my country" (p. 66). This study resonates with the point Allport made a few sentences earlier in the same chapter: "If a person is anti-Jewish, he is likely to be anti-Catholic, anti-Negro, anti any out-group" (1954, p. 66). If our attitudes are so highly inter-correlated, and if Allport's assertion is correct, then if we improved attitudes towards one outgroup, would this lead to improved attitudes to other outgroups? Research on the *secondary transfer effect* addresses precisely this research question.

The secondary transfer effect (Pettigrew, 2009) describes the phenomenon whereby coming into contact with a primary outgroup has an effect on one's attitudes towards other, secondary outgroups not involved in the contact. In this chapter, we will provide an extensive review of the sparse literature on the secondary transfer effect. We start our discussion with a brief exposition of Allport's (1954) *contact hypothesis*, after which we discuss early research on secondary transfer effects and then review more recent research on this topic. Next, we will turn our attention to the two main purported mediating processes, attitude generalization and deprovincialization, after which we will discuss a third, less tested mediator, intergroup empathy. We then review possible moderators of the link between primary outgroup contact and secondary outgroup attitude as well as the link between primary and secondary outgroup attitudes. Lastly, we turn our attention to some limitations of extant research on the secondary transfer effect, and then suggest some issues for future research in this domain.

Intergroup contact theory and the secondary transfer effect

Intergroup contact theory

In *The Nature of Prejudice*, Allport (1954) set out what was to become one of the most influential hypotheses in social psychology today, the *Contact Hypothesis*. Favoring parsimony, the hypothesis states that when two social groups come into contact under the conditions of equal status, collaborative work towards a common goal, and when contact is sanctioned by authorities, there will be a reduction in intergroup prejudice. Cross-group friendship has been highlighted as, and shown to be, an especially potent form of intergroup contact as it is said to embody most of Allport's facilitating conditions (Davies, Tropp, Aron, Pettigrew, & Wright, 2011; Hamberger & Hewstone, 1997; Pettigrew, 1997; see chapter by Davies, Wright, Aron & Comeau, this volume). With 50 years of research confirming that contact is associated with reduced intergroup animosity (see Brown & Hewstone, 2005; Dovidio, Gaertner, & Kawakami, 2003; Pettigrew & Tropp, 2006) there is little doubt left as to its effectiveness at improving intergroup relations. Indeed, the amount of work available that supports the contact hypothesis, and the progress made in understanding its mechanisms, has been argued to surely afford Allport's "hypothesis" the title of a bona fide *theory* (Hewstone, 2009; Hewstone & Swart, 2011).

One of the earliest questions that faced social psychologists interested in intergroup contact was that of attitude generalization; if contact theory is to have wider consequences its effects need to generalize. Three forms of attitude generalization have been identified in the literature (Pettigrew, 1998) and their effect size estimated by Pettigrew and Tropp (2006) in their authoritative meta-analysis of over 500 studies: (a) whether attitudes towards an outgroup generalize across situations, (b) whether a change in attitudes towards one outgroup member generalizes to the outgroup as a whole, and (c) whether attitudes generalize from one outgroup to another, uninvolved outgroup. We will briefly discuss the first two forms of attitude generalization before focusing in this chapter on the third aspect of attitude generalization, namely generalization across multiple outgroups.

Attitude generalization across situations

Minard (1952), who studied the behavior of White miners towards their Black colleagues in a coal mine in West Virginia, observed that while race relations were friendly below ground, lack of contact and segregation were the norm above ground. Similarly, Harding and Hogrefe (1952) found in their study of White department store employees that equal status contact with Blacks at work increased willingness to work with Blacks, but had no effect on willingness to accept other kinds of interracial relationships (see Amir, 1969, for a review). Pettigrew and Tropp (2006) tested this form of attitude generalization meta-analytically using 17 tests from 9 samples. They found that intergroup contact effects did indeed generalize across situations ($r = -.244, p < .001$).

Attitude generalization from an outgroup member to the outgroup as a whole

This is the most widely studied type of generalization and, despite earlier pessimism (e.g., Amir, 1969; Hewstone & Brown, 1986), there is now extensive evidence demonstrating generalization from specific individuals to the outgroup as a whole (see Brown & Hewstone, 2005, for a review; see also Pettigrew & Tropp, 2006).

A large number of studies have shown that this member-to-outgroup generalization is most likely to happen when categories are salient during contact (see Hewstone & Brown, 1986) and when the encountered group member is typical of the group in general (see Rothbart & John, 1985). For example, Wilder (1984), manipulated both the behavior (pleasant vs. unpleasant) and the typicality (typical/atypical) of an outgroup member in a contact situation and found that, only when the encountered group member behaved in a pleasant way and was typical of her group, did ratings of the outgroup in general become more favorable. Similarly, Van Oudenhoven, Groenewoud, and Hewstone (1996) demonstrated that Dutch students' evaluations of Turkish people in general were more positive after a cooperative interaction with a Turkish confederate when his nationality was explicitly mentioned during the interaction than when it was not mentioned. Similarly, a series of correlational studies found that contact was more strongly associated with positive outgroup attitudes for respondents who reported having been aware of the group memberships during contact (e.g., Brown, Vivian, & Hewstone, 1999; Voci & Hewstone, 2003). Based on 1,164 tests, Pettigrew and Tropp (2006) found a reliable relationship between contact with an individual outgroup member and prejudice towards the outgroup as a whole ($r = -.213$, $p < .001$). Thus, there is substantial evidence that creating awareness of social categories during contact, either by making categories explicitly salient or by presenting representative outgroup members, can lead to generalized attitude change.

Evidence for the secondary transfer effect

Initial evidence from three studies conducted in the 1970s is consistent with the secondary transfer effect, but not necessarily conclusive. First, in one of the earliest studies showing support for secondary transfer effects of contact, Weigert (1976) found that for Black soldiers, the forming of friendships with White soldiers stationed in Germany was associated with less prejudice towards German civilians even after controlling for demographics, ideological orientation, and – most impressively – previous contact with Germans. Second, Clement, Gardner, and Smythe (1977) found that Canadian Anglophones who reported having had more contact with French Quebecers while on an excursion to Quebec showed improved attitudes towards French Quebecers, as well as European French people, when compared with those who (a) reported having had less contact during the trip, and (b) a control group who did not partake in the excursion. Third, Caditz (1976) found that, of her 204 participants sampled from an American politically liberal organization, those who moved in more religiously diverse circles were more supportive of policies aimed at racial integration than those who were part of more homogeneous friendship networks.

Analyzing data from several European national probability samples, Pettigrew (1997) found that measures of cross-group friendships with immigrants found in each country predicted more favorable attitudes towards both those immigrant groups as well as towards a variety of other immigrant outgroups, even those not found in the respondent's own country. Pettigrew noticed that it was not just intergroup friendships that showed wider attitude influence; intergroup contact as co-workers was also associated, albeit to a lesser degree, with improved attitudes towards a variety of outgroups.

More recently, Eller and Abrams (2004, Study 1) provided the first longitudinal test of the secondary transfer effect. Using a small sample size of 34 British undergraduates, they were able to show that having more French friends directly predicted less prejudiced attitudes towards Algerians 6 months later. Corroborating Pettigrew's (1997) assertion that intergroup friendships are an especially effective form of intergroup contact, general contact with French people at University failed to improve attitudes towards Algerians. More impressively, Van Laar, Levin, Sinclair, and Sidanius (2005) collected longitudinal data spanning a period of 5 years based on over 2100 students at University of California (UCLA), Los Angeles. Among other hypotheses, the researchers investigated the effects of living with White, Latino, African American, and Asian American outgroup roommates on attitudes towards the respective groups. The authors found that those participants who were randomly assigned a Latino roommate during their second and third year at UCLA not only held less prejudiced attitudes towards Latinos during their fourth year, but their attitudes towards African Americans also showed improvement. A similar, reciprocal relationship held for those who were randomly assigned an African American roommate, in that respondents' attitudes towards Latinos improved as well. What is more, the authors were able to control for both previous contact and attitudes towards the various outgroups.

Pettigrew and Tropp's (2006) meta-analysis reported on 18 samples that tested this relatively understudied form of attitude generalization from primary to secondary outgroups; they found a small but significant effect size ($r = -.19, p < .001$). Of these 18 tests, 14 were taken from relatively loosely controlled studies that were therefore not able to rule out possible alternative explanations (Pettigrew, 2009).

One of the most fundamental questions facing contact research is that of causal order: does contact reduce prejudice, or do less prejudiced people seek more contact (see Hodson, Costello, & MacInnis, this volume)? Evidence shows that there is typically a bi-directional relationship between contact and prejudice, with the negative path from contact to prejudice being the stronger relationship (Pettigrew & Tropp, 2006; Swart et al., 2011). In terms of the secondary transfer effect, do less prejudiced people seek contact from a wider pool of outgroups? Tausch, Hewstone, Kenworthy, Psaltis, Schmid, Popan et al. (2010) tested a two-wave longitudinal model whereby attitudes at wave 1 predicted contact with members of the secondary outgroup one year later. They found that none of their attitude measures predicted contact with either the primary or secondary outgroups. From this analysis, we have the first evidence showing that less prejudiced people do *not* necessarily seek more intergroup contact with diverse groups. While this provides the first tentative evidence for the causal order from more contact to less prejudice, more research is needed to verify this causal relationship.

Having established the existence of a direct relationship between primary outgroup contact and secondary outgroup attitudes, researchers next sought to uncover the mechanism(s) whereby contact is able to have such widespread influence. We now turn our attention to the mediators of the secondary transfer effect.

Mediators of the secondary transfer effect

It was not until twelve years after Pettigrew's (1997) initial study that the first formal paper studying the *secondary transfer effect* and its underlying mechanisms appeared (Pettigrew, 2009). Pettigrew (2009) investigated two of his mediational hypotheses, namely the attitude generalization and deprovincialization hypotheses (Pettigrew, 1997). In this next section, we will explore both of these hypotheses and the support that has amounted for each. Next, we investigate the first evidence for Pettigrew's (1997) third hypothesized mediational process of the secondary transfer effect, that of intergroup empathy.

The attitude generalization hypothesis

Based on research concerning attitude generalization – a process whereby attitudes towards an object generalize to other, similar objects (Fazio, Eiser, & Shook, 2004; Shook, Fazio, & Eiser, 2007) – the attitude generalization hypothesis describes a process by which attitudes towards a primary outgroup mediates the relationship between primary outgroup contact and secondary outgroup attitudes (Pettigrew, 2009; Tausch et al., 2010). In other words, this hypothesis predicts that the beneficial effects of contact with the primary outgroup on attitudes towards the primary outgroup will generalize to attitudes towards secondary outgroups (often even after controlling for prior contact with the secondary outgroups; see Figure 4.1, paths a through b). In the relatively sparse literature on the secondary transfer effect, this mediational hypothesis has received the most support (Al Ramiah, 2009; Harwood, Paolini, Joyce, Rubin, & Arroyo, 2011; Lolliot, Schmid, Hewstone, Swart, & Tausch, 2011; Pettigrew, 2009; Schmid, Hewstone, Küpper, Zick, & Wagner, 2012; Tausch et al., 2010). Furthermore, attitude generalization has also been shown to play a role in improving attitudes towards secondary outgroups when an intergroup contact scenario is simply imagined (Harwood et al., 2011), rather than based on actual, face-to-face contact. Attitude generalization is now, as we shall argue, an important and robust mechanism underlying secondary transfer effects. We consider, first, cross-sectional evidence and then more compelling longitudinal and experimental evidence for mediation of the secondary transfer effect via attitude generalization. We also consider reverse secondary transfer effect models whereby we test whether contact with a secondary outgroup can improve attitudes towards the primary outgroup as mediated by secondary outgroup attitudes.

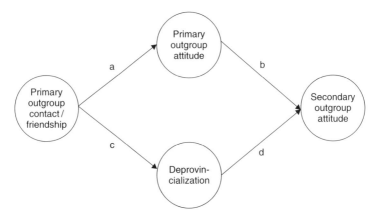

Figure 4.1 Structural model illustrating the attitude generalization and deprovincialization hypotheses

Analyzing two German national probability surveys, Pettigrew (2009) found that attitudes towards immigrants mediated the relationship between having more immigrant friends and improved attitudes towards two other outgroups, homosexuals and the homeless. Al Ramiah (2009) found support for the attitude generalization hypothesis in two of her three sample groups. She studied intergroup contact between three ethnic groups in Malaysia who were taking part in a three-month nation-building program of 'National Service' camps run for young people. Participants were randomly assigned to camps and participation was mandatory. She found that for ethnic Malay and Chinese respondents, camp contact with the respective outgroup not only improved attitudes towards that outgroup, but attitudes towards Indians also showed improvement. Attitudes towards the primary outgroup (Malays for Chinese respondents, and vice versa) mediated this relationship. What is impressive about this study is that the contact was a result of mandatory participation in a structured contact intervention (thus removing concerns about self-selection), and these effects were evident even after controlling for prior attitudes towards the secondary outgroups. Thus, Al Ramiah provides a stricter test of the attitude generalization hypothesis than typically found in cross-sectional studies.

Tausch and colleagues (2010) found support for the attitude generalization hypothesis in all three of their cross-sectional studies. Lending further confidence to the attitude generalization hypothesis, these three studies showed consistent support in diverse contexts ranging from Cyprus (Study 1) to Northern Ireland (Study 2) to America (Study 3). Furthermore, by controlling for contact with the secondary outgroups (Studies 2 and 3) as well as social desirability effects (Study 3) these studies helped rule out two important concerns: (1) that those who have more contact with one outgroup are likely to have more contact with other outgroup members, and (2) that the secondary transfer effect is a result of people not wanting to be seen as overtly prejudiced.

Even though these studies used powerful statistical techniques to investigate the hypothesized relationships between the variables, they remain nonetheless cross-sectional: one cannot confidently claim causality between variables in cross-sectional studies. Therefore, we now turn our attention to those few studies reporting longitudinal and experimental evidence, both methodologies permitting more confidence in inferences about the causal relationship between the variables under consideration (MacCallum & Austin, 2000).

In addition to the direct relationship from primary outgroup contact to secondary outgroup attitudes reported on earlier, Eller and Abrams (2004) provided initial longitudinal support for the attitude generalization hypothesis. Eller and Abrams also showed that having more French friends improved British students' attitudes towards Algerians six months later by increasing affective ties to French people; the mediation, however, failed to reach significance. Tausch et al. (2010, Study 4), using a second Northern Ireland sample, did, however, test and find support for the attitude generalization hypothesis using a two-wave longitudinal design. In other words, contact with the ethno-religious outgroup at wave 1 improved attitudes towards racial minorities one year later by improving attitudes towards the ethno-religious outgroup, even after previous contact with and attitudes towards racial minorities were controlled for.

Lastly, Harwood and colleagues (2011) provided the first experimental evidence for the attitude generalization hypothesis. An imagined contact paradigm asserts that imagining a contact scenario with an outgroup member is enough to improve attitudes towards that outgroup (see Crisp, Stathi, Turner, & Husnu, 2008), a contention that has received support (Crisp, Husnu, Meleady, Stathi, & Turner, 2010; see also Crisp & Turner, this volume). Harwood et al. (2011) instructed 128 American undergraduates to imagine one of three scenarios: (1) a positive or (2) negative interaction with an illegal immigrant (primary outgroup), or (3) an outdoor scene (control group). After the imagination exercise, they assessed participants' attitudes towards various outgroups. The authors found that those who imagined a positive interaction with an illegal immigrant also showed improved attitudes towards a handful of the secondary outgroups, with the relationship being mediated by attitudes towards illegal immigrants. They did not, however, control for previous contact with the secondary outgroups. We return to this study below, and speculate as to why the effects of primary-outgroup contact generalized to some, but not all, secondary outgroups.

Additional support for the attitude generalization hypothesis comes from reverse secondary transfer effect models. These models test if contact with secondary outgroups improves attitudes towards the primary outgroup, with secondary outgroup attitudes mediating the relationship. Essentially, these reverse models provide another test for the secondary transfer effect and the attitude generalization hypothesis by using another outgroup as the focal outgroup. The few studies that have tested these reverse models found that attitudes towards the secondary outgroup did indeed mediate the relationship between secondary outgroup contact and primary outgroup attitudes (Schmid, Hewstone, & Tausch, 2012; Tausch et al., 2010). Even though these reverse models tend to yield weaker secondary transfer effects,[1] the finding that attitudes towards the secondary outgroups also mediate the relationship between secondary outgroup contact and primary outgroup attitudes provides additional support for the attitude generalization hypothesis.

We have now reviewed the basic literature on attitude generalization as one of the mechanisms by which the secondary transfer effect works. As encouraging as these findings are, some methodological concerns remain. We now consider two of the most pertinent threats to the validity of the attitude generalization hypothesis, namely shared method variance and *the secondary contact problem* (Tausch et al., 2010).

Threats to the attitude generalization hypothesis

The use of similar measures may inflate the relationship between the variables being considered (Podsakoff, MacKenzie, Lee, & Podsakoff, 2003) resulting in undue confidence in the relationship(s) between the variables under consideration. This is a valid concern for research regarding the secondary transfer effect as many of the studies reported here used the same rating scales when measuring attitudes towards the various primary and secondary outgroups. It could also be the case that people who have more contact with one outgroup will tend to have more contact with other outgroups, also known as the secondary contact problem (Tausch et al., 2010). In this section, we briefly evaluate concerns relating to both these forms of potential bias and evaluate the extent to which they limit the conclusions we can draw about secondary transfer effects.

As mentioned, most research on the secondary transfer effect has relied on using the same attitudinal measures when measuring attitudes towards the primary and secondary outgroups (Al Ramiah, 2009; Harwood et al., 2011; Lolliot et al., 2011; Tausch et al., 2010). For example, Tausch et al. (2010) and Harwood et al. (2011) both used feeling thermometers when measuring attitudes towards the various outgroups under investigation. Research reported by Pettigrew (2009) helps to reduce concerns about shared method variance. He found strong evidence for the attitude generalization hypothesis using different attitude scales when investigating the secondary transfer effect between Germans' contact with and attitudes towards immigrants (the primary outgroup), and their attitudes towards homosexuals, and the homeless (secondary outgroups). Schmid et al. (2012) conducted a large cross-national survey of eight European countries using different measures for attitudes towards primary (immigrants) and secondary (homosexuals and Jews) outgroups. The use of different measures helps reduce concerns relating to shared method bias. Neither the study by Pettigrew (2009) nor that by Schmid et al. (2012), however, controlled for contact with the secondary outgroups, leaving them prone to concerns about selection biases. Using British students, Lolliot et al. (2011) were able to show that friendships with Asians improved attitudes towards gay men, lesbian women and the homeless via improved attitudes towards Asians using not only different measures for the primary and secondary outgroups, but also when controlling for contact with the secondary outgroups. Similarly, Schmid et al. (2012, Study 2) showed in a study conducted in

Northern Ireland, that intergroup friendships with people from the other religious community (i.e., Catholics for Protestant respondents, and Protestants for Catholic respondents) improved attitudes towards immigrants and homosexuals – measured using feeling thermometers – by increasing the perceived group variability of the ethno religious outgroup. Perceived ethno-religious variability still mediated the relationship between friendships with people from the other ethno-religious community and attitudes towards gay men and immigrants even after controlling for contact with the secondary outgroups. Even though these studies afford us more confidence in the attitude generalization processes, they need to be replicated both longitudinally and experimentally before we can confidently rule out any possible spurious effects owing to shared method biases.

The deprovincialization hypothesis

Pettigrew (1997) stated that cross-group contact (especially in the form of cross-group friendships) leads ingroup members to realize that the ingroup is not the only yardstick by which to judge the social world. He termed this broadening of perspective *deprovincialization*. In addition to broadening one's gaze beyond the ingroup's norms, customs, and lifestyles, intergroup contact serves to humanize outgroup members and distance oneself from the ingroup (see Figure 4.1, paths c through d). In short, Pettigrew states that intergroup contact leads ingroup members to have a less provincial view of the world. To date, the deprovincialization hypothesis has received mixed support, with some studies providing confirming evidence (Pettigrew, 2009; Tausch et al., 2010, Study 1), and others not (Tausch et al., 2010, Studies 2–4). As will be discussed, one possible reason for these inconsistent results is that most studies testing the deprovincialization hypothesis used a narrow operationalization of the process, namely ingroup identification (Pettigrew, 2009) or ingroup attitude (Tausch et al., 2010). We will first discuss the mixed evidence for the deprovincialization hypothesis in the context of the secondary transfer effect. We will then discuss multiculturalism and social identity complexity as alternative conceptualizations of the deprovincialization hypothesis.

Mixed evidence for the deprovincialization hypothesis

Pettigrew (2009) provided the first evidence for the deprovincialization hypothesis. He found that identification with Germany significantly mediated the relationship between Germans' positive contact with German immigrants and their attitudes towards homosexuals and the homeless. Positive contact with immigrants predicted lower identification with Germany, which, in turn, was associated with improved secondary outgroup attitudes. Pettigrew did concede, however, that German identity was a weaker mediator of the secondary transfer effect than was attitude generalization. Tausch et al. (2010, Study 1) also reported evidence for the deprovincialization hypothesis; they found that for Greek and Turkish Cypriots in Cyprus ingroup attitude (operationalized as private collective self-esteem) mediated the relationship between contact with the primary outgroup (i.e., Turkish/

Greek Cypriots, respectively) and attitudes towards mainland Turks/Greeks (i.e., Greeks in Greece, or Turks in Turkey). Thus, contact with the Cypriot outgroup predicted lower private collective self-esteem which, in turn, predicted more positive attitudes towards the mainland (secondary) outgroup. Contrasting the mediation effects of attitude generalization and deprovincialization, Tausch et al. (2010) also found that attitudes toward the primary outgroup were a stronger mediator of the secondary transfer effect than were ingroup attitudes.

In their remaining three studies, however, Tausch et al. (2010) failed to find evidence for the deprovincialization hypothesis. Using feeling thermometers (Studies 2, 3 and 4) and private collective self-esteem (Study 4) as an indicator of ingroup attitude, contact with the primary outgroup reliably failed to predict attitudes towards the ingroup in all three studies, while in only two of their four studies did ingroup attitude predict outgroup attitudes (Studies 2 and 3). In their longitudinal study (Study 4), neither the ingroup feeling thermometer nor the measure of private collective self-esteem was predicted by contact, nor did they predict outgroup attitudes. The tenuous relationship between contact, ingroup attitude and outgroup attitudes is not as surprising as one may think. Brewer (1999) highlights the finding that the relationship between ingroup and outgroup attitudes varies across studies, even though it has predominantly been thought to be negative and ethnocentric, where ingroup attachment is associated with outgroup derogation. However, discrimination in favor of the ingroup over outgroups may be just that – preferential treatment of the ingroup, rather than outgroup derogation. Brewer goes on to say that, "most contemporary research on intergroup relations, prejudice, and discrimination appears to accept, at least implicitly, the idea that ingroup favoritism and outgroup negativity are reciprocally related" (1999, p. 430).

In light of this evidence, as well as Pettigrew's (1997) wider-reaching definition of deprovincialization, it remains questionable whether research focusing more narrowly on ingroup attitude as a mediator of secondary transfer effects has, to date, adequately operationalized deprovincialization (see also Tausch et al., 2010). We thus argue that exploring other aspects of Pettigrew's (1997) deprovincialization hypothesis may prove more fruitful. In the next section, we review two alternative accounts to studying the deprovincialization hypothesis, one based on multiculturalism, and the other operationalizing deprovincialization as social identity complexity.

Theoretical extensions of the deprovincialization hypothesis: multiculturalism and social identity complexity

Multiculturalism: Adopting a multicultural outlook is said to nurture an acceptance of and appreciation for minority groups' identities and cultures (Verkuyten, 2005). This loose definition of multiculturalism seems to resonate with Pettigrew's (1997) proposal that intergroup contact results in a reappraisal of the ingroup's norms, values and customs. Intergroup contact has been associated with an increased endorsement of multiculturalism (Verkuyten, Thijs, & Bekhuis, 2010), which itself has been associated with improved outgroup attitudes (Verkuyten,

2005). By extension, understanding the world as a multicultural place should lead to a greater acceptance of a wider range of outgroups and not just a primary outgroup. Therefore, use of multiculturalism as a mediator seems to provide a compelling test for Pettigrew's (1997) deprovincialization hypothesis.

Testing this hypothesis using White students attending a British university, Lolliot et al. (2011) found that multiculturalism – measured by three items taken from Verkuyten et al. (2010) – mediated the relationship between cross-group friendships with Asians (primary outgroup) and improved attitudes towards homosexual men and women, but not towards the homeless. The mediation remained significant while controlling for previous contact with the secondary outgroups. Thus this study provided the first evidence that intergroup contact with a primary outgroup can help people develop a multicultural outlook, which, in turn, improves attitudes towards other, secondary outgroups (Lolliot et al., 2011). It should be kept in mind that multiculturalism is of primary relevance to inter-ethnic groups, or groups with an established culture. While we acknowledge that the homeless do indeed have a culture (see Ravenhill, 2008; Wasserman & Clair, 2010), their cultural practices may differ substantially from other social groups' cultural practices. Such a discrepancy could offer an explanation as to why multiculturalism did not mediate the relationship between contact with Asians and attitudes towards the homeless. Multiculturalism, as a result, may only be useful when considering social groups that have salient or recognised cultural practices.

Social identity complexity: A person's social identity complexity refers to their cognitive representation of the interrelationships between their multiple ingroup identities (Brewer & Pierce, 2005; Roccas & Brewer, 2002). Put differently, people who are high in social identity complexity realize that they may share ingroup membership with another person on one category (for example, two people may both be social psychologists) but may perceive that person as an outgroup member on another category (e.g., one social psychologist may be a Democrat while the other is a Republican). People with low social identity complexity, on the other hand, will only consider Democrat (or Republican) social psychologists as part of their ingroup.

In a footnote, Pettigrew (2009) mentioned the possibility that social identity complexity might be a good proxy for deprovincialization (see also Brewer, 2008, for a more complete theoretical exposition of deprovincialization in terms of social identity complexity). Pettigrew's (1997) original formulation of the deprovincialization hypothesis refers to a *reappraisal* of the ingroup; social identity complexity seems to be well suited for the task, as individuals who have more intergroup contact tend to have more a more complex social identity which, in turn, is related to less prejudicial attitudes (Brewer & Pierce, 2005; Roccas & Brewer, 2002; Schmid, Hewstone, Tausch, Cairns, & Hughes, 2009).

In two correlational studies conducted in different contexts – Germany and Northern Ireland – Schmid et al. (2012) provided the first empirical test of this hypothesis in the context of the secondary transfer effect. In Study 1, conducted with a large sample of adults in Germany, they found that positive intergroup contact with (non-German) Western Europeans improved Germans' attitudes towards people of Turkish and Russian descent; both paths were mediated by social identity complexity. In a second study using a large sample of adults from both Catholic and Protestant communities in Northern Ireland, Schmid et al. (2012, Study 2) examined the relationship between the number of ethno-religious outgroup friends and attitudes towards immigrants and homosexuals. The analyses revealed that social identity complexity, once again, acted as an intervening mechanism in the generalization of attitudes to the non-target outgroups, even after controlling for direct contact with each of the secondary outgroups. Thus it seems that part of the secondary transfer effect of contact can be explained by variations in cognitive re-structuring of one's social identity, that is, social identity complexity.

Empathy as a mediator of secondary transfer effects

Pettigrew (1997), considering the role of perspective taking in the secondary transfer effect, proposed that cross-group friendships lead to increased perspective taking abilities (see Reich & Purbhoo, 1975). Pettigrew (1997) did not, however, specify how perspective taking may improve attitudes beyond the contacted (i.e., primary) outgroup to secondary outgroups. In this section, we will first define what we mean by empathy before discussing research involving empathy and wider attitude generalization. We then end this section by exploring the role of empathy in the secondary transfer effect.

Following Pettigrew's (1997) emphasis on perspective taking, we will also focus our review on this type of intergroup empathy (for a full review of the affective empathy states, see Batson & Ahmad, 2009). Perspective taking – a cognitive form of empathy – denotes the ability to put oneself in another's shoes; to see the world through their eyes. If a person asks, while putting him- or herself in the other's shoes, "How would *I* feel if *I* were in their situation?", then they are engaging in *imagine-self* perspective taking. On the other hand, a person engages in *imagine-other* perspective taking if they try to understand what goes through the target person's head, i.e., the person whose shoes they are filling.

Owing to space restrictions, unless otherwise specified, we will use the term *empathy* to refer to both perspective taking states.

Empirical evidence shows that empathy is associated with improved attitudes towards a variety of outgroups, ranging from ethnic groups (Swart, Hewstone, Christ, & Voci, 2010, 2011) to convicted murderers (Batson, Polycarpou, Harmon-Jones, Imhoff, Mitchener, Bednar et al., 1997, Study 4). The positive effects of empathy have also been shown to generalize from a single outgroup member to the outgroup as a whole (Batson et al., 1997). Furthermore, empathy has also been associated with pro-social behavior benefitting the group for which empathy is felt (Batson, Chang, Orr, & Rowland, 2002). Extending this previous research, we are interested in the possibility that empathy improves attitudes beyond a target (primary) outgroup to other, secondary outgroups. Three relevant studies offer inconsistent evidence of whether empathy does improve intergroup attitudes to secondary outgroups, one study showing support (Galinsky & Moskowitz, 2000, Study 1) and two not (Shih et al., 2009; Vescio, Sechrist, & Paolucci, 2003). Galinsky and Moskowitz (2000, Study 1) found that participants who adopted an imagine-self perspective while writing an essay on a day in the life of an elderly person – when compared to stereotype suppression and control groups – showed improved attitudes towards the elderly (the primary outgroup) as well as more positive evaluations of African Americans (secondary outgroup). Shih et al. (2009) and Vescio et al. (2003), on the other hand, did not find any wider attitude generalization effects for participants in their empathy condition, who were instructed to adopt an imagine-other perspective for their primary outgroups, when compared to participants in other conditions.

It is interesting to note that the two studies using an imagine-other perspective (Shih et al., 2009; Vescio et al., 2003) did not find wider attitude generalization effects while the study that used the imagine-self perspective (Galinsky & Moskowitz, 2000) did. The two perspective taking states appear to have surprisingly different consequences on our psychological processes (Ames, Jenkins, Banaji, & Mitchell, 2008; Galinsky, Ku, & Wang, 2005; Ruby & Decety, 2004), although it may be argued that the different methodologies used in these three studies could have led to a more personalized (Shih et al., 2009; Vescio et al., 2003) or depersonalized (Galinsky & Moskowitz, 2000) experience with the target outgroup possibly leading to the inconsistent results. One common factor between the three studies is that none of them investigated how empathy may be elicited by intergroup contact; therefore, they cannot be taken to measure secondary transfer effects of contact. In the next section, we explore possible ways in which empathy may mediate secondary transfer effects.

Empathy and the secondary transfer effect

There is a small but growing body of research that suggests that empathy mediates the effects of intergroup contact on outgroup attitudes (Aberson & Haag, 2007; Harwood, Hewstone, Paolini, Voci, 2005; Hodson, 2008; Pagotto, Voci, & Maculan, 2010; Pettigrew & Tropp, 2008; Swart et al., 2010, 2011). From the previous section on the attitude generalization hypothesis, we know that attitudes towards a primary outgroup generalize to other outgroups. Therefore, empathy may influence attitudes towards secondary outgroups *through* attitudes towards

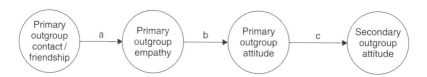

Figure 4.2 Structural model illustrating how intergroup contact with a primary outgroup can improve attitudes towards secondary outgroups through the double mediated mechanisms of primary outgroup empathy and primary outgroup attitudes

the primary outgroup, with empathy itself being influenced by intergroup contact (see Figure 4.2).

In other words, intergroup contact may improve attitudes to secondary outgroups by increasing levels of empathy towards the primary outgroup (path a), which then may improve attitudes towards the primary outgroup (path b). These improved attitudes towards the primary outgroup should then generalize to the secondary outgroups (path c). Lolliot et al. (2011) have collected evidence for such a double mediated path in their recent research using a sample of Catholic and Protestant students in Northern Ireland. They found that cross-group friendships with the ethno-religious outgroup increased respondents' empathy felt for the ethno-religious outgroup. These heightened empathic feelings, in turn, reduced prejudice towards the secondary outgroups (i.e., racial minorities and homosexual men) with this path mediated by improved attitudes to the primary ethno-religious outgroup.

In addition to the above model, empathy towards the primary outgroup may also influence attitudes towards secondary outgroups by first eliciting a greater empathic response towards these secondary outgroups (see Figure 4.3). In this model, contact with a primary outgroup may induce empathy towards a primary outgroup (path a) which will lead to more empathic feelings for other outgroups (path b). These heightened empathic feelings towards the secondary outgroups should then improve attitudes towards the secondary outgroups (path c).

Vezzali and Giovannini (2011) simultaneously tested the two double-empathy mediation secondary transfer effect models we have just described. Furthermore, they expanded on these two models by including intergroup anxiety as a potential mediator of the secondary transfer effect. Using a sample of 175 Italian high school students, Vezzali and Giovannini tested if the relationship between contact with immigrants (their primary outgroup) and attitudes towards immigrants was mediated by an increase in perspective taking and a reduction in anxiety towards immigrants. Having found significant mediations for these primary transfer effects, they next tested two secondary transfer effect models – one for each of their secondary outgroups (the disabled and homosexuals). First (see Figure 4.2), they explored if the reduced social distance towards immigrants that was associated with more intergroup contact with immigrants – as mediated by reduced anxiety and increased perspective taking towards immigrants – was associated with reduced social distance towards homosexuals and the disabled (i.e., their secondary outgroups). The data supported this model even after controlling for secondary outgroup contact, anxiety and perspective taking. Secondly (see Figure 4.3), they tested if contact with the

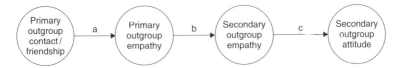

Figure 4.3 Structural model illustrating how intergroup contact with a primary outgroup can improve attitudes towards secondary outgroups through the double mediated mechanisms of primary and secondary outgroup empathy

primary outgroup increased perspective taking and reduced anxiety towards each of the secondary outgroups (as mediated by perspective taking and anxiety, respectively, towards the primary outgroup), and if this increase in empathy and reduction in anxiety towards the secondary outgroups would reduce social distance towards the secondary outgroups (i.e., the second double mediated model described above). Once again, their data supported this hypothesis for both secondary outgroups. Not only is this study the first to show the two above-described double mediation paths, it is also the first to show both perspective taking and intergroup anxiety as mediators of the secondary transfer effect. These effects are quite noteworthy as the available sample was quite small and the models tested rather complex. This makes detecting these effects difficult. Having said this, this study remains cross-sectional, and therefore needs to be verified using longitudinal and experimental designs.

Given the complex causal relationships between these various variables, however, it will be necessary to undertake either experimental or longitudinal research to determine the relative merits of these two models.

Summary of the mediators of the secondary transfer effect

Having reviewed the literature on the three main proposed mediating processes thought to underlie the secondary transfer effect, we find substantial support for the attitude generalization hypothesis, mixed support for the deprovincialization hypothesis, and initial evidence for the mediating role of intergroup empathy. Attitude generalization has received consistent support as a process explaining secondary transfer effects of contact. Our confidence in this hypothesis is bolstered by the finding that primary outgroup attitudes remain a significant mediator of the link between primary outgroup contact and secondary outgroup attitudes after controlling for a number of demographic variables (Pettigrew, 2009; Schmid et al., 2012), right wing authoritarianism (Pettigrew, 2009), and social desirability (Tausch et al., 2010, Study 3). Furthermore, we were able to systematically rule out concerns that the mediation is due to shared method biases. We can therefore confidently state that attitude generalization is a robust mediator of the secondary transfer effect.

The deprovincialization hypothesis, on the other hand, has received mixed results in the literature. This comes as no surprise given the inconsistent relationship between ingroup attitude and outgroup attitudes (Brewer, 1999), as well as inconsistent operationalizations of deprovincialization. Rather than relying on measures of ingroup attitude or evaluation, we have argued that future research may consider operationalizing deprovincialization in terms of multiculturalism and social identity complexity. Whereas the former speaks to Pettigrew's (1997, 1998) notion of intergroup contact widening an individual's perspective on ingroup norms, values and lifestyles, the latter speaks to the notion of ingroup reappraisal. Although initial evidence for both mediational processes exists, it remains for future research to replicate their involvement in secondary transfer effects.

With the relative paucity of tests for the role of empathy within secondary transfer effects, the two models proposed in this section need to be tested empirically.

One of the most prevalent concerns relating to empathy, however, is the nature and history of intergroup relations as inducing empathy for an outgroup may prove difficult in contexts that are characterized by a history of conflict. Furthermore, intergroup relations that are characterized by extreme levels of intergroup violence may induce a negative empathic response, such as pleasure in the outgroup member's misfortune (see, for example, work on intergroup schadenfreude; Spears & Leach, 2004). Despite the present lack of clarity, empathy remains a potentially powerful mediator of the effects of intergroup contact on outgroup attitudes, with the full extent of its effects still to be rigorously tested.

Moderators of the secondary transfer effect

Most research on processes associated with the secondary transfer effect has focused on understanding *how* it works, i.e., processes that mediate the secondary transfer effect. From these mediational analyses, however, a new set of questions has emerged, many of which point towards moderation processes that explain *when* secondary transfer effects may come about. In this section, we will cover some of the moderation hypotheses that have been proposed as well as review the first studies that have investigated them. We will argue that exploring moderation effects can help us understand both how societal influences and dispositional effects can intersect, providing a more complete understanding of the secondary transfer effect.

Moderators of the primary outgroup contact to primary outgroup attitude link and beyond

Asbrock, Christ, Hewstone, Pettigrew, and Wagner (2011) were able to show stronger secondary transfer effects for secondary outgroups that were rated as similar to a primary outgroup on the warmth and competence dimensions of Fiske, Cuddy, Glick, and Xu's (2002) Stereotype Content Model. The researchers also hypothesized that a similarity gradient would only be evident for direct contact, while extended contact – knowing that an ingroup friend has an outgroup friend(s) – would predict improved attitudes towards all secondary outgroups. Arguing that extended contact influences intergroup norms (see Turner, Hewstone, Voci, & Vonofakou, 2008; Wright, Aron, McLaughlin-Volpe, & Ropp, 1997), and that norms are not group-specific, changing attitudes towards one outgroup would then be extended to a wider range of outgroups through a change in norms. This is exactly what Asbrock, Christ, Hewstone et al. (2011) found in their German sample. While direct contact with foreigners in Germany (primary outgroup) was directly associated with improved attitudes to all secondary outgroups (with the exception of attitudes towards Jews), this direct link was stronger for those groups rated more (Muslims, homeless people, homosexuals) than those rated less (non-traditional women, Jews) similar in terms of the warmth and competence dimensions of the stereotype content model (Fiske et al., 2002) to the primary outgroup. Confirming their second hypothesis, there were no differences between the strength of the generalization paths for extended contact when comparing similar and dissimilar outgroups. Asbrock, Christ, Hewstone et al. (2011) did not, however, control for direct or extended contact with the secondary outgroups, nor did they test their hypothesis using attitudes towards the primary outgroup as a mediator. Asbrock, Christ, Hewstone et al. (2011), did, however, find a second moderator of the secondary transfer effect for extended contact. Corroborating previous findings (Christ et al., 2010), Asbrock, Christ, Hewstone et al. (2011) showed that extended contact with their primary outgroup was especially effective in improving secondary outgroup attitudes for those individuals who had less direct contact with the primary outgroup than those who had more direct contact.

In the literature considering intergroup contact and prejudice, research has recently focused on the interplay between individual difference measures and intergroup contact. Social dominance orientation is a construct that has received particular interest as a potential moderator of intergroup contact effects (Asbrock, Christ, Duckitt, & Sibley, 2011; Dhont & Van Hiel, 2009; Hodson, 2008). Social dominance orientation is an individual difference measure tapping into an individual's support for an ideology of inequality. More specifically, it measures the extent to which an individual views different groups in society as being hierarchically structured or not, and is a strong predictor of intergroup prejudice (Altemeyer, 1998; Pratto, Sidanius, & Levin, 2006; Pratto, Sidanius, Stallworth, & Malle, 1994). While some authors argue that intergroup contact is especially effective at reducing prejudice for people high in social dominance orientation (Dhont & Van Hiel, 2009; Hodson, 2008), others hypothesize that highly socially dominant individuals may be more resistant to the beneficial effects of intergroup contact (Asbrock, Christ, Duckitt et al., 2011). These studies have found support for their respective hypotheses, leaving the role of social dominance orientation as a moderator of intergroup contact effects unclear.

For example, Hodson (2008), using samples of convicts from two British prisons, tested the hypothesis that individuals high in social dominance orientation benefit the most from intergroup contact. In both studies, Hodson showed that intergroup contact was associated with less ingroup bias – a measure created by subtracting outgroup attitude from ingroup attitude – for individuals high in social dominance. Intergroup contact had no effect on ingroup bias for those low in social dominance orientation. Dhont and Van Hiel (2009) obtained similar interaction effects between contact and social dominance orientation in one of two studies conducted in Belgium (Study 2). They found that for individuals high in social dominance, the positive relationship between positive contact and attitudes was stronger, and the negative relationship between negative contact and attitudes was stronger than for low social dominance orientation scorers.

Asbrock, Christ, Duckitt et al. (2011), however, argue that intergroup contact may hold beneficial effects for individuals low in social dominance orientation. They argue that since prejudice functions as a strategy to enforce the social hierarchies that are important to socially dominant individuals, individuals high in social dominance orientation may be particularly reluctant to change attitudes that help maintain the perceived social hierarchy. Using longitudinal (Study 1) and cross-sectional (Study 2) designs, Asbrock, Christ, Duckitt et al. found evidence for the second social dominance orientation moderation hypothesis whereby contact was only associated with less prejudice for individuals low in social dominance orientation and not for individuals high in social dominance orientation while controlling for right-wing authoritarianism in Study 1. While the interaction effect fell just short of significance ($p < .07$) in their year-long two-wave longitudinal analysis, the pattern of relationships for high and low socially dominant individuals remained the same. Asbrock, Christ, Duckitt et al. (Study 2) cross-sectionally replicated the findings of their first study by showing that contact was more strongly associated with a reduction in prejudice for individuals low in social dominance orientation than those who were high in social dominance orientation; contact was still significantly associated with a reduction in prejudice for individuals high in social dominance orientation. Potential reasons for the discrepancies between studies could be a result of either the different type of samples employed or the items used to measure social dominance orientation. Therefore, it remains for future research to disentangle these effects.

Social dominance orientation has important implications for the secondary transfer effect because of its established close association with intergroup prejudice. Schmid et al. (2012) recently investigated social dominance orientation as a moderator of the secondary transfer effect. Using a large multinational sample drawn from eight European countries, they examined the relationship between contact with immigrants (the primary outgroup), and attitudes towards two secondary outgroups – Jews and homosexuals – mediated by attitudes towards the primary outgroup. They further tested whether the relationship between primary outgroup contact and primary outgroup attitudes was moderated by social dominance orientation. Analyzing data from all eight countries simultaneously, Schmid et al. (2012) found, as had Asbrock, Christ, Duckitt et al. (2011), that primary outgroup contact was more strongly related with more positive primary outgroup attitudes for individuals low in social dominance orientation, while the relationship fell short of significant for individuals high in social dominance orientation ($p = .07$). Moreover, Schmid et al.'s study (2012) revealed a moderated mediation of primary outgroup contact effects on secondary outgroup attitudes. They found that for individuals who scored low in social dominance orientation, effects emerged between contact with the primary outgroup and attitudes towards both secondary outgroups, mediated by attitudes towards the primary outgroup. The link between contact with the primary outgroup and attitudes towards the secondary outgroups for individuals high in social dominance orientation was also mediated by attitudes towards the primary outgroup, albeit to a weaker degree.

In not only finding a significant moderation effect, but a moderated mediation effect, Schmid et al. (2012) provide the first evidence for a more refined understanding of the mechanisms underlying the secondary transfer effect. Therefore, contact may be primarily associated with more positive attitudes towards secondary outgroups for people who are low to medium in social dominance orientation, but people who show high levels of social dominance orientation might be more resistant, though not impervious, to the otherwise powerful generalized effects of contact.

Moderators of the primary to secondary outgroup attitude link

Pettigrew (2009) noticed that attitudes generalized more readily between certain outgroups. He hypothesized that a similarity gradient may help explain this phenomenon. At this point, it may be useful to apply Goffman's (1963) typology of social stigma to the secondary transfer effect. Goffman's typology categorizes social stigma as falling into one of three types (which we have re-labeled in more acceptable contemporary language); "tribal stigma" (e.g., devalued ethnic, racial or religious groups; henceforth referred to as *category stigma*), "abominations of the body" (e.g., physically handicapped groups; henceforth referred to as *physical stigma*) and "blemishes of individual character" (e.g., homosexuals, homeless, drug-addicts; henceforth referred to as *character stigma*). Early studies on the secondary transfer effect mainly show attitude generalization within the same type of stigma, chiefly concerning category stigma; for example, attitude generalization from French Canadians towards European French (Clement et al., 1977). There is evidence, however, of attitudes generalizing across types of stigma, such as from an ethnic outgroup attitude (category stigma) to attitudes towards homosexual men (character stigma); (Lolliot et al., 2011; Schmid et al., 2012; Schmid et al., in press; Tausch et al., 2010). The natural question then is: why do we see attitude generalization between seemingly unrelated groups? Similarity gradients may go some way to explaining when and why we see, in terms of Goffman's (1963) stigma typology, inter-category attitude generalization.

Pettigrew (2009) does admit that it is difficult to define precisely what is meant by "similarity." He argued that it could range from similarity in dominant stereotypes to prior experiences with the outgroups. There are plenty of studies that show that objects that appear similar to each other do show stronger attitude generalization effects than dissimilar attitude objects, including evidence from a diverse set of empirical paradigms: mere exposure effects (Monahan, Murphey, & Zajonc, 2000; Zajonc, 2001); attitude generalization from a single group member to the outgroup as a whole (Brown & Hewstone, 2005; Hewstone & Brown, 1986); implicit attitude generalization (Ranganath & Nosek, 2008); group entitativity (Crawford, Sherman, & Hamilton, 2002); and objects in a computer game (Fazio et al., 2004; Shook et al., 2007).

Pettigrew (2009) makes reference to findings from other areas of social psychology that may help explain why we see wider attitude generalization even between unrelated outgroups (Martin & Hewstone, 2008). Martin, Laing, Martin and Mitchell (2005) found that participants who scrutinized an argument in favor of voluntary euthanasia not only showed attitude change to euthanasia in the direction of the argument, but a similar attitude change was also witnessed towards abortion. Similarly, Martin and Hewstone (2008) showed that participants who read an argument put forward by a minority group in favor of euthanasia showed attitude change to both voluntary euthanasia and genetic screening.

Martin et al. (2005) argue that the attitudes generalized from their direct measure (voluntary euthanasia) to their indirect measure (pro-abortion) because, as in Martin and Hewstone's (2008) study, both attitudinal objects referred to a common superordinate theme: the control of life. Therefore, testing for a similarity gradient seems highly relevant in the context of secondary transfer effects.

Initial evidence for a similarity gradient can be inferred from a study by Swart (2008). In two South African samples – one using White and the other Colored (persons of mixed racial heritage) South African respondents – Swart found seemingly contradictory secondary transfer effects. For his White sample, cross-group friendships with Colored South Africans improved attitudes towards Black South Africans (persons of black African ancestry), via improved attitudes towards Colored South Africans (while controlling for friendships with Black South Africans). The reverse model also found support for the secondary transfer effect whereby contact with Black South Africans improved attitudes towards Colored South Africans via improved attitudes towards Black South Africans (while controlling for friendships with Colored South Africans). For his Colored South African sample, however, cross-group friendships with White South Africans predicted less prejudiced attitudes towards White South Africans, but these attitudes failed to generalize towards Black South Africans (while controlling for friendships with Black South Africans). Testing the reverse model, Swart found similar results in that cross-group friendships with Black South Africans, although associated with less prejudiced attitudes towards Black South Africans, failed to improve attitudes towards White South Africans (while controlling for friendships with White South Africans). In explaining why secondary transfer effects were witnessed for the White sample and not for the Colored sample, Swart hypothesizes that Colored and Black South Africans seem to share greater historical and political similarity than White and Black South Africans share. These results are also in line with Tropp and Pettigrew's (2005) findings that contact functions differently for majority versus minority groups.

While Swart's (2008) findings provide preliminary evidence for a similarity gradient, two studies have directly tested this moderation hypothesis (Harwood et al., 2011; Lolliot et al., 2011). To gauge the similarity between their primary and secondary outgroups,[2] Harwood and his colleagues (2011) asked three undergraduates – who did not form part of the sample pool – to rate how similar a set of 20 outgroups were to illegal immigrants (their primary outgroup). Harwood and colleagues found stronger secondary attitude generalization effects among the 42 American undergraduates in the positive imagine contact condition who rated the secondary outgroups as more similar to the primary outgroup (illegal immigrants) than those who rated them as dissimilar.

The Harwood study relied on an externally provided measure of intergroup similarity. Intergroup similarity ratings were provided by a set of raters who were not involved in the study. Would we still see evidence for a similarity gradient if we asked the participants themselves to judge between-group similarity? Lolliot et al. (2011) asked White South African respondents if they thought White South Africans (the ingroup) treated Black and Colored South Africans similarly or differently. In line with their hypotheses, they found a moderation effect whereby respondents who thought that the ingroup treated the two outgroups similarly showed stronger secondary transfer effects than those who thought the two out-groups were treated dissimilarly by the ingroup. Following this line of reasoning, it might be useful to acquire information regarding the "level" of discrimination that each group is perceived to experience as this could be another path along which our attitudes generalize.

Schmid et al. (in press) propose that individuals may perceive secondary out-groups as belonging to an overarching, shared minority group, which may explain attitude generalization between seemingly "disparate" groups. Previous research seems to support such a hypothesis. Van Laar et al. (2005), for example, explain their reciprocal secondary transfer effect between Latinos and African Americans in terms of the two outgroups sharing a similar lower social status than White Americans. Thus, it seems that there is indeed a stimulus gradient in effect, inas-much as groups that are perceived to be similar on some dimension tend to show stronger secondary transfer effects. As encouraging as these findings are, more research needs to be done in this area. Do attitudes generalize more strongly for novel outgroups versus groups that have a long history in the country? Tausch et al. (2010, Study 3), for example, reported that among American students the stron-gest secondary transfer effects occurred towards a relatively small and unknown secondary outgroup (Asian Indians), while Schmid et al. (2012, Study 2) found that in Northern Ireland, attitudes did generalize from the ethno-religious out-group (either Catholics or Protestants) to racial minorities and homosexuals, but not towards Travellers – an outgroup that has had a long history characterized by marginalization in that country (Redmond, 2008).

Summary of moderators of the secondary transfer effect

Moderation hypotheses seem to be particularly important to the secondary transfer effect as they help explain (a) when we may see cross-category attitude generalization and (b) when stronger or weaker secondary transfer effects may occur. Speaking to the first point, some of the studies reported here have con-sidered similarity gradients as a moderator of the secondary transfer effect. With evidence mounting that similarity gradients do indeed moderate the secondary transfer effect, this is an exciting area for future research. Regarding the latter point, and corroborating previous research on primary transfer effects (primary outgroup contact improving primary outgroup attitudes), social dominance ori-entation helps to explain when we see stronger or weaker secondary transfer effects. Schmid et al. (in press) found that intergroup contact seems to be benefi-cial only for individuals low in social dominance orientation, while individuals high in social dominance orientation seem to be more resistant to the beneficial effects of intergroup contact (see Asbrock, Christ, Duckitt et al., 2011). It must be kept in mind that there is also evidence for contact being especially effec-tive for highly socially dominant individuals (Dhont & Van Hiel, 2009; Hodson, 2008; Hodson et al., this volume). While Schmid et al.'s (in press) findings are impressive owing to the breadth and size of their sample, the study does have its limitations. Firstly, the study employed a cross-sectional design. Secondly, the study used a two-item measure of social dominance orientation. Therefore, the discrepancy between the findings that highly social dominant people are more receptive to the beneficial effects of intergroup contact (Dhont & Van Hiel, 2009; Hodson, 2008; Hodson et al., this volume) or are more resistant to the effects of intergroup contact (Asbrock, Christ, Duckitt et al., 2011; Schmid et al., in press) could be a result of either the different types of samples employed or the items used to measure social dominance orientation. For example, Hodson (2008) used British convicts as his sample group. Prisons are typically characterized by very clear group hierarchies and so social dominance tends to be a highly salient phenomenon in these environments. In the Dhont and Van Hiel (2009) study, participants were recruited by asking students to administer questionnaires to their adult neighbors. As a result, their sample appears to be slightly skewed towards individuals from higher socio-economic backgrounds. On the other hand, even though Asbrock, Christ, Duckitt et al. (2011) used more representative samples, they used a three-item measure of social dominance orientation whereas Hodson (2008) used the full 16-item social dominance orientation scale and Dhont and Van Hiel (2009) used a 14-item version. Therefore, it is important that future research clarifies the relationship between intergroup contact and attitudes towards outgroups as moderated by social dominance orientation. All in all, while research has only begun to scratch the surface of what promises to be a very fruitful field for future research, more research exploring and expanding on similarity gradients and social dominance orientation as moderators of the secondary transfer effect needs to be conducted, preferably using longitudinal and experimental designs. Below, we will explore other potential moderators of the secondary transfer effect.

Limitations and directions for future research

We turn now to some of the potential limitations of the work done on the secondary transfer effect and consider some promising directions for future research in this area.

Limitations of current research

Study design

One of the most concerning threats to the validity of the secondary transfer effect is that of study design. Much like the majority of research investigating intergroup contact theory (see Hewstone & Swart, 2011), most of the research reported in this chapter has relied on cross-sectional data. There is initial evidence of the secondary transfer effect in more restrictive longitudinal designs (Eller & Abrams, 2004; Pettigrew, 2009; Tausch et al., 2010, Study 4; Van Laar et al., 2005) and in more controlled experiments (Clement et al., 1977; Galinsky & Moskowitz, 2000; Harwood et al., 2011); these studies, however, remain few and far between. Echoing Pettigrew's (2008) call for more longitudinal studies testing contact theory in general, longitudinal designs are needed to more thoroughly investigate the secondary transfer effect. The longitudinal designs that have shown the secondary transfer effect (Eller & Abrams, 2004; Pettigrew, 2009; Tausch et al., 2010) are, however, lacking in one main respect: they rely on two waves of data (with the exception of Van Laar et al., 2005). Testing the secondary transfer effect and its mediators inherently requires at least three waves of data in order to test the effect of contact on the mediators (for example, primary outgroup attitudes) from wave 1 to wave 2, and then the effect of the mediators on the outcome variables from wave 2 to 3 (Cole & Maxwell, 2003). To our knowledge, no three-wave longitudinal study has been conducted testing the secondary transfer effect and its mediators. Furthermore, more detailed multi-wave longitudinal studies will help test reverse secondary transfer effect models more accurately.

Longitudinal designs, as powerful as they are, cannot strictly test causal hypotheses (Cliff, 1983). Therefore, future research also needs to test the secondary transfer effect using experimental designs. Because one can manipulate contact conditions in experimental designs, they provide more confidence in the causal nature of the secondary transfer effect. Neither of the two experimental designs (Galinsky & Moskowitz, 2000; Harwood et al., 2011) covered in this review, however, manipulated direct contact. It should also be noted that Clement et al. (1977) found evidence for the secondary transfer effect using a quasi-experimental design – an experimental design that does not randomly assign participants to different conditions (Crano & Brewer, 1986) – comparing those students who went on a school trip to Quebec (contact condition) with students who did not attend the excursion[3] (control group). The relative lack of experimental studies exploring the secondary transfer effect deserves attention.

Secondary outgroup contact measures

Most research on the secondary transfer effect that has measured contact with the secondary outgroup has relied on relatively simple measures of contact, i.e., single item measures of secondary outgroup contact (for two exceptions, see Lolliot et al., 2011; Swart, 2008). Models testing reverse secondary transfer effects – where secondary outgroup contact predicts primary outgroup attitudes – have, to date, resulted in weak effects. This could be because of (a) the relatively small number of contact items used, and (b) the reliance on general quantity and quality of contact measures rather than measures of cross-group friendships. Including more detailed secondary contact measures would allow researchers to test reverse secondary transfer effect models more convincingly. Most research that has measured contact with the secondary outgroups has measured it using quantity and quality of general contact. Having established intergroup friendships as a powerful predictor of intergroup attitudes (see Hamburger & Hewstone, 1997; Pettigrew, 1997), using friendships with the secondary outgroup as a predictor of secondary outgroup attitudes would also provide a more thorough test of the secondary transfer effect.

Directions for future research

We see several exciting directions for future research on the secondary transfer effect. We first discuss potential mediators of the secondary transfer effect after which we explore possible moderators. We end this section by briefly discussing the secondary transfer effect in terms of different attitudinal measures.

Additional mediators of the secondary transfer effect

The theoretical extensions suggested in this chapter provide a good starting point for the next generation of research on the secondary transfer effect. The hypotheses regarding our revised deprovincialization theory – involving multiculturalism and social identity complexity – as well as those regarding the role of empathy in the secondary transfer effect need to be (a) replicated, and (b) tested using longitudinal and experimental designs.

In addition to the two models offered above, empathy as a mediator of the secondary transfer effect has a number of avenues which need exploring. Firstly, research needs to tease out the effects that the different forms of perspective taking – imagine-other and imagine-self – could have on wider attitude generalization. While both perspective taking states elicit an affective empathic response (Finlay & Stephan, 2000), they may have different consequences for attitude formation and change. Secondly, current research has focused mainly on cognitive forms of empathy and the secondary transfer effect, leaving the affective forms untested. Given that affective processes have received strongest support in research on mediators of direct contact effects (Pettigrew & Tropp, 2008), the role of empathic concern in the secondary transfer effect needs to be explored.

Gaertner and Dovidio's (2000) dual identity model also suggests an important mediator of secondary transfer effects. The dual identity model states that a more inclusive super-ordinate identity that both in- and outgroups can ascribe to *without* forsaking members' respective sub-group identities is beneficial for intergroup relations. Because the dual identity model aims at producing a shared identity that both ingroup and outgroup members can identify with, it can also be considered a process of deprovincialization as it could be argued to measure ingroup reappraisal. In addition, creating a shared ingroup identity has been associated with an increase in self-disclosure with (previous) outgroup members (Dovidio, Gaertner, Validzic, Matoka, Johnson, & Frazier, 1997), and therefore may affect attitudes towards the secondary outgroups via intergroup empathy as well.

Lastly, and given its powerful mediating effects uncovered in research towards *primary* outgroups (Pettigrew & Tropp, 2008; Stephan & Stephan, 1985), intergroup anxiety is an obvious candidate as a mediator of the secondary transfer effects (see Vezzali & Giovannini, 2011, for the first evidence of anxiety's role in the secondary transfer effect).

Additional moderators of the secondary transfer effect

As with the attitude generalization hypothesis, similarity gradients may help uncover stronger attitude generalization effects from primary outgroup empathy to secondary outgroup attitudes. Batson et al. (1997) hypothesized that the positive effects of empathy will generalize from a single outgroup member to the outgroup as a whole if the person's outgroup membership is a salient component of their plight. Therefore, the positive effects of empathy should generalize to secondary outgroups if the secondary outgroup is understood to suffer a similar type of discrimination as the primary outgroup. Similarly, the *amount* or *level* of stigma may moderate the relationship between a mediator (such as primary outgroup attitudes or empathy) and secondary outgroup attitudes. For instance, if two outgroups are seen as experiencing similar levels of discrimination (i.e., two outgroups may experience different *types* of discrimination, but if the individual perceives them as both experiencing high *levels* of their respective discrimination), then the positive effects of contact may generalize from the primary outgroup to a secondary outgroup. Thinking back to Goffman's (1963) stigma typology, this moderated mediation hypothesis could help explain possible inter-category attitude generalization effects as mediated by empathy towards a primary outgroup. While Lolliot et al. (2011) provide initial evidence for the level of stigma moderating the attitude generalization path, more research needs to replicate this finding.

Attitude strength may help us uncover when attitudes generalize more strongly. Since attitude strength increases with the amount of exposure to the attitude object (Krosnick & Petty, 1995), if an individual has had little contact with an outgroup (see Christ et al., 2010, and Vonofakou, Hewstone, & Voci, 2007, for evidence of intergroup contact increasing attitude strength), their attitudes towards that outgroup may be more malleable. Therefore, we hypothesize that attitude strength could act as a potential moderator such that intergroup contact with a primary outgroup will show stronger secondary transfer effects for attitudes towards secondary outgroup(s) that are low in attitude strength than those that are held strongly.

An individual's need for cognition (Cacioppo & Petty, 1982) – an individual difference measure that measures a person's enjoyment and willingness to engage in thinking – may also moderate secondary transfer effects. Individuals low in need for cognition have been shown to be more prejudiced (Waller, 1993) and rely more on stereotyping (Schaller, Boyd, Yohannes, & O'Brien, 1995). Therefore, intergroup contact may be especially effective for individuals who score low on the need for cognition measure as they may show more blanket attitude generalization effects than individuals who are high in their need for cognition. Similarly, need for closure – a construct that measures an individual's preference for definite answers and the avoidance of ambiguity (Kruglanski & Webster, 1996) – could moderate secondary transfer effects. While need for closure has been positively associated with prejudice (Roets & Van Hiel, 2006; Van Hiel, Pandelaere, & Duriez, 2004), Dhont, Roets, and Van Hiel (2011) showed that intergroup contact was especially effective at improving intergroup attitudes for participants who scored high in need for closure than for low scorers. They hypothesized that individuals high rather than low in their need for closure would gain more certainty from an intergroup encounter which would reduce anxiety. This reduction in anxiety would then mediate the relationship between contact and prejudice. This is exactly what they found; anxiety was a stronger mediator of intergroup contact effects for those high rather than low in need for closure (Dhont et al., 2011, Studies 4 and 5). By simple extension then, individuals who are high in need for closure should show wider attitude generalization effects than those who do not need closure, a process that would also be mediated by a reduction in intergroup anxiety.

Concluding remarks

Societies are becoming more diverse. For example, citizens from more than 170 countries worldwide reside in London alone (Vertovec, 2007). As technology increases, international transport becomes more feasible, and international boarders more permeable, it is with little surprise that we read: "There are far more international migrants in the world today than ever previously recorded, and their number has increased rapidly in the last few decades" (International Organization for Migration, 2010, p. 3). Therefore, it is no wonder that some authors refer to modern cities as "super-diverse" (Vertovec, 2007; see also Benedictus, 2006). The obvious challenge, then, is for societies to find some way in which this myriad of social groups can function peacefully. With growing evidence for the existence of secondary transfer effects, intergroup contact, although not a panacea for prejudice (Hewstone, 2003), seems to be even more suited for this task than previously thought. Given the implications of the secondary transfer effect for improving intergroup relations beyond what was previously thought possible, attention does need to be focused on policy development within our diversifying societies (Brown & Hewstone, 2005; Pettigrew, 2008). The development of theories relating to the secondary transfer effect, such as deprovincialization for example, provides useful backdrops against which policy development can take place.

Looking further than community-based intergroup relations, there is great current interest across a number of social and behavioral sciences in the concept of "cosmopolitanism." This work concerns its ethical and philosophical dimensions, especially regarding questions of how to live as a "citizen of the world," in open acceptance of diversity and with a willingness to engage with others (e.g., Appiah, 2006; see Vertovec, 2010). If intergroup contact can improve attitudes beyond an immediately contacted outgroup – which the research reported in this chapter attests to – then intergroup contact represents one of the most powerful tools available for improving intergroup relations in the world's growing cosmopolitan societies.

Acknowledgment

Miles Hewstone's contribution to this chapter was funded, in part, by a grant on 'Ethno-religious diversity and trust in residential and educational settings' from the Leverhulme Trust, UK.

Notes

1 Most studies testing the secondary transfer effect have, owing to space constructions, had to rely on general contact quantity scales when measuring contact with the secondary outgroups (see Lolliot et al., 2011; Swart, 2008, for two exceptions), while contact with the primary outgroup has usually been measured using intergroup friendship scales which show stronger intergroup contact effects (Hamberger & Hewstone, 1997; Pettigrew, 1997).
2 Harwood et al. (2011) intentionally left the term "similarity" undefined in order to make the similarity judgments as global a measure as possible (see Pettigrew, 2009).
3 See Dhont, Roets, and Van Hiel, 2011 (Study 3) for a true experimental version of this design. Dhont et al. randomly allocated Belgian school students involved in an intercultural exchange program to either go on a 1-week school trip to Morocco (contact condition) or to stay behind. Students who participated in the week-long trip showed significantly less prejudice towards the outgroup than control participants did.

References

Aberson, C. L., & Haag, S. C. (2007). Contact, perspective taking, and anxiety as predictors of stereotype endorsement, explicit attitudes, and implicit attitudes. *Group Processes & Intergroup Relations, 10*, 179–201.

Allport, G. W. (1954). *The nature of prejudice.* Reading, MA: Addison-Wesley.

Al Ramiah, A. (2009). *Intergroup relations in Malaysia: Identity, contact and threat.* (Unpublished doctoral dissertation). Oxford University, Oxford.

Altemeyer, B. (1998). The other "authoritarian personality." In M. Zanna (Ed.), *Advances in experimental social psychology* (Vol. 30, pp. 47–92). San Diego, CA: Academic Press.

Ames, D. L., Jenkins, A. C., Banaji, M. R., & Mitchell, J. P. (2008). Taking another person's perspective increases self-referential neural processing. *Psychological Science, 19*, 642–644.

Amir, Y. (1969). Contact hypothesis in ethnic relations. *Psychological Bulletin, 71*, 319–342.

Appiah, K. A. (2006). *Cosmopolitanism: Ethics in a world of strangers.* New York, NY: Norton.

Asbrock, F., Christ, O., Duckitt, J., & Sibley, C. G. (2011). Differential effects of intergroup contact for authoritarians and social dominators: A dual process model perspective. *Personality and Social Psychology Bulletin.* Advanced online publication.

Asbrock, F., Christ, O., Hewstone, M., Pettigrew, T. F., & Wagner, U. (2011). *Comparing the secondary transfer effect of direct and extended intergroup contact: The generalization of positive attitudes and its limitations.* Manuscript submitted for publication.

Batson, C. D., & Ahmad, N. Y. (2009). Using empathy to improve intergroup attitudes and relations. *Social Issues and Policy Review, 3*, 141–177.

Batson, C. D., Chang, J., Orr, R., & Rowland, J. (2002). Empathy, attitudes, and action: Can feeling for a member of a stigmatized group motivate one to help the group? *Personality and Social Psychology Bulletin, 28*, 1656–1666.

Batson, C. D., Polycarpou, M. P., Harmon-Jones, E., Imhoff, H. J., Mitchener, E. C., Bednar, L. L., Klein, T. R., & Highberger, L. (1997). Empathy and attitudes: Can feeling for a member of a stigmatized group improve feelings toward the group? *Journal of Personality and Social Psychology, 72*, 105–118.

Benedictus, L. (2006). All together now. *The Guardian*, 23 January. Retrieved on August 29, 2011 from http://www.guardian.co.uk/uk/2006/jan/23/britishidentity.features118?INTCMP=ILCNETTXT3487

Brewer, M. B. (1999). The psychology of prejudice: Ingroup love or outgroup hate? *Journal of Social Issues, 55*, 429–444.

Brewer, M. B. (2008). Deprovincialization: Social identity complexity and outgroup acceptance. In U. Wagner, L. Tropp, G. Finchilescu, & C. Tredoux (Eds.), *Emerging research directions for improving intergroup relations – Building on the legacy of Thomas F. Pettigrew* (pp. 160–176). Oxford, UK: Blackwell.

Brewer, M. B., & Pierce, K. P. (2005). Social identity complexity and outgroup tolerance. *Personality and Social Psychology Bulletin, 31*, 428–437.

Brown, R., & Hewstone, M. (2005). An integrated theory of intergroup contact. In M. Zanna (Ed.), *Advances in experimental social psychology* (Vol. 37, pp. 255–343). San Diego, CA: Academic Press.

Brown, R., Vivian, J., & Hewstone, M. (1999). Changing attitudes through intergroup contact: The effects of group membership salience. *European Journal of Social Psychology, 29*, 741–764.

Cacioppo, J. T., & Petty, R. E. (1982). The need for cognition. *Journal of Personality and Social Psychology, 42*, 116–131.

Caditz, J. (1976). Ethnic identification, interethnic contact, and belief in integration. *Social Forces, 54*, 632–645.

Christ, O., Hewstone, M., Tausch, N., Wagner, U., Voci, A., Hughes, J., & Cairns, E. (2010). Direct contact as a moderator of extended contact effects: Cross-sectional and longitudinal impact on outgroup attitudes, behavioral intentions, and attitude certainty. *Personality and Social Psychology Bulletin, 36*, 1662–1674.

Clement, R., Gardner, R. C., & Smythe, P. C. (1977). Interethnic contact: Attitudinal consequences. *Canadian Journal of Behavioral Science, 9*, 205–215.

Cliff, N. (1983). Some cautions concerning the application of causal modeling methods. *Multivariate Behavioral Research, 18*, 115–126.

Cole, D. A., & Maxwell, S. E. (2003). Testing mediational models with longitudinal data: Questions and tips in the use of structural equation modeling. *Journal of Abnormal Psychology, 112*, 558–577.

Crano, W. D., & Brewer, M. B. (1986). *Principles and methods of social research.* Boston: Allyn and Bacon, Inc.

Crawford, M. T., Sherman, S. J., & Hamilton, D. L. (2002). Perceived entitativity, stereotype formation, and the interchangeability of group members. *Journal of Personality and Social Psychology, 83*, 1076–1094.

Crisp, R. J., Husnu, S., Meleady, R., Stathi, S., & Turner, R. N. (2010). From imagery to intention: A dual route model of imagined contact effects. *European Review of Social Psychology, 21*, 188–236.

Crisp, R. J., Stathi, S., Turner, R. N., & Husnu, S. (2008). Imagined intergroup contact: Theory, paradigm, and practice. *Social and Personality Psychology Compass, 3*, 1–18.

Davies, K., Tropp, L. R., Aron, A., Pettigrew, T. F., & Wright, S. C. (2011). Cross-group friendships and intergroup attitudes: A meta-analytic review. *Personality and Social Psychology Review, 15*, 332–351.

Dhont, K., Roets, A., & Van Hiel, A. (2011). Opening closed minds: The combined effects of intergroup contact and need for closure on prejudice. *Personality and Social Psychology Bulletin, 37*, 514–528.

Dhont, K., & Van Hiel, A. (2009). We must not be enemies: Interracial contact and the reduction of prejudice among authoritarians. *Personality and Individual Differences, 46*, 172–177.

Dovidio, J. F., Gaertner, S. L., & Kawakami, K. (2003). Intergroup contact: The past, present, and the future. *Group Processes & Intergroup Relations, 6*, 5–21.

Dovidio, J. F., Gaertner, S. L., Validzic, A., Matoka, K., Johnson, B., & Frazier, S. (1997).

Extending the benefits of recategorization: Evaluations, self-disclosure, and helping. *Journal of Experimental Social Psychology, 33*, 401–420.

Eller, A., & Abrams, D. (2004). Come together: Longitudinal comparisons of Pettigrew's reformulated intergroup contact model and the common ingroup identity model in Anglo-French and Mexican-American contexts. *European Journal of Social Psychology, 34*, 229–256.

Fazio, R. H., Eiser, J. R., & Shook, N. J. (2004). Attitude formation through exploration: Valence asymmetries. *Journal of Personality and Social Psychology, 87*, 293–311.

Finlay, K. A., & Stephan, W. G. (2000). Improving intergroup relations: The effects of empathy on racial attitudes. *Journal of Applied Social Psychology, 30*, 1720–1737.

Fiske, S. T., Cuddy, A. J. C., Glick, P., & Xu, J. (2002). A model of (often mixed) stereotype content: Competence and warmth respectively follow from perceived status and competition. *Journal of Personality and Social Psychology, 82*, 878–902.

Gaertner, S. L., & Dovidio, J. F. (2000). *Reducing intergroup bias: The common ingroup identity model.* Hove: Psychology Press.

Galinsky, A. D., Ku, G., & Wang, C. S. (2005). Perspective-taking and self-other overlap: Fostering social bonds and facilitating social coordination. *Group Processes & Intergroup Relations, 8*, 109–124.

Galinsky, A. D., & Moskowitz, G. B. (2000). Perspective-taking: Decreasing stereotype expression, stereotype accessibility, and in-group favoritism. *Journal of Personality and Social Psychology, 78*, 708–724.

Goffman, E. (1963). *Stigma: Notes on the Management of Spoiled Identity.* Englewood Cliffs, NJ: Prentice Hall.

Hamberger, J., & Hewstone, M. (1997). Inter-ethnic contact as a predictor of prejudice: Tests of a model in four Western European nations. *British Journal of Social Psychology, 36*, 173–190.

Harding, J., & Hogrefe, R. (1952). Attitudes of white department store employees toward Negro co-workers. *Journal of Social Issues, 8*, 18–28.

Harwood, J., Hewstone, M., Paolini, S., & Voci, A. (2005). Grandparent-grandchild contact and attitudes toward older adults: Moderator and mediator effects. *Personality and Social Psychology Bulletin, 31*, 393–406.

Harwood, J., Paolini, S., Joyce, N., Rubin, M., & Arroyo, A. (2011). Secondary transfer effects from imagined contact: Group similarity affects the generalization gradient. *British Journal of Social Psychology, 50*, 180–189.

Hewstone, M. (2003). Intergroup contact: Panacea for prejudice? *Psychologist, 16*, 352–355.

Hewstone, M. (2009). Living apart, living together? The role of intergroup contact in social integration. *Proceedings of the British Academy, 162*, 243–300.

Hewstone, M., & Brown, R. (1986). Contact is not enough: An intergroup perspective on the "contact hypothesis." In M. Hewstone, & R. Brown (Eds.), *Contact and conflict in intergroup encounters* (pp. 1–44). Oxford: Basil Blackwell.

Hewstone, M., & Swart, H. (2011). Fifty-odd years of inter-group contact: From hypothesis to integrated theory. *British Journal of Social Psychology, 50*, 374–386.

Hodson, G. (2008). Interracial prison contact: The pros for (socially dominant) cons. *British Journal of Social Psychology, 47*, 325–351.

International Organization for Migration (2010). *World migration report 2010. The future of migration: Building capacities for change.* Retrieved from http://publications.iom.int/bookstore/free/WMR_2010_ENGLISH.pdf

Krosnick, J. A., & Petty, R. E. (1995). Attitude strength: An overview. In R. E. Petty, & J.

A. Krosnick (Eds.), *Attitude strength: Antecedents and consequences* (pp. 1–24). Hillsdale, NJ: Erlbaum.

Kruglanski, A. W., & Webster, D. M. (1996). Motivated closing of the mind: "Seizing" and "Freezing." *Psychological Review, 103*, 263–283.

Lolliot, S., Schmid, K., Hewstone, H., Swart, H., & Tausch, N. (2011). *Mediators and moderators of secondary transfer effects in intergroup contact.* Manuscript in preparation.

MacCallum, R. C., & Austin, J. T. (2000). Applications of structural equation modeling in psychological research. *Annual Review of Psychology, 51*, 201–226.

Martin, R., & Hewstone, M. (2008). Majority versus minority influence, message processing and attitude change: The source-context-elaboration model. *Advances in Experimental Social Psychology, 40*, 237–326.

Martin, P. Y., Laing, J., Martin, R., & Mitchell, M. (2005). Caffeine, cognition, and persuasion: Evidence for caffeine increasing the systematic processing of persuasive messages. *Journal of Applied Social Psychology, 35*, 160–182.

Minard, R. D. (1952). Race relations in the Pocahuntas coal fields. *Journal of Social Issues, 8*, 29–44.

Monahan, J. L., Murphey, S. T., & Zajonc, R. B. (2000). Subliminal mere exposure: Specific, general, and diffuse effects. *Psychological Science, 11*, 462–466.

Pagotto, L., Voci, A., & Maculan, V. (2010). The effectiveness of intergroup contact at work: Mediators and moderators of hospital workers' prejudice towards immigrants. *Journal of Community & Applied Social Psychology, 20*, 317–330.

Pettigrew, T. F. (1997). Generalized intergroup contact effects on prejudice. *Personality and Social Psychology Bulletin, 23*, 173–185.

Pettigrew, T. F. (1998). Intergroup contact theory. *Annual Review of Psychology, 49*, 65–85.

Pettigrew, T. F. (2008). Future directions for intergroup contact theory and research. *International Journal of Intercultural Relations, 32*, 187–199.

Pettigrew, T. F. (2009). Secondary transfer effect of contact: Do intergroup contact effects spread to noncontacted outgroups? *Social Psychology, 40*, 55–65.

Pettigrew, T. F., & Tropp, L. R. (2006). A meta-analytic test of intergroup contact theory. *Journal of Personality and Social Psychology, 90*, 751–783.

Pettigrew, T. F., & Tropp, L. R. (2008). How does intergroup contact reduce prejudice? Meta-analytic tests of three mediators. *European Journal of Social Psychology, 38*, 922–934.

Podsakoff, P. M., MacKenzie, S. B., Lee, J. Y., & Podsakoff, N. P. (2003). Common method biases in behavioral research: A critical review of the literature and recommended remedies. *Journal of Applied Psychology, 88*, 879–903.

Pratto, F., Sidanius, J., & Levin, S. (2006). Social dominance theory and the dynamics of intergroup relations: Taking stock and looking forward. *European Review of Social Psychology, 17*, 271–320.

Pratto, F., Sidanius, J., Stallworth, L. M., & Malle, B. F. (1994). Social dominance orientation: A personality variable preceding social and political attitudes. *Journal of Personality and Social Psychology, 67*, 741–763.

Ranganath, K. A., & Nosek, B. A. (2008). Implicit attitude generalization occurs immediately: Explicit attitude generalization takes time. *Psychological Science, 19*, 249–254.

Ravenhill, M. (2008). *The culture of homelessness.* Aldershot, Hampshire: Ashgate Publishing Company.

Redmond, A. (2008). "Out of Site, Out of Mind": An Historical Overview of Accommodating Irish Travellers' Nomadic Culture in Northern Ireland. *Shared Space, 5*, 59–73.

Retrieved 11 June, 2010 from http://www.community-relations.org.uk/fs/doc/shared-space-issue-chapter5-59-73-web.pdf

Reich, C., & Purbhoo, M. (1975). The effects of cross-cultural contact. *Canadian Journal of Behavioural Science, 7*, 313–327.

Roccas, S., & Brewer, M. B. (2002). Social Identity Complexity. *Personality and Social Psychology Review, 6*, 88–106.

Roets, A., & Van Hiel, A. (2006). Need for closure relations with authoritarianism, conservative beliefs and racism: The impact of urgency and permanence tendencies. *Psychologica Belgica, 43*, 235–252.

Rothbart, M., & John, O. P. (1985). Social categorization and behavioral episodes: A cognitive analysis of the effects of intergroup contact. *Journal of Social Issues, 41*, 81–104.

Ruby, P., & Decety, J. (2004). How would *you* feel versus how do you think *she* would feel? A neuroimaging study of perspective-taking with social emotions. *Journal of Cognitive Neuroscience, 16*, 988–999.

Schaller, M., Boyd, C., Yohannes, J., & O'Brien, M. (1995). The prejudiced personality revisited: Personal need for structure and formation or erroneous group stereotypes. *Journal of Personality and Social Psychology, 68*, 544–555.

Schmid, K., Hewstone, M., Küpper, B., Zick, A., & Wagner, U. (in press). Secondary transfer effects of intergroup contact: A cross-national comparison in Europe. *Social Psychology Quarterly.*

Schmid, K., Hewstone, M., Tausch, N., Cairns, E., & Hughes, J. (2009). Antecedents and consequences of social identity complexity: Intergroup contact, distinctiveness threat, and outgroup attitudes. *Personality and Social Psychology Bulletin, 35*, 1085–1098.

Schmid, K., Hewstone, M., & Tausch, N. (2012). Secondary transfer effects of intergroup contact: Deprovincialization via social identity complexity and attitude generalization via perceived outgroup variability. Manuscript in preparation.

Shih, M., Wang, E., Bucher, A. T., & Stotzer, R. (2009). Perspective taking: Reducing prejudice towards general outgroups and specific individuals. *Group Processes & Intergroup Relations, 12*, 565–577.

Shook, N. J., Fazio, R. H., & Eiser, J. R. (2007). Attitude generalization: Similarity, valence, and extremity. *Journal of Experimental Social Psychology, 43*, 641–647.

Spears, R., & Leach, C. W. (2004). Intergroup schadenfreude: Conditions and consequences. In L. Z. Tiedens, & C. W. Leach (Eds.), *The social life of emotions: Studies in emotion and social interaction* (pp. 336–355). New York, NY: Cambridge University Press.

Stephan, W. G., & Stephan, C. W. (1985). Intergroup anxiety. *Journal of Social Issues, 41*, 157–175.

Swart, H. (2008). *Affective mediators of intergroup contact: Cross-sectional and longitudinal analyses in South Africa* (Unpublished doctoral dissertation). Oxford University, Oxford.

Swart, H., Hewstone, M., Christ, O., & Voci, A. (2010). The impact of crossgroup friendships in South Africa: Affective mediators and multigroup comparisons. *Journal of Social Issues, 66*, 309–333.

Swart, H., Hewstone, M., Christ, O., & Voci, A. (2011). Affective mediators of intergroup contact: A three-wave longitudinal study in South Africa. *Journal of Personality and Social Psychology, 101*, 1221–1238.

Tausch, N., Hewstone, M., Kenworthy, J. B., Psaltis, C., Schmid, K., Popan, J. R., Cairns, E., & Hughes, J. (2010). Secondary transfer effects of intergroup contact: Alternative accounts and underlying processes. *Journal of Personality and Social Psychology, 99*, 282–302.

Tropp, L. R., & Pettigrew, T. F. (2005). Relationships between intergroup contact and prejudice among minority and majority status groups. *Psychological Science, 16*, 951–957.

Turner, R. N., Hewstone, M., & Voci, A. (2007). Reducing explicit and implicit outgroup prejudice via direct and extended contact: The mediating role of self-disclosure and intergroup anxiety. *Journal of Personality and Social Psychology, 93*, 369–388.

Turner, R. N., Hewstone, M., Voci, A., & Vonofakou, C. (2008). A test of the extended intergroup contact hypothesis: The mediating role of intergroup anxiety, perceived ingroup and outgroup norms, and inclusion of the outgroup in the self. *Journal of Personality and Social Psychology, 95*, 843–860.

Van Hiel, A., Pandelaere, M., & Duriez, B. (2004). The impact of need for closure on conservative beliefs and racism: Differential mediation by authoritarian submission and authoritarian dominance. *Personality and Social Psychology Bulletin, 30*, 824–837.

Van Laar, C., Levin, S., Sinclair, S., & Sidanius, J. (2005). The effect of university roommate contact on ethnic attitudes and behaviour. *Journal of Experimental Social Psychology, 41*, 329–345.

Van Oudenhoven, J. P., Groenewoud, J. T., & Hewstone, M. (1996). Cooperation, ethnic salience and generalization of interethnic attitude. *European Journal of Social Psychology, 26*, 649–661.

Verkuyten, M. (2005). Ethnic group identification and group evaluation among minority and majority groups: Testing the multiculturalism hypothesis. *Journal of Personality and Social Psychology, 88*, 121–138.

Verkuyten, M., Thijs, J., & Bekhuis, H. (2010). Intergroup contact and ingroup reappraisal: Examining the deprovincialization hypothesis. *Social Psychology Quarterly, 73*, 398–416.

Vertovec, S. (2007). Super-diversity and its implications. *Ethnic and Racial Studies, 30*, 1024–1054.

Vertovec, S. (2010). Cosmopolitanism. In K. Knott, & S. McLoughlin (Eds.), *Diasporas: Concepts, identities, intersections*. London, England: Zed Books.

Vescio, T. K., Sechrist, G. B., & Paolucci, M. P. (2003). Perspective taking and prejudice reduction: The mediational role of empathy arousal and situational attributions. *European Journal of Social Psychology, 33*, 455–472.

Vezzali, L., & Giovannini, D. (2011). Secondary transfer effect of intergroup contact: The role of intergroup attitudes, intergroup anxiety, and perspective taking. *Journal of Community & Applied Social Psychology, 22*, 125–144.

Vonofakou, C., Hewstone, M., & Voci, A. (2007). Contact with out-group friends as a predictor of meta-attitudinal strength and accessibility of attitudes towards gay men. *Journal of Personality and Social Psychology, 92*, 804–820.

Waller, J. (1993). Correlation of need for cognition and modern racism. *Psychological Reports, 73*, 542.

Wasserman, J. A., & Clair, J. M. (2010). *At home on the street: People, poverty, and a hidden culture of homelessness*. Covent Garden, London: Lynne Rienner Publishers.

Weigert, K. M. (1976). Intergroup contact and attitudes about a third group: A survey of Black soldiers' perceptions. *International Journal of Group Tensions, 6*, 110–124.

Wilder, D. A. (1984). Intergroup contact: The typical member and the exception to the rule. *Journal of Experimental Social Psychology, 20*, 177–194.

Wright, S. C., Aron, A., McLaughlin-Volpe, T., & Ropp, S. A. (1997). The extended contact effect: Knowledge of cross-group friendships and prejudice. *Journal of Personality and Social Psychology, 73*, 73–90.

Zajonc, R. B. (2001). Mere exposure: A gateway to the subliminal. *Current Directions in Psychological Science, 10*, 224–228.

5   The role of group power in intergroup contact

Tamar Saguy, Linda R. Tropp, and Diala Hawi

In November, 2005, an Israeli peace center brought together Palestinian and Israeli architecture students to design hypothetical joint-housing projects. In the course of the encounters, the students learned about housing prototypes in Palestinian and Israeli societies, and then worked in mixed Palestinian-Israeli groups to design a building that could house both Palestinian and Israeli families. Interviews with the participants a few months later revealed that while the project seemed to have a positive impact on the perceptions and feelings of Israelis, who reported enjoyment and satisfaction with the encounters, it did little to change those of the Palestinians, whose main reactions were frustration and disappointment (Zandberg, 2006; see Nadler & Saguy, 2004).

These different reactions of Israelis and Palestinians are in line with findings from an extensive meta-analysis of the contact literature (Tropp & Pettigrew, 2005; see also Pettigrew & Tropp, 2006), summarizing over five hundred studies across a wide range of contexts and countries. Although contact was related to improved attitudes among members of both advantaged and disadvantaged groups, it was found to be significantly less effective for improving the outgroup attitudes of disadvantaged group members than those of advantaged group members[1] (Tropp & Pettigrew, 2005). Furthermore, optimal conditions in the contact situation (e.g., cooperation, equal status, institutional support; see Allport, 1954) were found to facilitate the effect of contact *only* for members of advantaged groups; the presence of these conditions did not have a significant impact on disadvantaged group members involved in intergroup contact.

Despite the richness of the contact literature (see Brown & Hewstone, 2005), few studies offer explanations for these power-based differences in the efficacy of contact. Because differences in group power have traditionally been considered an obstacle that should be overcome in contact situations, the emphasis has been on creating and maintaining equal status between interacting group members (Allport, 1954; Amir, 1969). This emphasis resulted in limited understanding of how power dynamics, those that mark the relations between the groups *outside* of the encounter, might still impact processes that occur *within* contact situations, even when attempts are made to achieve equal status (see Foster & Finchilescu, 1986; Riordan, 1978). Moreover, the vast majority of studies on intergroup contact have examined the responses of advantaged and disadvantaged group members separately from one another (Tropp & Pettigrew, 2005), offering few opportunities to test the role of group power on the effects of intergroup contact.

More recently, researchers have begun to consider differences in how advantaged versus disadvantaged group members approach, experience, and are affected by intergroup contact (see Devine & Vasquez, 1998; Shelton, Richeson, & Vorauer, 2006; Tropp, 2006). For instance, findings from a U.S. national survey show that while positive effects of contact are typically observed among White Americans, they are significantly inhibited among Black Americans who perceive high levels of discrimination against their racial group (Tropp, 2007). Experimental and diary studies further indicate that exposure to prejudice and discrimination can undermine minorities' willingness to engage in contact with members of the advantaged majority group (Shelton & Richeson, 2006; Tropp, 2003). Still, such findings offer little information regarding the ways in which group differences in power are enacted in contact settings, or how intergroup contact can either perpetuate or ameliorate group differences in power.

In the this chapter, we review emerging evidence that can advance our understanding of the intersection of power and contact between groups. We begin by considering how psychological processes associated with group position (i.e., advantaged versus disadvantaged group membership) relate to how people approach contact situations in terms of their goals and preferences for the content of intergroup encounters. We then describe research that links the consequences of intergroup contact to power asymmetries between groups and to processes that promote social change. We conclude by discussing the implications of this work for research and practice on improving intergroup relations.

Group position and approaches to intergroup relations

Without exception, societies are hierarchically organized such that at least one group controls a greater share of valued resources (e.g., political power, economic wealth, educational opportunities) than do other groups (Jackman, 2001; Sidanius & Pratto, 1999). Group-based hierarchy is reflected in almost every aspect of social life, from poverty rates and school attrition rates to prison sentences and mortality rates – favoring members of advantaged over disadvantaged groups (Feagin, 2006; Jackman, 2001; Smooha, 2005; Ulmer & Johnson, 2004). Members of disadvantaged groups, compared with members of advantaged groups, also encounter discrimination and social injustice in a wide range of domains, such as when interviewing for jobs and being quoted a price for a house or a car (e.g., Ayres, 1991; Bertrand & Mullainathan, 2004). The differential control over resources accompanied by differential social treatment produces divergent daily realities for members of advantaged and disadvantaged groups. Whereas members of disadvantaged groups find many doors to economic opportunities closed, have a difficult time climbing the social ladder, and experience legal authorities as a source of intimidation, advantaged group members experience far more economic security, opportunities to advance, and social acceptance (Jones, Engelman, Turner, & Campbell, 2009).

Because advantaged and disadvantaged group members encounter vastly different realities, they also tend to view the status quo in different ways. Members of advantaged groups, who benefit both practically and psychologically from hierarchical social arrangements, are likely to perceive the status quo as reasonable and even "natural", and to have little opposition to group-based hierarchy. Instead, because they have more to gain from changes toward greater equality, members of disadvantaged groups are generally more likely to perceive the status quo as problematic and to desire a change in current social arrangements. These group-based orientations toward the status quo are implicated in prominent theories of intergroup relations such as the Group Position Model (Blumer, 1958; see also Bobo, 1999; Bobo & Hutchings, 1996), Social Dominance Theory (Sidanius & Pratto, 1999), Realistic Group Conflict Theory (LeVine & Campbell, 1972; Sherif, 1966) and Social Identity Theory (Tajfel & Turner, 1979), and are supported empirically. For example, Pratto, Sidanius, Stallworth, and Malle (1994) demonstrate that individuals who hold more power in society tend to view the social hierarchy as natural and necessary, while members of disadvantaged groups are more likely to see the hierarchy as in need of change. This effect has been replicated in a variety of intergroup contexts including ethnic groups in Israel (Saguy, Dovidio, & Pratto, 2008, Study 2), India (Saguy, Tausch, Dovidio, Pratto, & Singh, 2010) and the US (Pratto et al., 1994), and also among experimental groups for whom group position was experimentally manipulated (Saguy et al., 2008, Study 1).

Consistent with their group-based motivations toward the status quo, advantaged group members are likely to behave in ways that would help them maintain their relative dominance and undermine change, such as by promoting ideologies that make hierarchy seem legitimate and reasonable (Jackman, 2001; Reicher, 2007; Sidanius & Pratto, 1999). By contrast, members of disadvantaged groups are more likely to engage in behaviors that would challenge current social arrangements, such as by supporting or participating in collective action efforts aimed at promoting equality (van Zomeren, Postmes & Spears, 2008; Simon & Klandermans, 2001). These different tendencies also manifest themselves in the psychological needs that members of advantaged and disadvantaged groups bring to relations with each other. Positions of disadvantage pose a threat to one's status and power and motivate people to seek empowerment and voice in relations with the advantaged group; by contrast, positions of advantage pose a threat to one's moral image and motivate people to seek acceptance from the disadvantaged (Shnabel & Nadler, 2008; Shnabel, Nadler, Ullrich, Dovidio, & Carmi, 2009).

Studies conducted across different intergroup contexts reveal that advantaged and disadvantaged group members tend to further differ in what they regard as the preferred form of intergroup relations (see Dovidio, Gaertner & Saguy, 2009; Hornsey & Hogg, 2000). Advantaged group members show relatively strong support for relations in which differences between groups are minimized and the emphasis instead is on common ties among the groups within one, superordinate, category (e.g., "we are all Americans, rather than Blacks and Whites"); (Wolsko, Park, Judd, & Wittenbrink, 2000). Conversely, even though they might also appreciate commonalities, members of disadvantaged groups show a consistent preference for relations through which group differences are also acknowledged and valued (Richeson & Nussbaum, 2004; Verkuyten, 2005; Wolsko et al., 2000). For example, native-Dutch (the advantaged majority) have been shown to prefer assimilation of immigrants to the host culture, whereas immigrants prefer to become part of the dominant (host) culture while retaining their original cultural identity (van Oudenhoven, Prins, & Buunk, 1998; see also Pfafferott & Brown, 2006; Verkuyten, 2006). Similarly, Blacks in the U.S. have been shown to endorse an emphasis on racial identities more than colorblindness, whereas Whites tend to endorse colorblindness more than Blacks (Ryan, Hunt, Weible, Peterson, & Casas, 2007; see also Dovidio, Gaertner, & Kafati, 2000).

These group-based preferences for emphasizing common ties or differences can be seen, at least to some extent, as strategic – that is, serving motivations for social change among disadvantaged groups and for stability among advantaged groups. In order to advance action that could bring about social change, some conditions must be met. As proposed by Social Identity Theory (Tajfel & Turner, 1979), when disadvantaged group members come to think of the social hierarchy as legitimate and just, they become less motivated to support efforts toward social change (Wright, 2001). This notion is echoed in System Justification Theory (Jost, Banaji, & Nosek, 2004), which asserts that disadvantaged and advantaged group members alike are motivated to justify and defend the existing system (Jost, 2001; Jost, Burgess, & Mosso, 2001). Beyond the recognition of injustice, disadvantaged group members must also be strongly committed to their group in order to collectively challenge their group's inferior position in the social hierarchy (Doosje, Ellemers, & Spears, 2002; Veenstra & Haslam, 2000; Wright & Tropp, 2002). Thus, factors that both promote the legitimacy of the hierarchical system and loosen disadvantaged group members' ties with their group can jointly work to undermine potential for social change.

As discussed by Wright and Lubensky (2009), a focus on commonalities across groups can provoke a reduction in identification with one's own group, including less commitment to the ingroup's goals, norms, and particular interests. Furthermore, the focus on commonalities can reduce the salience of group differences, including those pertaining to status and power, thereby rendering potential injustices less apparent (Saguy et al., 2009). Taken together, these perspectives suggest that an emphasis on similarities and commonalities may better serve advantaged group members' motivation to maintain the status quo, whereas attention to differences and inequalities can serve disadvantaged group members' motivation for social change (see Wright & Lubensky, 2009). We next consider how these different orientations toward commonality and difference may inform group members' goals and preferences in intergroup contact.

Group position and goals in intergroup contact

The contact that has traditionally been considered "optimal" for changing attitudes involves a focus on a common goal, or cooperation between groups (see Allport, 1954; Sherif, 1966). However, intergroup contact can take different forms, and given their different orientations toward intergroup relations, advantaged and disadvantaged group members may differ in their preferences for addressing commonalities versus group differences during intergroup contact.

Consistent with these ideas, Tropp and Bianchi (2007) found that disadvantaged group members responded more positively to intergroup contact than advantaged group members when an outgroup member explicitly mentioned how group membership might be relevant to a future interaction. When the outgroup member (confederate) mentioned how "Whites" or "ethnic minorities" might have different ideas during the upcoming task, ethnic minority participants expressed more interest in interacting with the outgroup member than did ethnic majority participants. These findings suggest that, in contact settings, members of disadvantaged groups positively value an acknowledgement of group differences (Eggins, Haslam, & Reynolds, 2002) and the preservation of their group identity (Hornsey & Hogg, 2000), whereas advantaged group members may be relatively more threatened by discussions of group difference (see also Trawalter & Richeson, 2008).

Indeed, due to legacies of disadvantage and a stronger motivation for change, disadvantaged group members may be more likely than advantaged group members to want intergroup encounters to bring to light differences in the experiences and positions of the groups (Maoz, 2011). As suggested previously, this focus could serve the disadvantaged group's interest in drawing attention to structural inequalities and the need for social change. In contrast, members of advantaged groups might be more in favor of attending to commonalities during contact, through which group members could engage in discussions of similarities without addressing potential differences between the groups. This focus can not only promote affection between the groups but also disguise power relations, which together can reduce the likelihood of resistance and undermine social change (Jackman, 2001).

Still, while advantaged and disadvantaged group members may diverge in their willingness to emphasize differences, they may diverge less when it comes to emphasizing commonalities. Beyond serving the needs of the advantaged group, an intergroup encounter that focuses on commonalities could also, at least partially, serve the interests of the disadvantaged groups, particularly if issues of power are also addressed. By emphasizing common connections between the groups while simultaneously making group disparities salient, members of disadvantaged groups could sensitize the advantaged group to issues of common humanity and social injustice. Consequently, advantaged group members' support for social change toward equality can potentially increase the more they come to know and care about the concerns of the disadvantaged (see Dixon et al., 2010b; Saguy et al., 2008). Thus, whereas members of advantaged and disadvantaged groups may differ in their tendencies to emphasize aspects that distinguish their group identities (such as differences in group power), they can have similar tendencies to focus on aspects that they share (such as national or cultural commonality).

In summary, the content of cross-group interactions can be viewed as strategic and functional for serving group-based goals. This proposition can have important implications for understanding how group members approach and experience intergroup encounters. As a function of group position, group members may perceive certain types of encounters as more beneficial to their group than other types and, consequently, would have different preferences for the content of discussions during intergroup contact. Moreover, the desire for certain contents is likely to increase the more goals regarding the status quo (i.e., change vs. stability) are pronounced. Finally, if a focus on particular content serves the interest of those who wish to stabilize the status quo, then encounters that focus on such content should ultimately reduce the chances of social change to occur. In the remainder of this chapter, we present evidence in line with these ideas.

Perceptions of group benefit

Given the different goals advantaged and disadvantaged group members have regarding the status quo, certain types of interaction contents may be more in line with the needs of advantaged group members and some may better meet the needs of disadvantaged group members. An interaction content that involves a focus on differences in terms of illegitimate power asymmetries (e.g., job opportunities favoring majority over minority group members) can serve the group-based interests of disadvantaged groups, whereas an interaction content that centers on commonalities in terms of dimensions that people from different ethnic groups share can serve the group-based interests of advantaged groups. As suggested previously, the focus on commonalities might also be beneficial for promoting the interests of disadvantaged groups by sensitizing advantaged group members to issues of social inequality. Thus, although for disadvantaged group members, a focus on power differences during contact (*power-focused contact*) may be perceived as more beneficial than a focus on commonalities (*commonality-focused contact*), both advantaged and disadvantaged group members may perceive comparable benefits in commonality-focused contact.

Recent evidence provides support for these propositions. White and Latino Americans were presented with one of two intergroup contact programs (presented as a list of discussion topics), focused either on commonalities or on power differences (Saguy & Dovidio, 2011). The topics presented in the power-focused contact condition were linked to social disparities between the groups (e.g., "Discussing ways to fight past and current discrimination against minority groups") and the commonality-related topics emphasized salient, shared cultural aspects with no reference to power (e.g., "Discussing interests and hobbies that members of different ethnic groups in America share in common"). Participants were asked to evaluate whether discussing the topics in a future intergroup encounter could benefit their own ethnic group.

As predicted, for Latinos, power-focused contact was rated as more likely to benefit the ingroup than commonality-focused contact; by contrast, for Whites, commonality-focused contact was rated as more likely to benefit the ingroup than power-focused contact. There was also a significant difference between Whites and Latinos in the perception of power-focused contact as beneficial to the ingroup, but there was no significant difference between the groups in the perceptions of commonality-focused contact as beneficial to the ingroup (see Figure 5.1). We further examined whether advantaged and disadvantaged group members recognize the potential benefits of commonality-focused or power-focused contact for the outgroup. Latinos believed that Whites would benefit more from commonality-focused contact than from power-focused contact, whereas Whites believed that Latinos would benefit more from power-focused contact than from commonality-focused contact. As such, endorsement of these contents reflects common strategic orientations in cross-group interactions, such that group members not only recognize potential benefits to their own group as a result of each type of contact, but they also seem to recognize potential benefits for the outgroup.

These results were replicated in a laboratory experiment in which group position was manipulated by giving one group control over valued resources (experimental credit) for both groups (Saguy & Dovidio, 2011). Participants believed they were about to interact with members of the other group and were presented with the list of topics to be discussed. Consistent with the results involving Whites and Latinos, members of the low power group believed their group would benefit more from discussing power over commonalities, with no differences between the groups obtained with regard to perceptions of benefits due to commonalities. Furthermore, and consistent with the previous study, members of the low power group believed that high power group members would benefit more from discussing commonalities than from discussing power. As expected, the opposite pattern was obtained for the high power group, who believed that low power group members would benefit more from discussing power than from discussing commonalities.

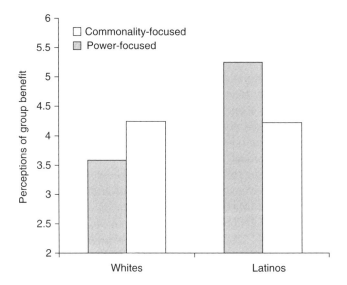

Figure 5.1 Perceptions of ingroup benefit as a function of group position and contact type (Saguy & Dovidio, 2011)

Preferences for the content of cross-group interactions

Given that advantaged and disadvantaged group members are aware of the utility that different types of interaction content have for serving both the ingroup's and the outgroup's needs, they may also exhibit corresponding preferences for the content of interactions between their groups. Saguy et al. (2008) provided support for these ideas in a variety of intergroup settings. In a laboratory study (Saguy et al., 2008, Study 1), group power was manipulated by giving one group (the advantaged group) control over a resource that was desired by both groups (i.e., course credits, which are the incentive for participating in studies), while the disadvantaged group had no control over the resource. As they approached intergroup contact, both groups showed an equivalent interest in discussing topics of commonality. However, advantaged group members exhibited significantly less interest in discussing power differences between the groups than did disadvantaged group members, whereas disadvantaged group members displayed equivalent interest in talking about commonality and difference. Moreover, disadvantaged group members' greater preference for discussing differences in power was mediated by their greater motivation for a change in the power structure, relative to the advantaged group members. These findings were replicated with groups differing in social status in Israel, including Ashkenazim (Jews of American or European descent) and Mizrahim (Jews of Asian or African descent); (Saguy et al., 2008, Study 2). In addition, members of the advantaged group who identified more strongly with their group displayed even greater interest in talking about commonality, whereas highly identified disadvantaged group members showed a greater preference for talking about differences (Saguy et al., 2008, Study 2).

These ideas are further supported by data collected in field settings involving actual encounters between advantaged and disadvantaged groups. In an analysis of conflict resolution workshops involving Israelis and Palestinians, Rouhana and Korper (1997) found that Israeli participants (i.e., advantaged group members) expressed desire to participate in the workshop if the interactions were based on interpersonal processes that could lead to attitude change, whereas Palestinians wanted to address structural and political issues during the encounters (see Maoz, 2011; Nadler & Saguy, 2004, for additional qualitative evidence). Related findings were observed in a study of interactions between Jewish and Arab educators (Maoz, 2000). When discussing issues related to the educational system, a topic clearly common to both groups, Jewish participants were more active and dominant in the interactions, whereas Arabs were passive and uninvolved. However, when the discussion shifted to issues concerning the political conflict in the region, Arabs were more involved in the interaction and also expressed more positive attitudes towards it (Maoz, 2000).

Taken together, the findings reviewed thus far suggest that group position shapes group members' goals and preferences regarding the *content* of cross-group interactions. Furthermore, these different preferences seem strategic and functional for serving group-based needs, in light of prior work on group-based motivations (Bobo, 1999) and related behaviors (Dovidio et al., 1997). We next describe work that provides support for the strategic way in which group members approach situations of contact.

Strategies in cross-group interactions

To empirically establish the strategic nature of the preferences to discuss power and commonalities, Saguy and Dovidio (2012) examined these preferences under insecure status relations. According to Tajfel and Turner (1979; see also Bettencourt et al., 2001; Ellemers, Van Knippenberg, & Wilke, 1990), group members' reactions to the status quo depend on the extent to which they perceive the status relations to be stable and legitimate, that is, secure. When status relations are secure, alternatives to the existing status relations do not seem viable or right. As a result, members of advantaged groups perceive little threat to their relatively superior position, and members of disadvantaged groups have little faith that attempts to advance their status would be fruitful. In contrast, when the status relations are perceived as unstable and illegitimate, not only that the hierarchy might change, such change has moral justification. Consequently, advantaged group members might be particularly inclined to defend their insecure status while disadvantaged group members are likely to be particularly motivated to engage in attempts to advance their group's position. Nadler and Halabi (2006) provided elegant support for these ideas by examining Arabs' reactions to help offered by Jews. Arabs in Israel are a low status minority, who generally perceive their status relative to Jews to be illegitimate. Results demonstrated that under unstable (compared with stable) status relations, Arabs in Israel were more likely to reject help offered by an Israeli Jew – help which could work to sustain the status hierarchy by fostering Arabs' dependency on Jews. Ironically, Israeli Jews were particularly likely to offer such dependency-oriented help to Arabs when their advantaged group's position was perceived as unstable (Halabi, Dovidio, & Nadler, 2008).

According to this analysis, when group members perceive the status relations to be insecure, they will be more likely to enact strategies to advance (for low status groups) or protect (high status groups) their status. In keeping with this, if the group-based preferences for interaction content described earlier are indeed strategic, they would be more pronounced under insecure status relations. That is, when they believe a change is possible, and morally justified, disadvantaged group members should engage more strongly in behaviors that can advance change, such as raising attention to power. By contrast, advantaged group members should be more defensive of their group status and more inclined to engage in behaviors that could preserve the status quo.

To test these predictions, students from the University of Connecticut (a high ranked, public research university in Connecticut), were led to believe that they were about to interact with either students from Yale university (a more prestigious school in the same state) or with students from Eastern Connecticut College (a school with lower prestige in the same state). These expectations constituted the group position manipulation by creating an advantaged position (when expecting to interact with Eastern Connecticut students) versus a disadvantaged position (when expecting to interact with Yale students). Similar to previous studies, participants were asked to rate the degree to which they would like to discuss different topics during the interaction, some addressing commonalities, and some addressing differences in status. Prior to choosing topics, participants read a newspaper article describing the differences in status between alumni of the two schools, that were portrayed as either enduring (stable condition) or likely to change (unstable condition), and as either legitimate or not. The findings revealed that disadvantaged group members' desire to discuss power differences during the interaction was most pronounced when the status relations were both unstable and illegitimate. Mediation analysis further revealed that this greater desire to address status differences was largely due to a heightened motivation for social change. By contrast, advantaged group members showed a stronger desire to discuss commonalities over power differences, and this tendency somewhat increased when the status relations were both unstable and illegitimate.

These findings support the notion that goals involved in status relations relate to the way group members approach and react to situations of intergroup contact. A goal of challenging current status relations might lead to a stronger focus on *power differences* whereas a goal of maintaining power could be reflected in an emphasis on *commonalities*. In the next section we examine the utility of these strategies by considering the consequences of intergroup contact for the stability or malleability of power relations between groups.

Consequences of intergroup contact for social equality and social change

A focus on commonalities has consistently been shown to relate to more positive outgroup attitudes (Gaertner & Dovidio, 2000), to foster more personalized and intimate cross-group interactions (Dovidio, Gaertner, Validzic, Matoka, Johnson, & Frazier, 1997), and to promote prosocial behavior across group lines (Nier, Gaertner, Dovidio, Banker, & Ward, 2001). Nevertheless, commonality-focused interactions can impact outcomes that go beyond attitudes and emotions (see Dixon, Durrheim, & Tredoux, 2005). For example, coming to like members of the disadvantaged group might relate to stronger support on part of advantaged group members for policies that could advance equality. Nevertheless, and as described earlier, such encounters might divert disadvantaged group members' attention from issues related to social inequality, thereby influencing their awareness and motivation to promote change. In this section we review findings that demonstrate the relationship between intergroup contact and perceptions and behaviors related to social inequality and social change.

Research on members of advantaged groups has generally shown that positive contact experiences with the disadvantaged predicts greater support for egalitarian policies (see Pettigrew & Tropp, 2011). For example, the more White South Africans had positive contact with Blacks, the less opposed they were to compensatory policies that could promote Black advancement (e.g., scholarships for underrepresented students) and to preferential policies for Blacks such as affirmative action (Dixon et al., 2010b). In a survey of Jewish-Israelis, Maoz and Ellis (2008) have shown that participation in structured encounters with Palestinians predicted increased willingness to compromise and make reparations. Studies in Western Europe and the United States further find that contact with immigrants is significantly associated with greater support for pro-immigration practices (e.g., Hayes & Dowds, 2006; Pettigrew, Wagner, & Christ, 2007; see also Pettigrew, 1997).

Research on members of disadvantaged groups, which has been relatively scarce in contact research (Tropp & Pettigrew, 2005), has begun to reveal a more complex picture regarding contact and dimensions related to equality and social change. Wright and Lubensky (2009) found that among African Americans and Latinos, positive contact with Whites was associated with more positive attitudes toward Whites, but also with less support for collective action to advance equality. Similar findings were obtained among Arabs in Israel, for whom contact with Jews predicted better attitudes toward Jews, but also reduced support for policies that could advance the positions of Arabs – an effect mediated by reduced awareness of structural inequalities between the groups (Saguy et al., 2009). In a survey of Black South Africans, positive contact with Whites was associated with decreased support for social policies that could potentially enhance racial equality (Dixon, Durrheim, & Tredoux, 2007), and with decreased perceptions of racial discrimination (Dixon et al., 2010a). Taken together, these findings suggest that positive contact may not only encourage minorities to feel more favorably towards advantaged groups, but can have the unintended consequence of diminishing their perceptions of discrimination and their inclination to challenge the status quo (Dixon, Tropp, Durrheim, & Tredoux, 2010c).

These ideas were further tested in a laboratory experiment in which different types of contact, either focused on commonalities or differences in power, were manipulated and perceptions regarding inequality were subsequently measured (Saguy et al., 2009). College students were randomly assigned to either an advantaged or a disadvantaged group. The advantaged group was given the opportunity to assign extra course credits to the two groups. Before the advantaged group members allocated the credits, members of both groups interacted, with instructions to focus on either intergroup commonalities or differences. Results demonstrated that commonality-focused interactions, compared with differences-focused interactions, produced more positive intergroup attitudes among both advantaged and disadvantaged group members. In addition, commonality-focused contact was related to reduced awareness of the inequality in the study among members of both groups. Moreover, members of the disadvantaged group expected the advantaged group to distribute the credits in a more equitable fashion, following commonality-focused than following differences-focused interactions. Mediation analysis revealed that this expectation was explained by improved intergroup attitudes and reduced awareness of inequality. These findings complement the cross-sectional data reviewed above, showing that positive contact predicts reduced perceptions of discrimination (Dixon et al., 2010a).

The laboratory experiment further enabled examination of whether the disadvantaged group members' expectations for equality were met by the behavior of the advantaged group. Results showed that following difference-focused contact, advantaged group members were substantially biased in the allocation of credits, just as disadvantaged group members anticipated. However, after commonality-focused contact, although disadvantaged group members expected a more equal distribution of credits, advantaged group members were just as biased in this condition as in the difference-focused condition. This effect is consistent with theories of group position indicating that advantaged groups are motivated to maintain their power (Blumer, 1958; Sidanius & Pratto, 1999). Furthermore, whereas members of advantaged groups may support equality in principle, which likely corresponds to an attitudinal outcome of favorable contact, they may still demonstrate resistance to creating equality in practice (Durrheim & Dixon, 2004; Jackman & Crane, 1986).

Taken together, the findings reviewed in this section suggest that experiences of positive, commonality-focused contact can affect how disadvantaged group members view social inequality and their own disadvantage. Because perceiving one's group as disadvantaged is a key predictor of collective resistance (Simon & Klandermans, 2001; van Zomeren et al., 2008), the impact of contact on such perceptions might work to impede the potential for change among members of disadvantaged groups. Moreover, the harmony created by contact, as reflected in improved attitudes, might predict greater stated support for equality among members of advantaged groups, but not necessarily egalitarian actions. Implications of this work for designing contact interventions and future contact research are discussed in the next section.

Conclusions

In this chapter we provided a framework for understanding how power relations impact the dynamics of intergroup contact. Traditionally, contact research has granted limited attention to the ways in which differences in group power impact the dynamics of intergroup contact. For over fifty years, the assumption seems to have been that advantaged and disadvantaged group members alike benefit from contact that is generally pleasant and focuses on goals that the groups share in common. Consistent with this view, contact interventions were typically constructed to diminish power differences between groups during the intergroup encounter. The research reviewed in this chapter demonstrates a number of key points regarding the intersection of power and intergroup contact.

First, advantaged and disadvantaged group members bring different *goals and preferences* to intergroup contact. Whereas members of both groups may see benefits in a focus on communalities, the desire to address differences in power is typically stronger among members of disadvantaged groups. A primary implication of these findings is that the perspectives of *both* advantaged and disadvantaged group members are important to consider when studying and designing intergroup encounters. A focus on cooperative elements can be successful in inducing a pleasant atmosphere, yet, if it involves no reference to power, it might better serve the interests and goals of members of advantaged groups than of members of disadvantaged groups. Thus, if intergroup contact is solely focused on commonalities – such as having Palestinians and Israelis work together on joint projects (see Maoz, 2011) or play soccer together on the same team (Peres Center for Peace, 2008), members of disadvantaged groups might end up feeling that the interaction was less satisfying, productive, or worthwhile than advantaged group members.

Second, the findings reviewed in this chapter suggest that the harmony created by positive contact, in the form of improved attitudes, might inadvertently impede chances for change toward equality. The orientations of both disadvantaged and advantaged groups can contribute to this "irony of harmony." Harmony-inducing strategies can turn disadvantaged group members' attention away from social inequalities and lead them to view the advantaged group as generally fair and egalitarian. Both of these outcomes can lead disadvantaged group members to relax their efforts to promote change toward equality. At the same time, for members of advantaged groups, improved attitudes resulting from positive contact do not necessarily translate into more egalitarian intergroup behavior (Durrheim & Dixon, 2004).

Future research might examine the processes through which intergroup harmony impedes egalitarian actions on the part of advantaged groups members. One possibility is that when intergroup relations are positive, members of advantaged groups feel less urgency to make changes in the social system. Having positive interactions with the disadvantaged may have helped them to fulfill their needs to feel accepted and to have their moral image restored (Shnabel et al., 2009). Positive interactions in which members of the disadvantaged group appear content may also reduce advantaged group members' concerns about social inequality and make actual egalitarian behavior seem less necessary.

Future work might also examine the effects of commonality-focused contact over time, especially among members of disadvantaged groups. Disadvantaged group members may at first become optimistic about group relations through positive contact and the advantaged group's benevolence. In the longer term, however, disadvantaged group members may become "disillusioned" if repeated positive contact experiences do not correspond to achieving any real change. In addition, their situation might actually stagnate or get worse rather than improve if members of the advantaged group feel no pressure or urgency to be truly egalitarian. This cycle of events could in turn produce greater distrust, disillusionment, and resentment, which might eventually fuel more extreme forms of conflict. This possibility points to the potential fragility of harmony created by contact that focuses merely on commonalities, and to the need to develop interventions that would help achieve both improved intergroup attitudes and greater steps toward social equality.

It is important to note that the findings reviewed in this chapter do not indicate that commonality-based contact *necessarily* undermines efforts toward equality. The critical factor likely involves the nature of the positive contact and how this intergroup harmony is achieved. For instance, although an emphasis on commonalities that are unrelated to social inequalities may deflect attention from group disparities, common identities structured around a sense of morality and shared humanity would likely bring illegitimate disparities to light. Such a commonality focus could also motivate members of advantaged and disadvantaged groups to work together to eradicate social inequities. But, we wish to highlight that, both theoretically and practically, an emphasis on commonality and intergroup harmony in and of itself does not necessarily lead to intergroup equality (see Dixon et al., 2007).

In conclusion, the work reported in this chapter joins recent accounts in integrating intergroup contact with insights from work on social change (Dixon et al., 2005; Dixon et al., 2010c; Reicher, 2007; Wright & Lubensky, 2009). There are many clear positive consequences of optimal contact on intergroup attitudes, and these effects have been shown to generalize across context and time (see Pettigrew & Tropp, 2011). Nevertheless, solely promoting more harmonious relationships can distract attention away from inequity and impede, in the long run, fundamental structural changes in society. Recognition of this potential contradiction between the positive attitudinal outcomes of contact and the motivating factors for social change is of crucial importance when considering the wide implementation of contact interventions (Brown & Hewstone, 2005; Paluck & Green, 2009). If such interventions inadvertently work to undermine efforts toward social change, they may, ultimately contribute to the stability of status relations and the corresponding manifestations of social inequality and injustice. Understanding the complexity and range of consequences of what is typically considered "optimal" contact is thus essential for creating a society that is both inclusive and just in structure and practice, not only in principle.

Note

1. We use the terms "advantaged" and "disadvantaged" to refer to differences between the groups in power and/or status. Whereas differences in group power often involve differential control over valuable resources (Sidanius & Pratto, 1999), differences in group status could be also symbolic and involve differential prestige and value associated with each group (Tajfel & Turner, 1979). By using the terms advantaged and disadvantaged, we refer to differences in the relative position of each group within the social hierarchy (Bobo, 1999), which could be due to power, status, or as in most intergroup contexts, both.

References

Allport, G. W. (1954). *The nature of prejudice.* Reading, MA: Addison-Wesley.
Amir, Y. (1969). Contact hypothesis in ethnic relations. *Psychological Bulletin, 71,* 319–342.
Ayres, I. (1991). Fair driving: Gender and race discrimination in retail car negotiations. *Harvard Law Review, 104,* 817–872.
Bertrand, M., & Mullainathan, S. (2004). Are Emily and Greg more employable than Lakisha and Jamal? *American Economic Review, 94,* 991–1013.
Bettencourt, B. A., Charlton, K. D., Dorr, N., & Hume, D. L. (2001). Status differences and in-group bias: A meta-analytic examination of the effects of status stability, status legitimacy, and group permeability. *Psychological Bulletin, 127,* 520–542.
Blumer, H. (1958). Race prejudice as a sense of group position. *Pacific Sociological Review, 1,* 3–7.

Bobo, L. D. (1999). Prejudice as group position: Microfoundations of a sociological approach to racism and intergroup relations. *Journal of Social Issues, 55*, 445–472.

Bobo, L., & Hutchings, V. L. (1996). Perceptions of racial group competition: Extending Blumer's theory of group position to a multiracial social context. *American Sociological Review, 61*, 951–972.

Brown, R., & Hewstone, M. (2005). An integrative theory of intergroup contact. In M. Zanna (Ed.), *Advances in experimental social psychology* (Vol. 37, pp. 255–343). San Diego, CA: Academic Press.

Devine, P. G., & Vasquez, K. A. (1998). The rocky road to positive intergroup relations. In J. L. Eberhardt, & S. T. Fiske (Eds.), *Confronting racism: The problem and the response* (pp. 234–262). Thousand Oaks, CA: Sage.

Dixon, J. A., Durrheim, K., & Tredoux, C. (2005). Beyond the optimal strategy: A "reality check" for the contact hypothesis. *American Psychologist, 60*, 697–711.

Dixon, J. A., Durrheim, K., & Tredoux, C. (2007). Intergroup contact and attitudes toward the principle and practice of racial equality. *Psychological Science, 18*, 867–872.

Dixon, J., Durrheim, K., Tredoux, C., Tropp, L., Clack, B., & Eaton, E. (2010a). A paradox of integration? Interracial contact, prejudice reduction and blacks' perceptions of racial discrimination. *Journal of Social Issues, 66*, 401–416.

Dixon, J., Durrheim, K., Tredoux, C., Tropp, L., Clack, B., Eaton, E., & Quale, M. (2010b). Challenging the stubborn core of opposition to equality: Racial contact and policy attitudes. *Political Psychology, 31*, 831–855.

Dixon, J., Tropp, L. R., Durrheim, K., & Tredoux, C. (2010c). "Let them eat harmony": Prejudice reduction and the political attitudes of historically disadvantaged groups. *Current Directions in Psychological Science, 19*, 76–80.

Doosje, B., Ellemers, N., & Spears, R. (1999). Commitment and intergroup behaviour. In N. Ellemers, R. Spears, & B. Doosje (Eds.), *Social identity: Context, commitment and content* (pp. 84–107). Oxford, England: Blackwell.

Dovidio, J. F., Gaertner, S. L., & Kafati, G. (2000). Group identity and intergroup relations: The Common In-Group Identity Model. In S. R. Thye, E. J. Lawler, M. W. Macy, & H. A. Walker (Eds.), *Advances in group processes* (Vol. 17, pp. 1–34). Stamford, CT: JAI Press.

Dovidio, J. F., Gaertner, S. L., & Saguy, T. (2009). Commonality and the complexity of "We": Social attitudes and social change. *Personality and Social Psychology Review, 13*, 3–20.

Dovidio, J. F., Gaertner, S. L., Validzic, A., Matoka, K., Johnson, B., & Frazier, S. (1997). Extending the benefits of re-categorization: Evaluations, self-disclosure and helping. *Journal of Experimental Social Psychology, 33*, 401–420.

Durrheim, K., & Dixon, J. A. (2004). Attitudes in the fibre of everyday life: Desegregation and the discourse of racial evaluation. *American Psychologist, 59*, 626–636.

Eggins, R. A., Haslam, S. A., & Reynolds, K. J. (2002). Social identity and negotiation: Subgroup representation and superordinate consensus. *Personality and Social Psychology Bulletin, 28*, 887–899.

Ellemers, N., Van Knippenberg, A., & Wilke, H. (1990). The influence of permeability of group boundaries and stability of group status on strategies of individual mobility and social change. *British Journal of Social Psychology, 29*, 233–246.

Feagin, J. R. (2006). *Systematic racism: A theory of oppression.* New York: Routledge.

Foster, D., & Finchilescu, G. (1986). Contact in a "non-contact" society: The case of South Africa. In M. Hewstone, & R. Brown (Eds.), *Contact and conflict in intergroup encounters* (pp. 119–136). Oxford, England: Basil Blackwell.

Gaertner, S. L., & Dovidio, J. F. (2000). *Reducing intergroup bias: The common ingroup identity model*. Philadelphia, PA: Psychology Press.

Halabi, S., Dovidio, J. F., & Nadler, A. (2008). When and how high status groups offer help: Effects of social dominance orientation and status threat. *Political Psychology, 29*, 841–858.

Hayes, B. & Dowds, L. (2006). Social contact, cultural marginality, or economic self-inter-est? Attitudes towards immigrants in Northern Ireland. *Journal of Ethnic and Migration Studies, 32*, 455–476.

Hornsey, M. J., & Hogg, M. A. (2000). Assimilation and diversity: An integrative model of subgroup relations. *Personality and Social Psychology Review, 4*(2), 143–156.

Jackman, M. R. (2001). License to kill: Violence and legitimacy in expropriative social relations. In J. T. Jost, & B. Major (Eds.), *The psychology of legitimacy: Emerging per-spectives on ideology, justice, and intergroup relations* (pp. 437–467). New York: Cam-bridge University Press.

Jackman, M. R., & Crane, M. (1986). Some of my best friends are black . . .: Interracial friendship and whites' racial attitudes. *Public Opinion Quarterly, 50*, 459–486.

Jones, J. M., Engelman, S., Turner, C., & Campbell, S. (2009). Worlds apart: The univer-sality of racism leads to divergent social realities. In S. Demoulin, J. P. Leyens, & J. F. Dovidio (Eds.), *Intergroup misunderstandings: Impact of divergent social realities* (pp. 117–134). Philadelphia, PA: Psychology Press.

Jost, J. T. (2001). Outgroup favoritism and the theory of system justification: An experi-mental paradigm for investigating the effects of socio-economic success on stereotype content. In G. Moskowitz (Ed.), *Cognitive social psychology: The Princeton symposium on the legacy and future of social cognition.* Hillsdale, NJ: Erlbaum.

Jost, J. T., Banaji, M. R., & Nosek, B. A. (2004). A decade of system justification theory: Accumulated evidence of conscious and unconscious bolstering of the status quo. *Politi-cal Psychology, 25*, 881–919.

Jost, J. T., Burgess, D., & Mosso, C. O. (2001). Conflicts of legitimation among self, group, and system. In J. T. Jost, & B. Major (Eds.), *The psychology of legitimacy* (pp. 363–388). New York: Cambridge University Press.

LeVine, R. A., & Campbell, D. T. (1972). *Ethnocentrism: Theories of conflict, ethnic atti-tudes, and group behavior.* New York: Wiley.

Maoz, I. (2000). Power relations in intergroup encounters: A case study of Jewish-Arab encounters in Israel. *International Journal of Intercultural Relations, 24*, 259–277.

Maoz, I. (2011). Does contact work in protracted asymmetrical conflict? Appraising 20 years of reconciliation-aimed encounters between Israeli Jews and Palestinians. *Journal of Peace Research, 48*, 115–125.

Maoz, I., & Ellis, D. G. (2008). Intergroup communication as a predictor of Jewish-Israeli agreement with integrative solutions to the Israeli–Palestinian conflict: The mediating effects of out-group trust and guilt. *Journal of Communication, 58*, 490–507.

Nadler, A., & Halabi, S. (2006). Inter-group helping as status relations: Effects of status stability, identification and type of help on receptivity to high status group's help. Journal of Personality and Social Psychology, 91, 97–110.

Nadler, A., & Saguy, T. (2004). Reconciliation between nations: Overcoming emotional deterrents to ending conflicts between groups. In H. Langholtz & C. E. Stout (Eds.), *The Psychology of Diplomacy* (pp. 29–46). New York: Praeger.

Nier, J. A., Gaertner, S. L., Dovidio, J. F., Banker, B. S., & Ward, C. M. (2001). Changing interracial evaluations and behavior: The effects of a common group identity. *Group Processes and Intergroup Relations, 4*, 299–316.

Paluck, E. L., & Green, D. P. (2009). Prejudice reduction: What works? A critical look at evidence from the field and the laboratory. *Annual Review of Psychology, 60*, 339–367.

Pfafferott, I., & Brown, R. (2006). Acculturation preferences of majority and minority adolescents in Germany in the context of society and family. *International Journal of Intercultural Relations, 30*, 703–171.

Peres Center for Peace. (2008). Retrieved on March 1, 2008, from http://www.peres-center.org

Pettigrew, T. F. (1997). Generalized intergroup contact effects on prejudice. *Personality and Social Psychology Bulletin, 23*, 173–185.

Pettigrew, T. F., & Tropp, L. (2006). A meta-analytic test of intergroup contact theory. *Journal of Personality and Social Psychology, 90*, 751–783.

Pettigrew, T. F., & Tropp, L. R. (2011). *When groups meet: The dynamics of intergroup contact*. New York: Psychology Press.

Pettigrew, T. F., Wagner, U., & Christ, O. (2007). Who opposes immigration? Comparing German with North American findings. *Du Bois Review, 4*, 19–39.

Pratto, F., Sidanius, J., Stallworth, L. M., & Malle, B. F. (1994). Social dominance orientation: A personality variable predicting social and political attitudes. *Journal of Personality and Social Psychology, 67*, 741–763.

Reicher, S. (*2007*). Rethinking the paradigm of prejudice. *South African Journal of Psychology, 37*, 820–834.

Richeson, J. A., & Nussbaum, R. J. (2004). The impact of multiculturalism versus colorblindness on racial bias. *Journal of Experimental Social Psychology, 40*, 417–423.

Riordan, C. (1978). Equal-status interracial contact: A review and revision of the concept. *International Journal of Intercultural Relations, 2*, 161–185.

Rouhana, N. N., & Korper, S. H. (1997). Power asymmetry and goals of unofficial third party intervention in protracted intergroup conflict. *Peace and Conflict: Journal of Peace Psychology, 3*, 1–17.

Ryan, C. S., Hunt, J. S., Weible, J. A., Peterson, C. R., & Casas, J. F. (2007). Multicultural and colorblind ideology, stereotypes, and ethnocentrism among Black and White Americans. *Group Processes and Intergroup Relations, 10*, 617–637.

Saguy, T., & Dovidio, J. F. (2012) Insecure status relations shape preferences for the content of intergroup contact. Manuscript submitted for publication.

Saguy, T., & Dovidio, J.F. (2011). The content of contact and perceptions of group-based benefits. Unpublished manuscript.

Saguy, T., Dovidio, J. F., & Pratto, F. (2008). Beyond contact: Intergroup contact in the context of power relations. *Personality and Social Psychology Bulletin, 34*, 432–445.

Saguy, T., Tausch, N., Dovidio, J. F., & Pratto, F. (2009). The irony of harmony: Intergroup contact can produce false expectations for equality. *Psychological Science, 20*, 114–121.

Saguy, T., Tausch, N., Dovidio, J. F., Pratto, F., & Singh, P. (2010). Tension and harmony in intergroup relations. In M. Mikulincer, & P. R. Shaver (Eds.), *Human aggression and violence: Causes, manifestations, and consequences* (pp. 333–348). Washington, DC: American Psychological Association.

Shelton, J. N., & Richeson, J. A. (2006). Ethnic minorities' racial attitudes and contact experiences with white people. *Cultural Diversity and Ethnic Minority Psychology, 12*, 149–164.

Shelton, J. N., Richeson, J. A., & Vorauer, J. D. (2006). Threatened identities and interethnic interactions. *European Review of Social Psychology, 17*, 321–358.

Sherif, M. (1966). *In common predicament: Social psychology of intergroup conflict and cooperation*. Boston: Houghton Mifflin.

Shnabel, N., & Nadler, A. (2008). A needs-based model of reconciliation: Satisfying the differential emotional needs of victim and perpetrator as a key to promoting reconciliation. *Journal of Personality and Social Psychology, 94*, 116–132.

Shnabel, N., Nadler, A., Ullrich, J., Dovidio, J. F., & Carmi, D. (2009). Promoting reconciliation through the satisfaction of the emotional needs of victimized and perpetrating group members: The needs-based model of reconciliation. *Personality and Social Psychology Bulletin, 35*, 1021–1030.

Sidanius, J., & Pratto, F. (1999). *Social dominance: An intergroup theory of social hierarchy and oppression.* New York: Cambridge University Press.

Simon, B., & Klandermans, B. (2001). Politicized collective identity: A social-psychological analysis. *American Psychologist, 56*, 319–331.

Smooha, S. (2005). *Index of Arab-Jewish relations in Israel 2004.* Haifa: The Jewish-Arab Center, University of Haifa.

Tajfel, H., & Turner, J. C. (1979). An integrative theory of intergroup conflict. In W. G. Austin, & S. Worchel (Eds.), *The social psychology of intergroup relations* (pp. 33–48). Monterey, CA: Brooks/Cole.

Trawalter, S., & Richeson, J. A. (2008). Let's talk about race, baby! When Whites'and Blacks' interracial contact experiences diverge. *Journal of Experimental Social Psychology, 44*, 1214–1217.

Tropp, L. R. (2003). The psychological impact of prejudice: Implications for intergroup contact. *Group Processes & Intergroup Relations, 6*, 131–149.

Tropp, L. R. (2006). Stigma and intergroup contact among members of minority and majority status groups. In S. Levin, & C. van Laar (Eds.), *Stigma and group inequality: Social psychological perspectives* (pp. 171–191). Mahwah, NJ: Erlbaum.

Tropp, L. R. (2007). Perceived discrimination and interracial contact: Predicting interracial closeness among Black and White Americans. *Social Psychology Quarterly, 70*, 70–81.

Tropp, L. R., & Bianchi, R. A. (2007). Interpreting references to group membership in context: Feelings about intergroup contact depending on who says what to whom. *European Journal of Social Psychology, 37*, 153–170.

Tropp, L. R., & Pettigrew, T. F. (2005). Relationships between intergroup contact and prejudice among minority and majority status groups. *Psychological Science, 16*, 951–956.

Ulmer, J., & Johnson, B. D. (2004). Sentencing in context: A multilevel analysis. *Criminology, 42*, 137–177.

van Oudenhoven, J. P., Prins, K. S., & Buunk, B. (1998). Attitudes of minority and majority members towards adaptation of immigrants. *European Journal of Social Psychology, 28*, 995–1013.

van Zomeren, M., Postmes, T., & Spears, R. (2008). Toward an integrative social identity model of collective action: A quantitative research synthesis of three socio-psychological perspectives. *Psychological Bulletin, 134*, 504–535.

Veenstra, K., & Haslam, A. (2000). Willingness to participate in industrial protest: Exploring social identification in context. *British Journal of Social Psychology, 39*, 153–172.

Verkuyten, M., (2005). Ethnic group identification and group evaluation among minority and majority groups: Testing the multiculturalism hypothesis. *Journal of Personality and Social Psychology, 88*, 121–138.

Verkuyten, M. (2006). Multicultural recognition and ethnic minority rights: A social identity perspective. In W. Stroebe, & M. Hewstone (Eds.), *European review of social psychology* (Vol. 17, pp. 148–184). New York: Psychology Press.

Wolsko, C., Park, B., Judd, C. M., & Wittenbrink, B. (2000). Framing interethnic ideology: Effects of multicultural and color-blind perspectives on judgments of groups and individuals. *Journal of Personality and Social Psychology, 78*, 635–654.

Wright, S. C. (2001). Restricted intergroup boundaries: Tokenism, ambiguity and tolerance of injustice. In J. T. Jost, & B. Major (Eds.), *The psychology of legitimacy* (pp. 223–256). Cambridge University Press.

Wright, S. C., & Lubensky, M. (2009). The struggle for social equality: Collective action vs. prejudice reduction. In S. Demoulin, J. P. Leyens, & J. F. Dovidio (Eds.), *Intergroup misunderstandings: Impact of divergent social realities* (pp. 291–310). New York: Psychology Press.

Wright, S. C., & Tropp, L. R. (2002). Collective action in response to disadvantage: Intergroup perceptions, social identification, and social change. In I. Walker, & H. Smith (Eds.), *Relative deprivation: Specification, development, and integration* (pp. 200–236). Cambridge: Cambridge University Press.

Zandberg, E. (2006). *Non-cooperative housing*. Retrieved March, 1, 2008, from http://www.haaretz.com

Part III
Building intimacy in intergroup contact

Preludes and processes

6 Imagined intergroup contact

Refinements, debates, and clarifications

Richard J. Crisp and Rhiannon N. Turner

In this chapter we review, discuss and advance a new implementation of intergroup contact theory. *Imagined intergroup contact* is "the mental simulation of a social interaction with a member or members of an outgroup category" (Crisp & Turner, 2009, p. 234). Our proposition is that simply imagining intergroup contact can produce more positive perceptions of outgroups. Recent research has supported this proposition: Imagined contact improves both explicit and implicit attitudes, it reduces stereotyping and intergroup anxiety, and it promotes and enhances intentions to engage in future contact.

We do not advocate imagined contact as a replacement for existing contact-based approaches. Rather, we believe it has two principal uses. First, it is a means of accessing the benefits of contact when actual or extended contact are impossible or impractical (as in contexts of extreme segregation). Second, it is a pre-contact tool for practitioners and policymakers, a way of introducing the *concept* of contact to individuals prior to more involving interventions. It can work as the "first step" on the road to reconciliation and reduced prejudice, so that when extended or actual contact interventions are implemented those participating will be more likely to do so with an open mind and a positive disposition.

In what follows we give a brief introduction to imagined intergroup contact and address three current issues. First, we discuss recent empirical findings supporting the idea that imagined contact may be an effective pre-contact tool for encouraging greater interest in, and engagement with, outgroups. Second, we explore whether imagined contact works through the same underlying processes as extended and actual contact, when these processes diverge, and the implications of this theoretical analysis for developing integrated contact interventions. Finally, we describe some recent debates in the literature that have focused on the efficacy and applicability of imagined contact, provide some important clarifications, and suggest future directions for imagined contact research and practice.

Origins and rationale

Allport's (1954) contact hypothesis presented a simple idea: bringing together members of different groups under appropriate conditions will lead to more positive intergroup relations. Decades of research has confirmed this hypothesis.

Intergroup contact can improve intergroup attitudes in many different contexts: between younger and older people, host communities and immigrants, straight and gay people, people of different races and nationalities, and towards people with illnesses such as AIDS (see Pettigrew & Tropp, 2006). Studies have shown that positive contact not only generates more positive attitudes towards outgroups, but also that it breaks down outgroup stereotypes (Paolini, Hewstone, Cairns, & Voci, 2004), and promotes forgiveness for past wrongdoings (Tam, Hewstone, Kenworthy, & Cairns, 2009). The hypothesis is now a sophisticated theoretical account of the antecedents, processes and outcomes associated with social contact, one that is built upon the firm bedrock of over 500 supportive studies (Pettigrew & Tropp, 2006).

We now know a great deal about when, whether and how contact exerts its positive effects. However, recent advances have seen the theory evolve and extend in scope beyond Allport's original vision. One new focus has been on developing our understanding of the different *types* of contact that are effective at reducing prejudice. Pettigrew (1998), for example, proposed that intergroup contact based on long-term close relationships rather than initial acquaintanceship would be most successful at reducing prejudice, a premise that has received extensive empirical support over the past decade (Levin, van Laar, & Sidanius, 2003; Pettigrew, 1997). Cross-group friendship works through developing more positive *feelings* about outgroup members, as well as increasing *knowledge* about the outgroup. For instance, it reduces intergroup anxiety, the negative arousal experienced at the prospect of contact by individuals who have little experience with the outgroup (Paolini et al., 2004), it promotes the reciprocal disclosure of personal information between group members (Turner, Hewstone, & Voci, 2007), and it generates intergroup trust (Tam, Hewstone, Kenworthy, & Cairns, 2009) and empathy (Tam et al., 2007).

Our research has contributed to this focus on new forms of contact, but from a different perspective. While intimate forms of contact like cross-group friendship are a highly effective means of reducing prejudice, they do come with a proviso: they can only reduce prejudice when social groups and group members are afforded the *opportunity* to engage in contact (e.g., Phinney, Ferguson, & Tate, 1997; Turner, Hewstone, Voci, Paolini, & Christ 2007; Turner, Hewstone, Voci, & Vonofakou, 2008). Unfortunately, there are many examples where the local intergroup relations afford few such opportunities. In the United States, for example, segregation of Latino and White communities remains pervasive (Martin, 2006) and the average White person lives in a predominantly White neighborhood with less than 10 percent Black residents (Logan, 2001). Many Catholic and Protestant communities in Belfast, Northern Ireland, comprise a very low percentage of residents from the other community, and only 5 percent of Northern Irish children attend mixed Catholic-Protestant schools (Census, 2001). High quality contact has an undoubtedly positive impact on intergroup perceptions, but the question remains: what if actual contact cannot be achieved in these highly segregated contexts?

In fact, even when groups are in close physical proximity, research has shown that this in itself is not enough to promote high quality contact. Sometimes groups are in the same place, at the same time, but have no inclination, nor motivation, to engage in any meaningful contact (compounded by the fact that, psychologically speaking, we have a tendency to interact mainly with those similar to ourselves, especially with regard to age, race, and gender; Graham & Cohen, 1997). Take, for example, the UK. At the time of the last Census (2001), 4.7 million British people belonged to a minority ethnic group, 8.8 million belonged to a minority religious group, and 3.5 million reported being gay or lesbian. In other words, the UK is composed of a diverse array of social groups, which surely provides many opportunities for interactions and the development of close relationships between members of different groups. However, despite this diversity, there is considerable evidence to suggest that these opportunities for contact are not always pursued (see Cameron & Turner, 2010, for a review). In sum, even though many countries are becoming increasingly multicultural, and communities progressively diverse, people often live "parallel lives" (Cantle, 2001), engaging in little or no meaningful social interaction with members of groups other than their own.

So while we know a great deal about the benefits of contact between members of different groups, one of the biggest challenges facing social scientists and policymakers is how to improve relations when opportunities for contact are minimal; or how to stimulate an interest in contact where opportunities do exist, but existing prejudices or uncertainties prevent them from being realised. We believe that *imagined contact* could offer a way of addressing these issues.

A brief introduction to imagined contact

Our proposition is that simply imagining contact can produce more positive perceptions of outgroups (Crisp & Turner, 2009, in press). The idea is that when people imagine intergroup contact they engage in conscious processes that parallel those involved in actual contact. They may, for example, actively think about what they would learn about the outgroup member, how they would feel during the interaction, and how this would influence their perceptions of the outgroup member and the outgroup more generally. In turn, this should lead to more positive evaluations of the outgroup, similar to the effects of face-to-face contact.

In empirical work on imagined contact, participants have been given a very simple task:

> We would like you to take a minute to imagine yourself meeting [an outgroup] stranger for the first time. Imagine that the interaction is positive, relaxed and comfortable.

This simple phrase includes two key elements that we have found to be critical. First is the instruction to engage in a simulated encounter. We have found that running through the mental script of an interaction is essential. In contrast, simply thinking of an outgroup member in the absence of any simulated interaction has no positive effects on attitudes (Turner, Crisp, & Lambert, 2007, Experiment 2). Second is a positive tone. We know that this is important for direct contact, and it is likely to be even more important for imagined contact (to safeguard against negative stereotypes unduly influencing the envisaged encounter). Empirically, research has shown that imagined contact works better when it is positive compared to neutral (Stathi & Crisp, 2008, Experiment 1).

Control conditions are critical to experimental investigations using the imagined contact paradigm. We have typically used a version of the following in order to create a pleasant scene (akin to a positive interaction), but with no reference to groups:

> We would like you to take a minute to imagine an outdoor scene. Try to imagine aspects of the scene (e.g., is it a beach, a forest, are there trees, hills, what's on the horizon?).

Mindful that this might not control for more generalized positive effects of social interaction *per se*, research has also used a version simulating positive social interaction with a member of a non-relevant group (i.e., a positive interaction with a non-relevant stranger versus a positive interaction with a relevant stranger); (Stathi & Crisp, 2008, Experiment 2). This rules out positive affect arising from generalized social interaction as an explanation for imagined contact effects. The use of varied control conditions has also ruled out informational load (Turner, Crisp et al., 2007, Experiment 1), stereotype priming (Turner, Crisp et al., 2007, Experiment 2), as well as positive affective priming and non-relevant social interaction (Stathi & Crisp, 2008, Experiment 2). For a full account of the different instructional task variants and control conditions, see Crisp, Stathi, Turner, and Husnu (2008).

In-depth reviews of imagined contact, which focus on both theoretical underpinnings (Crisp & Turner, 2009) and technical details of task variants (Crisp et al., 2008), can be found elsewhere. However, a brief outline of key studies is illustrative. The simple instructions described above have a unique, positive impact on a range of outcomes associated with more positive intergroup relations. For instance, in three studies, Turner, Crisp et al. (2007) found that imagined contact with an outgroup member led to more positive outgroup evaluations, as well as greater perceived outgroup variability. Two studies found that young participants who imagined a scenario in which they participated in a short positive interaction with an older person showed less subsequent ingroup favoritism. This was the case whether participants imagined contact compared to simply imagining an outdoor scene (Experiment 1) or compared to simply thinking about an older person, without any interaction involved (Experiment 2). In a third study, we focused on attitudes of heterosexual men towards homosexual men. Participants who imagined talking to a homosexual man on a train subsequently evaluated homosexual men in general more positively, and stereotyped homosexual men less (perceived less homogeneity), than participants who imagined an outdoor scene.

Subsequent studies have offered further support for the imagined contact proposition, ruled out alternative explanations, and developed an understanding of the theoretical processes and practical scope of the approach. For instance, one early concern was that demand characteristics could play a role in explaining the effect. Perhaps the imagined contact effect is not about imagining contact at all, but just about participants guessing what the task is *meant* to do? We have, however, found no evidence to suggest that imagined contact effects could be explained by demand characteristics. Typically, no participants report any awareness of the experimental hypotheses at feedback. For instance, in Turner, Crisp et al. (2007) only four participants out of seventy nine across the three studies reported any suspicion about the purpose of the experiment and not one participant successfully identified the aims. Nonetheless, in order to better rule out this explanation we have examined the effects of imagined contact on implicit measures of attitudes (Turner & Crisp, 2010). Whereas explicit attitudes are conscious, deliberative and controllable (and are usually captured by traditional self-report measures), implicit attitudes are unintentionally activated by the mere presence (actual or symbolic) of an attitude object, and are therefore less likely to be influenced by social desirability than are explicit measures. We asked young participants to imagine talking to an older stranger using the same instructions as in Turner, Crisp et al. (2007) before completing an explicit outgroup attitude measure and a measure of implicit attitudes, the implicit association test (IAT) (Greenwald, McGhee, & Schwartz, 1998). Participants who had imagined contact with an older person subsequently showed not only more positive explicit, self-reported, outgroup attitudes towards older people in general, but also more positive *implicit* outgroup attitudes on a young-old version of the IAT (Experiment 1). In a subsequent study, non-Muslim students who imagined interacting with a Muslim showed more positive implicit outgroup attitudes on a non-Muslim – Muslim version of the IAT (Experiment 2).

Other research has shed light on *how* and *when* imagined contact promotes more positive attitudes towards outgroups. Stathi and Crisp (2008) showed that imagined contact encourages the projection of positive traits from the self to ethnic and national outgroups (using a trait attribution task where participants were required to tick traits that applied to themselves, and also whether the same list of traits applied to the outgroup). This was especially the case under conditions that made the self salient (i.e., when the self was thought about before the group, rather than vice-versa). This finding was consistent with what we know about social projection – it is a process through which traits and attitudes are attributed to others and can constitute a fundamental "cognitive basis for ingroup favoritism" (p. 42; Robbins & Krueger, 2005; see also Cadinu & Rothbart, 1996). Ingroup bias occurs because projection of positive self traits to similar others (i.e., the ingroup) is generally stronger for ingroups than outgroups (Clement & Krueger, 2002). Imagined contact, like real contact, appears to break down the boundaries that prevent positive projection to outgroup members.

As well as cognitive processes like projection, our research has established emotion-based routes to reduced prejudice, namely reduced intergroup anxiety (Turner, Crisp et al. 2007). This is the negative emotional reaction that can occur at the prospect of having to engage in an intergroup encounter, which is most likely to arise where there has been minimal previous contact and when there are large differences in status (Stephan & Stephan, 1985). Finally, imagined contact can also reduce the impact of negative self-stereotypes on quantitative performance (the *stereotype threat* effect) (Steele, 1997). Research has found that older people (all aged over 60 years old) who imagined a short social interaction with a young stranger (compared to control) were subsequently immune to the depleting effects of a threat comparison (i.e., a stated comparison of older peoples' performance with younger people) on cognitive test performance (Abrams et al., 2008; Crisp & Abrams, 2008).

Three current issues

Our aim in this chapter is to address three current issues and debates surrounding imagined contact. First, we outline new findings that have supported the notion that imagined contact could be usefully applied as a pre-contact tool for promoting a more positive orientation to engaging in actual contact. Second, with growing empirical support for imagined contact effects, an important question is whether and how the approach is distinct from existing contact strategies, and what implications this theoretical analysis might have for future research and implementation. Finally, we discuss the prospects for applying imagined contact as an educational strategy, answering recent critiques about the technique's applicability with children, and clarify what we expect to be the optimal procedures to ensure maximal effectiveness of the approach.

Imagined contact as a pre-contact tool

Imagined contact can improve outgroup attitudes (Turner, Crisp et al., 2007; Turner & Crisp, 2010; Stathi & Crisp, 2008). However, we have suggested that its principal value (and wider applicability) may be in its ability to encourage people to seek out contact, remove contact inhibitions that go hand in hand with existing prejudices, and prepare people to engage outgroups with an open mind (Crisp & Husnu, 2011; Crisp & Turner, 2009, 2010; Crisp, Husnu, Meleady, Stathi, & Turner, 2010). It may literally "unfreeze" rigid conceptions of intergroup relations (Kruglanski, 1989), and initiate the action needed to instigate actual intergroup contact. In this way, imagined contact might be highly effective as a "first step" in the pursuit of more positive intergroup relations, a *pre-contact* tool that can enhance intentions to engage in future contact.

Empirical studies have begun to offer some support for the idea of imagined contact as a preparatory measure, and helped to elucidate the mechanisms involved. In this section we first describe some recent research supporting the idea that imagined contact can encourage intentions to engage in future contact. Second, we describe research that is supporting the idea that, once contact has been initiated, having previously imagined contact will help the interaction proceed in a positive manner (i.e., avoiding potential misinterpretations that could blight the encounter and worsen relations).

Encouraging intentions

We believe that one of the most tangible benefits of imagined contact will be its ability to break inhibitions that go hand in hand with existing prejudices and encourage people to engage positively with outgroup members. We know that imagining an event reliably increases the perceived likelihood that the event will occur, and that individuals will be more likely to carry out behaviors in the pursuit of objectives that they have imagined obtaining (Carroll, 1978). Imagined contact may have a similar impact on intentions to engage in future outgroup contact. One way in which imagined contact might therefore be usefully applied is immediately before an intervention that involves direct contact.

A recent study by Husnu and Crisp (2010b) has supported the idea that imagined contact represents an important way of encouraging intentions to engage in future contact. We tested the approach in the inter-ethnically divided island of Cyprus, a context defined by extremely low levels of contact, but where the recent opening of the "green line" border between northern and southern Cyprus presents an opportunity for contact – should members of either side wish to take it. It was therefore an ideal setting in which to test the idea that imagined contact could stimulate intentions to engage in future contact.

To explore the issue of whether imagined contact could promote a greater interest in actual contact we adapted a measure of behavioral intentions used previously by Ratcliff, Czuchry, Scarberry, Thomas, Dansereau, and Lord (1999). Specifically we used two questions to measure intentions to engage in future contact. Participants were asked: "Next time you find yourself in a situation where you could interact with a Greek Cypriot person," 1. "How likely is it that you would strike up a conversation?" and 2. "How interested would you be in striking up a conversation?" We asked Turkish Cypriots to imagine a positive encounter with a Greek Cypriot, and then we asked them to complete the above questions. We found that imagining contact (compared to a control scene where participants were asked to imagine "walking in the outdoors") did lead to a greater interest in the prospect of engaging with Greek Cypriots, and higher likelihood estimates that they would indeed do so. This study provides some preliminary support for the idea that imagined contact could be usefully applied as a way of encouraging people to seek, or at least to not avoid, intergroup contact when they might otherwise have had no positive disposition towards it at all.

Improving interactions

Encouraging people to engage in contact where they might have otherwise avoided it is only half the battle. Once in a contact situation there is great potential for things to go wrong. One characteristic associated with lower levels of intergroup contact is higher intergroup anxiety (Plant & Devine, 2003). Intergroup anxiety can arise as a consequence of negative expectations of rejection or discrimination during cross-group interactions, or fears that the interaction partner, or the respondents themselves, may behave in an incompetent or offensive manner (Richeson &

Shelton, 2003; Stephan & Stephan, 1985; Vorauer, Hunter, Main, & Roy, 2000). These fears may lead people to avoid intergroup contact, but if we do succeed in bringing groups together, they can also blight the subsequent encounters. It has been found, for example, that the more negative White people's expectations were about interacting with Black people, the more they reported avoiding inter-racial encounters (Plant & Devine, 2003). Similarly, people often explain their failure to initiate intergroup contact in terms of their fear of being rejected by the outgroup member (Shelton & Richeson, 2005). So even if contact is initiated, intergroup anxiety may increase the likelihood that individuals will enter the encounter with negative feelings. In turn, this increases the likelihood that group members will interpret the interaction in a negative light, with negative consequences for intergroup relations.

If, however, participants first spend some time imagining a *positive* encounter their levels of anxiety will be lower, and their attitudes more positive, when they subsequently enter the interaction. We have seen that imagined contact reduces anxiety about the prospect of future intergroup encounters (Turner, Crisp et al., 2007). If interacting participants spend some time imagining intergroup contact before personally engaging in such an encounter, their levels of intergroup anxiety will be lower, and their expectations more positive, when they subsequently embark on the encounter. This should increase the likelihood that actual intergroup contact, when it is introduced, will result in strong, positive and long-lasting attitude change. Imagined contact may therefore increase the chances that a subsequent intergroup encounter will be of a high quality and result in further positive attitude change. Examining the direct behavioral impact of imagined contact will therefore be an important focus for future research.

Imagined, extended and actual contact

Imagined contact is a form of indirect contact, and in this it has much in common with extended contact. According to the *extended* contact hypothesis, learning that an ingroup member has a close relationship with an outgroup member can vicariously improve one's own attitudes towards the outgroup (Wright, Aron, McLaughlin-Volpe, & Ropp, 1997; see also Davies, Wright, Aron, & Comeau, this volume). Extended contact has been found to exert a positive impact on attitudes and outgroup stereotyping via the development of positive attitudinal ingroup norms, similarity to self and reduced anxiety with both children (Cameron, Rutland, Brown, & Douch, 2006) and adults (Paolini et al., 2004; Turner, Crisp et al., 2007; Turner & Christie, 2010). There are undoubted benefits of extended contact, and situations in which it literally extends the power and scope of the contact hypothesis.

An important line of future research concerns a direct comparison of imagined contact and extended contact. This is crucial because if the similarities and differences between these two types of intervention can be identified, it will help practitioners to target interventions in intergroup contexts where they will be most likely to benefit intergroup relations. So how might we expect these two interventions to compare to one another?

First, while extended and imagined contact are both "indirect" in that they do not require actual contact between the perceiver and a member of the outgroup, there is a fundamental distinction between the approaches. Like imagined contact, one does not need to engage in contact oneself to reap the benefits of extended contact, however, actual contact is still required *somewhere* in one's wider social network (be it with one's friend, family member or just another ingroup member). In contrast, imagined contact requires no experience, actual or vicarious. In fact, it is conceivable that someone can imagine a positive encounter with an outgroup member having never had any experience of contact oneself, or never having known anyone else who has had any experience of contact. In highly segregated settings such as Northern Ireland one simply may not know of *anyone* who knows an outgroup member, and in these situations imagined contact might therefore be the most viable strategy. Of course, in such contexts one must be careful that imagined contact is not principally based on negative outgroup stereotypes (which are more likely to inform imagined encounters where there is no basis for actual experience). In such contexts there is a greater need to ensure that imagined contact is properly structured and instructed so as to ensure a positive imagined encounter (see Stathi & Crisp, 2008).

Second, one might also expect imagined contact to have a more powerful impact than extended contact because imagined contact involves the *self*, with attitudes based on personal experiences tending to be stronger, more accessible, and more persistent than those based on second-hand experience (Fazio, Powell, & Herr, 1983). However, imagined contact may also be more susceptible to interference from previous negative contact experiences. If an individual has previously experienced negative contact, it may be difficult to overcome these memories and imagine a positive encounter. An advantage of extended contact is that it is likely that vicarious positive experiences will be a more powerful antidote to negative experiences than imagined positive experiences. This is because, while both imagined and extended contact are indirect, the very boundary conditions that define extended contact (i.e., the requirement for some actual contact somewhere in one's social network) is also the thing that makes it more grounded in actual experience.

Third, imagined and extended contact may also be distinct in terms of their underlying mechanisms, particularly regarding their impact on perceptions of *ingroup norms*. In extended contact, participants learn about an ingroup member behaving positively towards an outgroup member, apparently reflecting positive regard. This positive model constitutes an ingroup norm that uniquely mediates extended contact, but not actual contact (Turner et al., 2008). This is because extended contact involves a perceptual focus on another ingroup member, while actual contact does not. In actual contact the perceiver is focused on the outgroup, and has no ingroup "model" from which to derive a behavioral norm. Since the instructional set used in imagined contact, like actual contact, focuses participants on the outgroup, it is likely that ingroup norms will be unaffected. In contrast, given that extended *and* imagined contact involves a focus on the outgroup, mechanisms that involve changing perceptions of outgroup members, such as lowered intergroup anxiety, outgroup norms, and increased intergroup trust, should explain the effect of both. This highlights a similarity between *actual* and imagined contact that extended contact does not share: the mental simulation of one's *personal* engagement with the outgroup.

The prevalence of the norm mechanism in extended contact suggests another distinction between the two approaches: the impact of ingroup identification. Extended contact may be particularly effective among people who highly identify with the ingroup. People who highly identify with the ingroup are more likely to adopt the characteristics and norms of the ingroup rather than acting as an idiosyncratic individual (Spears, Doosje, & Ellemers, 1997). Extended contact (but not imagined contact) is likely to operate via the ingroup norm mechanism, because it involves a focus on how other ingroup members react to the outgroup. Extended contact should therefore be particularly effective at reducing prejudice among people who are either chronically or temporarily highly committed to the ingroup, for whom group norms are particularly influential. In contrast, because ingroup norms are less likely to play a role in driving the effects of imagined contact, high identification is not likely to have these positive impacts. In fact, research has shown entirely opposing effects of identification on imagined contact. Stathi and Crisp (2008) found that lower identifiers were *more* likely to project positive self traits to the outgroup – a mechanism partly responsible for defining evaluative impressions. This is consistent with what we know about projection: it is more likely to occur when the personal self is salient, and this is less likely when the collective self is salient. Therefore, through different mechanisms (social norms and projection), identification should have distinguishing effects on extended and imagined contact.

Finally, although there are these important differences, there is also a common mechanism that provides a powerful point of synthesis between the two approaches. Extended contact involves observing, or learning of, the positive behavior of another person towards the outgroup. This reduces fears and inhibitions (e.g., Turner, Hewstone, Voci et al., 2007; Turner, Crisp et al., 2007) and should therefore increase self-efficacy about performing the same behavior oneself. Imagined contact similarly reduces intergroup anxiety (Turner, Crisp et al., 2007), and there is evidence that imagining achieving some goal increases the likelihood of the individual actually working towards achieving that goal (Carroll, 1978). As discussed above, reduced anxiety should make participants feel more positive and comfortable about the prospect of actual contact, so both imagined and extended contact should increase the likelihood that intergroup contact will be instigated. Moreover, when an intergroup encounter occurs, the interaction is likely to run more smoothly, be more successful, and therefore improve intergroup attitudes further. This should increase the likelihood that, when the opportunities *do* arise, acquaintance contact will develop into long-lasting friendships.

If, as we discussed earlier, imagined contact could provide an important means of preparing people for contact, an intriguing possibility is that imagined, extended and actual contact might form a continuum of psychological interventions that are maximally effective at different stages of social integration (see Crisp & Turner,

2009). At early stages of co-existence there may be high segregation and little opportunity for contact. In this situation imagined contact may be the only viable intervention to help encourage attitude change and intentions to engage in preliminary contact (or ensure that when that contact does occur, it does so with open minds and an increased chance of success). At intermediate stages when boundaries have begun to permeate, and some positive interactions initiated, extended contact will work well to reinforce the impact of isolated (but known) contact encounters. Increasing extended contact may then lead to a cascade of positive interactions, along with all the benefits associated with actual intergroup contact. These include lower levels of intergroup anxiety (Paolini et al., 2004; Turner, Hewstone, Voci et al., 2007), increased mutual self-disclosure with outgroup members, and higher levels of intergroup empathy and trust (Tam et al., 2009; Turner, Hewstone, Voci et al., 2007), more positive outgroup attitudes (e.g., Pettigrew, 1997; Pettigrew & Tropp, 2006) and a greater desire to approach, rather than avoid, outgroup members (Tam et al., 2009). Developing the best implementation of imagined contact, in conjunction with existing approaches, is the focus of the final section.

Practical application

To date, research on imagined contact has been conducted almost exclusively in a laboratory setting. However, for a number of reasons, we believe that it contains all of the essential ingredients for an effective anti-prejudice intervention that could be applied in an educational setting.

First, as we have outlined above, imagining a positive interaction with an outgroup member has a whole host of benefits, including more positive explicit and implicit outgroup attitudes, more positive behavioral tendencies, and less intergroup anxiety towards a range of outgroups (e.g., Abrams et al., 2008; Husnu & Crisp, 2010a; Stathi & Crisp, 2008; Turner, Crisp et al., 2007; Turner & Crisp, 2010). Imagined contact is therefore capable of combating pervasive prejudices from several angles for maximum effectiveness.

Second, imagined contact also involves only a short, simple task, and can therefore be implemented with ease and little expense. It is important to note that this does not mean that one session will be enough to overturn years of ingrained prejudice. Like any intervention strategy, imagined contact may require multiple sessions to develop sustainable changes in attitudes and behavior. As Crisp and Turner (2009) note:

> We do not advocate imagined contact as a replacement for existing interventions. . . . Rather, we assert that the value in imagined contact is in its ability to encourage people to seek out contact, to remove inhibitions associated with existing prejudices, and to prepare people to engage outgroups with an open mind. We argue that imagined contact could be highly effective as a first step on the route toward reconciliation and reduced prejudice, on a *continuum of contact* that provides a road map for the use of multiple contact strategies in improving intergroup relations (p. 231).

Third, while we advocate integrated strategies, we also note some clear advantages of imagined contact over existing interventions used in schools, and the need to ensure that integrated interventions are properly tested for both individual and combined effectiveness. Currently many schools use multicultural curricula programs, which involve teaching children about the culture and lifestyle of minority groups (e.g., Sleeter & Grant, 1994). However, such interventions often fail to work because they are based on the erroneous assumption that children will passively 'soak up' positive information about outgroup members and change their attitudes accordingly (e.g., Koeller, 1977; Lessing & Clarke, 1976; see also Aboud & Spears Brown, this volume). In reality, people tend to forget, distort, or ignore information that contradicts existing attitudes (Neuberg, 1996; Rothbart & John, 1985). The multicultural curricula approach also focuses on changing beliefs or knowledge rather than feelings and emotions regarding other groups, and it is the latter which are most likely to influence intergroup relations (Pettigrew & Tropp, 2008). To change intergroup attitudes an approach is required which not only actively challenges existing attitudes, but also changes participants' emotional reactions to the outgroup. Imagined contact does both of these things. While imagining contact, participants are likely to think about what they would learn about the outgroup member, how they would feel during the interaction, and how this would influence their perceptions of that outgroup member and the outgroup more generally. These processes help to reduce anxiety and negative expectations about contact (e.g., Turner, Crisp et al., 2007), while generating positive emotions like empathy (Turner & Christie, 2010).

Research with children illustrates some of the challenges facing education-based interventions. Findings have shown that children's friendship groups often do not reflect the ethnic make-up of the school. Indeed, cross-race friendships have been shown to be relatively uncommon among second grade (aged 7 and 8) and sixth grade (aged 11 and 12) students (Aboud & Sankar, 2007), are less durable than same-race friendships, and tend to decline between the ages of 6 and 12 (Aboud, Mendelson, & Purdy, 2003). Research by Graham and Cohen (1997) provides stark evidence for this: in a setting in which half the children enrolled in the school were African American, older African American children (approximately 12 years) were significantly more likely to form same-race and less likely to form cross-race friendships, than younger African American children.

Several factors may explain these trends. First, people may feel anxious about interacting with outgroup members. Plant and Devine (2003) and Shelton and Richeson (2005) have found that participants explain their failure to initiate intergroup contact in terms of their fear of being rejected by outgroup members. Second, individuals may perceive there to be negative ingroup norms about interacting with outgroup members. Castelli, De Amicis, and Sherman (2007), for example, found that pre-school (aged 4–5) and first grade children (aged 5–6) preferred same-group friends who are 'loyal' to their ingroup and are friends with other ingroup members rather than outgroup members. Third, individuals may perceive there to be too many differences between ingroup and outgroup members. Verkuyten and Steenhuis (2005) found that one of the reasons for not forming cross-group friendships most often cited by teenagers was perceived differences in background.

Despite the enormous potential of imagined contact as an applied intervention, the published research to date has been conducted almost exclusively in the laboratory. As Bigler and Hughes (2010) note, in the field different people may react differently to imagined contact. This is something that all intervention strategies must strive to address. In adapting imagined contact from an experimental paradigm to a practical method for promoting tolerance we must endeavor to tailor interventions to match the characteristics of different people's experience, motivations and perspectives (see Stathi & Crisp, 2008, for some progress in this regard). This is a key challenge for practitioners and policymakers in developing imagined contact as a workable intervention for use in schools, institutions and organizations.

Nonetheless, there has been some preliminary research in educational settings. Turner, West, and Christie (in press) found that imagining a positive encounter with a fellow student who is an asylum seeker predicted greater trust, and empathy, more positive attitudes and behavioral tendencies towards asylum seekers among 16–18-year-old British high school students. The technique used here was similar to the task used in laboratory studies. However, Cameron and colleagues (2011) have recently developed a different version of an imagined contact task that can be used with primary school children. Children aged between 5 and 10 were given a large picture of a park setting and laminated pictures of park related objects (e.g., swings, a dog, a bench) and a photograph of themselves and a physically disabled child of their gender. They were then asked to spend three minutes using these pictures and photographs to create a story that featured the participant themselves and a disabled child. After this time, children were asked a series of questions by the researcher about the activity regarding what they had imagined. Compared to those in a control condition, children showed less bias against the disabled generally, and viewed disabled children as being warmer and more competent. Further studies, like this, will be invaluable for determining the best and most effective means of applying imagined contact to classroom settings.

Conclusions

In this chapter we have described the theoretical basis, emerging support, and practical potential of a new intervention strategy for improving intergroup relations: imagined intergroup contact. We described recent empirical findings supporting the effectiveness of imagined contact as a pre-contact tool to encourage future contact intentions. We presented a theoretical analysis of the underlying mechanisms that distinguish imagined from extended contact. Finally, we outlined some key issues for future efforts to apply imagined contact to classroom settings. Imagined contact is a simple yet effective means of promoting more positive intergroup relations, a firmly grounded intervention with significant potential for policymakers and educators. We believe it holds huge potential as a theoretical paradigm and applied intervention for those of us seeking a solution to the problem of prejudice, and we look optimistically forward to future research that will help clarify, define and refine this testament to the inherent power and flexibility of the contact hypothesis.

References

Aboud, F. E., Mendelson, M. J., & Purdy, K. T. (2003). Cross-race peer relations and friendship quality. *International Journal of Behavioural Development, 27*, 165–173.

Aboud, F. E., & Sankar, J. (2007). Friendship and identity in a language-integrated school. *International Journal of Behavioral Development, 31*, 445–453.

Abrams, D., Crisp, R. J., Marques, S., Fagg, E., Bedford, L., & Provias, D. (2008). Threat inoculation: Experienced and imagined intergenerational contact prevent stereotype threat effects on older people's math performance. *Psychology and Aging, 23*, 934–349.

Allport, G. W. (1954). *The nature of prejudice.* Reading, MA: Addison-Wesley.

Bigler, R. S., & Hughes, J. M. (2010). Reasons for skepticism about the efficacy of simulated social contact interventions. *American Psychologist, 65*, 132–133.

Cadinu, M. R., & Rothbart, M. (1996). Self-anchoring and differentiation processes in the minimal group setting. *Journal of Personality and Social Psychology, 70*, 661–677.

Cameron, L., Rutland, A., Brown, R., & Douch, R. (2006). Changing children's intergroup attitudes towards refugees: Testing different models of extended contact. *Child Development, 77*, 1208–1219.

Cameron, L., Rutland, A., Turner, R. N., Blake, B., Holman-Nicolas, R., & Powell, C. (2011). Changing attitudes with a little imagination: Imagined contact effects on young children's implicit attitudes. *Anale de Psicologia, 27*, 708–717.

Cameron, L., & Turner, R. N. (2010). The application of diversity-based interventions to policy and practice. In R. J. Crisp (Ed.), *The Psychology of Social and Cultural Diversity* (pp. 322–352). Oxford: SPSSI-Blackwell.

Cantle, T. (2001). *Community Cohesion: A Report of the Independent Review Team.* UK: The Home Office.

Carroll, J. S. (1978). The effort of imagining an effect on expectations for the event: An interpretation in terms of the availability heuristic. *Journal of Experimental Social Psychology, 14*, 88–96.

Castelli, L., De Amicis, L., & Sherman, S. J. (2007). The loyal member effect: On the preference for ingroup members who engage in exclusive relations with the ingroup. *Developmental Psychology, 43*, 1347–1359.

Census (2001). *National statistics government website: Neighbourhood Statistics.* Retrieved July 24, 2006, from http://neighbourhood.statistics.gov.uk.

Clement, R. W., & Krueger, J. (2002). Social categorization moderates social projection. *Journal of Experimental Social Psychology, 38*, 219–231.

Crisp, R. J., & Abrams, D. (2008). Improving intergroup attitudes and reducing stereotype threat: An integrated contact model. In W. Stroebe, & M. Hewstone (Eds.), *European Review of Social Psychology* (Vol. 19, pp. 242–284). Hove, E. Sussex: Psychology Press.

Crisp, R. J., & Husnu, S. (2011). Attributional processes underlying imagined contact effects. *Group Processes and Intergroup Relations, 14*, 275–287.

Crisp, R. J., Husnu, S., Meleady, R., Stathi, S., & Turner, R. N. (2010). From imagery to intention: A dual route model of imagined contact effects. In W. Stroebe, & M. Hewstone (Eds.), *European Review of Social Psychology* (vol. 21, pp. 188–236). Hove, E. Sussex: Psychology Press.

Crisp, R. J., Stathi, S., Turner, R. N., & Husnu, S. (2008). Imagined intergroup contact: Theory, paradigm, and practice. *Social and Personality Psychology Compass, 2*, 1–8.

Crisp, R. J., & Turner, R. N. (2009). Can imagined interactions produce positive perceptions? Reducing prejudice through simulated social contact. *American Psychologist, 64*, 231–240.

Crisp, R. J., & Turner, R. N. (2010). Have confidence in contact. *American Psychologist, 65*, 133–134.

Crisp, R. J. & Turner, R. N. (in press). The imagined contact hypothesis. In J. Olson & M. P. Zanna (Eds.). *Advances in Experimental Social Psychology* (vol. 46). Orlando, FL: Academic Press.

Fazio, R. H., Powell, M. C., & Herr, P. M. (1983). Toward a process model of the attitude-behavior relation: Accessing one's attitude upon mere observation of the attitude object. *Journal of Personality and Social Psychology, 44*, 723–735.

Graham, J. A., & Cohen, R. (1997). Race and sex as factors in children's sociometric ratings and friendship choices. *Social Development, 6*, 355–372.

Greenwald, A. G., McGhee, D. E., & Schwartz, J. L. K. (1998). Measuring individual differences in implicit cognition: The implicit association test. *Journal of Personality and Social Psychology, 74*, 1464–1480.

Husnu, S., & Crisp, R. J. (2010a). Elaboration enhances the imagined contact effect. *Journal of Experimental Social Psychology, 46*, 943–950.

Husnu, S., & Crisp, R. J. (2010b). Imagined intergroup contact: A new technique for encouraging greater inter-ethnic contact in Cyprus. *Peace & Conflict: Journal of Peace Psychology, 16*, 97–108.

Koeller, S. (1977). The effect of listening to excerpts from children's stories about Mexican-Americans on the attitudes of sixth graders. *Journal of Educational Research, 70*, 329–334.

Kruglanski, A. W. (1989). *Lay epistemics and human knowledge: Cognitive and motivational bases.* New York: Plenum.

Lessing, E. E., & Clarke, C. C. (1976). An attempt to reduce ethnic prejudice and assess its correlates in a junior high school sample. *Educational Research Quarterly, 1*, 3–16.

Levin, S., van Laar, C., & Sidanius, J. (2003). The effects of ingroup and outgroup friendships on ethnic attitudes in college: A longitudinal study. *Group Processes and Intergroup Relations, 6*, 76–92.

Logan, J. (2001). *Ethnic diversity grows, neighborhood integration lags behind.* Albany, NY: State University of New York at Albany, Lewis Mumford Center.

Martin, M. E. (2006). *Residential segregation patterns of Latinos in the United States, 1990–2000.* New York: Routledge.

Neuberg, S. L. (1996). Expectancy influences in social interaction: The moderating role of social goals In J. A. Bargh, & P. M. Gollwitzer (Eds.), *The psychology of action: Linking cognition and motivation to behavior* (pp. 529–552). New York: Guilford Press.

Paolini, S., Hewstone, M., Cairns, E., & Voci, A. (2004). Effects of direct and indirect cross-group friendships on judgments of Catholics and Protestants in Northern Ireland. The mediating role of an anxiety-reduction mechanism. *Personality and Social Psychology Bulletin, 30*, 770–786.

Pettigrew, T. F. (1997). Generalized intergroup contact effects on prejudice. *Personality and Social Psychology Bulletin, 23*, 173–185.

Pettigrew, T. F. (1998). Intergroup contact theory. *Annual Review of Psychology, 49*, 65–85.

Pettigrew, T. F., & Tropp, L. R. (2006). A meta-analytic test of intergroup contact theory. *Journal of Personality and Social Psychology, 90*, 751–783.

Pettigrew, T. F., & Tropp, L. R. (2008). How does intergroup contact reduce prejudice? Meta-analytic tests of three mediators. *European Journal of Social Psychology, 38,* 922–934.

Phinney, J. S., Ferguson, D. L., & Tate, J. D. (1997). Intergroup attitudes among ethnic minority adolescents: A causal model. *Child Development, 68,* 955–969.

Plant, E. A., & Devine, P. G. (2003). The antecedents and implications of interracial anxiety. *Personality and Social Psychology Bulletin, 29,* 790–801.

Ratcliff, C. D., Czuchry, M., Scarberry, N. C., Thomas, J. C., Dansereau, D. F., & Lord, C. G. (1999). Effects of directed thinking on intentions to engage in beneficial activities: Actions versus reasons. *Journal of Applied Psychology, 29,* 994–1009.

Richeson, J. A., & Shelton, J. N. (2003). When prejudice does not pay: Effects of interracial contact on executive function. *Psychological Science, 14,* 287–290.

Robbins, J. M., & Krueger, J. I. (2005). Social projection to ingroups and to outgroups: A review and meta-analysis. *Personality and Social Psychology Review, 9,* 32–47.

Rothbart, M., & John, O. P. (1985). Social categorization and behavioral episodes: A cognitive analysis of the effects of intergroup contact. *Journal of Social Issues, 41,* 81–104.

Shelton, J. N., & Richeson, J. A. (2005). Intergroup contact and pluralistic ignorance. *Journal of Personality and Social Psychology, 88,* 91–107.

Sleeter, C. E., & Grant, C. A. (1994). *Making choices for multi-cultural education.* New York: Macmillan.

Spears, R., Doosje, B., & Ellemers, N. (1997). Self-stereotyping in the face of threats to group status and distinctiveness: The role of group identification. *Personality and Social Psychology Bulletin, 23,* 538–553.

Stathi, S., & Crisp, R. J. (2008). Imagining intergroup contact promotes projection to outgroups. *Journal of Experimental Social Psychology, 44,* 943–957.

Steele, C. M. (1997). A threat in the air: How stereotypes shape the intellectual identities and performance of women and African Americans. *American Psychologist, 52,* 613–629.

Stephan, W. G., & Stephan, C. W. (1985). Intergroup anxiety. *Journal of Social Issues, 41,* 157–176.

Tam, T., Hewstone, M., Harwood, J., Voci, A., & Kenworthy, J. (2007). Intergroup contact and grandparent-grandchild communication: The effects of self-disclosure on implicit and explicit biases against older people. *Group Processes and Intergroup Relations, 9,* 413–430.

Tam, T., Hewstone, M., Kenworthy, J., & Cairns, E. (2009). Intergroup trust in Northern Ireland. *Personality and Social Psychology Bulletin, 35,* 45–59.

Turner, R. N., & Crisp, R. J. (2010). Imagining intergroup contact reduces implicit prejudice. *British Journal of Social Psychology, 49,* 129–142.

Turner, R. N., Crisp, R. J., & Lambert, E. (2007). Imagining intergroup contact can improve intergroup attitudes. *Group Processes and Intergroup Relations, 10,* 427–441.

Turner, R. N., Hewstone, M., & Voci, A. (2007). Reducing explicit and implicit prejudice via direct and extended contact: The mediating role of self-disclosure and intergroup anxiety. *Journal of Personality and Social Psychology, 93,* 369–388.

Turner, R. N., Hewstone, M., Voci, A., Paolini, S., & Christ, O. (2007). Reducing prejudice via direct and extended cross-group friendship. *European Review of Social Psychology, 18,* 212–255.

Turner, R. N., Hewstone, M., Voci, A., & Vonofakou, C. (2008). A test of the extended intergroup contact hypothesis: The mediating role of intergroup anxiety, perceived ingroup and outgroup norms, and inclusion of the outgroup in the self. *Journal of Personality and Social Psychology, 95*, 843–860.

Turner, R. N., West, K., & Christie, Z. (in press). Outgroup trust, intergroup anxiety, and outgroup attitude as mediators of the effect of imagined intergroup contact on intergroup behavioural tendencies. *Journal of Applied Social Psychology.*

Verkuyten, M., and Steenhuis, A. (2005). Preadolescents' understanding and reasoning about asylum seeker peers and friendships. *Journal of Applied Developmental Psychology, 26*, 660–679.

Vorauer, J. D., Hunter, A. J., Main, K. J., & Roy, S. A. (2000). Meta-stereotype activation: Evidence from indirect measures for specific evaluative concerns experienced by members of dominant groups in intergroup interaction. *Journal of Personality and Social Psychology, 78*, 690–707.

Wright, S. C., Aron, A., McLaughlin-Volpe, T., & Ropp, S. A. (1997). The extended contact effect: Knowledge of cross-group friendships and prejudice. *Journal of Personality and Social Psychology, 73*, 73–90.

7 Intergroup contact across time
Beyond initial contact

Tessa V. West and John F. Dovidio

Intergroup friendship has a profound effect on improving intergroup relations. Yet, compared to the substantial literature on intergroup contact generally, little is known about the dynamics of intergroup interaction beyond initial contact, how people form friendships across group lines, and how this process might differ from developing intragroup friendships. Indeed, interracial interactions are fundamentally distinct from intraracial ones in terms of the cognitive, affective, perceptual, and behavioral processes. This chapter examines the dynamics of anticipated and initial intergroup interaction and extends this work to investigations of contact between roommates of the same or different race/ethnicity over time. We present empirical evidence of how these dynamics change as a function of the orientations that people bring to these interactions and emergent qualities of the social exchange across multiple stages during intergroup, compared to intragroup, dyadic interactions. We conclude by identifying avenues for future research to help illuminate the underlying psychological mechanisms that shape interpersonal perceptions and, ultimately, intergroup relations.

Intergroup contact represents the most widely researched and empirically-supported way of creating more positive intergroup attitudes and harmonious intergroup relations (Allport, 1954; Pettigrew & Tropp, 2006, 2008, 2011). Moreover, this body of research reveals that intergroup friendship is, cross-culturally, one of the most potent elements of contact for reducing intergroup bias (Pettigrew, 1997, 1998). Merely learning that another ingroup member has a friend in an outgroup is sufficient to improve attitudes toward the outgroup overall (the *extended contact effect*); (Wright, Aron, McLaughlin-Volpe, & Ropp, 1997). Nevertheless, forming intergroup friendships is not easy. In the US, for example, contact between Whites and Blacks is limited substantially by widespread residential and occupational segregation (Massey, 2001). Moreover, Whites and Blacks are often motivated to avoid contact (Gaertner & Dovidio, 1986; Plant & Butz, 2006; Mallet, Wilson, & Gilbert, 2008). When interracial contact does occur, these interactions are characterized by high levels of tension (W.G. Stephan & C.W. Stephan, 1985, 2000) and suspicion (Dovidio, Gaertner, Kawakami, & Hodson, 2002), and they are cognitively taxing (Shelton, Richeson, & Vorauer, 2006). Interactions between members of different groups are much more fragile and easier to disrupt than are interactions between two people who are members of the same group. Thus, whereas previous work amply documents the benefits of cross-group friendships for intergroup relations, the present chapter focuses on the dynamics shaping how racial and ethnic majority- and minority-group members in the US overcome these barriers and form intergroup friendships over time.

The approach we adopt in this chapter reflects the recent emphasis on the importance of what transpires in interpersonal interactions in intergroup relations. Traditionally, research on racial/ethnic group relations has emphasized the *intrapersonal* processes, such as stereotyping and prejudice (Dovidio, Brigham, Johnson, & Gaertner, 1996) or contextual factors, such as the optimal prerequisite conditions for intergroup contact (Pettigrew, 1998; Pettigrew & Tropp, 2006), on relations between groups. Although it is an area attracting increasing attention, still comparatively little work has investigated the nature of intergroup interactions from a more interpersonal perspective (Richeson & Shelton, 2010).

An *interpersonal* perspective considers how relationships between individuals are shaped *jointly* by the interpretations and responses of each person during their interaction. It considers how, within a given interaction, an individual's own outcomes are not only shaped by their own characteristics (e.g., agreeableness) but also by their partner's qualities (e.g., their partner's agreeableness). Studying interpersonal relations from an *intergroup* perspective further recognizes how people's sense of social identity and their partners' group membership and identity influence the nature and outcomes of interactions (Richeson & Shelton, 2010; Page-Gould, Mendoza-Denton, & Tropp, 2008). The experiences of two individuals interacting with each other can be substantially shaped in different ways by their group memberships. For example, during an interaction between a majority and a minority group member, the minority person's outcome might be largely influenced by the majority member's level of prejudice, but, because of differences in social power between the groups, the majority member's outcome might be affected to a much lesser extent by the minority member's biases.

This chapter emphasizes the unique value of studying dyadic interactions from the perspectives of both participants simultaneously for understanding intergroup relations. In particular, we consider how interpersonal processes shape the nature and outcomes of intergroup interactions. Specifically, we examine the dynamics of dyadic intergroup interactions – social exchanges between members of two different groups – on the development of intergroup friendships. Our focus is on sustained interactions, typically within the context of college roommate relationships. Our goal is to provide a framework for understanding how different factors contribute to intergroup dynamics at different stages in interactions.

The remainder of this chapter considers analytic approaches, conceptual issues, and empirical findings relating to the development of intergroup friendships over time. In our framework, we take an interpersonal perception approach by focusing on subjective experiences and person perception at three levels: (a) how Whites and minorities *perceive themselves* in such interactions; (b) how Whites and minorities *perceive each other*; and (c) how Whites and minorities *are perceived by each other*. In the next section of the chapter, we provide a brief overview of our analytical approach. After that, we present a conceptual framework for understanding how intergroup interactions unfold across time. We discuss the intra- and interpersonal processes that characterize interracial interactions: how expectations are shaped as people approach these encounters, and how such expectations influence reciprocal responses in brief interactions between new acquaintances. We then focus specifically on how the psychological processes observed during brief interactions may change over time to predict friendship development. We conclude the chapter by discussing several avenues of future research.

Analytic framework

We adopt a dyadic approach to examine friendship formation within the context of race relations in the US. To date, most studies of intergroup friendships have adopted a cross-sectional approach (Shelton, West, & Trail, 2010), which limits an understanding of the unfolding processes involved in intergroup relationship formation. Friendship is an inherently interpersonal phenomenon that develops over a period of time: The thoughts, feelings, and behaviors of one partner in the relationship are interdependent with those of the other. Recent advances in the analysis of dyadic data have enabled intergroup researchers to not only expand beyond the individual to the interpersonal, but to examine these interpersonal processes dynamically as they change across time (Kenny, Kashy, & Cook, 2006).

Much of the work on the development of cross-race friendships that we discuss in this chapter utilizes the Actor-Partner Interdependence Model (APIM); (Kashy & Kenny, 2000; Kenny & Acitelli, 2001). The APIM is an analytical framework that can be used to ask theoretical questions about the interdependence between partners, and thus represents a tool for exploring the interpersonal processes that characterize interracial friendship development. As illustrated in Figure 1, within the APIM an individual's own outcome is predicted by factors that vary at two levels: at the level of the *actor* and at the level of the *partner.*

Everyone is both an actor and a partner in the APIM framework. *Actor effects* refer to the influence of respondents' intrapersonal processes on their own outcomes. They represent the effects on an interaction of qualities that an individual (the respondent) brings to an interaction, such as his or her attitudes or contact experience. These factors can influence, for example, how anxious the individual feels, willingness to disclose personal information, and how responsive the person is in the interaction. Partner effects represent the influence of the partners' qualities on the respondent. For instance, the partner's attitudes or contact experience can determine how anxious the respondent feels and how self-disclosing the respondent is during the interaction. It is important to note that the same behavior, such as a respondent's level of self-disclosure, can be the product of both actor and partner effects. As another example, illustrated in Figure 1, in an investigation of whether anxiety predicts individuals' perceptions of closeness with their partners, anxiety would be studied both in terms of (a) the effect of the respondent's own anxiety on his or her feelings of closeness (the *actor effect*), and (b) the effect of the partner's anxiety on the respondent's feelings of closeness (the *partner effect*).

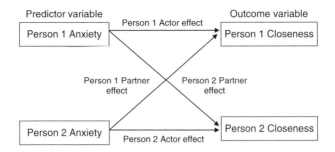

Figure 7.1 The Actor-Partner Interdependence Model

In the APIM, outcomes are jointly determined by predictors at the actor and partner levels, and so the pattern of actor and partner effects provides insight into the dynamic and reciprocal nature of the interaction.

When applied to dyadic relations involving members of majority and minority groups, the APIM can answer questions such as: (a) Does the process of friendship development differ for people in same-race dyads compared to cross-race ones? (b) Does the process differ for Whites and racial/ethnic minorities within same-race dyads, as well as within cross-race dyads? The APIM allows researchers to simultaneously examine these questions pertaining to the race composition of dyads.

The APIM can also be used to examine how different psychological factors at the levels of the actor and partner contribute to intergroup friendship development. When data are collected longitudinally, it is possible to examine two different types of individual-level predictors, time-invarying and time-varying predictors. The distinction between time-varying and time-invarying variables is a methodological one. *Time-invarying* predictors are those that, because of their presumed nature or the plan of the researcher, are measured only once in the study. For example, because a person's sex is unlikely to change over the course of a study (although it is possible), it is typically considered a time-invariant predictor and measured only once. Other predictors are classified as time-invariant not because they cannot change but because the design of the study does not allow for consideration of a change. For example, Page-Gould et al. (2008) examined how individuals' levels of race-based rejection sensitivity measured prior to contact influenced the process of friendship development. Although race-based rejection sensitivity can vary across time and as a function of the interaction, methodologically this is a time-invariant predictor because the researchers measured it only once, at the beginning of the study. *Time-varying* predictors are conceived to potentially vary and are thus measured more than once during the study. Anxiety is often considered a time-varying predictor of friendship development because its level and influence can change over time and it is measured at multiple time points.

In the APIM, both time-varying and time-invariant predictors can be considered simultaneously, and at the level of the actor and the partner. In addition, dyad level-predictors are those that vary between dyads, such as the racial composition of the dyad (i.e., same-race compared to mixed-race), or as another example, how long dyad members have known each other. We apply an approach whereby both individual-level and dyad-level factors are included in studying the dynamics of friendship formation between roommates of different racial and ethnic groups.

Taken together, the APIM is an analytical approach that, when applied to longitudinal data, helps researchers identify the process by which friendships develop. Predictors of friendship formation are simultaneously examined at the levels of the actor, partner, and relationship. Moreover, the APIM can be used to answer several questions related to the longitudinal nature of the data, such as what predicts linear and non-linear growth in friendship, and what predicts day-to-day stability in friendship.

Understanding intergroup interactions at multiple stages: anticipated and initial interaction

Traditionally, much of the research on intergroup relations has focused on the general orientations that members of minority and majority groups have toward one another, such as intergroup attitudes (Dovidio et al., 1996; Johnson & Lecci, 2003; Talaska, Fiske, & Chaiken, 2008) and motivations (Dunton & Fazio, 1997; Plant & Devine, 2003), without actual or even anticipated interaction. More recently, attention has shifted to appreciating the complex nature of actual interactions (Richeson & Shelton, 2010) and how experiences in these exchanges are shaped by and, in turn, shape intergroup relations more generally (Dovidio et al., 2002). However, this work has focused largely on the earliest stages of interaction; that is, the responses of people as they approach an interaction and the initial, relatively brief contact between members of different groups who are strangers.

In general, this research shows that intergroup interactions at the earliest stages – in the anticipation of interaction and in initial contact – differ fundamentally from intragroup interactions in two critical ways: Expectations of others and the amount of anxiety experienced. These two elements, separately and in combination, exert systematic influences that can create barriers to the formation of intergroup friendships, leading members of different groups to avoid interacting with one another and creating fragile relations between them in initial encounters. We consider these processes as people approach new interactions and engage in initial interactions with strangers from another group.

Anticipating interaction

As people approach interactions, the mere information that their partner is a member of their own group or another group arouses differential expectations and affective reactions. Generally, people anticipate outgroup (vs. ingroup) members to behave less positively to them personally, and to be less likely to share their attitudes and values (Robbins & Krueger, 2005). In addition, people anticipate outgroup members to display bias toward their group (Judd, Park, Yzerbyt, Gordijn,

& Muller, 2005). As a consequence of these negative expectations, people are less trusting of outgroup than ingroup members (Foddy, Platow, & Yamagishi, 2009), and are vigilant to cues of bias from outgroup members (Vorauer, 2006; see also Vorauer, this volume). With respect to race, Shelton and Richeson (2005) found that both Whites and Blacks were personally interested in intergroup interaction, but avoid such interaction because they anticipate that their overtures would be rejected by members of the other group. Thus, people not only perceive ingroup members more favorably, they also have negative expectations about how outgroup members will treat them.

Perceiving others as members of another group rather than as a member of one's own group (or as a unique individual) also has a systematic effect on affective responses (see Gaertner & Dovidio, 2000). In part as the result of heightened vigilance and negative expectations (Plant, Butz, & Tartakovsky, 2008), intergroup interactions are characterized by much higher levels of intergroup anxiety than are exchanges between members of the same group (Stephan & Stephan, 1985, 2000). Within the U.S., interethnic contact, in particular, is often marred by anxiety and distrust (Dovidio et al., 2002; Plant & Butz, 2006), and thus both Whites and Blacks experience heightened anxiety in interracial compared to intraracial interactions, but for somewhat different reasons. Whites' anxiety may relate to increased cognitive demand associated with not wanting to appear biased (Dovidio & Gaertner, 2004; Richeson & Shelton, 2003; Richeson & Trawalter, 2005; Shelton, 2003), whereas Blacks' anxiety and arousal may be related to vigilance in detecting bias (Vorauer, 2006) and ways of coping with anticipated prejudice and discrimination (Hyers & Swim, 1998). Feelings of anxiety in anticipation of interaction, in turn, motivate members of majority and minority groups to avoid intergroup interaction (Plant, 2004; Plant & Butz, 2006).

Initial interaction

For a range of different reasons, members of different groups cannot always avoid intergroup interaction and may sometimes seek such encounters. They not only typically enter intergroup interactions with more negative expectancies and greater levels of anxiety than they do for intragroup interactions, but these biases take on a dynamic nature in social exchange. Specifically, people have more favorable orientations toward ingroup than outgroup members (Tajfel & Turner, 1979); they are more positive, both explicitly and implicitly, in their evaluations of ingroup members (Otten & Moskowitz, 2000). Cognitively, people process information more deeply for ingroup than for outgroup members (Van Bavel, Packer, & Cunningham, 2008), have better memory for information about ways ingroup members are similar and outgroup members are dissimilar to the self (Wilder, 1981), and remember less positive information about outgroup members (Howard & Rothbart, 1980). Although the consequences of these cognitive processes are studied for individual-level outcomes, they can also influence complex interpersonal dynamics and interpersonal outcomes. For example, when individuals enter interracial interactions, their cognitive biases shape their own behaviors as well as their perceptions of their partners, which can in turn influence their partners' perceptions of them.

Differential expectations leading up to interactions can engage people to make different attributions for the behaviors of ingroup and outgroup members. Positive behaviors and successful outcomes are more likely to be attributed to internal, stable characteristics of ingroup than outgroup members, whereas negative outcomes are more likely to be ascribed to the personalities of outgroup than ingroup members (Hewstone, 1990). Group-based expectancies shape the perception of emotional behaviors displayed by both ingroup (Beaupré & Hess, 2003) and outgroup (Hugenberg & Bodenhausen, 2003) members, often in a stereotype-confirming manner.

As a consequence of systematic biases in the ways people interpret the behaviors of ingroup and outgroup members, interracial interactions are not only characterized by a higher level of anxiety, but also, individuals make more negative attributions for their partners' anxiety in interracial relative to same-race interactions (West, Shelton, & Trail, 2009). In mixed-race interactions, the attributions that individuals make tend to refer to the cross-race nature of the interaction (Richeson & Trawalter, 2005) and are interpreted in ways consistent with negative expectancies of intergroup relations (Shelton & Richeson, 2005). For instance, whereas both Whites and Blacks attribute nonverbal cues related to high levels of anxiety (e.g., self-touch, inconsistent gaze, closed posture) displayed by another person of the same race primarily as an indication of mere anxiety, these same behaviors demonstrated by a member of the other race is interpreted as unfriendliness as well (Dovidio, West, Pearson, Gaertner, & Kawakami, 2007). Thus, both Blacks and Whites tend to conflate cues of anxiety with indications of dislike, but only when the other person is of a different race.

Understanding what guides attributions of partners' behaviors, and the systematic misinterpretations of cues such as manifestations of anxiety, can have both immediate and longer-term effects on dyadic and group relations. Pearson, West, Dovidio, Powers, Buck, and Henning (2008), for example, showed that intergroup interactions are substantially more fragile than intragroup exchanges. Whereas a slight (1-second) delay in audio-visual feedback between interactants over closed-circuit television, which was imperceptible to participants, had no detrimental effect on same-race dyadic relations, it had a significant adverse effect on cross-race dyadic interactions. Of particular importance was how this delay led participants in cross-race interactions to perceive their rapport more negatively, compared to a control condition. Participants in cross-race, but not same-race interactions, became more anxious as a function of the delay, and they perceived more anxiety in their partner. However, it was the perception of partner's anxiety, not their personally experienced anxiety, that primarily mediated the lower level of rapport. This finding is thus consistent with the study of Dovidio et al. (2007) of biases in perceptions of nonverbal cues of anxiety, again showing that perceived anxiety carries surplus meaning in cross-race interaction that disrupts rapport-building.

Interventions that alter people's expectations as they enter intergroup interactions can improve initial contact experiences. For instance, inducing members of different groups to attend to their similarities rather than their more typical focus on dissimilarities produces smoother and more favorable initial interactions between members of different races (Mallett et al., 2008). In addition, reminding people of personal experiences in which intergroup contact went better than they expected leads people to be more relaxed in intergroup interactions, anticipate more positive responses from members of other groups, produce more satisfying interactions with other outgroup members, and increase motivation to engage in cross-group contact in the future (Mallett & Wilson, 2010).

We have briefly reviewed the interpersonal processes that characterize initial interracial interactions. In the remainder of the chapter, we focus on whether these same processes sustain themselves as interactions unfold across time.

Understanding intergroup interactions at multiple stages: interactions over time

Given the importance of friendships to social life and the current prominence of cross-group friendships for promoting more positive relations between groups, research on friendship formation, in general, is surprisingly limited. Research on the development of intergroup friendships is even rarer. In the next section, we offer a brief overview of general processes in friendship formation.

Processes in friendship formation over time

Research on the process by which friendships develop has highlighted the interdependence between individual, dyadic, and situational factors that determine the course of a personal relationship. Although initial models of friendship development focused primarily on the role of disclosure in predicting intimacy in the early stages of friendship development (see Reis, Collins, & Berscheid, 2000 for a review), other models of relationship development have focused on determinants of intimacy beyond self-disclosure, including responsiveness to nonverbal cues (Patterson, 1982).

In terms of process, models of friendship development have focused on the cognitive, affective, and behavioral processes that occur during repeated interactions with new college friends (Hays, 1985). Importantly, as relationships progress from casual acquaintanceship to close friendships, benefits of the relationship transform from reflecting self-interest (i.e., what will I get out of the relationship?), to reflecting interpersonal and reciprocal interests (Levinger & Snoek, 1972). The transformation from individual to personal friendships creates substantial self-other overlap in self-concept, which is associated with greater relationship satisfaction and intimacy (see A. Aron, McLaughlin-Volpe, Mashek, Lewandowski, Wright, & E.N. Aron, 2004).

In addition, as Hays' (1985) work has demonstrated, the factors that individuals bring with them to new relationships largely influence the trajectory of that relationship. Hays specifically examined individuals' motivation to develop a new friendship, as well as personality factors, such as shyness. Within the context of intergroup friendships, it is important to consider individual-level factors that uniquely influence behavioral and perceptual processes, such as those that may alter individuals' feelings of anxiety during their interactions, their perceptions of their partners' anxiety, and the behaviors associated with their anxiety. The next section thus considers, theoretically, how intergroup contact and interaction may unfold over time.

Intergroup interactions across time

As we noted earlier, the dynamics of initial interactions between members of different races are more challenging and tenuous than those between members of same races. Nevertheless, it is possible that the forces that disrupt initial intergroup interactions may weaken over time. Repeated interactions with an outgroup member, especially when the quality of these interactions is positive, can reduce intergroup anxiety, increase perspective taking and empathy, and improve interpersonal and intergroup relations substantially (Turner, Hewstone, Voci, & Vonofakou, 2008). As a consequence, it is likely that through repeated interaction over a period of time, members of different races may relatively quickly overcome initial negative group-based perceptions and expectancies and form friendships as readily as do members of the same racial group.

In support of this hypothesis, Page-Gould et al. (2008) found that Whites experienced heightened levels of anxiety during an initial interaction with an outgroup member, but their anxiety decreased over the course of subsequent interactions with the same person. Moreover, structured contact (i.e., contact in the lab in which participants were given specific tasks to do together, such as playing the game Jenga together) facilitated prejudice reduction, mediated by anxiety reduction. Similarly, Shook and Fazio (2008b) found that not only Whites' intergroup anxiety reduced over time when they had an ethnic minority roommate, but automatically activated racial attitudes also became less negative.

Alternatively, the biases that individuals bring with them to intergroup interactions, and those that shape perceptions made during interactions, may continue to exert an influence on perceptions made over time. In this case, building directly on initial intergroup biases, dynamics between partners from different social groups may consistently worsen over time. Furthermore, there may be additional qualities of extended interaction over time that can exacerbate intergroup tensions. Briefly, in structured laboratory interactions individuals are able to regulate (to some degree) their behaviors toward their partners by not explicitly expressing negative feelings such as distrust or dislike. However, the ability to regulate one's true thoughts and emotions may weaken over time, particularly as regulatory cognitive resources that inhibit bias diminish with time (Shelton, West, & Trail, 2010), resulting in a "leaking out" of behaviors that are reflective of these thoughts and emotions.

Initial attempts to suppress negative thoughts and feelings often produce an amplified, "rebound" effect when cognitive resources are depleted (see Monteith, Sherman, & Devine, 1998, for a review). If group boundaries remain salient during intergroup interactions, the negative thoughts and feelings that character-ize intergroup encounters at the initial interaction stage will either be maintained or they will increase. In either case, such thoughts and feelings will eventually be expressed through behaviors, which will in turn be perceived by partners. This rather grim hypothesis has received some support in the finding that individuals are more satisfied and more likely to continue living with a same-raced roommate than a different-raced one (Shook & Fazio, 2008a, 2008b; Trail, Shelton, & West, 2009).

As these alternative hypotheses and conflicting data suggest, the question of whether repeated outgroup interactions will lead to friendship formation cannot be answered with a simple "yes" or "no." How and why Whites and minorities become friends represent complicated processes that involve both the cognitive orientations and affective reactions that individuals bring with them to such inter-actions and the perceptual, cognitive, and affective processes that occur during these interactions. We posit that to understand the longitudinal trajectory of inter-group friendship formation, it is important to study both intrapersonal and inter-personal processes, as well as the interplay between them. In the remainder of this section, we first highlight the unique opportunities that studying college room-mates have for testing theories of intergroup relations, and then we review current findings about processes that determine the development of interracial friendships over a period of time.

Why study roommates?

Much of the recent research on intergroup contact (Binder et al., 2009) has revealed the causal role of frequent, positive contact with members of other groups for improving intergroup attitudes, not only with respect to the specific individuals involved in contact but also to their group as a whole (van Laar, Levin, & Sida-nius, 2008), as well as to other minority groups (Pettigrew, 1997). In addition, many of the intrapersonal processes that benefit from repeated direct contact also profit from repeated contact over time. For example, Turner et al. (2008) demon-strated that intergroup contact reduces subsequent intergroup anxiety, increases the inclusion of the outgroup in the self, and alters norms about the outgroup.

In much of the longitudinal study of interracial interactions, researchers have relied upon college roommates as a population for examining relationship devel-opment. Research examining repeated contact with roommates differs from work on repeated contact with outgroup members in general because it allows for the examination of how contact with a specific outgroup member over time facilitates friendship formation with that outgroup member.

Although studying college roommate relations represents a restricted contact context – college students are more highly educated and liberal than others in the general population – there are also several important methodological advan-tages (see Shook & Fazio, 2008a, 2008b; Van Laar, Levin, Sinclair, & Sidan-ius, 2005). First, college roommates are often randomly assigned to live together with respect to race or ethnicity thus circumventing problems of self-selection.

Second, the living conditions of college dormitories represent optimal conditions of contact: Roommates are of equal status in the context of the living environment, they have the common goal of getting along with one another (especially given the small living space they share), they have equal access to resources within the college community, and they have the sanction of authorities (Allport, 1954). Third, researchers have access to the amount and quality of contact between roommates before they move in together and can monitor friendship formation from the time of initial contact. Fourth, roommate relations are consequential ones for college students; the quality of roommate relations affects the physical health and psychological well-being of college students (Joiner, Vohs, & Schmidt, 2000).

Even though college roommate living environments typically exist under optimal conditions of contact for psychological research, simply living with someone of a different race is not sufficient to facilitate interracial friendship formation. Such situations can be hugely demanding forms of contact, particularly for people who have strong racial bias and little previous intergroup contact. In fact, day-to-day contact can make interracial relations even worse given the intensity of these interactions. Mixed-race roommate relationships are generally less satisfying (Shook & Fazio, 2008b), are more likely to dissolve (Shook & Fazio, 2008a), and demonstrate steeper declines over time (Trail et al., 2009) than do same-race ones. Thus, studying roommates provides opportunities to understand both harmonious and contentious intergroup relations. The next section summarizes the results of a series of studies that have investigated the influence of both emergent (time-varying) processes – those that arise through repeated interactions between roommates – and influences related to the qualities that individuals bring to their exchange (time-invarying factors).

Friendship development between roommates of the same or different races

The research on intergroup interactions at varying stages of intergroup contact – anticipated contact, initial contact, and repeated contact with members of another group – triangulates on the importance of a perceiver's own anxiety and perceptions of the partner's anxiety in these encounters. In this section, building on Hays's (1985) general framework of how dyadic and individual factors shape the development of friendships, we illustrate how affective and perceptual processes that occur during repeated interactions predict friendship development between roommates of the same race or of different races. We first review two studies of friendship development between roommates of the same or different races that demonstrate the pivotal roles of self-reported anxiety and perceptions of the partner's orientations. Then, in two additional studies, we consider factors particularly relevant in the intergroup domain (i.e., concerns with appearing prejudiced and perceptions of commonality) that individuals bring with them to their dyadic relations and that can moderate the trajectory of intergroup friendship development.

Anxiety and friendship development

West, Shelton et al. (2009) investigated the role of the experience of anxiety in friendship development in same- and cross-race roommates, during the first weeks of roommates living together. Within the first week of the semester, college students who had been randomly assigned to same-race and cross-race roommate dyads made daily ratings of their own felt anxiety (e.g., how anxious, nervous, and uncomfortable they felt) and interest in living together in the future. These ratings began shortly after the roommates moved in together and continued for 15 consecutive days. Using APIM (Kenny et al., 2006), we treated anxiety experienced by the respondent on one day as the predictor of reported anxiety levels the following day, both the respondent's own anxiety (the *actor* effect), and the anxiety level of the respondent's partner (i.e., the *partner* effect). Because anxiety is often perceived as rejection in interracial interactions (Pearson et al., 2008), it was hypothesized that partner's self-reported anxiety, above and beyond respondents' own self-reported anxiety, would have detrimental effects, but mainly for individuals in cross-race dyads. That is, the main prediction was that in cross-race roommate dyads, but not in same-race roommate dyads, greater anxiety experienced *by the roommate* would negatively predict the respondent's subsequent interest in living together again (over and above any effect of the respondent's level of anxiety).

In general, across roommate pairs of the same race or of different races, one's own anxiety experienced one day predicted one's own anxiety the following day, and greater self-reported anxiety predicted respondents' lower desire to live with their roommate in the future (i.e., an actor effect). Moreover, as hypothesized, there were additional dynamics that were unique to cross-race roommate dyads. Only in cross-race roommate dyads did the respondent's anxiety experienced one day carry over to predict their roommates' anxiety the following day (i.e., a partner effect). That is, there was a "contagion" of anxiety between roommates of different races but not between roommates of the same race. Also, in cross-race roommate dyads, the more *one's roommate was anxious* across the 15-day period of the study, the less the respondent desired to live with that roommate in the future. In contrast, in same-race roommate dyads, greater anxiety reported by one's roommate was related to a greater desire by the respondent to live with the roommate in the future. This pattern of results was similar for White and racial minority participants.

Overall, the findings of West, Shelton et al. (2009) demonstrate that not only does partner anxiety linger in cross-race interactions to influence how people feel the following day, the attributions for it appear to harm the process of friendship development. The finding that same-race roommates' anxiety positively predicted respondents' interest in living together is similar to the finding in Pearson et al. (2008) in which same-race pairs reacted positively to the one-second delay. Perhaps people in same-race pairs not only make attributions for their partners' anxious behaviors that are relationship-enhancing, but they also engage in compensatory behaviors during their interactions with their anxious roommates. In interracial interactions, compensatory behaviors may be less likely, which, coupled with elevated feelings of anxiety, put these interactions at a great disadvantage relative to same-race ones.

Anxiety and its social manifestations represent one class of behaviors that people can exhibit in their interactions. Individuals can also engage in actions that are even more directly communicative of intentions to promote greater intimacy or create greater social distance. The next study we report thus expands upon the previous research on the experience of anxiety to perceptions of people's own and their roommate's behaviors.

Intimacy-related behaviors and intragroup and intergroup roommate relations

Trail et al. (2009) investigated how differences in partners' intimacy-building behaviors (e.g., perceptions of the partner smiling, talking, appearing engaged and interested) and intimacy-distancing behaviors (e.g., perceptions of the partner fidgeting, avoiding eye contact, concealing opinions) contribute to differences in friendship development between same-race and cross-race roommate dyads. This research drew upon additional data from respondents in the previous study, who completed diaries of the experiences across 15 days soon after they met their roommates.

The main hypothesis was that the lower quality of relationship between interracial than intraracial roommate dyads would be mediated by a range of different behaviors exhibited in these interactions and particularly with respect to perceptions of the roommate's behaviors. Quality of relationship was represented by positive orientations toward the roommate and their connection (e.g., "I like my roommate"; "I want to live together in the future").

The distinction between distancing and building behaviors is particularly important in the context of interracial relationships because Whites and ethnic minorities often have ambivalent attitudes about interacting with one another (Dovidio & Gaertner, 2004), and subtle prejudice is conveyed more through the absence of intimacy-building behaviors than through the presence of intimacy-distancing ones. As such, it was expected that intimacy-building behaviors would play a more prominent role in explaining differences between the quality of cross-race and same-race relationships than would intimacy-distancing behaviors.

As expected, the quality of roommate relationships was higher for same-race than for cross-race roommate dyads. Furthermore, consistent with the hypotheses, both minorities and Whites in cross-race roommate pairs perceived fewer intimacy-building and more intimacy-distancing behaviors than did Whites and minorities in same-race roommate pairs. In addition, although intimacy-distancing behaviors remained relatively constant for both same-race and cross-race roommate dyads, intimacy-building behaviors declined over time particularly for Whites and minorities in cross-race pairs. This finding is supportive of the prediction that interracial dyads would be characterized more by subtle expressions of bias (the absence of intimacy-building behaviors) than by more overt bias (intimacy-distancing behaviors).

Further supportive of the hypotheses, Trail et al. (2009) also found that differences in the quality of interracial roommate relationships (i.e., the desire to live together again, liking of the roommate) are due, in part, to perceptions of the partners' behaviors. Specifically, perceptions of roommates' intimacy-building and, to a weaker extent, intimacy-distancing behaviors mediated the difference in relationship quality (i.e., desire to live together again, satisfaction with the relationship, and perceptions of support) between same-race and cross-race dyads. In addition, we found evidence for both actor and partner effects of the mediators: The respondent's perceptions of the partner's behaviors and the partner's perceptions of the respondent's behaviors both predicted the respondent's report of relationship quality.

Taken together, these results suggest that, in addition to the general negative impact of perceived anxiety of one's roommate in interracial dyads, perceptions of the roommate's display of intimacy-distancing and especially intimacy-building behaviors are critical determinants of lower quality relations between roommates of the different racial/ethnic group status than of the same group.

These first two studies that we reviewed in some detail did not consider how the individual-level factors that individuals bring with them to interracial interactions can, in time, influence the dynamics of the relationship. The next two studies illustrate how individual-level factors can differentially moderate the trajectory of friendship development between roommates of the same or of different races.

Concerns with appearing prejudiced and friendship development

Drawing on additional data from respondents in the previous two studies, Shelton et al. (2010) examined how Whites' and minorities' concerns with appearing prejudiced, measured at the start of the semester, predicted changes in self-reported anxiety (i.e., actor effects) and perceptions of those individuals by their roommates, over the course of 15 days.

In initial interracial interactions, concerns with appearing prejudiced have positive effects on liking and rapport building. For example, individuals who are more strongly concerned about appearing biased behave more positively toward their roommates of a different race, and when they do experience negative feelings during their interactions, they are better able to monitor these emotions. Indeed, Shelton (2003) found that Blacks liked Whites who tried not to be prejudiced during an interaction more than they liked Whites who did not. Over time, however, the monitoring of one's thoughts and feelings may break down, leading individuals to express the anxiety that they are successful at "holding in" during the very early stages of the interaction. Shelton et al. (2010) investigated both Whites' and minorities' concerns with appearing prejudiced on their self-ratings of anxiety, their perceptions of their partners' anxiety-related behaviors (e.g., fidgeting), and their liking of their roommate.

Overall, in Shelton et al. (2010), Whites and minorities who were more concerned with appearing prejudiced felt more anxious during their interactions with their roommates, and the level of anxiety did not change. In addition, a partner effect for concerns with appearing prejudiced was found for Whites and minorities in cross-race dyads. Specifically, for Whites and minorities high on concerns with appearing prejudiced, their anxious behaviors began to "leak out" after about 10 days of living together. Beginning on the tenth day of the study, respondents in cross-race interactions began to perceive their roommates, particularly those roommates who were more concerned with appearing prejudiced at the beginning of the study, as more anxious. By the end of the study (i.e., by the 15th day), individuals in cross-race roommate relationships who had roommates higher on concerns with appearing prejudiced also liked those roommates significantly less.

These results indicate the importance of examining how intrapersonal factors can have very different effects on the dynamics of relationships during the initial stages of the relationship than in later stages. Concerns with appearing prejudiced at the beginning of the study did not show a relationship with anxiety-related behaviors until several days into the study, and then only, as expected, in cross-race roommate dyads. Nevertheless, this emergence of anxiety-related behaviors was related to less liking of roommates of a different race at the end of the study. Thus, to the extent that efforts to control one's bias can eventually increase anxiety-related behaviors, presumably as people struggle to inhibit prejudice, attempts to control one's bias may backfire and undermine the development of cross-group friendships between roommates.

Given all of the potential negative intra- and interpersonal processes that can occur during the development of interracial roommate relationships, how then can these roommate pairings result in successful friendship development? We considered this question in the next section.

Commonality and intergroup friendship formation

The ways people conceive of one another at the very outset of their interaction can systematically influence the nature and outcome of their exchange. For instance, focusing people on the similarities, rather than dissimilarities, between them and members of another group reduces intergroup anxiety, creates more positive expectancies, and facilitates smoother intergroup interactions (Mallett et al., 2008). In West, Pearson, Dovidio, Shelton, and Trail (2009), we examined how individuals' common in-group identity framework – that is, the way in which people think about racial categories in the context of a larger, superordinate category (i.e., college students on campus; see Gaertner & Dovidio, 2000) – influences changes in intergroup anxiety and, consequently, friendship development. The Common Ingroup Identity model (Gaertner & Dovidio, 2000) proposes that incorporating members of different groups into a common, inclusive identity can extend the benefits of within-group categorization to members of racial out-groups. Typically, research utilizing a common in-group identity framework has experimentally manipulated or primed commonality, and then examined perceptions made in brief, one-time-only interactions. However, in our research we treated commonality orientation as an individual difference trait that can influence individuals', as well as their roommates', anxiety and perceptions of friendship development over time.

In West, Pearson et al. (2009), college students completed measures of commonality at the beginning of the semester (e.g., "Regardless of our racial/ethnic group, it usually feels as though we are all members of one group"). For the next 5.5 weeks, they completed twice-weekly measures of friendship formation and anxiety experienced in the context of roommate interactions.

Although both same-race and cross-race roommates generally showed a decline in friendship over a period of time, stronger perceptions of commonality between members of different racial and ethnic groups on campus, relative to seeing people mainly in terms of their different-group memberships, buffered the decline in friendships among roommates of different races. For cross-race roommate dyads, when either the respondent or his or her roommate strongly perceived commonality among the groups at the beginning of the semester (i.e., both actor and partner effects), roommates were able to sustain their friendship six weeks into the semester. When commonality perceptions were initially weak, friendship in interracial dyads declined across the same period. Furthermore, consistent with the research implicating the role of perceptions of the partner's anxiousness in initial intergroup responses (Pearson et al., 2008) and contact across time between roommates of different races (West, Shelton et al., 2009), these effects were mediated by roommates' anxiety.

Overall, these results demonstrate that commonality perceptions not only have intrapersonal effects on intergroup anxiety, but interpersonal ones as well – although roommates likely never discussed their commonality perceptions with each other, these perceptions positively influenced the trajectory of their friendship from the perspectives of both partners. What is not clear in this study, as well as in our other studies of roommate relationships, is how this repeated interracial interaction over time generalizes to affect attitudes toward the other group as a whole and orientations to other members of the group. Our research has focused primarily on roommates' dyadic interactions and their orientations to each other.

Although the development of an intergroup friendship is typically one of the most potent contributors to reductions of bias toward other members of the group (Pettigrew, 1998; Pettigrew & Tropp, 2011), friendship formation between roommates may be limited in its effects on intergroup relations, depending on the processes by which this friendship is achieved. In particular, to the extent that intergroup friendship formation occurs when roommates think primarily in terms of common group identity (West, Pearson ct al., 2009), the salience of their separate racial group memberships may be greatly diminished. A key element for generalizing the positive effects of an intergroup encounter to more favorable attitudes toward the group as a whole is maintaining the salience of the different group identities, which provides the associative links to other group members (see Brown & Hewstone, 2005). Thus, although friendship formation between roommates can reduce intergroup bias generally (Shook & Fazio, 2008a, 2008b; Van Laar et al., 2005), it may be less effective if the friendship is achieved and maintained by ignoring or dismissing their different group identities. Given the social importance of racial group memberships, it is unlikely that race will cease to be a factor altogether in roommate relationships. Nevertheless, future research might consider more directly how the dynamics of friendship formation between room-mates might be different or similar to other forms of contact in how it influences, in time, the ways people think about, feel about, and act toward other members of the roommate's racial group.

Summary and future directions

Despite the importance of intergroup friendships for improving intergroup rela-tions generally (Pettigrew, 1997; Wright et al., 1997), to date there has been limited research examining intergroup friendship formation, the processes that critically shape the development across group lines, and how these processes may differ from those underlying intragroup friendship formation. This chapter thus considered, both theoretically and empirically, these issues.

Building on research that examines anticipated and initial intergroup contact, we emphasized the importance of social expectations, anxiety, and the different attributions people make for this anxiety in intergroup compared to intragroup exchanges. In general, people have more negative expectations for intergroup than intragroup interaction (Mallett et al., 2008; Shelton & Richeson, 2005) and expe-rience greater levels of anxiety in anticipation of and during intergroup contact (Plant, 2004; Stephan & Stephan, 2000). Both negative expectations and anxiety lead people to avoid interaction with members of other groups, and when these interactions do occur they are more fragile and cognitively and emotionally taxing than intragroup interactions (Pearson et al., 2008; Richeson & Shelton, 2010). As a consequence, intergroup friendships are more difficult to establish and sustain over time (Shook & Fazio, 2008a, 2008b) than are intragroup friendships.

Guided by the Actor-Partner Interdependence Model, we proposed that in both initial and sustained interaction it is important to consider how individuals per-ceive themselves, perceive their partners, and are perceived by their partners in social exchanges. These three different types of perceptions uniquely influence evaluations of the relationship and ultimately the development of cross-group friendships.

With respect to intergroup contact, perceptions of one's partner's anxiety, whether in terms of global impressions (Shelton et al., 2010) or perceptions of specific behaviors (Trail et al., 2009), have particularly strong effects on initial intergroup reactions and on friendship formation longer-term, above and beyond perceivers' own thoughts and feelings. Moreover, the perceived or actual anxi-ety of one's partner impairs relations only for interactions between members of different groups, not for members of the same racial or ethnic group (West, Shel-ton et al., 2009). The potential misattribution of anxiety in which anxiety is seen as unfriendliness, which is theorized to occur reciprocally between majority and minority group members (West, Shelton et al., 2009), can create a cascading effect producing an especially pronounced decline in feelings of friendship between members of different groups (West, Shelton et al., 2009).

The studies of roommate relations reported in this chapter add an important element to the study of intergroup interaction through longitudinal analyses: the dimension of time and the role of intervening processes. Besides revealing more negative trajectories for relationships between roommates of the same race than of different races, this work illuminates how emergent qualities of an interaction (time-varying factors) influence subsequent interaction processes and outcomes. This research triangulates on the importance of anxiety, particularly perceptions of a partner's anxiety, on the erosion of intergroup relationships across time. Furthermore, the trajectory of influences that develop throughout the course of sustained interaction can be substantially altered by intrapersonal (time-invarying) factors that people bring with them to the interactions. For instance, concerns about appearing prejudiced have a detrimental effect on intergroup roommate relations, while perceptions of different groups belonging to a common superordinate identity promotes friendship between cross-race roommate pairs across time.

There is considerable research examining the importance of intergroup anxiety on intergroup relations, but most of that research has focused primarily on how people personally experience anxiety. The research reviewed in the current chapter is supportive of this work on experienced arousal, but it also consistently implicates the critical role of the partner's anxiety and what that signals to interactants. Given the importance of perceptions of others' anxiety – which is generally even more influential than one's own experienced anxiety – in intergroup interactions, future research might productively consider the processes that shape these perceptions. We suggest three potential questions to pursue in this direction: (a) What factors influence, and potentially bias, perceptions of the partner's anxiety? (b) Is accuracy in these perceptions beneficial? and (c) What kinds of interventions can facilitate more positive intergroup interaction, both for initial and sustained contact?

With respect to the first question, future research might investigate the cognitive and motivational mechanisms that influence the processes of interpersonal perception. As we reviewed in this chapter, in the expectation and initial stage of interracial interactions, perceptions of one's partner are largely guided by cognitive biases that typically lead to negative outcomes for the self or the relationship. However, whether these cognitive biases continue to exert the same influences on the process of perception remains unexplored. The degree to which cognitive biases influence interpersonal perceptions may depend on individuals' motivations and goals. Although the interplay between cognitive and motivational biases have received a great deal of attention in other perceptual domains (see Kunda, 1990, for a review), to date there has been little research in the intergroup domain concerning how individuals' goals and motivations, as well as situational factors, influence judgments made during interactions. Understanding these processes, and how they may differ for intergroup and intragroup interactions, can help illuminate the intergroup dynamics that occur within contact situations.

In terms of the second question we posed, considerable attention has been devoted in social psychology to the detrimental effects of biases in perceptions of members of other groups (Dovidio & Gaertner, 2010), but relatively little work has considered the "flip side" of this issue – the assumption that accuracy in perceptions is beneficial to intergroup relations (cf. Pearson et al., 2008). On the surface, it may seem as though accuracy would positively benefit both partners, given the importance of overcoming communication roadblocks that characterize intergroup interactions. Indeed, there is some evidence that accurate impression formation has positive effects on social judgments and behavior in the context of interracial interactions (Vorauer, 2006; see Chapter 2 by Vorauer, this volume). In addition, the inability of Whites to "read" minorities accurately contributes to minorities' mistrust of Whites and the societal institutions with which they are associated (Pearson, Dovidio, & Gaertner, 2009).

However, accuracy in perceptions is not necessarily the best way of creating and sustaining positive relations, whether intergroup or interpersonal. There is a well-replicated finding in the domain of romantic relationships that evaluations that are overly positive are more beneficial to both partners in the relationship than are evaluations that are completely grounded in reality (see Murray, 1999, for a review). Thus, creating positive biases, rather than true accuracy, may ultimately be critical in creating the quality of intergroup contact that is instrumental for improving intergroup relations generally (West, Pearson et al., 2009).

The literature on interpersonal relationships, however, suggests a more complex process – one involving accuracy on some dimensions and positive bias on others. Fletcher and Kerr (2010) recently demonstrated that in personal relationships it is important to have *tracking accuracy* – to know on average how one's partner is feeling and to know that partner's ups and downs – and *positivity* – to see one's partner more positively than that partner actually is. Applying Fletcher's theorizing to the development of cross-race friendships, it may be beneficial to the relationship as a whole for Whites and minorities to understand how their partners are feeling on a day-by-day basis – to know if they are feeling particularly anxious on one day and calm the next – but, at the same time, to also overestimate their partner's acceptance and friendliness toward them. Future research might therefore investigate directly whether these processes, which have been studied primarily in within-group personal relationships, apply to cross-group friendship formation, and ultimately to intergroup relations generally.

Although the Contact Hypothesis (Allport, 1954; Pettigrew, 1998) identifies the types of conditions (e.g., cooperative interdependence) that are critical to establish for contact to improve relations between groups, applying work on interpersonal relations to contact can suggest other types of interventions to promote intergroup friendship with sustained interaction. For example, the research we have presented in this chapter demonstrates the pivotal role of perceptions of a partner's anxiety, especially for members of different groups, in the development of relationships. Anxiety perceived in members of another group, but not in members of one's own group, is interpreted as signs of unfriendliness and rejection (Dovidio et al., 2007).

Although anxiety is generally higher in intergroup than intragroup interactions (Stephan & Stephan, 1985, 2000), to promote more positive intergroup interactions it may be possible to influence the attributions that interactants make for the other's anxiety. Indeed, utilizing the classic misattribution of arousal paradigm, Richeson and Trawalter (2005) demonstrated that individuals who re-attribute their *own* anxiety experienced during interracial interactions to features of the context (i.e., to the one-way mirror in the room rather than to the interracial nature of the interaction) experience their intergroup interaction more positively. The work we have presented suggests that an intervention altering perceptions of the partner's, rather than one's own, anxiety would have particular benefits for inter-action with a member of another group.

In conclusion, a more comprehensive understanding of relations between groups and how to improve them involves consideration of interpersonal as well as intrapersonal (e.g., stereotyping, prejudice) and intergroup (e.g., structural) processes. How members of different groups perceive and respond to each other both shape and are shaped by intergroup relations more generally. Moreover, to understand the dynamics of intergroup relations, it is important to study how inter-actions unfold. The trajectories of intergroup interactions are determined not only by the intrapersonal factors (e.g., intergroup stereotypes and other expectations) that people bring to their interactions with members of other groups, but also by factors (e.g., anxiety and perceptions of anxiety) that emerge during the course of the interaction and change over time. Integrating work on intergroup behavior, which identifies the importance of intergroup friendships for improving inter-group attitudes, and interpersonal relations, which illuminates how people form and maintain friendships, can help illuminate ways to promote enduring positive relations and bridge the "racial divide."

References

Allport, G. W. (1954). *The nature of prejudice*. Reading, MA: Addison-Wesley.

Aron, A., McLaughlin-Volpe, T., Mashek, D., Lewandowski, G., Wright, S.C., & Aron, E. N. (2004). Including others in the self. *European Review of Social Psychology, 15*, 101–132.

Beaupré, M. G., & Hess, U. (2003). In my mind, we all smile: A case of in-group favorit-ism. *Journal of Experimental Social Psychology, 39*, 371–377.

Binder, J., Zagefka, H., Brown, R., Funke, F., Kessler, T., Mummendey, A., Maquil, A., Demoulin, S., & Leyens, J-P. (2009). Does contact reduce prejudice or does prejudice reduce contact? A longitudinal test of the contact hypothesis among majority and minor-ity groups in three European countries. *Journal of Personality and Social Psychology, 96*, 843–856.

Brown, R., & Hewstone, M. (2005). An integrative theory of intergroup contact. In M. P. Zanna (Ed.), *Advances in experimental social psychology* (Vol. 37, pp. 255–343). San Diego, CA: Academic Press.

Dovidio, J. F., Brigham, J. C., Johnson, B. T., & Gaertner, S. L. (1996). Stereotyping, prejudice, and discrimination: Another look. In C. N. Macrae, M. Hewstone, & C. Stan-gor (Eds.), *Foundations of stereotypes and stereotyping* (pp. 276–319). New York: Guilford.

Dovidio, J. F., & Gaertner, S. L. (2004). Aversive racism. In M. P. Zanna (Ed.), *Advances in experimental social psychology* (Vol. 36, pp. 1–51). San Diego, CA: Academic Press.

Dovidio, J. F., & Gaertner, S. L. (2010). Intergroup bias. In S. T. Fiske, D. Gilbert, & G. Lindzey (Eds.), *Handbook of social psychology* (Vol. 2, 5th ed, pp. 1084–1121). New York: Wiley.

Dovidio, J. F., Gaertner, S. L., Kawakami, K., & Hodson, G. (2002). Why can't we just get along? Interpersonal biases and interracial distrust. *Cultural Diversity and Ethnic Minority Psychology, 8*, 88–102.

Dovidio, J. F., West, T. V., Pearson, A. R., Gaertner, S. L., & Kawakami, K. (2007, October). *Racial prejudice and interracial interaction*. Paper presented at the annual meeting of the Society for Experimental Social Psychology, Chicago, IL.

Dunton, B. C., & Fazio, R. H. (1997). An individual difference measure of motivation to control prejudiced reactions. *Personality and Social Psychology Bulletin, 23*, 316–326.

Fletcher, G. J. O., & Kerr, P. S. G. (2010). Through the eyes of love: Reality and illusion in intimate relationships. *Psychological Bulletin, 136*, 627–658.

Foddy, M., Platow, M. J., & Yamagishi, H. (2009). Group-based trust in strangers: The role of stereotypes and expectations. *Psychological Science, 20*, 419–422.

Gaertner, S. L., & Dovidio, J. F. (1986). The aversive form of racism. In J. F. Dovidio, & S. L. Gaertner (Eds.), *Prejudice, discrimination, and racism* (pp. 61–89). Orlando, FL: Academic Press.

Gaertner, S. L., & Dovidio, J. F. (2000). *Reducing intergroup bias: The Common Ingroup Identity Model,* Philadelphia, PA: The Psychology Press.

Hays, R. B. (1985). A longitudinal study of friendship development. *Journal of Personality and Social Psychology, 48*, 909–924.

Hewstone, M. (1990). The "ultimate attribution error"? A review of the literature on intergroup causal attribution. *European Journal of Social Psychology, 20*, 311–335.

Howard, J. M., & Rothbart, M. (1980). Social categorization for in-group and out-group behavior. *Journal of Personality and Social Psychology, 38*, 301–310.

Hugenberg, K., & Bodenhausen, G. V. (2003). Facing prejudice: Implicit prejudice and the perception of facial threat. *Psychological Science, 14*, 640–643.

Hyers, L., & Swim, J. (1998). A comparison of the experiences of dominant and minority group members during an intergroup encounter. *Group Processes and Intergroup Relations, 1*, 143–163.

Johnson, J. D., & Lecci, L. (2003). Assessing anti-White attitudes and predicting perceived racism: The Johnson-Lecci scale. *Personality and Social Psychology Bulletin, 29*, 299–312.

Joiner, T. E., Jr., Vohs, K. D., & Schmidt, N. B. (2000). Social appraisal as correlate, antecedent, and consequence of mental and physical health outcomes. *Journal of Social and Clinical Psychology, 19*, 336–351.

Judd, C. M., Park, B., Yzerbyt, V., Gordijn, E. H., & Muller, D. (2005). Attributions of intergroup bias and outgroup homogeneity to ingroup and outgroup others. *European Journal of Social Psychology, 35*, 677–704.

Kashy, D. A., & Kenny, D. A. (2000). The analysis of data from dyads and groups. In H. T. Reis, & C. M. Judd (Eds.), *Handbook of research methods in social and personality psychology* (pp. 451–477). New York, NY: Cambridge University Press.

Kenny, D. A., & Acitelli, L. K. (2001). Accuracy and bias in the perception of the partner in a close relationship. *Journal of Personality and Social Psychology, 80*, 439–448.

Kenny, D. A., Kashy, D. A., & Cook, W. L. (2006). *Dyadic data analysis*. New York: Guilford.

Kunda, Z. (1990). The case for motivated reasoning. *Psychological Bulletin, 108*, 480–498.

Levinger, G., & Snoek, J. D. (1972). *Attraction and relationship: A new look at interpersonal attraction.* Morristown, NJ: General Learning Press.

Mallett, R. K., & Wilson, T. D. (2010). Increasing positive intergroup contact. *Journal of Experimental Social Psychology, 46*, 382–387.

Mallett, R. K., Wilson, T. D., & Gilbert, D. T. (2008). Expect the unexpected: Failure to anticipate similarities when predicting the quality of an intergroup interaction. *Journal of Personality and Social Psychology, 94*, 265–277.

Massey, D. S. (2001). Residential segregation and neighborhood conditions in U. S. metropolitan areas. In N. J. Smelser, W. J. Wilson, & F. Mitchell (Eds.), *Racial trends and their consequences* (Vol. 1, pp. 391–434). Washington, DC: National Academy Press.

Monteith, M. J., Sherman, J. W., & Devine, P. G. (1998). Suppression as a stereotype control strategy. *Personality and Social Psychology Review, 2*, 63–82.

Murray, S. L. (1999). The quest for conviction: Motivated cognition in romantic relationships. *Psychological Inquiry, 10*, 23–34.

Otten, S., & Moskowitz, G. B. (2000). Evidence for implicit evaluative in-group bias: Affect-based spontaneous trait inference in a minimal group paradigm. *Journal of Experimental Social Psychology, 36*, 77–89.

Page-Gould, E., Mendoza-Denton, R., & Tropp, L. R. (2008). With a little help from my cross-group friend: Reducing anxiety in intergroup contexts through cross-group friendship. *Journal of Personality and Social Psychology, 95*, 1080–1094.

Patterson, M. L. (1982). A sequential functional-model of nonverbal exchange. *Psychological Review, 89*, 231–249.

Pearson, A. R., Dovidio, J. F., & Gaertner, S. L. (2009). Teaching & learning guide for: The nature of contemporary prejudice: Insights from aversive racism. *Social and Personality Psychology Compass, 3*, 1–9.

Pearson, A. R., West, T. V., Dovidio, J. F., Powers, S. R., Buck R., & Henning, R. (2008). The fragility of intergroup relations: Divergent effects of delayed audiovisual feedback in intergroup and intragroup interaction. *Psychological Science, 19*, 1272–1279.

Pettigrew, T. F. (1997). Generalized intergroup contact effects on prejudice. *Personality and Social Psychology Bulletin, 23*, 173–185.

Pettigrew, T. F. (1998). Intergroup Contact Theory. *Annual Review of Psychology, 49*, 65–85.

Pettigrew, T. F., & Tropp, L. (2006). A meta-analytic test of intergroup contact theory. *Journal of Personality and Social Psychology, 90*, 751–783.

Pettigrew, T. F., & Tropp, L. R. (2008). How does contact reduce prejudice? Meta- analytic tests of three mediators. *European Journal of Social Psychology, 38*, 922–934.

Pettigrew, T. F., & Tropp, L. R. (2011). *When groups meet: The dynamics of intergroup contact*. New York: Psychology Press.

Plant, E. A. (2004). Responses to interracial interactions over time. *Personality and Social Psychology Bulletin, 30*, 1458–1471.

Plant, E. A., & Butz, D. A. (2006). The causes and consequences of an avoidance-focus for interracial interactions. *Personality and Social Psychology Bulletin, 32*, 833–846.

Plant, E. A., Butz, D. A., & Tartakovsky, M. (2008). Interethnic interactions: Expectancies, emotions, and behavioral intentions. *Group Processes & Intergroup Relations, 11*, 555–574.

Plant, E. A., & Devine, P. G. (2003). The antecedents and implications of interracial anxiety. *Personality and Social Psychology Bulletin, 29*, 790–801.

Reis, H. T., Collins, W. A., & Berscheid, E. (2000). The relationship context of human behavior and development. *Psychological Bulletin, 126*, 844–872.

Richeson, J. A., & Shelton, J. N. (2003). When prejudice does not pay: Effects of interracial contact on executive function. *Psychological Science, 14*, 287–290.

Richeson, J. A., & Shelton, J. N. (2010). Prejudice in intergroup dyadic interactions.

In J. F. Dovidio, M. Hewstone, P. Glick, & V. M. Esses (Eds.), *Handbook of prejudice, stereotyping, and discrimination*. Thousand Oaks, CA: Sage.

Richeson, J. A., & Trawalter, S. (2005). Why do interracial interactions impair executive function? A resource depletion account. *Journal of Personality and Social Psychology, 88*, 934–947.

Robbins, J. M., & Krueger, J. I. (2005). Social projection to ingroups and outgroups: A review and meta-analysis. *Personality and Social Psychology Review, 9*, 32–47.

Shelton, J. N. (2003). Interpersonal concerns in social encounters between majority and minority group members. *Group Processes and Intergroup Relations, 6*, 171–185.

Shelton, J. N., & Richeson, J. A. (2005). Intergroup contact and pluralistic ignorance. *Journal of Personality and Social Psychology, 88*, 91–107.

Shelton, J. N., Richeson, J. A., & Vorauer, J. D. (2006). Threatened identities and inter-ethnic interactions. In W. Stroebe, & M. Hewstone (Eds.), *European review of social psychology* (Vol. 17, pp. 312–358). New York: Psychology Press.

Shelton, J. N., West, T. V., & Trail, T. E. (2010). Concerns with appearing prejudiced: Implications for anxiety during daily interracial interactions. *Group Processes and Intergroup Relations, 13*, 329–344.

Shook, N. J., & Fazio, R. H. (2008a). Interracial roommate relationships: A comparison of interracial and same-race living situations. *Group Processes and Intergroup Relations, 11*, 425–437.

Shook, N. J., & Fazio, R. H. (2008b). Interracial roommate relationships: An experimental field test of the contact hypothesis. *Psychological Science, 19*, 717–723.

Stephan, W. G., & Stephan, C. W. (1985). Intergroup anxiety. *Journal of Social Issues, 41*, 157–175.

Stephan, W. G., & Stephan, C. W. (2000). An integrated threat theory of prejudice. In S. Oskamp (Ed.), *Reducing prejudice and discrimination* (pp. 23–46). Hillsdale, NJ: Erlbaum.

Tajfel, H., & Turner, J. C. (1979). An integrative theory of intergroup conflict. In W. G. Austin, & S. Worchel (Eds.), *The social psychology of intergroup relations* (pp. 33–48). Monterey, CA: Brooks/Cole.

Talaska, C. A., Fiske, S. T., & Chaiken, S. (2008). Legitimating racial discrimination: Emotions, not beliefs, best predict discrimination in a meta-analysis. *Social Justice Research, 21*, 263–296.

Trail, T. E., Shelton, J. N., & West, T. V. (2009). Interracial roommate relationships: Negotiating daily interactions. *Personality and Social Psychology Bulletin, 35*, 671–684.

Turner, R. N., Hewstone, M., Voci, A., & Vonofakou, C. (2008). A test of the extended intergroup contact hypothesis: The mediating role of perceived ingroup and outgroup norms, intergroup anxiety and inclusion of the outgroup in the self. *Journal of Personality and Social Psychology, 95*, 843–860.

Van Bavel, J. J., Packer, D. J., & Cunningham, W. A. (2008). The neural substrates of ingroup bias. *Psychological Science, 19*, 1131–1139.

Van Laar, C., Levin, S., & Sidanius, J. (2008). Ingroup and outgroup contact: A longitudinal study of the effects of cross-ethnic friendships, dates, roommate relationships, and participation in segregated organizations. In U. Wagner, L. R. Tropp, G. Finchilescu, & C. Tredoux (Eds.), *Improving intergroup relations: The legacy of Thomas F. Pettigrew* (pp. 127–142). Malden, MA: Blackwell.

Van Laar, C., Levin, S., Sinclair, S., & Sidanius, J. (2005). The effect of university roommate contact on ethnic attitudes and behavior. *Journal of Experimental Social Psychology, 41*, 329–345.

Vorauer, J. D. (2006). An information search model of evaluative concerns in intergroup interaction. *Psychological Review, 113*, 862–886.

West, T. V., Pearson, A. R., Dovidio, J. F., Shelton, J. N., & Trail, T. (2009). Superordinate identity and intergroup roommate friendship development. *Journal of Experimental Social Psychology, 45*, 1266–1272.

West, T. V., Shelton, J. N., & Trail, T. E. (2009). Relational anxiety in interracial interactions. *Psychological Science, 20*, 289–292.

Wilder, D. A. (1981). Perceiving persons as a group: Categorization and intergroup relations. In D. L. Hamilton (Ed.), *Cognitive Processes in Stereotyping and Intergroup Behavior* (pp. 213–57). Hillsdale, NJ: Erlbaum.

Wright, S. C., Aron, A., McLaughlin-Volpe, T., & Ropp, S. A. (1997). The extended contact effect: Knowledge of cross-group friendships and prejudice. *Journal of Personality and Social Psychology, 73*, 73–90.

8 Positive and negative intergroup contact among children and its effect on attitudes

Frances E. Aboud and Christia Spears Brown[1]

The study of ethnic divisions around the world is now more urgently leading to programs to enhance respect and inclusion. Childhood is thought to be the proper age to create experiences that enhance respect and inclusion, because children may be more flexible than adolescents and adults. Likewise, intergroup contact is seen to be the best means to achieve this end. Yet the evidence in favor of contact in childhood is not as clear-cut as we may wish. In this chapter we critically review and analyze the evidence regarding the effects on respectful attitudes of different types of contact (such as contact that arises by attending integrated schools, contact that is vicariously experienced by watching cross-group friendships on television, and learning about negative contact through classroom discussion about racism). Our objective is to provide a corpus of programs found to be effective regarding inclusive contact and respectful attitudes with children in the 3 to 8 year age range. We build on four prior reviews of interventions to modify children's attitudes, namely, Aboud (2009), Aboud and Levy (2000), Pfeifer, Brown, and Juvonen (2007), and Tropp and Prenovost (2007), though none focused on the early childhood years.

Our eventual goal is to evaluate programs that develop respect and inclusion. While some such programs exist and have been evaluated, most of the current research on contact and attitudes fulfills a preliminary objective. This objective is to identify promising determinants of attitude change or prevention, which can then be implemented in larger-scale, longer-duration programs. Studies often use a correlational design, measuring naturally-occurring contact and attitudes and examining the strength and reliability of their association. If children who have positive and high-quality contact also have respectful attitudes, then high-quality contact might be considered a source of the respect. A weakness of correlational designs is that it is unclear whether positive contact leads to respect, or whether children with positive intergroup attitudes seek out children from other groups. This confound is particularly limiting in studies involving one-time assessments, but also exists in longitudinal designs (although longitudinal studies can help examine whether respect increases after the onset of contact). Experimental designs have also been used, by manipulating positive or negative contact and examining its effects on attitudes, to more directly test the causal sequence. Experimental designs not only help to identify the causal role of contact; if realistic, they can also serve as an analogue for a real-life program. For example, experimental studies that expose children to a short scripted video in which two men from different ethnic groups interact (Castelli, De Dea, & Nesdale, 2008) or that have cross-ethnic pairs of children interact to select playmates (Leman & Lam, 2008) serve as analogues for larger scale programs that use contact to change attitudes. One concern with experimental studies, however, is that many are not very realistic and thus have limited external validity. Those with an ambition to evaluate a program would firstly, and with some success, want to employ the two preliminary designs, correlational and experimental, prior to developing, implementing, and evaluating a longer-term program.

We have organized our chapter to include studies that use correlational designs, experimental analogues, and effectiveness evaluations for the three types of contact most commonly examined – positive direct contact, media-mediated indirect contact, and discussions about negative contact (to be explained below). We present the theoretical underpinnings of contact, and then critically analyze studies with a view to assessing whether they identify promising determinants for an attitude-change program. However, attitudes and contact among children may vary with age and ethnic status. So our first section covers some of the descriptive designs used to outline age and ethnic differences among children. For the purposes of this paper, the term "ethnicity" refers to social categories of people who share an ethnic, language or religious affiliation or background. The term "ingroup" refers to the child's own group; "outgroups" refer to groups other than the child's own, regardless of whether the child actually likes or identifies with one. These groupings are usually identified by the adults in the community and so will be used here without other assumptions. The conclusion will be that children from the ethnic majority need programs aimed at reducing rather than preventing prejudice and discrimination by 4 years of age, as that is the age when bias can emerge.

Are children respectful and inclusive?

Majority White children in general appear to be less respectful in their attitudes toward ethnic minorities, but more inclusive in their contact, than one might expect. This chapter will use the constructs of attitudes and contact as key variables. We have adopted their broadest definition in order to expand the scope of research included here. So "respectful attitudes," or its opposites "prejudice" and "bias," may be measured as a set of positive and negative evaluations made by children about their ingroup and another group (i.e., an outgroup). Typically, attitudes have been measured by explicitly asking children to assign positive and negative evaluations to none, some, most, or all of the children from their own and other ethnic groups. Attitudes have also been measured by asking children about their intentions to keep social distance from other ingroup and outgroup members. Implicit attitudes have also been assessed with children using category judgments (Dunham, Baron, & Banaji, 2006) or priming procedures (Williams, Steele, & Durante, 2009). They are called "implicit" attitudes because children presumably do not know that their ethnic attitudes are under scrutiny and so are unlikely to control them for purposes of self-presentation. As of now, researchers are still debating what implicit attitudes reflect – overlearned category associations or personal beliefs. Existence of explicit and implicit attitudes suggests that children have two or more sets of attitudes, referred to as dual attitudes (Wilson, Lindsey, & Schooler, 2000); perhaps one was acquired in the early years without much thought and another developed more slowly with input from many sources and processes.

In general, children from majority White ethnic groups prefer their ingroup to their outgroup by 3 to 4 years of age. Shortly thereafter, children begin to show negative attitudes or prejudices toward members of visible minority ethnic groups, but this declines across middle childhood for some (but not all) children (Aboud, 2008). Prejudices may rise again in adolescence, particularly among groups who seek a source of positive and shared identity (Teichman, Bar-Tal, & Abdolrazeq, 2007). Children may only gradually with age develop prejudice toward less visible minority groups. Children from visible ethnic minorities tend to show little consensus in their attitudes, with some preferring their own group, some preferring the majority White group, and others being unbiased; their popularity with peers often increases if they are the same race as their teacher and classmates (Jackson, Barth, Powell, & Lochman, 2006). For example, African Americans in the United States tend to show more ingroup bias with age. Because of these differences among children from different ethnic groups and because of the age at which prejudices emerge, most interventions and programs seek to reduce prejudice and discrimination in White ethnic majority children starting from 4 years of age.

A second key construct in this research is contact in its different forms. Contact can be either direct or indirect. Direct contact can be operationalized as participating in integrated schooling, by having an outgroup peer relationship, or having a cross-group social interaction such as talking or helping. Indirect contact (also referred to as vicarious or extended contact) is defined as knowing, or being told about, an ingroup member who is friends with an outgroup member (Wright, Aron, McLaughlin-Volpe, & Ropp, 1997). Indirect contact typically involves the child being exposed to contact via media, such as television or books – a common source of contact for youngsters. Both direct and indirect contact can be either inclusive and positive or negative and discriminatory. Inclusive or positive direct contact is typically marked by friendships; this meets the conditions for Allport's equal-status contact and Pettigrew's (1998) friend contact in which the six known qualities of friendship such as companionship, loyalty and intimacy are met (e.g., Aboud, Mendelson, & Purdy, 2003). Negative or discriminatory direct contact can include exclusion, name-calling, and avoidance (e.g., Aboud & Joong, 2007; Killen & Stangor, 2001; Verkuyten, Kinket, & van der Wielen, 1997).

In studies that examine positive direct contact, children tend to show fairly high levels of outgroup peer play and friendship at 3 to 8 years of age, though at slightly lower levels than ingroup contact (Finkelstein & Haskins, 1983; Fishbein & Imai, 1993). Positive outgroup contact declines over the middle-childhood years in public schools (ages approximately 5 to 12 years); (Aboud et al., 2003; Hallinan & Teixeira, 1987). Those who do have a cross-ethnic friend report little difference in the quality of the friendship compared to a matched same-ethnic friend (Aboud et al., 2003). In terms of negative direct contact, physical and verbal bullying are high in middle childhood. Verbal bullying increases quickly after 7 or 8 years of age, whereas exclusion and other forms of relational bullying peak after 10 years (Aboud & Miller, 2007; Verkuyten et al., 1997). Verbal discrimination, in the form of nasty name-calling, increases in primary school, with 30 percent of children in grades 3 and 4, and more than 50 percent of children in grades 5 and 6 saying they were bullied in the past month. In a mixed ethnic school, 16 percent said that skin color was the source of the bullying; other ethnic attributes such as nationality, language and religion were also targeted (Aboud & Miller, 2007).

In contrast to direct contact, indirect contact is measured or manipulated in terms of knowing that an ingroup peer has an outgroup friend (Wright et al., 1997). This is viewed as positive indirect contact. Negative indirect contact may be experienced by children who witness an incident of intergroup bullying (60 percent in the past month in one study, Aboud & Miller, 2007). Interestingly, knowing that an ingroup peer called an outgroup member a nasty name led to more outgroup respect and vicarious anger in one experimental analogue study of young adults (Finlay & Stephan, 2000).

Age differences in indirect contact among children have been measured infrequently. Within integrated schools, children generally have direct contact with cross-ethnic friends, so indirect contact by itself is difficult to extract. However, when Aboud, Friedmann, and Smith (2011) studied peer contact in an integrated school with segregated classrooms, they found some evidence of indirect contact among 25 percent of students. Over the course of the year, second graders translated these indirect contacts into direct contacts or dropped them, whereas fourth graders continued to increase their set of indirect contacts.

The mechanisms by which contact affects attitudes, and their important social psychological mediators, are discussed throughout this volume. They include affective variables such as reduced anxiety about being in an unfamiliar place with outgroup peers and including the outgroup in the concept of oneself (e.g., Turner, Hewstone, Voci, & Vonofakou, 2008). There are also frequently studied social-cognitive variables, such as attention to individual rather than ethnic category differences, multiple simultaneous classification, and perspective-taking reconciliation (e.g., Aboud, 2003; Bigler, Brown, & Markell, 2001). All three of these social-cognitive variables have been associated with reductions in prejudice. Consequently, training these skills is seen as one way of enhancing the value of direct and indirect contact on attitudes and has been integrated into several prejudice-reduction programs with some success (e.g., Aboud & Fenwick, 1999). However, emphasizing individual differences with no discussion of how they supersede ethnicity is ineffective (Levy, West, Bigler, Karafantis, Ramirez, & Velilla, 2005). In contrast, training children to decategorize and focus on individual differences instead of ethnicity is effective (Aboud & Fenwick, 1999), possibly because without the training children do not yet have the requisite social-cognitive skills. Likewise, perspective taking by itself may serve only to strengthen ingroup norms of exclusion (Abrams, Rutland, Pelletier, & Ferrell,

2009), whereas perspective-taking along with reconciliation of ethnic differences might serve to alert children to the value of appreciating differences. Even though these skills are acquired during middle childhood, they may be trained in slightly younger children.

This brief overview of age differences in prejudice, contact, and mediators of the two sets the stage for a more critical look at how children benefit from the three types of contact most frequently evaluated in the literature: (1) positive direct contact, such as classroom-based cross-ethnic dyads, (2) indirect contact, specifically media-mediated contact, and (3) negative contact, combining direct and indirect such as learning about prejudice and how to respond to it.

Direct contact

Theoretical bases

Direct contact with an ethnic group other than one's own is now considered the most successful means to enhance positive attitudes among children and adults (Pettigrew & Tropp, 2006). Hypotheses were derived from Allport's (1954) contact theory, which proposed that people would come to like one another under conditions of cooperative and equal-status contact. This spawned a great deal of research on cooperative learning groups, both experimental analogue research with university students and field research in schools. Reviews of studies on cooperative learning groups (e.g., Slavin, Hurley, & Chamberlain, 2003) provide convincing evidence that cooperative learning programs yield academic and intergroup benefits. We found, however, very few primary source studies published in the past 30 years with young children ages 3 to 8 years, or even primary school children up to 12 years of age. One critical issue has been the extent to which liking for one's group-mates generalizes to other outgroup members.

Pettigrew (1998) extended the work of Allport by pointing out that if contact provided opportunities for friendship, it would lead to positive attitudes. As the gold standard of equal-status contact, friendship embodies much more than cooperation, and opportunities for friendship require more than simply classroom cooperation. In fact, opportunities for out-of-class voluntary contact and opportunities for dyadic closeness might be prerequisites for the formation of friendship (Aboud & Sankar, 2007). In the past 20 years, research on friendship among children has provided a theoretical basis for proposing mediators of the link between contact and positive attitudes. For example, among young children, similarities in activity preferences (such as types of play) are more important for friendship formation than ethnic or attitude similarity. Children seek and expect from a friend qualities such as companionship, emotional security, loyalty, help, intimacy, and self-validation (Aboud et al., 2003). Consequently, a cross-ethnic friend who provides these socially supportive qualities is likely to embody the conditions we know are important for reducing bias.

Kenworthy, Turner, Hewstone, and Voci (2005) elaborated on this point by proposing a set of psychological mediators that are responsible for linking collaborative and friendly contact with respect and inclusion. They considered cognitive mediators, such as learning personal information about outgroup individuals, which allows for a reduction of the outgroup homogeneity effect (i.e., greater attention to individual over ethnic differences). They also considered affective mediators, such as the anxiety-reducing role of collaborative contact. If bias is maintained by feelings of threat and anxiety (Stephan & Stephan, 2000), then close and friendly contact that reduces anxiety and the fear of bullying could be responsible for prejudice reduction. Similarly, if bias is maintained by a stereotypic view of the other, then the intimacy and self-disclosure that are part of close contact could reduce bias. Other psychological mediators known to be associated with respect and inclusion among children, such as perspective-taking, empathy and multiple classification might also increase as a result of close and friendly contact and thus be responsible for reduced bias.

Empirical evidence

Correlational evidence comes from naturalistic designs in which children's contact, either the type or amount of contact, is correlated with their ethnic attitudes. A review of the literature revealed seven studies with at least some children in the age range of 3 to 8 years (Aboud et al., 2003; Graham & Cohen, 1997; Howes & Wu, 1990; Farhan, 2008; Feddes, Noack, & Rutland, 2009; McGlothlin & Killen, 2006; Turner, Hewstone, & Voci, 2007), and several studies with only older children (Stringer, Irwing, Giles, McClenahan, Wilson, & Hunter, 2009; Turner et al., 2008).

Among these studies, overall contact was associated with more positive attitudes, and when it was higher quality contact or contact with an outgroup friend, it was associated with even more positive attitudes (Aboud et al., 2003; Turner et al., 2007). Using the minimal criterion for direct contact, some researchers obtain records regarding the proportion of outgroup peers in a school, class or neighborhood (Rutland, Cameron, Bennett, & Ferrell, 2005), or ask children about the presence of outgroup peers in social contexts such as their town, school, neighborhood, family and sports teams (McGlothlin & Killen, 2006). However, these measures are, strictly speaking, merely "opportunities for contact" rather than actual contact. For example, Rutland et al. (2005) assessed the positive and negative evaluations of White British children 3 to 5 years of age toward African Caribbean British, South Asian British and East Asian British. Negative bias toward African Caribbean British was higher in all-White and majority-White preschools, but non-existent in the mixed site. These studies highlight how opportunities for contact sometimes lead to more positive attitudes and sometimes do not, most likely because an opportunity for contact does not necessitate actual contact.

High quality contact is often defined as having a mutual friendship in which the friend is seen to provide important experiences that might mediate contact's impact on attitudes. These experiences go beyond what Allport called equal-status and cooperative contact, but capitalize on Pettigrew's (1998) notion of friendship. This type of high quality contact is associated with very positive attitudes because it allows, for example, for the inclusion of the outgroup in the definition of the self, enhances intimacy and self-disclosure, and reduces anxiety by providing emotional security. Four studies, in particular, address potential mediators: Aboud et al. (2003), Farhan (2008), and Turner et al. (2007, 2008). So far, there has been some support for cross-ethnic friendships leading to increases in perceptions of similarity (Farhan, 2008; Turner et al., 2008), intimacy (Aboud et al., 2003; Turner et al., 2007), and anxiety reduction (Turner et al., 2007), which in turn result in more positive attitudes about the ethnic outgroup in general. Importantly, cross-ethnic friendships appear to be more than token in nature; they show the same quality as same-ethnic friendships, though they tend to be less stable (Aboud et al., 2003; Aboud & Sankar, 2007).

Less evidence exists for the impact of peer norms on friendship or attitudes or as a mediator of the friendship-attitude link. However, peer norms do appear to be important in fostering the *avoidance* of such friendships. For example, work by Castelli, De Amicis, and Sherman (2007) and Abrams et al. (2009) reveals that young children, and children with a competitive view of ethnic relations, perceive negative norms for cross-ethnic friendships. In other words, children reported that peers would disapprove of cross-ethnic playmates. This appears, however, to be a case of pluralistic ignorance (Prentice & Miller, 1993), as many of the respondents themselves favored such friendships. Consequently, peer norms of exclusion may be exaggerated and difficult to overcome.

Listening to children talk about whom to select as playmates provides some insight on peer norms for contact. Leman and Lam (2008) paired 7- and 8-year-olds with an outgroup or ingroup peer and asked them to discuss and agree on whom to select as a playmate. When paired with a same-ethnic peer, British minority children tended to agree on an ingroup member over 50 percent of the time, whereas White British pairs agreed on an ingroup peer 90 percent of the time. However, when paired with a cross-ethnic peer, 30 percent of the White-minority pairs could not even agree on the choice of a playmate. Those who did agree on a choice were more likely to select a White playmate (46 percent) over an Asian one (24 percent in White-Asian pairs) or over a Black Caribbean playmate (20 percent in White-Caribbean pairs). Minority ethnic playmates were selected in less than 25 percent of these discussions. This suggests why the number of cross-ethnic friends declines with age: children begin discovering and conforming to the social norms regarding desirable playmates (typically White children), and minority children who want to be integrated find themselves excluding their own ingroup peers.

Experimental analogue evidence for the effects of contact comes from three studies in which authority support for contact was manipulated via teachers' attention to groupings (Bigler et al., 2001; Bigler, Jones & Lobliner, 1997; Patterson & Bigler, 2006). In these summer school studies, half the children were randomly assigned to wear a blue shirt and the other half to wear a red shirt for 3 weeks. The teacher, an authority figure, ignored the distinctions among color groups in one condition and used the shirt colors to organize children's activities in the other condition. Older children's bias in the first two studies was affected by the teacher's attention to color groups (Bigler et al., 1997, 2001). However, the 3- to

7-year-olds showed ingroup bias on six of the eight measures regardless of the teachers' attention to color (Patterson & Bigler, 2006). Thus, in contrast to the older students' attention to authority support or lack of support for color categories, younger children attended to color regardless. However, children were rarely biased in actual peer play, so direct contact remained high. This suggests that older children may be more sensitive to authority support of contact when forming biases compared to younger children who attend to color categories regardless.

Only four articles reported an evaluation of larger-scale programs that were designed to promote contact with Allport's conditions of cooperation and equal-status contact (Bratt, 2008; Johnson, Johnson, Tiffany, & Zaidman, 1984; Ng & Lee, 1999; Oortwijn, Boekaerts, Vedder, & Fortuin, 2008). The American studies typically find more positive attitudes and cooperative behavior toward minority classmates, which do not always generalize to the group as a whole. The Ng and Lee study in Singapore found higher rates of cross-ethnic friends among 11-year-olds in cooperative than in regular classes. Further, minority ethnic children in cooperative learning classes were rated as more popular (e.g., selected by classmates as "liked") compared to peers in regular classes (Oortwijn et al., 2008). Conversely, the study conducted in Norway found no significant benefit of cooperative learning classes (Bratt, 2008). Taken together, this suggests it is common to find greater social inclusion of minority ethnic group members, without more overall positive attitudes toward the ethnic group.

Two studies compared existing programs in different schools with different levels of ethnolinguistic contact (Aboud & Sankar, 2007; Wright & Tropp, 2005). Instruction in the languages of the two contact groups was expected to enhance friendship and attitudes. Although language proficiency might facilitate contact, raising the status of the minority language group through authority support could be a stronger influence. Attitudes were more positive when children attended an integrated ethnic and language program than when they simply had contact without language integration (Wright & Tropp, 2005). Likewise, children in two-language schools had equal numbers of high quality friends from both language groups (Aboud & Sankar, 2007). Outgroup friendship was associated with stronger affiliative attitudes toward the outgroup as a whole. Despite these positive outcomes, we found no other studies on the effects of authority support for ethnic and language integration and none for religious integration.

In sum, there is considerable evidence that providing children with the opportunity for dyadic contact will lead to playmates and friendships. These peer relationships in turn promote positive attitudes. Indirect contact via an ingroup peer (e.g., when a child observes an ingroup peer positively interacting with an outgroup classmate) is not as easily studied independently of direct contact in that the indirect outgroup peer is also likely a direct contact. However, younger children as well as adolescents may benefit from indirect contact independently of direct contact. Evidence for indirect contact may be easier to demonstrate using media, as discussed in the next section. There is strong support for programs that integrate ethnic and language groups and provide authority support for minority status. Efforts to bring children together in cooperative learning groups may not

be useful with young children of 3 to 8 years. To make sure that contact conditions support respect and inclusion, we need more correlational and experimental
analogue research on positive and negative norms, and whether authority figures
can alter negative norms when they exist.

Media-mediated (or para-social) contact

By media-mediated contact, we mean contact via the media, usually in contexts where
no direct contact is available. Media-mediated contact is important because many
children live in homogeneous neighborhoods and cities where they have few contact
opportunities until they reach adolescence. Decades of research on reading books to
children or showing videos about those from a different culture (often referred to as
multicultural education), assuming that knowledge will be acquired and identification will be enhanced, have shown them to be consistently ineffective (Katz & Zalk,
1978; Kowalski, 1998; Wham, Barnhart, & Cook, 1996). Consequently, we focus
on media-mediated contact that includes a cross-ethnic friendship.

Theoretical bases

Wright and colleagues (1997) extended the value of direct contact by pointing out
that children may benefit from media-mediated contact, specifically if they see an
ingroup child who has a cross-ethnic friend. They assumed that people are motivated to expand their self-concepts by including the other in their sense of self.
This is measured by asking how close one feels to another. Wright et al. (1997)
point out that people easily "identify with" or feel close to an ingroup peer, and if
this peer is friends with an outgroup child, then the latter will become "included in
the self" (see also Davies, Wright, Aron, & Comeau, this volume).

   The theory provided an explanation for why learning about the outgroup alone
was ineffective; the missing link was the ingroup peer. Multicultural education,
when it simply provides information about another ethnic group, has the benefit of
allowing one to become familiar with an outgroup child, but lacks the benefits of
being mediated by processes associated with the ingroup peer. Through the eyes
of the ingroup peer, people find it easier to include the other in the self, reduce
anxiety about being within a strange culture, and infer positive peer norms supporting inclusion (Turner et al., 2008). For example, the mediator proposed by
Wright et al. (1997) is the "closeness" one feels to others, which first extends to
the ingroup peer and then the outgroup friend. It is reasonable to apply the mediators of indirect contact to indirect contact through television and stories. Such
contact also provides information about positive norms of association with other
groups, norms that children apparently think are negative and lead to disapproval
and exclusion (see Abrams, Rutland, & Cameron, 2003; Castelli et al., 2007). The
ingroup peer also serves as a role model to emulate in cross-ethnic encounters;
this would be evident in storybooks and video episodes. Moreover, the lack of
threat directed toward the ingroup peer might serve to reduce feelings of anxiety
in children about cross-ethnic encounters.

Empirical evidence

Books and video/television episodes are the common means for providing media-mediated, indirect contact with outgroup peers. The story unfolds through the eyes of an ingroup peer who has an outgroup friend or acquaintance. Two series of studies will be described: one concerns the use of storybooks with young children and the second examines televised or video programs such as *Sesame Street* worldwide. The former has been studied with a field experimental analogue design, implemented by a research assistant in classrooms over several weeks. The latter used program-effectiveness field trials with considerably less control over the exposure and after-viewing discussion. Nine studies included children 8 years and under (Aboud, 2002; Cameron, Rutland, Brown, & Douch, 2006; Cameron, Rutland, & Brown, 2007; Castelli et al., 2008; Cole, Arafat, Tidhar, Tafesh, Fox, Killen et al., 2003; Fluent Public Opinion, 2008; Kowalski, 1998; Persson & Musher-Eizenman, 2003; Wham et al., 1996).

To date, the strongest research to be evaluated on contact via storybooks was reported by Cameron et al. (2006, 2007). They used three storybooks about the friendship activities of an outgroup child (in this case a refugee) and his/her ingroup White British friend. The children ranged in age from 5 to 11 years, so books were altered for their age level and to express components of contact. The books were read by an assistant to small groups of children who each had their own book, and the reading was followed by a group discussion. Positive and negative evaluations of the refugee outgroup and the ingroup made after the 6-session intervention showed that the stories produced more positive outgroup evaluations than a no-story control condition. The most successful condition was one in which the story children's common group identity, namely their school affiliation, was highlighted along with their different ethnic identities. So although indirect contact with a refugee child through the reading and discussion of three storybooks enhanced outgroup attitudes, attention to the dual identity of the refugee produced the greatest difference. This effect seemed to be mediated by how closely children rated themselves to the refugees (aka inclusion of other in the self).

Several larger-scale educational programs have attempted to incorporate storybooks into classroom procedures. These were conducted over 40 years ago when multiethnic readers were used in second grade classrooms (Lichter & Johnson, 1969; Lichter, Johnson, & Ryan, 1973). The attitudes of children who read from books with pictures of both White and Black children for 4 weeks were compared with the attitudes of children who read from books with the usual all-White cast of characters. The studies yielded discrepant findings, one showing a benefit and one not. Several features of these studies would not be replicated today: one is that teachers were told not to initiate any talk about race, and the second was the forced-choice nature of attitude measures. However, a more recent attempt to implement a storybook program with children 6 to 10 years of age also resulted in little change in attitudes (Wham et al., 1996). In that 7-month program, parents were encouraged to read daily the designated books to their child and to talk about the story and answer their child's questions. The books were about children from another country and children with a different skin color. Kindergartners were more negative at pre-test than children from second and fourth grade; children became more negative toward those from another country over the 7 months, and slightly more positive to children with different skin color. Although the changes lacked statistical significance, they show that not all storybook interventions are effective at reducing bias.

Indeed, the Wham et al. (1996) study highlights a paradox. Kindergarteners are the age group most likely to receive such a program in the classroom (e.g., Kowalski, 1998), yet they might not extract the intended message for several reasons. Social-cognitive developmental theories have argued that as a result of their immature mindsets, young children often distort incoming information, even from parents and friends, to make it fit their own view (Bigler & Liben, 2006). This might result from an inability to take another person's perspective and reconcile differences. So it was not entirely surprising that children who listened to an adult reading stories about cross-ethnic friends did not extract the intended antibias message (Aboud, 2002). White Canadian children initially assumed that the adult was negative toward Blacks, and after hearing her read 4 books over 4 weeks, first graders inferred that she was more positive while kindergarteners inferred that she was more negative. A similar conclusion was drawn by Mares and Acosta (2008) who found that moral lessons about disability on television were not received as intended. Likewise Kowalski (1998) reported no benefits on American kindergarteners from a 4-month media exchange program with a Japanese school. These findings raise questions about how to make antibias messages more explicit, so that the effectiveness of the message is not solely dependent on children's limited perspective-taking and reconciliation abilities.

Television and videos have likewise been more or less successful in modifying the attitudes of young children. Most of the studies are effectiveness evaluations of locally produced *Sesame Street* programs around the world, such as in the Middle East and Kosovo. Many focus explicitly on intergroup relations with the aim of promoting respect and inclusion, such as *Jalan Sesama* in Indonesia. However, other studies have evaluated shorter video clips manipulating specific messages. Not all are effective with children under 7 years (e.g., Persson & Musher-Eizenman, 2003). However, Castelli et al. (2008) produced a video where the message was clear. They showed to children 3–7 years old brief videos of an encounter between an ingroup White Italian adult and a brown-skinned adult named Abdul. Verbal and nonverbal cues of closeness and distance were varied. Nonverbal cues produced a stronger effect: children who saw positive nonverbal behavior of the White Italian toward Abdul, regardless of verbal behavior, inferred more positive feelings in the White adult and expressed more positive attitudes themselves. The emphasis here on nonverbal cues is consistent with Castelli, Zogmaister, and Tomelleri's (2009) finding that preschool children's attitudes correlated more with their parents' implicit than explicit attitudes.

Sesame Street production teams in areas where there is ethnic division and conflict often create episodes around a theme of ethnic diversity and intergroup harmony. Several programs have recently been evaluated. The evaluation of *Rechov Sumsum/Shara'a Simsim* shown to Jewish Israeli, Palestinian Israeli, and

Palestinian children aged 3 to 6 years at school and at home is the most accessible publication (Cole et al., 2003). Over a 4 month period, 70 30-minute episodes were available, integrating serious educational messages with exposure to children from each ethnic group. Everyday lives of individual children, some contact between children, and cultural symbols were shown in an attempt to promote a more positive view of ethnic members, between-group similarities, and prosocial interaction. Although Jewish Israeli and Palestinian Israeli children showed pre-post increases in positive attitudes to the outgroup as measured by answers to open-ended questions about Arabs and Jews, Palestinian children did not. Only Jewish Israeli children showed an increase in perceived between-group similarities. Palestinian children showed an increase in their ability to identify Palestinian cultural symbols. Because most children resolved conflict vignettes in a prosocial way, there was no pre-post change here.

A Sesame television program in Kosovo evaluated the attitudes of 5–6-year- old Albanian and Serbian children after the conflict (Fluent Public Opinion, 2008). Children watched *Rruga Sesam/Ulica Sezam* at home no less than twice a week for six weeks. Control children did not watch the program. Overall, the increase in children's positive attitudes was 2.5 times higher in those who watched the program compared to controls. However, most of this was due to the Serbian Kosovar children; the Albanian Kosovar children showed a modest increase. Measures of positive attitudes consisted of recognition of group similarities, and close social distance with other ethnic and language groups (e.g., Roma-, Chinese-, Serbian- and Albanian-speaking).

As is usual with program effectiveness studies, there is little control over how much exposure each child receives. In Kosovo, parents were asked to keep diaries of viewing. Also because the programming is local, the messages and images of cross-ethnic contact vary across countries. Nonetheless, the results point to a mix of effects, with some positive change and some lack of change. Depending on each group's baseline, there might be different goals and different outcomes. The two studies described here showed greater effects on the majority or more powerful group – Jewish Israeli and Serbian Kosovar children – a finding paralled by general contact effects among adults (Tropp & Pettigrew, 2005). The Palestinian and Albanian Kosovar children may have lacked a secure identity and so attended to messages of ingroup pride.

Zielinska and Chambers (1995) point to several conditions of media messages that may enhance their value. They explain, for example, why some of the described studies resulted in positive outcomes and others in non-significant effects. Better outcomes result if the social messages of cooperation are enacted by viewers in post-viewing role-plays. Moreover, they advise that the social message portions not be mixed with and potentially swamped by literacy and numeracy lessons. Their unmixed messages did enhance prosocial free-play behavior, but whether post-viewing instruction entailed group cooperation or individual performance did not matter.

In summary, interventions and programs need to be explicit about their intended messages (e.g., that visible minority members are friendly and smart and make good friends), how these are communicated (verbally and visually), and the strategy for attitude or behavior change. Experimental analogue studies more explicitly described the theoretical constructs used to develop the intervention message than program evaluations, but were less explicit describing the process used to change attitudes. The experimental analogue studies used theoretical constructs such as indirect contact, but only rarely considered how attitudes would change with such mediators as positive ingroup and outgroup norms, anxiety reduction, and dual categorization. In contrast, the full-fledged programs provided a haphazard set of messages about everything from similar and positive everyday activities, and some contact along with cultural/religious symbols which could have enhanced stereotypes and a single identity. However, programs using visual media strategies have a more explicit theory of attitude change, namely education-entertainment communication theory (Slater & Rouner, 2002), which entails the use of verbal and nonverbal messages while arousing emotions such as curiosity, surprise, interest and excitement. It also implicitly includes constructs from cognitive elaboration theory of communication whereby the message and sender are varied according to how willing and able are the audience. There is inconsistent evidence on whether children are more or less willing than adults to process the message, but they are certainly less able. Their cognitive elaboration must therefore be encouraged with memorable episodes and ingroup senders. Cognitive elaboration is also enhanced by post-viewing discussions with peers and adults.

So, while media-mediated contact through storybooks and television has great potential, much more experimental work and program evaluations are needed to identify what works and why. It is clear that cross-ethnic friends need to be the central characters. However, a communication theory of attitude change for children should be elaborated, including features of the sender, such as ingroup or outgroup, and of the message (indirect contact vs. explicit antibias) suited to the social-cognitive skills of the child (see Figure 9.1 in Aboud, 2005, for a framework).

Negative contact

Studies that incorporate some form of negative contact vary considerably, differing in the degree to which they explicitly discuss prejudice and ethnicity. There are primarily three different approaches: those that discuss discrimination and prejudice explicitly, those that train children in empathy and other mediating cognitions to overcome prejudice, and those that train children in behavioral responses to counter bias and exclusion in school. However, they all take the view articulated by Derman-Sparks (Derman-Sparks & Phillips, 1997) that children should take responsibility for stopping prejudice and discrimination within their spheres of influence. Studies may use one approach singularly or use them in combination with one another.

Theoretical bases

Some researchers advocate discussing discrimination explicitly with children. For example, children may be told about the racial prejudice faced by famous African

Americans and the ways they overcame it (Hughes, Bigler, & Levy, 2007). The rationale is based on Bigler and Liben's (2006) developmental intergroup theory, which argues that children have already noticed differences in racial groups (e.g., in occupational prestige). They argue that children create their own explanations for the differences they notice (e.g., intrinsic differences in intelligence). By discussing discrimination explicitly, these studies provide children with an alternative explanation for the noticed differences in ethnic groups. Because the explanations for differences are not based on stereotypes, the rationale is that stereotypes will be reduced.

Developmental intergroup theory also incorporates features of social-cognitive developmental theory concerned with how children come to understand discrimination and psychological harm. Social-cognitive skills such as perspective-taking, empathy, and processing multiple attributes of people rather than solely their ethnicity may be central to the development of respect and inclusion. This forms the rationale for interventions that seek to enhance such skills. Without such skills, dual identities, shared identities, and common identities of cross-ethnic friends would be difficult.

A second approach, at times used in conjunction with explicit descriptions of discrimination, focuses on changing the group norm of exclusion. This approach attempts to reduce the degree to which negative contact is accepted within the school or group. Guided by social learning theory and peer socialization through co-construction (Grusec & Goodnow, 1994), these studies train children to confront bullies and people with biases. This can be done by providing role models for children or by having them role-play confrontation scenarios (Aboud & Miller, 2007). These studies are often categorized as anti-bullying programs, and are particularly relevant when the bullying is based on race or ethnicity.

Studies that explicitly discuss discrimination and exclusion are distinct from multicultural education (e.g., Perkins & Mebert, 2005). Multicultural education programs are based on the idea that ignorance of groups leads to prejudice, whereas knowledge leads to respect. These programs convey information on the positive attributes of a group and expand children's knowledge about that group. However, focusing on cultural rather than individual differences can result in the presentation of stereotypic information and is ineffective in improving positive attitudes (indeed, increased group knowledge is not strongly related to attitude change; Pettigrew & Tropp, 2008).

Empirical evidence

Formative descriptive research has provided the basis for these interventions, which then tested effects through experimental analogue designs. For example, children's reactions to racial prejudice and name-calling indicated that most were aware of it and had witnessed it. However children of different ages interpret discrimination differently (Brown & Bigler, 2005). For example, children as young as 5 can recognize explicit forms of bias like name-calling. Older children of 8 or 9 years, because of their more advanced social-cognitive and perspective-taking abilities, are better equipped to recognize more subtle forms of bias like exclusion and preferential treatment. Regardless of age, name-calling is often the most explicit and noticeable form of bias. In line with this, Aboud and Miller (2007) asked 8- to 11-year-old children about their exposure to bullying at school. Most children mentioned witnessing name-calling. In an unfortunate paradox, children reported feeling bothered by instances of negative contact, but remained silent. In fact, older children were more bothered but less likely to intervene to stop negative contact. This study highlights how normative are negative intergroup interactions. Children report that it is not their responsibility to stop name-calling ("none of my business") and less frequently that they fear retaliation and do not know what to say to stop it (Aboud & Miller, 2007). Because most children remain silent in the face of negative contact, the group norm of exclusion and name-calling is maintained.

The majority of research on negative contact uses an experimental analogue design. The strongest evidence comes from studies where stereotypes or racism are discussed explicitly. Aboud and Doyle (1996) pre-tested White 8–11-year-old children on their racial attitudes. Children who were categorized as low in prejudice were paired with a friend who was categorized as high in prejudice. Children were asked to discuss their positive and negative evaluations of different race individuals. Results indicated that the low prejudice children discussed cross-race similarity, specific positive outgroup members who refute negative evaluations, and negative evaluations of their White peers (e.g., they would point out instances of aggression by White children in their class). After these discussions, high prejudice children showed less bias than at pre-test, whereas their low prejudice partners continued to show low levels of bias. In a similarly effective study, children were led in an explicit discussion of historical racism. Hughes et al. (2007) read 6–11-year-old children biographies of famous White and African Americans. In the experimental condition, the biographies included references to discrimination faced by the African American at the hands of Whites. Results indicated that the White children showed fewer biases after the racism lessons than after control lessons. The impact of hearing about discrimination may be partly due to the children's emotional reaction, namely anger-inducing empathy, as demonstrated by Finlay and Stephan (2000). Their participants were White university students who read transcripts of African American peers' personal experiences of victimization. Developmental changes in anger-inducing empathy versus pity-inducing empathy to stories of discrimination and its impact on attitudes have not yet been systematically studied.

Research has established that children endorse or at least publicly accept the norm of exclusion; specifically, children seem to negatively evaluate ingroup members who befriend outgroup members. Castelli et al. (2007) found that 3–5-year-old children preferred a pictured ingroup child who played only with other ingroup peers and negatively evaluated the child who played with an outgroup peer. Similarly, Abrams and colleagues (2003, 2009) found that 5–9-year-old children were more positive toward biased than unbiased ingroup members. However, children inferred stricter norms of exclusion by their peers than they personally supported. They may arrive at this inference because of frequently observed incidents of name-calling and bullying that are not contradicted by peers or adults. Thus, they infer that public displays of discrimination are acceptable and perhaps the norm.

To alter the norm of exclusion, two studies attempted to train students in responding verbally to name-calling. Aboud and Miller (2007), for example, had 8–12-year-olds listen to audio taped name-calling scenarios. They then heard bystander role models give an anti-bullying response. Children became more assertive in their own role-played responses after hearing the role model. This was moderated by the age of the role model, with adult models being more effective in producing assertive response for children in grades 2–3, and peer models being more effective for children in grades 5–6. In an extension of this work, Lamb, Bigler, Liben, and Green (2009) taught children to respond to a bully (this study focused on bullying because of gender, but the techniques could easily be applied to race). Children either practiced their anti-bullying responses or heard a role model giving these responses. To test what had been learned, researchers observed children in actual scenarios in which bullying occurred, and they found that children who had practiced using anti-bullying responses did so more often than children who only heard models. Taken together, these two studies suggest that explicitly addressing *how* children should respond to negative contact can be effective, particularly when children listen to an effective model (i.e., adult models for younger children and peer models for older children) and then practice a co-constructed non-confrontational response.

Several larger scale studies have evaluated programs delivered to children in schools by teachers. One was based on changing the norm of exclusion by highlighting a common identity. Houlette, Gaertner, Johnson, Banker, Riek, and Dovidio (2004) evaluated the Green Circle Program with 6–7-year-olds. Specifically, facilitators focused on developing a common classroom identity among a racially diverse group of students and explicitly discussed how it feels to be excluded because of race or gender. Drawing on children's empathy toward people who may be excluded, they encouraged children to include in "their circle" people who are different from them. The effects were modest, but did indicate that children were more inclusive toward who could be their best friend. There were no other effects on attitudes toward children of different races or genders.

A program that also relied on empathy to promote inclusion, albeit with a considerably larger scope, aired cartoon video messages targeted to 3–4-year-olds on local television channels in Northern Ireland (Connolly, Fitzpatrick, Gallagher, & Harris, 2006). There were three objectives with the media messages: (a) increase children's awareness of exclusion, (b) increase their empathy toward the excluded, and (c) increase their willingness to include others different from themselves. Cartoons depicted children of different ethnic and religious backgrounds. Children saw the characters first exclude, and then include, the child who was different. Narration explicitly discussed why the child was excluded and why he or she should be included. A pilot evaluation was conducted with preschool children who watched the videos over 6 weeks along with teacher-guided discussion. Children who had viewed the cartoons recognized exclusion more, knew the excluded child would feel sad, and showed a small increase in their willingness to play with a cross-ethnic child. Control children who did not see the video showed no changes from pre-test to post-test. The results were similar in Connolly and Hosken (2006), in which 6–7-year-old children were shown still pictures of children excluding others. Although the videos were helpful, children needed more discussion to help them extract the intended message and practice inclusion behaviors.

Another school program attempted to enhance empathy by explicitly discussing prejudice and discrimination toward refugees. Turner and Brown (2008) evaluated a program called the Friendship Project designed to improve 9–11-year-old children's attitudes toward refugees. The program involved teachers in classrooms carrying out four specific lesson plans, with the goal of (a) teaching specific information about refugees, including any prejudices and discrimination they may have faced, and (b) changing the values of participants to foster openness and respect for others and to promote empathy skills. After the program, children's attitudes changed from slightly negative to slightly positive, but empathy did not change. The effects were short-lived, however, and were not maintained 7 weeks after the program. As most studies do not include such a post-test follow up, it may be that this lack of long-term effect is common.

Another teacher-delivered program was designed to strengthen the social-cognitive skill of processing individual information and weakening the use of stereotypes. Aboud and Fenwick (1999) evaluated a program with 10–12-year-olds called More than Meets the Eye. The 11-week program discussed the inaccuracy of stereotypes and included activities in which children learned names and individual preferences of unfamiliar, ethnically diverse children. Four months after the program, all intervention children showed more spontaneous processing of internal individual information than controls. Whites gave more positive evaluations and showed less bias toward Blacks, with effects being strongest among high prejudiced children.

Although the studies that attempt to either explicitly discuss negative contact or explicitly change the norms of exclusion and ingroup/outgroup classification show varying degrees of effectiveness, they are markedly more effective than studies that rely on multicultural education to expose children to different group cultures. For example, Perkins and Mebert (2005) interviewed children who attended preschools with multicultural curricula. They found that those children had more domain-specific knowledge about cultures but were no less biased than other preschool children (see also Gimmestad & De Chiara, 1982; Kowalski, 1998). London, Tierney, Buhin, Greco, and Cooper (2002) evaluated a multicultural curriculum based on a summer camp format for 10–13-year-olds. Children in the study showed a decrease in prejudice, but an increase in the belief of stereotypes. Thus, it appears that simply presenting information about an ethnic group does little to change attitudes; if any change occurs, it typically is in an increased endorsement of stereotypes.

In summary, interventions and programs are most effective by focusing on explicit discussions of historical and current discrimination, by explicitly pointing out similarities across groups and differences within groups to refute stereotypes, and by training children on specific behaviors to counteract the norms of exclusion. Simply discussing empathy and exclusion, without specific examples of discrimination and specific behaviors to enact when they encounter it, are not as effective. Indeed, programs that are the most concrete, such as those having children role-model inclusion and antibias behaviors instead of watching a video about other children, are the most effective, particularly for young children. This is likely due to children's limited social-cognitive skills, in which concrete behaviors and examples are easier to translate into behavior than more abstract concepts such as generalized empathy. Research suggests that the use of peers as agents of attitude change may be particularly effective. Future research should examine whether peers are effective in reducing bias because their opinions are in general highly valued in childhood, because they change the norm of accepted behavior, or because they match the social-cognitive skill level of the targeted children.

Conclusions

Findings with children in the 3 to 8 year range showed that direct and media-mediated contact can enhance respectful attitudes and inclusion, as do explicit discussions of exclusion and behavioral training to overcome it. Benefits of direct contact are the most clear-cut, and do not require special efforts such as cooperative learning groups to bring young children together. Wherever possible, children should be integrated in schools where language and comparative religious instruction confers equal status on participating students. However, direct contact is not feasible in many childhood settings. A strong alternative is contact through audio-visual media in which friendships between ingroup and outgroup peers form the story plot, that is, provide a vivid indirect contact experience. Likewise, vicariously experienced negative contact in the form of historical and contemporary discrimination can be introduced with sensitivity. The last two appear to be most beneficial when they also raise specific social-cognitive skills such as empathy, perspective taking and attention to multiple attributes, and when they provide opportunities for children to learn related behaviors.

More is known about the conditions for successful implementation of media-mediated, indirect contact. Storybook programs are still at the experimental analogue stage because we do not yet know the conditions or mediators for their success. Children under 8 years show a certain reluctance to extract the intended meaning of these books; consequently post-story discussions or training in perspective taking may be required to highlight the antibias message which is distorted or lost in the excitement. Behavioral enactment via role-plays may help to translate the messages into behavior and consolidate it. Discussions and role-plays may also enhance the effects of television episodes of ethnic diversity. Because *Sesame Street* is being produced worldwide along with outreach storybook materials, it can become a valuable source of evidence. Media programs need to converge on relevant theoretical frameworks that allow for generalizability. For example, constructs relevant to education-entertainment communication theory need to be combined with bias-reducing constructs such as indirect contact and perspective taking.

Negative contact is a valuable new avenue for the development of respect and inclusion. It appears that children as young as 5 or 6 understand discrimination and exclusion and have witnessed it. Small exposures appear to have a large impact because of the negative emotions aroused. However, large scale programs have not been as effective as hoped. So we may need more experimental analogue studies to identify promising components. Children between 5 and 8 years have social, cognitive and emotional limitations that require special tailoring of the message format. Generalized discussions are less effective than concrete and personalized experiences. Empathy is useful but only if it arouses anger rather than pity and only if it is connected to behaviors. Other social-cognitive skills may need explicit activities to strengthen their use as guides for behavior. Children benefit from older or same-age role models to help them co-construct a response that suits them. This is particularly so with public behaviors to address bullying.

Finally, our review of the evidence identified ingroup norms as a problematic area. In some research, it appears that young children assume high levels of ingroup norms in favor of exclusion. They may have misconstrued descriptive norms as indicative of prescriptive norms, or they may conceive of ethnic groups as competitive "teams." The lack of efforts by adults to address bullying confirms these norms. So even where there is authority support for contact, there may not be ingroup peer support. This obstacle needs to be addressed by all three types of programs.

Note

1 We would like to acknowledge the assistance of Una Quantitative Methods Learning Group. Una is a global learning initiative on children and ethnic diversity (see www.unaglobal. org) funded by the Bernard van Leer Foundation and the Atlantic Philanthropies.

References

Aboud, F. E. (2002). *Antibias messages and prejudice reduction in young children.* Paper presented at the Society for the Psychological Study of Social Issues, Toronto, June.
Aboud, F. E. (2003). The formation of ingroup favoritism and outgroup prejudice in young children: Are they distinct attitudes? *Developmental Psychology, 39,* 48–60.
Aboud, F. E. (2005). The development of prejudice in childhood and adolescence. In J. F. Dovidio, P. Glick, & L. A. Rudman (Eds.), *On the nature of prejudice: Fifty years after Allport* (pp. 310–326). Malden, MA: Blackwell.
Aboud, F. E. (2008). A social-cognitive developmental theory of prejudice. In S. M. Quintana & C. McKown (Eds.), *The handbook of race, racism, and the developing child* (pp. 55–71). Hoboken, NJ: Wiley.
Aboud, F. E. (2009). Modifying children's racial attitudes. In J. A. Banks (Ed.), *The Routledge international companion to multicultural education* (pp. 199–209). New York: Routledge.
Aboud, F. E., & Doyle, A. B. (1996). Does talk of race foster prejudice or tolerance in children? *Canadian Journal of Behavioural Science, 28,* 161–170.
Aboud, F. E., & Fenwick, V. (1999). Exploring and evaluating school-based interventions to reduce prejudice. *Journal of Social Issues, 55,* 767–785.

Aboud, F. E., Friedmann, J., & Smith, S. (2011). *Contact, attitudes, and ingroup norms for mixing in integrated schools.* Paper presented at Society for Research in Child Development Conference. Montreal, March 31.

Aboud, F. E., & Joong, A. (2007). Intergroup name-calling and conditions for creating assertive bystanders. In S. R. Levy, & M. Killen (Eds.), *Intergroup attitudes and relations in childhood through adulthood* (pp. 249–260). Oxford: Oxford University Press.

Aboud, F. E., & Levy, S. R. (2000). Interventions to reduce prejudice and discrimination in children and adolescents. In S. Oskamp (Ed.), *Reducing prejudice and discrimination* (pp. 269–293). Mahwah, NJ: Erlbaum.

Aboud, F. E., Mendelson, M. J., & Purdy, K. T. (2003). Cross-race peer relations and friendship quality. *International Journal of Behavioral Development, 27*(2), 165–173.

Aboud, F. E., & Miller, L. (2007). Promoting peer intervention in name-calling. *South African Journal of Psychology, 37*, 803–819.

Aboud, F. E., & Sankar, J. (2007). Friendship and identity in a language-integrated school. *International Journal of Behavioral Development, 31*, 445–453.

Abrams, D., Rutland, A., & Cameron, L. (2003). The development of subjective group dynamics: Children's judgments of normative and deviant in-group and out-group individuals. *Child Development, 74*, 1840–1856.

Abrams, D., Rutland, A., Pelletier, J., & Ferrell, J. M. (2009). Children's group *nous*: understanding and applying peer exclusion within and between groups. *Child Development, 80*, 224–243.

Allport, G. W. (1954/1979). *The nature of prejudice.* Cambridge, MA: Perseus Books.

Bigler, R. S., Brown, C. S., & Markell, M. (2001). When groups are not created equal: Effects of group status on the formation of intergroup attitudes in children. *Child Development, 72*, 1151–1162.

Bigler, R. S., Jones, L. C., & Lobliner, D. B. (1997). Social categorization and the formation of intergroup attitudes in children. *Child Development, 68*, 530–543.

Bigler, R. S., & Liben, L. S. (2006). A developmental intergroup theory of social stereotypes and prejudice. In R. V. Kail (Ed.), *Advances in child development and behavior* (Vol 34, pp. 39–89). San Diego: Elsevier.

Bratt, C. (2008). The Jigsaw Classroom under test: No effect on intergroup relations evident. *Journal of Community & Applied Social Psychology, 18*, 403–419.

Brown, C. S., & Bigler, R. S. (2005). Children's perceptions of discrimination: A developmental model. *Child Development, 76*, 533–553.

Cameron, L., Rutland, B., & Brown, R. (2007). Promoting children's positive intergroup attitudes towards stigmatized groups: Extended contact and multiple classification skills training. *International Journal of Behavioral Development, 31*(5), 454–466.

Cameron, L., Rutland, A., Brown, R., & Douch, R. (2006). Changing children's intergroup attitudes toward refugees: Testing different models of extended contact. *Child Development, 77*, 1208–1219.

Castelli, L., De Amicis, L., & Sherman, S. J. (2007). The loyal member effect: On the preference for ingroup members who engage in exclusive relations with the ingroup. *Developmental Psychology, 43*, 1347–1359.

Castelli, L., De Dea, C., & Nesdale, D. (2008). Learning social attitudes: Children's sensitivity to the nonverbal behaviors of adult models during interracial interactions. *Personality and Social Psychology Bulletin, 34*, 1504–1513.

Castelli, L., Zogmaister, C., & Tomelleri, S. (2009). The transmission of racial attitudes within the family. *Developmental Psychology, 45*, 586–591.

Cole, C. F., Arafat, C., Tidhar, C., Tafesh, W. Z., Fox, N. A., Killen, M., Ardila-Rey, A.,

Leavitt, L. A., Lesser, G., Richman, B. A., & Yung, F. (2003). The educational impact of *Rechov Sumsum/ Shara'a Simsim*: A *Sesame Street* television series to promote respect and understanding among children living in Israel, West Bank, and Gaza. *International Journal of Behavioral Development, 27*, 409–432.

Connolly, P., Fitzpatrick, S., Gallagher, T., & Harris, P. (2006). Addressing diversity and inclusion in the early years in conflict-affected societies: a case study of the media initiative for children in Northern Ireland. *International Journal of Early Years Education, 14*, 263–278.

Connolly, P., & Hosken, K. (2006). The general and specific effects of educational programmes aimed at promoting awareness of and respect for diversity among young children. *International Journal of Early Years Education, 14*, 107–126.

Derman-Sparks, L., & Phillips, C. B. (1997). *Teaching/learning anti-racism: A developmental approach.* New York: Teachers College, Columbia University.

Dunham, Y., Baron, A. S., & Banaji, M. R. (2006). From American city to Japanese village: a cross-cultural investigation of implicit race attitudes. *Child Development, 77*, 1268–1281.

Farhan, T. (2008). *Prejudice in school children: Causal analyses of possible factors of influence based on a longitudinal study.* Unpublished manuscript. Philipps University Marburg, Germany.

Feddes, A. R., Noack, P., & Rutland, A. (2009). Direct and extended friendship effects on minority and majority children's interethnic attitudes: A longitudinal study. *Child Development, 80*, 377–390.

Finkelstein, N. W., & Haskins, R. (1983). Kindergarten children prefer same-color peers. *Child Development, 54*, 502–508.

Finlay, K. A., & Stephan, W. G. (2000). Improving intergroup relations: The effects of empathy on racial attitudes. *Journal of Applied Social Psychology, 30*, 1720–1737.

Fishbein, H. D., & Imai, S. (1993). Preschoolers select playmates on the basis of gender and race. *Journal of Applied Developmental Psychology, 14*, 303–316.

Fluent Public Opinion (2008). *Assessment of educational impact of* Rruga Sesam *and* Ulica Sezam: Report of findings prepared for Sesame Workshop.

Gimmestad, B. J., & De Chiara, E. (1982). Dramatic plays: A vehicle for prejudice reduction in the elementary school. *Journal of Educational Research, 76*, 45–49.

Graham, J. A., & Cohen, R. (1997). Race and sex as factors in children's sociometric ratings and friendship choices. *Social Development, 6*, 355–372.

Grusec, J. E., & Goodnow, J. J. (1994). Impact of parental discipline methods on the child's internalization of values: A reconceptualization of current points of view. *Developmental Psychology, 30*, 4–19.

Hallinan, M. T., & Teixeira, R. A. (1987). Opportunities and constraints: Black-White differences in the formation of interracial friendships. *Child Development, 58*, 1358–1371.

Houlette, M. A., Gaertner, S. L., Johnson, K. M., Banker, B. S., Riek, B. M., & Dovidio, J. F. (2004). Developing a more inclusive social identity: An elementary school intervention. *Journal of Social Issues, 60,* 35–55.

Howes, C., & Wu, F. (1990). Peer interactions and friendships in an ethnically diverse school setting. *Child Development, 61*, 537–541.

Hughes, J. M., Bigler, R. S., & Levy, S. R. (2007). Consequences of learning about historical racism among European American and African American children. *Child Development, 78*, 1689–1705.

Jackson, M. G., Barth, J. M., Powell, N., & Lochman, J. E. (2006). Classroom contextual effects of race on children's peer nominations. *Child Development, 77*, 1325–1337.

Johnson, D. W., Johnson, R. T., Tiffany, M., & Zaidman, B. (1984). Cross-ethnic relationships: The impact of intergroup cooperation and intergroup competition. *Journal of Educational Research, 78*, 75–79.

Katz, P. A., & Zalk, S. R. (1978). Modification of children's racial attitudes. *Developmental Psychology, 14*, 447–461.

Kenworthy, J. B., Turner, R. N., Hewstone, M., & Voci, A. (2005). Intergroup contact: When does it work, and why? In J. F. Dovidio, P. Glick, & L. A. Rudman (Eds.), *On the nature of prejudice: Fifty years after Allport* (pp. 278–292). Malden, MA: Blackwell.

Killen, M., & Stangor, C. (2001). Children's social reasoning about inclusion and exclusion in gender and race peer group contexts. *Child Development, 72*, 174–186.

Kowalski, K. (1998). The impact of vicarious exposure to diversity on preschoolers' ethnic/racial attitudes. *Early Child Development & Care, 146*, 41–51.

Lamb, L., Bigler, R., Liben, L., & Green, V. (2009). Teaching Children to Confront Peers' Sexist Remarks: Implications for Theories of Gender Development and Educational Practice. *Sex Roles, 61*, 361–382.

Leman, P. J., & Lam, V. L. (2008). The influence of race and gender on children's conversations and playmate choices. *Child Development, 79*, 1329–1343.

Levy, S. R., West, T. L., Bigler, R. S., Karafantis, D. M., Ramirez, L., & Velilla, E. (2005). Messages about the uniqueness and similarities of people: Impact on U.S. Black and Latino youth. *Journal of Applied Developmental Psychology, 26*, 714–733.

Lichter, J. H., & Johnson, D. W. (1969). Changes in attitudes toward Negroes of White elementary school students after use of multiethnic readers. *Journal of Educational Psychology, 60*, 148–152.

Lichter, J. H., Johnson, D. W., & Ryan, F. L. (1973). Use of pictures of multiethnic interaction to change attitudes of White elementary school students toward Blacks. *Psychological Reports, 33*, 367–372.

London, L. H., Tierney, G., Buhin, L., Greco, D. M., & Cooper, C. J. (2002). Kid's College: Enhancing children's appreciation and acceptance of cultural diversity. *Journal of Prevention & Intervention in the Community, 24*, 61–76.

Mares, M-L., & Acosta, E. E. (2008). Be kind to three-legged dogs: Children's literal interpretations of TV's moral lessons. *Media Psychology, 11*, 377–399.

McGlothlin, H., & Killen, M. (2006). Intergroup attitudes of European American children attending ethnically homogeneous schools. *Child Development, 77*, 1375–1386.

Ng, M., & Lee, C. K. (1999, June). *The effects of cooperative learning on the cross-ethnic friendship choices of children.* American Education Research Association meetings, Montreal.

Oortwijn, M. B., Boekaerts, M., Vedder, P., & Fortuin, J. (2008). The impact of a cooperative learning experience on pupils' popularity, non-cooperativeness, and interethnic bias in multiethnic elementary schools. *Educational Psychology, 28*, 211–221.

Patterson, M. M., & Bigler, R. S. (2006). Preschool children's attention to environmental messages about groups: Social categorization and the origins of intergroup bias. *Child Development, 77*, 847–860.

Perkins, D. M., & Mebert, C. J. (2005). Efficacy of multicultural education for preschool children: A domain-specific approach. *Journal of Cross-Cultural Psychology, 36*, 497–512.

Persson, A., & Musher-Eizenman, D. R. (2003). The impact of a prejudice-prevention television program on young children's ideas about race. *Early Childhood Research Quarterly, 18*, 530–546.

Pettigrew, T. F. (1998). Intergroup contact theory. *Annual Review of Psychology, 49,* 65–85.

Pettigrew, T. F., & Tropp, L. R. (2006). A meta-analytic test of intergroup contact theory. *Journal of Personality and Social Psychology, 90,* 751–783.

Pettigrew, T. F., & Tropp, L. R. (2008). How does intergroup contact reduce prejudice? Meta-analytic tests of three mediators. *European Journal of Social Psychology, 38,* 922–934.

Pfeifer, J. H., Brown, C. S., & Juvonen, J. (2007). Teaching tolerance in schools: lessons learned since Brown *vs* Board of Education about development and reduction of children's prejudice. *Social Policy Report, 21,* Vol.2.

Prentice, D. A., & Miller, D. T. (1993). Pluralistic ignorance and alcohol use on campus: Some consequences of misperceiving the social norm. *Journal of Personality & Social Psychology, 64,* 243–256.

Rutland, A., Cameron, L., Bennett, L., & Ferrell, J. (2005). Interracial contact and racial constancy: A multi-site study of racial intergroup bias in 3–5 year old Anglo-British children. *Journal of Applied Developmental Psychology, 26,* 699–713.

Slater, M. D., & Rouner, D. (2002). Entertainment-education and elaboration likelihood: Understanding the processing of narrative persuasion. *Communication Theory, 12,* 173–191.

Slavin, R. E., Hurley, E. A., & Chamberlain, A. (2003). Cooperative learning and achievement: theory and research. In W. M. Reynolds, & G. E. Miller (Eds.), *Handbook of psychology: Educational psychology* (Vol.7 pp. 177–198). Hoboken, NJ: Wiley.

Stephan, W. G., & Stephan, C. W. (2000). An integrated threat theory of prejudice. In S. Oskamp (Ed.), *Reducing prejudice and discrimination* (pp. 23–45). Mahwah, NJ: Erlbaum.

Stringer, M., Irwing, P., Giles, M., McClenahan, C., Wilson, R., & Hunter, J. A. (2009). Intergroup contact, friendship quality and political attitudes in integrated and segregated schools in Northern Ireland. *British Journal of Educational Psychology, 79,* 239–257.

Teichman, Y., Bar-Tal, D., & Abdolrazeq, Y. (2007). Intergroup biases in conflict: Reexamination with Arab pre-adolescents and adolescents. *International Journal of Behavioral Development, 31,* 423–432.

Tropp, L. R., & Pettigrew, T. F. (2005). Relationships between intergroup contact and prejudice among minority and majority status groups. *Psychological Science, 16,* 951–957.

Tropp, L. R., & Prenovost, M. A. (2007). The role of intergroup contact in predicting children's interethnic attitudes evidence from meta-analytic and field studies. In S. R. Levy, & M. Killen (Eds.), *Intergroup attitudes and relations in childhood through adulthood* (pp. 249–260). Oxford: Oxford University Press.

Turner, R. N., & Brown, R. (2008). Improving children's attitudes toward refugees: An evaluation of a school-based multicultural curriculum and an anti-racist intervention. *Journal of Applied Social Psychology, 38,* 1295–1328.

Turner, R. N., Hewstone, M., & Voci, A. (2007). Reducing explicit and implicit outgroup prejudice via direct and extended contact: The mediating role of self-disclosure and intergroup anxiety. *Journal of Personality and Social Psychology, 93,* 369–388.

Turner, R. N., Hewstone, M., Voci, A., & Vonofakou, C. (2008). A test of the extended intergroup contact hypothesis: The mediating role of intergroup anxiety, perceived ingroup and outgroup norms, and inclusion of the outgroup in the self. *Journal of Personality and Social Psychology, 95,* 843–860.

Verkuyten, M., Kinket, B., & van der Wielen, C. (1997). Preadolescents' understanding of ethnic discrimination. *Journal of Genetic Psychology, 158,* 97–112.

Wham, M. A., Barnhart, J., & Cook, G. (1996). Enhancing multicultural awareness through storybook reading experience. *Journal of Research and Development in Education, 30*, 1–9.

Williams, A., Steele, J. R., & Durante, S. (2009). *The development of implicit racial bias among 6- and 9-year-olds: Is forced categorization by race a precondition for bias?* Manuscript, York University, Toronto.

Wilson, T. D., Lindsey, S., & Schooler, T. Y. (2000). A model of dual attitudes. *Psychological Review, 107*, 101–126.

Wright, S. C., Aron, A., McLaughlin-Volpe, T., & Ropp, S. A. (1997). The extended contact effect: Knowledge of cross-group friendships and prejudice. *Journal of Personality and Social Psychology, 73*, 73–90.

Wright, S. C., & Tropp, L. R. (2005). Language and intergroup contact: Investigating the impact of bilingual instruction on children's intergroup attitudes. *Group Processes and Intergroup Relations, 8*, 309–328.

Zielinska, I. E., & Chambers, B. (1995). Using group viewing of television to teach preschool children social skills. *Journal of Educational Television, 21*, 85–99.

9 Intergroup contact through friendship

Intimacy and norms

*Kristin Davies, Stephen C. Wright,
Arthur Aron, and Joseph Comeau*

After more than a half century of investigation, the Intergroup Contact Hypothesis (Allport, 1954), which posits that cross-group interaction can encourage positive intergroup attitudes, has emerged as social psychology's foremost strategy for reducing prejudice and improving interpersonal interaction across groups (see Dovidio, Glick, & Rudman, 2005; Pettigrew & Tropp, 2006). In one of the most important recent additions to this model, Pettigrew (1998) proposed that there is something special about friendship, making it the type of cross-group relationship most likely to produce positive intergroup attitude change. Furthermore, there is growing research evidence that friendship yields larger positive effects on intergroup attitudes than other less intimate forms of contact (e.g., Davies, Tropp, Aron, Pettigrew, & Wright, 2011).

This chapter focuses on this special cross-group relationship – friendship – and considers the psychology of those directly involved in the cross-group friendship as well as the impact of these friendships on those who merely observe them, what we have referred to as extended contact (Wright, Aron, McLaughlin-Volpe, & Ropp, 1997). We will discuss mechanisms that underpin the association between friendship and positive intergroup attitudes, focusing particularly on the role of intimacy-related processes. In addition, we will consider a variety of critical roles played by group norms in both direct and extended cross-group contact. In the case of direct contact, group norms have been implicated as motivators of cross-group interactions, as an important determinant of the success of these interactions in producing positive attitude change (as a moderator), and finally as a mechanism by which interpersonal friendships produce attitude change (as a mediator). In the case of extended contact, changes in perception of group norms have been described as one of a number of mechanisms that explain why simply observing the cross-group friendships of others can influence intergroup attitudes. We conclude with suggestions for future research directions.

Intergroup contact and friendship

Gordon Allport's (1954) Intergroup Contact Hypothesis is one of the oldest and best supported approaches in the scientific study of intergroup relations. The central premise is that under certain conditions, contact between individual members of differing social groups can lead to improved attitudes towards the partner's group. In his seminal volume *The Nature of Prejudice*, Allport (1954) built upon the work of other researchers of the time (e.g., Williams, 1947), laying out a comprehensive theory of the conditions most likely to produce optimal cross-group contact (i.e., the kind of contact most likely to produce positive attitude change). This initial theorizing stimulated what has become a vast literature that utilizes a wide variety of methods and measures to investigate the impact of contact across a range of groups in numerous locations around the world. The overall conclusion of an extensive meta-analytic review of this literature was that there is strong support for the positive effects of contact and for Allport's original model (Pettigrew & Tropp, 2006).

Although contact *generally* leads to improved attitudes towards the relevant outgroup, many contextual, group, and individual factors can undermine its success. Even in their earliest forms hypotheses concerning intergroup contact (e.g., Allport, 1954) recognized that simply bringing together members of groups with histories of negative, even hostile, intergroup relations has the potential to go very badly, and could serve to confirm rather than undermine negative views of the outgroup. We turn now to a brief discussion of factors likely to influence the ability of cross-group contact to encourage more positive attitudes towards outgroups. Following these descriptions, we consider friendship's apparent ability to offer a solution to some of the potential problems that may arise during cross-group contact.

Contextual factors

Recognizing the potential pitfalls inherent in cross-group contact, Allport's (1954) initial formulations proposed four primary necessary contextual conditions for successful contact: equal status, common goals, cooperation, and support of authorities and institutions. A comprehensive meta-analytic review (Pettigrew & Tropp, 2006) supports the claim that these conditions increase the likelihood that contact will produce positive attitudes, but they do not appear necessary for contact to be effective. We will return to one of Allport's key conditions later in the chapter as it bears directly on the issue of norms. However, Allport's focus on the contextual conditions for successful contact led many that followed to do the same, and for nearly 50 years the primary focus of contact research was to document the many factors that determined when cross-group contact would reduce prejudice and when it would not (see Pettigrew, 1986, for a review).

We should recall, however, that Allport penned his initial formulation of the hypothesis during a tumultuous time in American history, when the prototypical intergroup relationship of interest to social psychologists was the highly unequal and decidedly contentious relationship between Blacks and Whites in the US. Thus, the default assumption was that contact would be resisted, would be highly unequal when it did occur, and would usually serve to reify rather than undermine stereotypic representations of the outgroup. However, circumstances have changed dramatically. First, discussions of intergroup relations, even in the United States, are no longer entirely dominated by Black/White relations. Concerns have broadened to consider a wide range of groups, including group differences not based solely on race or ethnicity. In addition, many more people, at least consciously, espouse strong egalitarian values and see negative attitudes towards outgroups as inappropriate and even evil. How we got here and whether we can maintain and continue the positive movement are questions for another time, but what is striking is that even with these dramatic shifts, cross-group interactions remain a source of consternation for many people. Despite our often strongly professed desire to be free of constraints imposed by group differences, cross-group interactions remain more difficult (e.g., West, Shelton, & Trail, 2009; Vorauer & Kumhyr, 2001) and less frequent (e.g., Halualani, Chitgopekar, Morrison, & Dodge, 2004) than same-group interactions.

Group-level factors

More recently, researchers have focused on the influence of particular characteristics of the relevant groups that influence the outcomes of cross-group contact. One factor that has received considerable recent attention is group status. Generally, while contact can have a large positive influence on the attitudes of majority group members, the relationship between contact and attitudes, although still meaningful, is much weaker for minority group members (e.g., Tropp & Pettigrew, 2005). Of course, both majority and minority group members can be hampered by similar processes during cross-group interactions. For example, both majority and minority group members tend to explain their own lack of effort to engage in cross-group interactions on the basis of their fear of rejection by the other, while explaining the reluctance of outgroup members to engage in cross-group interactions as evidence of a lack of interest (Shelton & Richeson, 2005).

However, in other cases group status can affect the expectations and concerns that the individual brings to cross-group interactions and thus to the ways these interactions are experienced. In a review of their work, Shelton and Richeson (2006) describe ways in which Whites' (i.e., majority group) concerns about appearing prejudiced, and Blacks' (i.e., minority group) concerns about being the target of *prejudice*, differentially impact the contact experiences of members of these groups. Whites' efforts to appear non-prejudiced can lead them to be more liked by their Black interaction partners. However, the concerns that inspire these efforts also resulted in Whites feeling more *anxiety*, enjoying the interaction less, and being more cognitively depleted by the interaction. Meanwhile, expecting to be the target of prejudice resulted in Blacks enjoying the interaction less, feeling more negative effect, and feeling less authentic during cross-group interactions. Beyond this, research by Vorauer and colleagues (e.g., Vorauer & Turpie, 2004; see also Vorauer, this volume) shows that the strong desire not to appear prejudiced among majority group members who are actually low in prejudice can lead them to engage in hyper-vigilant self-regulatory efforts, which can serve to disrupt their default non-prejudiced thoughts and actions. The result is that they "choke" during cross-group interactions and, ironically, end up being less liked by the minority group individual than majority group members who actually do hold more prejudiced attitudes.

Equally ironic, Blacks who believe their partner harbors prejudice towards their group may engage in more socially engaging/affiliative behaviors, such as smiling and showing interest. The result is that their more prejudiced White partner experiences less *anxiety* and more enjoyment of the interaction than would a less prejudiced majority group member (Shelton & Richeson, 2006). Although a full review of this growing and increasingly complex literature on how intra-personal processes can influence cross-group interpersonal interactions is well beyond the scope of this chapter (see Shelton, Richeson, & Vorauer, 2006; West & Dovidio, this volume, for reviews), the broad conclusion that one might draw from this work is that cross-group interactions, although generally positive in terms of improving intergroup attitudes, can be complicated, psychologically demanding, and fraught with potential for miscommunication and misunderstanding.

Individual-level factors

At the level of the individual, it is not surprising that previous negative experiences with outgroup members can undermine future comfortable cross-group interactions. Experiences during past intergroup interactions predict the level of anxiety experienced during subsequent cross-group contact (e.g., Devine, Evett, & Vasquez-Suson, 1996; Stephan & Stephan, 1985). In turn, heightened anxiety can lead one to perceive outgroup members as very dissimilar to oneself and to see intergroup interactions as extremely difficult (Britt, Boniecki, Vescio, Biernat, & Brown, 1996). Apprehension about possible rejection by outgroup members, what Mendoza-Denton and colleagues have labeled *race-based rejection sensitivity* (Mendoza-Denton, Downey, Purdie, Davis, & Pietrzak, 2002), can lead minority group members to be overly vigilant for cues of prejudice and discrimination in cross-group interactions, leading to behaviors that are more affective and reactive, and to a general preference to avoid cross-group interactions altogether.

Thus, questions of how and why cross-group interactions can lead to more positive views of the outgroup and its members remain central to the psychological study of intergroup relations. Moreover, despite clear evidence of positive changes since Allport's initial theorizing, intergroup inequality and negative intergroup relations remain a critical issue across most societies, and it behooves us to continue to consider when and how some people are able to negotiate the obstacles and reap the benefits of cross-group contact.

The special nature of friendship contact

One of the key recent milestones in the understanding of cross-group contact came when Tom Pettigrew (1997), reporting on data from a large international European survey, pointed to the "special importance" of friendship as the most effective form of intergroup contact. Survey data spanning four European nations showed that having a cross-group friend was strongly associated with positive outgroup attitudes, much more so than having an acquaintance or co-worker from the outgroup. Pointing out that friendship involves longer-term contact and powerful affective connections that should inspire prejudice reduction, Pettigrew (1998) initially proposed that cross-group friendship (i.e., "friendship potential") should be added to Allport's original list as a fifth essential condition. We (Wright & van der Zande, 1999; Wright, Brody, & Aron, 2005) made an even stronger case for friendship, claiming that none of the previously described "necessary" and "facilitating" conditions are essential and that all should be understood to be conditions that improve the likelihood that contact will lead to feelings of interpersonal closeness and that these feelings are the primary determinant of effective cross-group contact. Pettigrew and Tropp (2006) have since demonstrated empirically that no specific condition need be considered essential, that even Allport's original conditions should be understood as merely facilitators. Our view is that what these situational conditions facilitate is a sense of interpersonal closeness.

In the decade that followed Pettigrew's (1997) initial investigation, a growing number of studies began to focus directly on cross-group friendship (e.g., Aberson, Shoemaker, & Tomolillo, 2004; Eller & Abrams, 2003; Jacobson & Johnson, 2006; Levin, van Laar, & Sidanius, 2003; McLaughlin-Volpe, Aron, Wright, & Reis, 2002; Page-Gould, Mendoza-Denton, & Tropp, 2008; R.N. Turner, Hewstone, & Voci, 2007; Wright, Aron, & Tropp, 2002). Pettigrew and Tropp (2006) analyzed a subset of studies in their large meta-analysis that specifically identified cross-group friendships, showing that contact that involved a close relationship typically yields larger positive effects than other forms of contact. More recently, Davies, Tropp, and colleagues (2011) expanded on this work by conducting a meta-analysis that focused specifically on studies that involved cross-group friendship. An extensive search process yielded a total of 135 individual studies. Of these 135 studies (with 208 individual samples, and 501 individual tests), more than half were conducted since the Pettigrew and Tropp meta-analysis. This analysis yielded effect sizes (mean $r = .258$ at the study level, $.236$ at the sample level, and $.236$ at the test level) very similar to those found for friendship in the Pettigrew and Tropp (2006) meta-analysis (e.g., mean r of $.246$ at the test level). The most reasonable conclusion appears to be that cross-group friendships do, in fact, represent a special kind of contact, one that has a particularly strong impact on intergroup attitudes. (More detailed findings from this work are presented at the end of the next section of this chapter.)

Building on this idea, researchers have sought to determine the underlying processes that might explain the special power of friendship to improve intergroup attitudes (see Brown & Hewstone, 2005; Davies et al., 2011; Wright, 2009; Wright et al., 2005). In this chapter, we will focus on two classes of mechanisms: (a) several that we will describe as intimacy-related mechanisms, and (b) mechanisms involving changes in one's perceptions of intergroup norms. However, before turning to these mechanisms, we will examine briefly the nature and psychological meaning of friendship.

The meaning of "friendship"

Friendship is an aspect of life that is highly valued by most people. In a study assessing beliefs about "what makes life meaningful" almost all respondents included friendship (Klinger, 1977). Fehr and Russell (1991) found that when asked to identify types of love, participants listed friendship more frequently than any other relationship. Thus, there is considerable consensus that friendships are important, but what do people mean when they call someone a "friend"? Tesch and Martin (1983) investigated how people define their friendships, and found that many responses addressed issues of reciprocity (i.e., dependability, caring, commitment and trust); others included discussions of compatibility, openness, acceptance and similarity; followed by descriptions of the individual as a good role model or as unique; finally others considered issues relating to time spent together. Furthermore, Tesch and Martin found few disparities in response content based on demographic factors such as age, gender or marital status, indicating that while friendship may involve a variety of features, people generally hold similar notions about what constitutes a friend.

The behaviors undertaken among friends clearly differ from those between strangers and acquaintances. Compared to interactions with strangers, interactions with friends are experienced as more valuable, and include more laughing, talking, and negative criticism and blame (Jormakka, 1976); are of higher communication quality and greater mutual control (Duck, Rutt, Hurst, & Strejc, 1991); and contain more expressions of both agreement and disagreement (Gottman, 1983). Friendship has also been clearly distinguished from general acquaintanceship. Compared to acquaintanceships, friendships include greater perceptions of cohesiveness between partners (Hindy, 1980). They involve more disclosure, greater trust, and more secrets and promises kept (Rotenberg, 1986); more positive comments directed at the partner and greater supportiveness (Berndt & Perry, 1986); greater reciprocity of positive behavior (Lederberg, Rosenblatt, Vandell, & Chapin, 1987); and greater mutuality and matching of affective expressions (Newcomb & Brady, 1982).

Duck (1983) has outlined various benefits of friendships, which include feelings of belonging, emotional integrity and stability, opportunities to talk about ourselves, assistance and support, reassurance of growth, opportunities to help and feel valuable, and finally, personality support (i.e., support of personal values and beliefs). According to Rubin (1985), "friends have a powerful effect on the development of a full, coherent, and satisfactory sense of self" (p. 12). She asserts that friendships allow us to test aspects of our identity. That is, friends are comfortable being honest in responding to our self-presentational efforts, and thus can provide useful information about who we are (and should be). Friendships can also help us to engage desired goals and pursue personal aspirations. Thus, we may attempt to befriend those who help us become the type of person we strive to be (see also Zhou & Wright, 2011). Friendships therefore create an opportunity for people to grow as individuals, and lead fuller, more satisfying lives.

In summary, friendships represent an enormously important element of human social life. They serve critical personal and social functions and thus most of us are

206 Kristin Davies et al.

highly motivated to seek and cultivate these relationships. Given this, those who study these relationships would probably not find it particularly surprising that when friendships do form across group boundaries they are particularly effective at altering the individual's understanding of their social as well as their personal world. In addition, given the recent focus within the friendship literature on the role that friendships play in defining and changing the self, it also appears that this literature might provide important insights into *why* friendship might be particularly effective in altering intergroup attitudes. Thus, we believe that the friendship literature will continue to be a very valuable source of novel ideas for research on intergroup relations generally and cross-group contact specifically. We turn now to research that has begun to investigate this connection, taking a closer look at potential connections between interpersonal processes and improved intergroup attitudes.

How or why does friendship improve intergroup attitudes? Intimacy-related mechanisms

An explanation for how cross-group contact can lead to improved attitudes about an entire outgroup must deal with the question of how the positive impressions and feelings that are developed for the single individual – the contact partner – can be transferred from that single individual to the outgroup as a whole. Given the powerful affective features of friendship (e.g., closeness, trust), it perhaps comes as no surprise that researchers (e.g., Paolini, Hewstone, Voci, Harwood, & Cairns, 2006; Pettigrew, 1998) have proposed that improved intergroup attitudes emerge when the strong affective bonds felt for the cross-group friend are "generalized" to the friend's group as a whole. This claim is consistent with evidence that stronger contact effects are found for measures of intergroup attitudes that focus on affect and emotions felt for the outgroup, as compared to measures that focus on more cognitive components of these attitudes (e.g., stereotypes); (see Pettigrew & Tropp, 2006; Tropp & Pettigrew, 2005). However, to say that positive affect is "generalized" from the individual to the group as a whole seems to address *what* is generalized, but still seems to leave unanswered the question of *how* and *why* this generalization occurs.

Inclusion of the outgroup in the self

In our own writing on this issue (Aron, McLaughlin-Volpe, Mashek, Lewandowski, Wright, & Aron, 2005; Brody, Wright, Aron, & McLaughlin-Volpe, 2008; Wright, 1997, 2009; Wright et al., 2002, 2005), we have proposed that one answer to this critical question can be provided by theorizing on the "inclusion of other in the self" (IOS), (A. Aron, E.N. Aron, Tudor, & Nelson, 2004; A. Aron, Mashek, & E.N. Aron, 2004). According to this model, as one develops feelings of closeness towards another person, one's cognitive representation of the self comes to overlap (share elements or activation potentials) with the cognitive representation of the friend, so that, along with other aspects of the friend, the friend's identities are treated to some extent as one's own. When the friend is an outgroup member, one of the available identities that can be included in the self is his/her group membership. Thus, through the interpersonal connection with an individual outgroup member (i.e., the inclusion of him/her in the self), the outgroup can become, to some extent, included in the self as well. There has been considerable correlational and experimental support for the central notions of this model, suggesting that subjective feelings of intimacy for another are associated with the inclusion of their resources, perspectives, and identities in the self (see A. Aron et al., 2004). Following this logic, in the case of cross-group friendships, it becomes probable that this inclusion could generalize from the outgroup individual to the outgroup as a whole.

Initial evidence of this possibility comes from a series of studies by McLaughlin-Volpe et al. (2002). In a first study, participants reported attitudes towards three target outgroups, as well as feelings of closeness for members of each of the outgroups. In this work, "closeness" was assessed using Aron, Aron, and Smollan's (1992) "Inclusion of Other in the Self" scale; a series of increasingly overlapping pairs of circles is depicted, with one circle representing "self" and the second representing "other" (in this case outgroup friend), and respondents select the pair of circles that they feel best represents their particular relationship. Findings revealed that high levels of closeness with one's closest outgroup friend *predicted* more positive attitudes for the entire outgroup of the friend. Furthermore, an additional study by the researchers revealed that a significant positive relationship between inclusion of an outgroup member in the self and positive attitude towards the outgroup remained significant even when the quantity of contact (i.e., number of cross-group interactions) was controlled for statistically. An interaction of contact quantity by closeness was also discovered, indicating that when closeness (i.e., IOS) to an outgroup interaction partner was high, having greater interactions was associated with having more positive attitudes towards the outgroup, but when closeness (i.e., IOS) to the partner was low, more interactions was associated with less positive attitudes.

Importantly, the theory also proposes that as the other is increasingly experienced as part of the self, the other is also treated more as one treats oneself (e.g., sharing valued resources, feeling pride in their accomplishments and sadness at their losses, etc.); (A. Aron, Mashek, & E.N. Aron, 2004). It follows then that as the outgroup is increasingly included in the self, it will also be experienced and treated more like the self (e.g., if the friend's group is threatened, one feels personally threatened; if the friend's group is supported, one feels personally supported). Thus, the transfer of positive thoughts, feelings and actions from the individual outgroup friend to the outgroup as a whole can be traced to a basic psychological process that accompanies the development of interpersonal closeness – the inclusion of the other in the self.

Self-disclosure

Another intimacy-related mechanism that has been shown to underlie the relationship between cross-group friendship and intergroup attitudes is *self-disclosure*.

Self-disclosure involves sharing with the other intimate and personal information that would not otherwise be easily known or discovered (Miller, 2002). Self-disclosure has been deemed "the primary route through which people develop intimacy in their relationships" (Fehr, 2004, p. 16; see also Altman & Taylor, 1973; Reis & Shaver, 1988). In a study investigating people's lay theories of prototypical friendship interactions, Fehr (2004) found that behaviors that involved social support and those describing self-disclosure (e.g., "If I talk, my friend will listen") were rated as most likely to produce a sense of intimacy. Importantly, the sharing of self-relevant information can also play a role in translating the positive feelings felt for the single outgroup friend into more positive attitudes about the outgroup as a whole. First, because self-disclosure appears to be central to the development and maintenance of strong feelings of interpersonal closeness, it may be critical in creating the self-other overlap that results from the inclusion of the other in the self, which, as described in the previous section, can lead to the inclusion of the outgroup in the self. Thus, self-disclosure may play an indirect role in the generalization process through its role in promoting the inclusion of the other in the self.

Given its critical import in the development of intimacy and feelings of closeness, it is perhaps not surprising that experimental research designed to test the impact of closeness in cross-group relationships on intergroup attitudes has often employed procedures that directly involve self-disclosure. For example, most of our own experimental research (e.g., Davies, Aron, Wright, Brody, & McLaughlin-Volpe, 2011; Wright et al., 2002, 2005) has used a closeness generation method developed by Aron and colleagues (A. Aron, Melinat, E.N. Aron, Vallone, & Bator, 1997) that has come to be known as the "Fast Friends Procedure." The procedure involves partners taking turns responding to a series of cards, the majority of which require that they answer questions that result in gradually escalating levels of self-disclosure. This procedure has been shown to be effective at producing strong feelings of interpersonal closeness between strangers in as little as 45 minutes, and has been employed in studies investigating a variety of topics including college adjustment among minority students (Mendoza-Denton & Page-Gould, 2008), hormonal effects of closeness (Brown et al., 2009), social anxiety (Kashdan & Roberts, 2006), and interpersonal cooperation (Cohen, Wildschut, & Insko, 2010).

Although we have supplemented this procedure with additional activities and sessions in some of our research (see Wright et al., 2005), there is evidence that the Fast Friends procedure can produce meaningful feelings of friendships between members of different ethnic groups in the laboratory (Wright, 2009), in interventions run in large class-room settings (Davies et al., 2011), and between police officers and community members in an intervention run during a "Citizen's Police Academy" program (e.g., Davies, Aron, Wright, Eberhardt, & Bergsieker, 2007). In every case, when intergroup attitudes were assessed as much as 4 weeks later, those partnered with an outgroup member (vs. those partnered with an ingroup member) were more positive about the outgroup. Page-Gould et al. (2008) have also used a friendship generating procedure that is very similar to the one we developed (Wright et al., 2002) and included the Fast Friends procedure. Their research shows that the resulting feelings of cross-group friendship can ameliorate feelings of intergroup anxiety and open the door for the development of intergroup trust and increase subsequent cross-group interactions. Given the critical role of mutual self-disclosure in the Fast Friends procedure, it appears that this sharing of important personal information may very well be a critical determinant of the positive change in intergroup attitudes found in all these studies.

Further evidence of the importance of self-disclosure was also found in our recent meta-analysis (Davies et al., 2011). One of the primary purposes of this work was to illuminate the mechanisms that might underpin the friendship-to-intergroup attitudes relationship by identifying precisely *which* aspects of friendship appear to be most strongly related to positive intergroup attitudes. To do this, we considered a variety of friendship assessments common in the intergroup contact literature, and examined whether these different operationalizations of cross-group "friendship" might produce different friendship/prejudice effect sizes. The results showed that measures of the intensity of behavioral interaction, like the amount of *self-disclosure* and *time spent* with outgroup friends, yielded larger friendship/positive intergroup attitude effects than assessment of the subjective experience of friendship (e.g., measures of felt closeness) or measures that assessed more quantitative aspects such as number or percentage of outgroup friends. Thus, this meta-analytic review pointed to the particular behaviors like self-disclosure as the means by which cross-group friendships improve intergroup attitudes. These behavioral aspects may be particularly important because time spent and level of self-sharing may each capture the individual's *engagement* in the relationship (see Fehr, 1996; Hays, 1984), and the degree to which he or she sees the friendship as valuable (see van Dick et al., 2004).

Other researchers have proposed and demonstrated additional routes by which self-disclosure might mediate the friendship/intergroup attitude relationship. For example, Miller and Ensari (e.g., Ensari & Miller, 2002; Miller, 2002) have proposed and tested a Personalization Model of contact that describes self-disclosure as a key process that promotes familiarity and individuation of the cross-group interaction partner. They theorize that this reduces the anxiety and discomfort that usually accompany intergroup interactions, which improves the processing of individuating information and decreases the degree to which negative outgroup stereotypes play a role in the interaction. In addition, they also describe an important role for trust. The logic is that receiving self-disclosing information implies that the discloser not only likes but also trusts the recipient of that disclosure. These perceived expressions of liking and trust lead to reciprocation of that liking and trust. Thus, according to this model, self-disclosure impacts intergroup attitudes in a number of ways including reducing anxiety, reducing stereotyping, and building trust. Similarly, R.N. Turner et al. (2007) found support for a model in which greater self-disclosure in cross-group friendships led to higher reported *empathy* for and *trust* of outgroup members, and increased the belief that contact with the outgroup is important. These, in turn, led to improved intergroup attitudes.

Finally, Shelton, Trail, West, and Bergsieker (2010) provide an interesting additional observation, pointing out that in cross-group interactions it may be

210 Kristin Davies et al.

particularly important to consider not only the degree of self-disclosure by individual partners but also their perceptions that the other is responsive to their overtures. That is, because trust, anxiety, and the possibility of rejection are especially high in cross-group interactions, not only how much one discloses but how positively responsive one's interaction partner seems, may be critical in determining whether these acts of self-disclosure strengthen or weaken trust and positive impressions of the outgroup member and the outgroup as a whole. This notion is consistent with the model of intimacy described by Reis and Shaver (1988), who argue that the impact of self-disclosure on intimacy depends upon the perceived responsiveness of the individual to whom one is self-disclosing.

In short, the mutual sharing of personal information has been shown not only to be evidence of a close interpersonal relationship, but also to be one of the key building blocks in the development, strengthening, and maintenance of closeness. However, most relevant to the current discussion, self-disclosure in cross-group relationships may also be critical in the process of generalizing interpersonal liking to improved attitudes towards the outgroup as a whole.

Potential relationships between cross-group friendships and intergroup norms

Thus far, we have considered cross-group friendships and how the intimacy that exists between friends might account for the positive impact that this form of contact has on intergroup attitudes. However, cross-group friendships can also influence an individual's perception of how members of her/his own group and members of the outgroup think about and relate to (or ought to relate to) members of the other group. In other words, cross-group friendships may provide new information about intergroup norms held by both the ingroup and the friend's group. In fact, the concept of group norms has been described in numerous theoretical accounts of cross-group contact (see Pettigrew, 1991, 1998), where norms are described as playing a variety of roles in the contact/intergroup attitudes relationship. We will first explore some of this theorizing about the numerous potential roles played by group norms in the relationship between cross-group friendship and intergroup attitude change. Second, we will introduce the concept of *extended contact*, a form of indirect cross-group contact in which the mere knowledge that an ingroup member has a close personal relationship with a member of the outgroup can lead to more positive attitudes about that outgroup. Here we will describe how changing perceptions of ingroup and outgroup norms may be a critical process that allows cross-group friendships to improve the attitudes not only of the friendship partners but of other group members who merely observe or even simply know about these relationships.

Norms are a group's shared understanding of the actions, thoughts, values and beliefs that a good member engages in or holds – "descriptive" or "informal" norms – or *should* engage in or hold – "injunctive" or "formal" norms (Cialdini, Kallgren, & Reno, 1991; Pettigrew, 1991). Various theoretical accounts of cross-group contact have proposed a number of functions that group norms may serve in determining whether and when cross-group interactions will lead to positive attitude change. However, to our knowledge, no single account has attempted to document and consider these many potential roles.

First, it is worth recognizing that norms can be considered in two different ways. The first is what might be called the actual or perhaps "objective" group norms, and the second is the individual's subjective perceptions of group norms. The former refers to observable consistency in the thoughts, values, and actions of a group that distinguish it from others. Groups, from large cultural groups to small friendship groups, develop idiosyncratic rules that guide members to demonstrate specific patterns of thoughts and actions that define and demonstrate their membership in that group. Although no group norm is universally followed by all members, there are measurable group-based differences in everything from clothing choice, to beliefs about what is funny, to how to raise a child. These normative rules are often followed by group members with little or no thought or consideration. In fact, in some cases, these normative ways of thinking and acting can be so widely shared within the ingroup that they come to be understood as just *the way* one thinks and behaves; they are not only "normal" they are simply the only way.

However, group norms need not go entirely unexamined; many are explicitly considered and intentionally followed. Group members are often well aware of their group's idiosyncrasies, and can compare their group's ways of thinking and acting to that of other groups. Group norms are often used as a means of differentiating the ingroup from the outgroup; defining "our" norms as superior to those of the outgroup provides a source of positive social comparisons. In addition, new members of the group will actively seek to fit in by intentionally learning and following the normative rules. Similarly, when one is unsure how to think and act in response to an unfamiliar situation, one will look to members of a relevant ingroup in an effort to determine what thoughts, feelings or actions are appropriate. Thus, group norms not only exist in an "objective" sense as measurable cross-group differences, they are also considered and understood by the individual members. It is these psychological manifestations of norms, the individual's perception of what a good member does (or ought to do), that will guide his/her thoughts and actions.

Much of the current theorizing about how norms influence intergroup relations is rooted in Self-Categorization Theory (J.C. Turner, Hogg, Oakes, Reicher, & Wetherell, 1987; J.C. Turner & Oakes, 1989; see also Terry & Hogg, 1996). Self-Categorization Theory shares with its predecessor Social Identity Theory (Tajfel & Turner, 1979) the critical differentiation between *personal identity* and *collective identity*. One's personal identity includes those aspects of the self-concept that define one as a unique and separate individual and includes personal characteristics and attributes. Collective identity, on the other hand, includes those aspects of the self that bind us and make us similar to others: our group memberships.

Self-Categorization Theory and Social Identity Theory use this distinction between personal and collective identities to elaborate a distinction between interpersonal and intergroup behavior, with interpersonal behavior being thoughts and actions that occur when one is focused on the personal identities of oneself and one's interactions partner. Conversely, intergroup behavior occurs when thoughts and actions are guided by recognition of the different group memberships of the self and those one is interacting with. Thus, when my group memberships are the salient self-representation, through a process of *self-stereotyping*, I take on the characteristic beliefs and actions of the ingroup, and I will respond as a good member of my group does or should (e.g., Jetten, Spears, & Manstead, 1997). Self-Categorization Theory also provides an explanation of how one comes to understand what the ingroup norms are. When a collective identity is salient, other ingroup members are seen to be interchangeable with self. As a result, relevant ingroup members can provide information about what I believe and how I behave. This process has been called *referent informational influence* (J.C. Turner, Wetherell, & Hogg, 1989). In other words, during intergroup interactions my thoughts and actions will be guided by my understanding of the relevant ingroup norms for interactions with members of the other group, and I often determine what these norms are by observing available ingroup members.

Likewise, these cross-group interactions are also guided by the actor's perceptions of outgroup norms. When group memberships are salient not only is the self understood in terms of my group membership, but the other is also represented in terms of his or her group membership. He or she is seen as an interchangeable prototype of the outgroup. Therefore, my expectations about how he or she is going to respond are determined by my beliefs about what is normative for a member of the outgroup. Thus, intergroup behavior is determined by actors' understanding of how *we* and *they* behave, that is, by what the actors believe is normative for the ingroup and the outgroup.

The multiple roles of group norms in cross-group contact

Given their prominent place in theorizing about intergroup relations (see Terry & Hogg, 2000) and their powerful influence on prejudice and intergroup behavior (see Crandall & Stangor, 2005; Stangor, Sechrist, & Jost, 2001), it is perhaps not surprising that norms have been mentioned as important contributors in a number of places in the relationship between cross-group contact and changes in intergroup attitudes. First, norms can be seen as antecedents that allow for the possibility that members of the two groups will engage in contact at all. Second, perceptions of both ingroup and outgroup norms can *moderate* the contact-prejudice effect, influencing whether a cross-group interaction will ultimately result in friendly feelings and prejudice reduction or not. Third, changes in perceptions of group norms have been described as a *mediator* of the contact-prejudice reduction effect. That is, positive contact produces changes in an individual's perception of ingroup and outgroup norms, and it is these changes that produce more positive intergroup attitudes. Finally, changing the individual's perception of the outgroup norms could be seen as an outcome itself, in that beliefs about what is normative for outgroup members can be seen as one part of what it means to be prejudiced.

Norms as antecedents to cross-group contact

The evidence for the general effectiveness of cross-group friendships to reduce prejudice is all but indisputable (e.g., Pettigrew & Tropp, 2006). However, what is less clear is why one would actively pursue the kinds of cross-group interactions that might actually lead to forming a friendship. This apparently critical question has received relatively little attention (see Esses & Dovidio, 2002, for an exception). Although much of our own work on this question has focused on intrapersonal motivations based on A. Aron and E.N. Aron's (1986) self-expansion model (see Wright, A. Aron, & Tropp, 2002), another clear candidate for a variable that should help to inspire positive cross-group interactions is ingroup norms. For example, Wright and Tropp (2005) investigated the impact of bilingual education on the attitudes and behavior of White English-speaking children. We found that compared to children in English-only classes, White children in bilingual classrooms not only demonstrated more positive attitudes towards Latino children, but also indicated greater interest in forming cross-group friendships. We interpreted this greater interest in befriending unfamiliar outgroup members as resulting in part from the more positive intergroup norms that emerge when both English and Spanish are used in the classroom. When the actions of the teacher and the classroom curriculum itself suggest that interactions between Whites and Latinos should be respectful and mutually helping, these messages about what is normative should foster a genuine interest in interactions with outgroup members.

Similarly, Tropp and Bianchi (2006) showed that perceptions of outgroup norms may also influence interest in cross-group interactions. In two studies involving ethnic minority students, they showed that interest in contact with majority group members was predicted by the degree to which the minority student perceived "valuing diversity" to be a normative attitude among majority group members (see also Pettigrew, Christ, Wagner, & Stellmacher, 2007). Thus, the first role for intergroup norms appears to be one of preparing the ground for cross-group interactions to occur in the first place. Messages that ingroup and outgroup norms support positive intergroup attitudes and cross-group interactions should increase motivation to engage in the kind of social interactions that should facilitate friendships.

In an effort to explore the development of cross-group friendships and to contrast this with the development of same-group friendships, we surveyed nearly 300 participants spanning a wide age range and representing a variety of ethnic backgrounds, all of whom currently had a cross-race friendship (Davies, 2009). Half the participants were asked to complete the survey reporting on their cross-race friendship, and the other half were asked to complete the same items reporting on a same-race friendship. They completed items tapping *recollections* of the support provided by ingroup and outgroup members during the *early* stages of the development of the friendships, as well as items tapping the *current* quality of the friendship and their intergroup attitudes. A number of the findings provide evidence of the importance of normative support not only during the formation of cross-race relationships but also in determining the quality of these relationships and the individual's intergroup attitudes down the line.

Among those describing a cross-race friendship, recollections of how much support was provided by one's own family (ingroup norms) and the partner's family (outgroup norms) predicted the participants' recalled feelings of closeness during the early stages of the relationship. However, importantly, these measures of recollections of ingroup support also predicted *current* feelings of closeness and the number of *current* friendship activities. Furthermore, a measure tapping recollections of more general support from the outgroup for the relationship (e.g., "other people from (the friend's) group would make the relationship difficult") showed that a perceived lack of outgroup support was associated with greater ingroup bias on a measure of *current* feelings or warmth for the ingroup and the outgroup (i.e., difference in warmth felt for own group versus friend's group). Finally, recalling greater support for a cross-race friendship by one's own family (ingroup norms) was associated with greater sympathy and admiration for the outgroup.

In comparing same-race and cross-race friendship development, we found that only for those describing a cross-race friendship were recollections that one's inner social circle (ingroup) initially approved of the friendship partner related to current *enjoyment of time* spent and *feeling comfortable* with the friend. When describing a same-race friendship the initial approval of one's social circle had a minimal (and non-significant) effect on these measures of current friendship quality. Similarly, recalling early family support for the relationship was more strongly related to current feelings of trust for the partner, for those describing a cross-race as compared to a same-race friendship. In other words, approval of one's social group appeared to have much less influence on friendship development and quality of *same-race* friendships, but was very important for the development and quality of a *cross-race* friendship.

Of course, these data are retrospective and correlational and future experimental research would be particularly helpful in untangling cause and effect relationships. However, it appears from the data currently available that perceptions of group norms (both ingroup and outgroup) may have an important influence on how (and perhaps whether) cross-group friendships develop and flourish.

It is important to recognize, however, that norms can produce precisely the opposite effect. Crandall, Eshleman, and O'Brien (2002) have shown quite convincingly that when ingroup norms support a negative representation of the outgroup, people will express more prejudice and direct more discriminatory actions towards the outgroup (see also Crandall & Stangor, 2005). It seems reasonable to assume that these negative norms would also serve to reduce interest and engagement in the kinds of positive interactions that would lead to cross-group friendships. In fact, even if the individual did not share the normative negative attitudes of the ingroup, the social pressure to conform might prevent positive social interactions in the absence of individual negative attitudes.

Norms as a moderator of contact effects

Exactly how specific beliefs about outgroup norms will influence the individual's behavior during cross-group interactions is a complex and interesting question in and of itself (see our description of *group-level factors* that influence contact effectiveness earlier in the chapter). However, what is clear is that the content of the individual's beliefs about the normative beliefs, attitudes, and behaviors of the outgroup will influence the quality of cross-group interactions and thus the likelihood that these interactions will lead to the development of relationships that will then improve intergroup attitudes. In fact, Vorauer and her colleagues (e.g., Vorauer & Turpie, 2004; see also Shelton et al., 2006) have shown that cross-group interactions are often influenced as much or more by what we believe "they" think about "our" group (i.e., meta-stereotypes) than the stereotypes *we* hold about the outgroup. So, for example, White majority group members can be made very uncomfortable and ineffective in interactions with members of an ethnic minority group if they believe that members of that minority group think that Whites are racists. These perceptions of the normative beliefs of minority group members set in motion cognitive and emotional processes (anxiety, social concerns, self-focused attention) that undermine their performance and subjective experience. Similarly, if an African American believes that it is normative for Whites to be prejudiced and discriminate against Blacks, this perception of negative outgroup norms can strongly influence their social interactions with Whites. Thus, the beliefs about what is normative for outgroup members that each partner brings to a cross-group contact situation will influence the interaction and thus will moderate the effects of these interactions on subsequent feelings towards the specific outgroup member and attitudes towards the outgroup as a whole.

Another example of this line of reasoning can be traced to Allport's (1954) initial formulation of the contact hypothesis, and particularly to one of his four conditions for "optimal" cross-group contact. Allport proposed that contact would lead to positive attitude change only when it received the active support of relevant local authorities, law, or custom (see Pettigrew & Tropp, 2006). In other words, the presence or absence of this kind of institutional support would moderate the impact of intergroup contact on intergroup attitudes. Although the language is slightly different, "support from local authorities, law, and customs" can easily be conceptualized as "normative support" (see Dovidio et al., 2003). To the degree that the local authorities are respected, they will have formidable power to influence the consensual understanding of what behaviors will be considered acceptable and appropriate for members of the group. Laws and customs reflect formal/injunctive norms. Thus, Allport appears to be describing norms as a moderator of the cross-group contact effects. In their extensive meta-analysis of contact, Pettigrew and Tropp (2006) tested the importance of Allport's four conditions (i.e., a "global test" of just those studies deliberately structuring all four conditions into the contact experience) and found substantial evidence that these conditions did moderate the impact of contact on intergroup attitudes. Specifically, they found particularly strong effects of institutional support, concluding that "further examination of Allport's conditions suggests that institutional support may be an especially important condition for facilitating positive contact effects" (p. 766).

It is not entirely clear whether the normative support for contact that is being described by Allport (1954) and by Pettigrew and Tropp (2006) should be understood to be ingroup norms, outgroup norms, both, or perhaps neither. It is also possible that what is being described is something akin to the concept of a *superordinate category norm*. Self-Categorization Theory (see Turner et al., 1987) points out that the relations between two groups are contained within and determined by their shared membership in a higher-level category. This superordinate category provides the context and norms that set the parameters for social comparisons made between the groups, as well as the range of intergroup behaviors that might be considered. For example, the school, the broader society, the nation, or the international community, set the parameters for interactions between subgroups of students, ethnic groups, regional groups, or nations respectively. To the degree that an ethnic group sees itself as part of a broader society that contains other ethnic groups, its interactions with those other ethnic groups are constrained by what it sees to be the normative rules for that broader society. Thus, perhaps what Allport and others have in mind is that the superordinate category that contains and constrains the two relevant subgroups of interest should be seen to have norms that support positive interactions and attitudes across groups.

Norms as mediators of the contact-prejudice reduction effect

Others have described a different role for norms. Instead of influencing whether contact will occur or whether it will reduce prejudice when it does occur, these researchers propose that the perceptions of group norms will change as a consequence of cross-group contact, and these changes in perceived group norms then influence intergroup attitudes. For example, Feddes, Noack, and Rutland (2009), in a longitudinal study of intergroup relations in a group of German middle schools, found that the number of Turkish friends that German children reported positively predicted their subsequent attitudes towards Turkish children. Importantly, they also measured the children's perceptions of both ingroup and outgroup norms and found that the change in these perceived intergroup norms partially mediated the longitudinal effect of the number of outgroup friends on intergroup attitudes. Using cross-sectional data, Carlson, Wilson, and Hargrave (2003) also examined the relationships between cross-group friendships, intergroup attitudes and perceptions of group norms in several middle schools in Texas with student populations that included primarily Hispanic and Black children or Hispanic and White children. Although they did not directly test the mediational effect of norms on the cross-group friendship-to-intergroup attitude relationship, they did show that perceptions of ingroup norms regarding cross-group contact was a significant predictor of intergroup attitudes, and when perceived ingroup norms was included in a multiple regression equation predicting intergroup attitudes, the number of cross-group friends was no longer a significant predictor.

It makes good sense that changes in perceptions of outgroup norms should mediate that relationship between cross-group friendships and attitudes towards the outgroup. To the degree that the outgroup friend is thought to be prototypical of the larger outgroup, his/her positive attitudes and actions could be interpreted as a demonstration of positive outgroup norms. Furthermore, a close cross-group friendship may also result in increased exposure to the outgroup friend's social network including additional members of the outgroup. To the degree that the "objective" outgroup norms for interacting with members of my group are more positive than I initially imagined (than my initial perceptions of what the outgroup norms were), I should be pleasantly surprised by these interactions and they should lead to a growing confidence that the outgroup is supportive of cross-group friendships and has a generally positive attitude towards the ingroup. Interestingly, this logic again points to the special benefits of friendship over other kinds of cross-group contact. Other forms of contact with outgroup members (e.g., workmates, neighbors, acquaintances) are more likely to be restricted to particular contexts and less likely to involve meeting and interacting with the partner's broader social network. Thus, these other forms of contact, although perhaps pleasant, should be less likely to lead to positive changes in the perceptions of outgroup norms.

The connection between cross-group friendships and changes in ingroup norms is perhaps less obvious. Why should my befriending an outgroup member lead me to believe that my own group holds a more positive view of the outgroup? There appear to be two possibilities for explaining this possibility. The first and most direct means would be through direct observation of the actions of other ingroup members in response to the individual's group friendship with an outgroup member. If she is not ostracized, or is even treated normally and pleasantly by the ingroup even as other members become aware of her friendship with an outgroup member, this could lead her to believe that the ingroup is more positive towards the outgroup and cross-group interactions than previously thought.

The second possible mechanism stems from research on self-anchoring (e.g., Otten & Bar-Tal, 2002; Otten & Epstude, 2006), which shows that under some circumstances we will use knowledge about the self to make inferences about the ingroup. The idea is that because the ingroup is "part of the self", our mental representations of the self and the ingroup overlap (see also Smith, Coats, & Walling, 1999; Tropp & Wright, 2001). One outcome of this, as described earlier, is that when my group membership becomes salient the characteristics of the ingroup become the characteristics of the self (self-stereotyping); (J.C. Turner et al., 1987). However, Otten and colleagues show that the opposite process can also occur, that at times the characteristics of the ingroup can be inferred from the characteristics of the self. That is, I not only assimilate myself to the ingroup, but can also assimilate the ingroup to match my understanding of the self. This process of self-anchoring occurs primarily when there is some degree of uncertainty or ambiguity about the ingroup. Thus, if individuals are unsure about the normative position of the ingroup regarding the outgroup and regarding cross-group friendships, they may use their own improving attitudes about the outgroup as a basis to infer more positive attitudes among the ingroup as a whole. In contrast, if the normative attitudes of the ingroup are widely known and clearly apparent, it is less likely that individuals could use their personal relationships with outgroup members and their own attitudes about the group as a basis for inferring ingroup norms.

Perceptions of outgroup norms as outcomes

One way to think about the perception of outgroup norms is as part of what it means to be prejudiced. Believing that negatively valued traits, beliefs, values and behaviors are normative for the outgroup is to some extent the essence of what it is to be prejudiced. Thus, if engaging in friendly cross-group contact and becoming close to an outgroup member leads one to see positive traits, beliefs, values and behaviors as more normative for the outgroup, one is by definition less prejudiced. We believe that this rather simple recognition that changing perceptions of outgroup norms is in fact prejudice reduction speaks to the critical importance of perceptions of norms in intergroup relations.

Extended contact (having an ingroup friend with a cross-group friendship)

In addition, changing perceptions of group norms has also been described as a critical mediator of at least one form of indirect cross-group contact. More than a decade ago, we proposed that direct personal interactions with an outgroup member might not be necessary to produce the positive changes in intergroup attitudes associated with cross-group contact (Wright et al., 1997). In proposing the extended contact hypothesis, we posited that the mere *knowledge* that an ingroup member has a close relationship with an outgroup member can lead to more positive intergroup attitudes. This type of indirect (or "extended") contact has important implications; it suggests that a relatively small number of cross-group friendships might produce meaningful reductions in prejudice among a much larger number of group members – that everyone need not have their own cross-group friendship for prejudice reduction to occur.

We introduced this idea with evidence from four studies. Two survey studies demonstrated that greater extended contact predicted more positive interethnic attitudes among White, Latino(a), and African American university students. In a "minimal group" experiment, participants were placed in groups based on an arbitrary object-estimation task, before observing an interaction between an ingroup and outgroup member. As predicted, participants who observed a friendly cross-group interaction subsequently evaluated the outgroup more positively than those who observed the neutral or hostile interaction. Finally, using a "mini-robbers cave" (very broadly modeled on the classic Sherif study); (Sherif, Harvey, White, Hood, & Sherif, 1961), we showed that after several hours in which ingroup solidarity and cross-group conflict were first created, the creation of a single positive cross-group relationship resulted in all group members reporting more positive attitudes and engaging in more positive behaviors toward the opposing group.

Subsequent research has supported these initial findings with numerous groups including Catholics and Protestants in Northern Ireland (Paolini, Hewstone, Cairns, & Voci, 2004), Germans' attitudes towards "foreigners" and Muslims (Pettigrew et al., 2007), White and South Asian high school students in Britain (R.N. Turner et al., 2007), and German and Turkish school children (Feddes et al., 2009).

Intervention studies have shown that extended contact can prevent the worsening of intergroup attitudes and in some cases improve attitudes among children towards immigrants (Liebkind & McAlister, 1999), children with disabilities (Cameron & Rutland, 2006), and ethnic outgroups and refugees (Cameron, Rutland, Brown, & Douch, 2006). Extended contact has even proven effective among authoritarian individuals, who report significantly less prejudice towards homosexuals when they have more heterosexual friends with homosexuals friends (Hodson, Harry, & Mitchell, 2009).

We initially proposed a number of mechanisms that might be responsible for the effectiveness of extended contact, and subsequent research has also provided support for these mechanisms (e.g., R.N. Turner et al., 2007; Wright et al., 2008) and suggested several others (e.g., Mazziotta, Mummendey, & Wright, 2011). For example, it appears that observing a cross-group friendship can reduce the anxiety that often accompanies thoughts about interacting with the outgroup and that this reduction in anxiety partially accounts for subsequent reductions in prejudice (e.g., R.N. Turner et al., 2007). In addition, the *inclusion of the outgroup in the self* mechanism described earlier in this chapter to explain direct cross-group friendships can be adapted to explain extended contact as well (e.g., Aron et al., 2005; Wright, 2009). The idea is that extended contact initiates a "transitive inclusion process", which works as follows: People spontaneously include ingroup members in the self because of their shared group membership (see Tropp & Wright, 2001; Smith et al., 1999). Observers spontaneously treat partners in a close relationship as a single cognitive unit (e.g., Sedikides, Olsen, & Reis, 1993). Therefore, the ingroup member in a cross-group friendship is to some degree part of the observer's self, and the outgroup member is understood to be part of that ingroup member's self, thus connecting the outgroup member to the self through his/her relationship with the ingroup member. If the outgroup member's group membership is salient and he or she is seen as a representative of the outgroup, this allows for the outgroup to be part of the self as well. This logic is consistent with Heider's (1958) balance theory. If unit relations exist between self and ingroup, between ingroup member and ingroup, between ingroup member and outgroup friend, and between outgroup friend and the outgroup, then a unit relationship exists between self and the outgroup (see also Andersen & Chen, 2002).

However, in introducing the concept of extended contact (Wright et al., 1997), we also proposed that another key mechanism by which knowledge of other ingroup members' cross-group friendships would improve intergroup attitudes was through *referent informational influence* and perception of ingroup norms. Observing the pleasant and supportive actions of an ingroup member involved in a cross-group friendship could lead observers to assume that ingroup norms support this kind of positive intergroup interactions. If the relevant group membership is salient and that particular collective identity is self-defining, the actions and apparent attitudes of the ingroup member should serve as a model for how the individual should think and act. Thus, changes in perceived ingroup norms resulting from extended contact should result in similar changes in one's own attitudes and actions towards that outgroup.

Similarly, observation of friendly behaviors of an outgroup member interacting with an ingroup member may serve to modify existing perceptions of *outgroup norms*. Often there is a perception that the outgroup holds negative views of the ingroup (e.g., Vorauer & Turpie, 2004) and that members of the outgroup are relatively uninterested in interacting with ingroup members (e.g., Shelton & Richeson, 2005). To the degree that the outgroup member involved in the observed cross-group friendship is seen to be representative of the outgroup, his or her actions may serve to undermine these perceptions of negative outgroup norms.

Importantly, the possibility of changing perceived group norms based on the behavior of particular individuals hinges on the salience of those individuals' group memberships. Whether we are talking about direct personal contact with an outgroup member or extended contact, if the group memberships of self and others are not prominently held in mind, then the actions of self and others will not be interpreted in group terms, and thus will not influence one's perception of group norms. Importantly, Wright and colleagues (1997) suggested that compared to one's own direct cross-group interactions, where the interaction is likely to involve both personal and collective identities, observing the cross-group interactions of others is likely to make group memberships particularly salient. Thus, extended contact may have an even stronger effect than direct personal contact on the perceptions of both ingroup and outgroup norms (see also Hewstone & Brown, 1986).

R.N. Turner, Hewstone, Voci, and Vonofakou (2008) investigated the role of intergroup norms as a mediator of the extended contact. In two studies, involving students at school or university, they found that awareness of others' cross-group friendships was associated with more positive perceptions of ingroup norms concerning the outgroup, which were in turn associated with more positive feelings for the outgroup. In fact, perceptions of ingroup norms was the most powerful mediator of the extended contact effect in both of these studies. They also found that extended contact was associated with more positive perceptions of outgroup norms concerning the ingroup, which were in turn associated with more positive attitudes towards the outgroup.

In a recent extension of this work, Sharp, Voci, and Hewstone (2011) investigated the possibility that one's own personal characteristics may influence how susceptible one may be to referent informational influence and the impact of norms. Along with measures of extended contact, direct contact and feeling thermometer ratings for two outgroups (Asians and gay men), the authors also instructed White university student participants to complete questionnaires assessing public self-consciousness (e.g., "I'm concerned about the way I present myself to others"; Fenigstein, Scheier, & Buss, 1975) and social comparison (e.g., "If I want to learn more about something, I try to find out what others think about it"; Gibbons & Buunk, 1999). The results of this innovative study indicated that although public self-consciousness played no role in the extended contact effect, a moderation effect was found such that extended contact was only associated with warmth for outgroups when social comparison was high.

We have recently replicated the basic extended contact effect in a study investigating attitudes of heterosexual university students towards gay men (Wright,

Davies, & Sanders, 2011), and like R.N. Turner et al. (2008) we focused on the mediating role of ingroup norms in explaining the impact of extended contact on attitudes towards the outgroup. Further, this research considered several different conceptualizations of ingroup norms. Perceived ingroup norms were measured in terms of how much the participant believed that most heterosexuals: a) accepted gay relationships, b) had positive feelings towards gay men, or c) approved of cross-group friendships with gay men. The results showed that each of these measures alone was a significant mediator of the effect of extended contact on attitudes towards gay men. When all three specific ingroup norms were included together in the analysis, both the perception that the ingroup had positive feelings towards gay men and that the ingroup approved of cross-group friendship, were significant independent mediators of the extended contact/intergroup attitude relationships. Thus, it appears that in some intergroup relationships there may be a number of relevant specific ingroup norms, and that some of these may have somewhat independent roles as mediators of the effect of extended contact on intergroup attitudes.

A second recent investigation of the mediating role of perceived ingroup norms in the extended contact effect (Comeau, 2010), replicated and extended existing findings. A survey of White, Chinese, and South Asian university students in Vancouver, Canada included measures of extended contact across ethnic groups, level of identification with their ethnic ingroup, perceptions of ingroup norms, and several measures of interethnic attitudes: feelings of warmth towards the ethnic outgroup, intention to interact with the ethnic outgroup, and for Whites a neo-racism scale. The findings replicated the now well-established extended contact effect. Knowing more ingroup members who had friendships with outgroup members was associated with more positive intergroup attitudes on all three measures. The findings extended previous work by showing that extended contact can influence intergroup attitudes in two understudied relationships: the attitudes of minority group members (Chinese & South Asian) towards a dominant outgroup (Whites), and even less studied, the attitudes of two minority groups towards each other.

This study also replicated R.N. Turner and colleagues' (2007) findings concerning the mediational role of ingroup norms, but also complicated this model somewhat by showing that the ingroup norms may only mediate the impact of extended contact on intergroup attitudes for those with some level of identification with the ingroup. In the majority of tests, ingroup identification moderated this effect, such that only for those with moderate or high levels of identification did ingroup norms emerge as a mediator of the extended contact/intergroup attitude relationship. Although extended contact did influence intergroup attitudes for those who indicated low identification with their ethnic ingroup, this effect was not mediated by differences in perceived ingroup norms for these low identifiers. In other words, ingroup norms appear to mediate the relationship between extended contact and prejudice, but only to the degree that the observer sees the ingroup to be an important self-representation (see also Mazziotta, 2011).

Finally, this work also points to another important role for extended contact. The study included a measure of intention to engage in direct contact with the outgroup, and findings support the idea that in addition to improving intergroup attitudes directly, extended contact may also have a positive indirect effect on intergroup attitudes by paving the way for interest in direct personal contact with the outgroup. When we combine this knowledge with our current focus on the importance of perceptions of group norms, an interesting potential model emerges. Extended and direct contact may be involved in a cyclical relationship, in which ingroup norms play a critical role in both directions. The logic is this: when normative intergroup attitudes are negative or ambiguous, if even a few individuals break with these existing norms and form cross-group friendships (direct contact), these examples of closeness across groups will be observed by others (extended contact). As shown, these extended contact experiences can lead observers to believe that there is greater normative support for cross-group contact. These changes in perceived norms not only lead directly to more positive attitudes, but also serve as one of the antecedents to direct contact (see Davies, 2009; Pettigrew et al, 2007; Tropp & Bianchi, 2006) making cross-group contact more likely. As the number of cross-group friendships increase, there is greater opportunity for extended contact and the resulting perception that contact is normative. What emerges is a virtuous spiral of extended and direct contact with perceptions of group norms as the psychological linchpin that drives the process.

To summarize, a growing number of studies suggest that the extended contact effect may be an effective method to improve intergroup attitudes. The notion that the mere *knowledge* of a cross-group relationship can have a positive influence on one's perspective of an outgroup is especially promising because this kind of contact is less likely to invoke intergroup anxiety. In addition, given that extended contact does not require the same degree of investment (both physical and emotional) typically found in direct friendships, it is likely to impact intergroup attitudes on a wider scale; one can acquire multiple "extended" friendships more easily and quickly than one can develop and maintain direct friendships. Furthermore, and directly relevant to the current focus of this chapter, there is growing evidence that one of the mechanisms underlying this extended contact effect is that the cross-group friendships of others appear to communicate that a more positive stance towards the other group is normative. Not only is one given evidence of the acceptability of close cross-group relationships among one's own group, but one may also learn about the willingness of the outgroup to forge meaningful close cross-group relationships as well.

Conclusions

In summary, intergroup contact via a close, intimate cross-group friendship appears to provide a special opportunity for both participants and observers to improve their attitudes and actions towards members of other groups. Growing evidence supports the claim that two particular psychological mechanisms may underpin the power of this particular relationship to improve attitudes. The first involves the psychology of *intimacy*. Here two processes seem particularly important. The first is the process by which the close other is included in the self, leading to a sense of overlap and self-sharing with the outgroup member which is then generalized to the outgroup as a whole. Thus, "they" become part of me and I, to some extent, begin to hold them in the same esteem as I hold myself. The second intimacy process is mutual self-disclosure. As I find out more about the outgroup and its members and share more of my own personal life with an outgroup member, I simultaneously alter the stereotypes I might hold about the outgroup and build a critical sense of trust.

The second key psychological mechanism powering the positive effects of cross-group friendships appears to be changes in the perception of *group norms*. What I believe is normative for both my own ingroup and the outgroup not only influences whether I will attempt to interact with members of the outgroup, it also influences whether a cross-group interaction, should one occur, will lead to the kind of liking that is critical for attitude change. Further, cross-group interactions, both my own and especially those of others that I observe, can influence the degree to which I think that my ingroup and members of the outgroup endorse and support cross-group interactions. Thus, ingroup and outgroup norms play multiple critical roles in the relationship between cross-group friendships and more positive intergroup relations.

Of course, continued research is necessary. Particularly useful will be experimental and longitudinal research that can help to more completely disentangle the direction of causality. Given the apparent cyclical relationships between extended and direct contact, and the multiple roles proposed for ingroup norms, longitudinal research may prove to be especially helpful in clarifying the overall process. Finally, it is also worth noting that there are other psychological processes that appear to complement intimacy and group norms as determinants of the effectiveness of cross-group contact. Determining the relative importance of each of these mediating processes, and the complex relationships that likely exist between these mediators, as well as the specific contexts in which each may play more or less primary roles, should keep researchers busy for quite some time. Nonetheless, as societies world-wide become increasingly diverse, as members of different groups increasingly share the same geographic areas, and as travel and technology bring all of us closer together, understanding the dynamics of interpersonal interactions across group boundaries and charting carefully the mechanisms that account for both positive and negative outcomes of these interactions becomes an increasingly complex yet essential task.

References

Aberson, C. L., Shoemaker, C., & Tomolillo, C. (2004). Implicit bias and contact: The role of interethnic friendships. *Journal of Social Psychology, 144*, 335–347.

Allport, G. W. (1954). *The nature of prejudice.* Reading, MA: Addison-Wesley.

Altman, I., & Taylor, D. A. (1973). *Social penetration: The development of interpersonal relationships.* New York: Holt, Rinehart & Winston.

Andersen, S. M., & Chen, S. (2002). The relational self: An interpersonal social-cognitive theory. *Psychological Review, 109*, 619–645.

Aron, A., & Aron, E. N. (1986). *Love as the expansion of self: Understanding attraction and satisfaction.* New York: Hemisphere.

Aron, A., Aron, E. N., & Smollan, D. (1992). Inclusion of Other in the Self Scale and the structure of interpersonal closeness. *Journal of Personality and Social Psychology, 63,* 596–612.

Aron, A., Aron, E. N., Tudor, M., & Nelson, G. (2004). Close Relationships as Including Other in the Self. In H. T. Reis, & C. E. Rusbult (Eds.), *Close relationships: Key readings* (pp. 365–379). Philadelphia, PA: Taylor & Francis.

Aron, A., Mashek, D., & Aron, E. (2004). Closeness as Including Other in the Self. In D. Mashek, & A. Aron (Eds.), *Handbook of closeness and intimacy* (pp. 27–41). Mahwah, NJ, US: Lawrence Erlbaum Associates.

Aron, A., McLaughlin-Volpe, T., Mashek, D., Lewandowski, G., Wright, S. C., & Aron, E. (2005). Including others in the self. *European Review of Social Psychology, 14,* 101–132.

Aron, A., Melinat, E., Aron, E. N., Vallone, R. D., & Bator, R. J. (1997). The experimental generation of interpersonal closeness: A procedure and some preliminary findings. *Personality and Social Psychology Bulletin, 23,* 363–377.

Berndt, T., & Perry, T. B. (1986). Children's perceptions of friendships as supportive relationships. *Developmental Psychology, 22,* 640–648.

Britt, T., Boniecki, K., Vescio, T., Biernat, M., & Brown, L. (1996). Intergroup anxiety: A person × situation approach. *Personality and Social Psychology Bulletin, 22*(11), 1177–1188.

Brody, S. M., Wright, S. C., Aron, A. & McLaughlin-Volpe, T. (2008). Compassionate love for individuals outside one's social group. In L. Underwood, S. Sprecher, & B. Fehr (Eds.), *The science of compassionate love: Research, theory, and applications* (pp. 283–308). Malden, MA: Wiley-Blackwell.

Brown, R., & Hewstone, M. (2005). An integrative theory of intergroup contact. In M. P. Zanna (Ed.), *Advances in Experimental Social Psychology* (Vol. 37, pp. 255–343). San Diego: Elsevier Academic Press.

Brown, S. L., Fredrickson, B. L., Wirth, M. M., Poulin, M. J., Meier, E. A., Heaphy, E. D., & Schultheiss, O. C. (2009). Social closeness increases salivary progesterone in humans. *Hormones and Behavior, 56,* 108–111.

Cameron, L., & Rutland, A. (2006). Extended Contact through Story Reading in School: Reducing Children's Prejudice toward the Disabled. *Journal of Social Issues, 62,* 469–488.

Cameron, L., Rutland, A., Brown, R., & Douch, R. (2006). Changing Children's Intergroup Attitudes Toward Refugees: Testing Different Models of Extended Contact. *Child Development, 77,* 1208–1219.

Carlson, C. I., Wilson, K. D., & Hargrave, J. L. (2003). The effect of school racial composition on Hispanic intergroup relations. *Journal of Social and Personal Relationships, 20,* 203–220.

Cialdini, R. B., Kallgren, C. A., & Reno, R. R. (1991). A focus theory of normative conduct. In M. P. Zanna (Ed.), *Advances in Experimental Social Psychology* (Vol. 24, pp. 201–234). San Diego, CA: Academic Press.

Cohen, T. R., Wildschut, T., & Insko, C. A. (2010). How communication increases interpersonal cooperation in mixed-motive situations. *Journal of Experimental Social Psychology, 46,* 39–50.

Comeau, J. (2010). *Ingroup norms mediate extended contact: But only if you identify with the ingroup.* Unpublished master's thesis, Simon Fraser University, Burnaby, BC, Canada.

Crandall, C. S., Eshleman, A., & O'Brien, L. (2002). Social norms and the expression and suppression of prejudice: The struggle for internalization. *Journal of Personality and Social Psychology, 82*, 359–378.

Crandall, C. S., & Stangor, C. (2005). Conformity and prejudice. In J. F. Dovidio, P. Glick, & L. A. Rudman (Eds.), *Fifty years after Allport* (pp. 295–309). Malden, MA, US: Blackwell Publishing.

Davies, K. M. (2009). *Identifying Key Themes in Cross-Group Friendship Formation.* unpublished doctoral dissertation. Stony Brook University, Stony Brook, NY.

Davies, K. M., Aron, A., Wright, S. C., Brody, S. & McLaughlin-Volpe, T. (2011). *The fast-friends project: Some initial results of an intergroup contact intervention.* Manuscript in preparation.

Davies, K. M., Aron, A., Wright, S., Eberhardt, J. L., & Bergsieker, H. (2007, June). *The fast friends project: Initial results of an intergroup contact intervention.* Paper presented at the annual meeting of the Canadian Psychological Association, Ottawa, ON, Canada.

Davies, K., Tropp, L. R., Aron, A., Pettigrew, T. F., & Wright, S. C. (2011). Cross-group friendships and intergroup attitudes: A meta-analytic review. *Personality and Social Psychology Review, 15*, 332–351.

Devine, P. G., Evett, S. R., & Vasquez-Suson, K. A. (1996). Exploring the interpersonal dynamics of intergroup contact. In R. M. Sorrentino, & E. T. Higgins (Eds.), *Handbook of motivation and cognition: Vol 3. The interpersonal context* (pp. 423–464). New York: Guilford Press.

Dovidio, J. F., Gaertner, S. L., & Kawakami, K. (2003). Intergroup contact: The past, present, and the future. *Group Processes & Intergroup Relations, 6*, 5–20.

Dovidio, J. F., Glick, P., & Rudman, L. A. (2005). Introduction: Reflecting on The Nature of Prejudice: Fifty Years after Allport. In J. F. Dovidio, P. Glick, & L. A. Rudman (Eds.), *On the nature of prejudice: Fifty years after Allport* (pp. 1–15). Malden: Blackwell Publishing.

Duck, S. W. (1983). *Friends, for life.* New York, NY: St. Martin's Press.

Duck, S. W., Rutt, D. J., Hurst, M., & Strejc, H. (1991). Some evident truths about conversations in everyday relationships: All communication is not created equal. *Human Communication Research, 18*, 228–267.

Eller, A., & Abrams, D. (2003). 'Gringos' in Mexico: Cross-sectional and longitudinal effects of language school-promoted contact on intergroup bias. *Group Processes & Intergroup Relations, 6*, 55–75.

Ensari, N., & Miller, N. (2002). The out-group must not be so bad after all: The effects of disclosure, typicality, and salience on intergroup bias, *Journal of Personality and Social Psychology, 83*, 313–329.

Esses, V. M., & Dovidio, J. F. (2002). The role of emotions in determining willingness to engage in intergroup contact. *Personality and Social Psychology Bulletin, 28*, 1202–1214.

Feddes, A. R., Noack, P., & Rutland, A. (2009). Direct and extended friendship effects on minority and majority children's interethnic attitudes: A longitudinal study. *Child Development, 80*, 377–390.

Fehr, B. (1996). *Friendship processes.* Thousand Oaks, CA: Sage.

Fehr, B. (2004). A prototype model of intimacy interactions in same-sex friendships. In D. J. Mashek, & A. Aron (Eds.), *Handbook of closeness and intimacy* (pp. 9–26). Mahwah, NJ: Lawrence Erlbaum Associates.

Fehr, B., & Russell, J. A. (1991). The concept of love viewed from a prototype perspective. *Journal of Personality and Social Psychology, 60*, 425–438.

Fenigstein, A., Scheier, M. F., & Buss, A. H. (1975). Public and private self-consciousness: Assessment and theory. *Journal of Consulting and Clinical Psychology, 43*, 522–527.

Gibbons, F. X., & Buunk, B. P. (1999). Individual differences in social comparison: Development of a scale of social comparison orientation. *Journal of Personality and Social Psychology, 76*, 129–142.

Gottman, J. M. (1983). How children become friends. *Monographs of the Society for Research in Child Development, 48*, 86.

Halualani, R., Chitgopekar, A., Morrison, J., & Dodge, P. (2004). Who's interacting? And what are they talking about? – intercultural contact and interaction among multicultural university students. *International Journal of Intercultural Relations, 28*, 353–372.

Hays, R. B. (1984). The Development and Maintenance of Friendship. *Journal of Social and Personal Relationships, 1*, 75–98.

Heider, F. (1958). *The psychology of interpersonal relations.* New York: John Wiley & Sons.

Hewstone, M., & Brown, R. (1986). Contact is not enough: An intergroup perspective on the "contact hypothesis." *Contact and conflict in intergroup encounters* (pp. 1–44). Cambridge, US: Basil Blackwell.

Hindy, C. G. (1980). Children's friendship concepts and the perceived cohesiveness of same-sex friendship dyads. *Psychological Reports, 47*, 191–203.

Hodson, G., Harry, H., & Mitchell, A. (2009). Independent benefits of contact and friendship on attitudes toward homosexuals among authoritarians and highly identified heterosexuals. *European Journal of Social Psychology, 39*, 509–525.

Jacobson, C. K., & Johnson, B. R. (2006). Interracial friendship and African American attitudes about interracial marriage. *Journal of Black Studies, 36*, 570–584.

Jetten, J., Spears, R., & Manstead, A. (1997). Strength of identification and intergroup differentiation: The influence of group norms. *European Journal of Social Psychology, 27*, 603–609.

Jormakka, L. (1976). The behaviour of children during a first encounter. *Scandinavian Journal of Psychology, 17*, 15–22.

Kashdan, T. B., & Roberts, J. E. (2006). Affective outcomes in superficial and intimate interactions: Roles of social anxiety and curiosity. *Journal of Research in Personality, 40*, 140–167.

Klinger, E. (1977). *Meaning and void: Inner experience and the incentives in people's lives.* Minneapolis, MN: University of Minnesota Press.

Lederberg, A. R., Rosenblatt, V., Vandell, D. L., & Chapin, S. L. (1987). Temporary and long-term friendships in hearing and deaf preschoolers. *Merrill-Palmer Quarterly, 33*, 515–533.

Levin, S., van Laar, C., & Sidanius, J. (2003). The effects of ingroup and outgroup friendship on ethnic attitudes in college: A longitudinal study. *Group Processes and Intergroup Relations, 6*, 76–92.

Liebkind, K., & McAlister, A. L. (1999). Extended contact through peer modelling to promote tolerance in Finland. *European Journal of Social Psychology, 29*, 765–780.

Mazziotta, A. (2011) *Vicarious intergroup contact effects: Applying Social-Cognitive Theory to intergroup contact research.* Unpublished doctoral dissertation. Friedrich-Schiller-Universität, Jena, Germany.

Mazziotta, A., Mummendey, A., & Wright, S. C. (2011). Vicarious contact can improve intergroup attitudes and prepare for direct contact. *Group Processes and Intergroup Relations, 14*, 255–274.

McLaughlin-Volpe, T., Aron, A., Wright, S. C., & Reis, H. T. (2002). Intergroup social interactions and intergroup prejudice: Quantity versus quality. Unpublished manuscript.

Mendoza-Denton, R., Downey, G., Purdie, V. J., Davis, A., & Pietrzak, J. (2002). Sensitivity to status-based rejection: Implications for African American students' college experience. *Journal of Personality and Social Psychology, 83*, 896–918.

Mendoza-Denton, R., & Page-Gould, E. (2008). Can cross-group friendships influence minority students' well-being at historically white universities? *Psychological Science, 19*, 933–939.

Miller, N. (2002). Personalization and the promise of contact theory. *Journal of Social Issues, 58*, 387–410.

Newcomb, A. F., & Brady, J. E. (1982). Mutuality in boys' friendship relations. *Child Development, 53*, 392–395.

Otten, S., & Bar-Tal, Y. (2002). Self-anchoring in the minimal group paradigm: The impact of need and ability to achieve cognitive structure. *Group Processes & Intergroup Relations, 5*, 267–284.

Otten, S., & Epstude, K. (2006). Overlapping mental representations of self, ingroup, and outgroup: Unraveling self-stereotyping and self-anchoring. *Personality and Social Psychology Bulletin, 32*, 957–969.

Page-Gould, E., Mendoza-Denton, R., & Tropp, L. R. (2008). With a little help from my cross-group friend: Reducing anxiety in intergroup contexts through cross-group friendship. *Journal of Personality and Social Psychology, 95*, 1080–1094.

Paolini, S., Hewstone, M., Cairns, E., & Voci, A. (2004). Effects of direct and indirect cross-group friendships on judgments of Catholics and Protestants in Northern Ireland: The mediating role of an anxiety-reduction mechanism. *Personality and Social Psychology Bulletin, 30*, 770–786.

Paolini, S., Hewstone, M., Voci, A., Harwood, J., & Cairns, E. (2006). Intergroup contact and the promotion of intergroup harmony: The influence of intergroup emotions. In R. Brown, & D. Capozza (Eds.), *Social identities: Motivational, emotional and cultural influences* (pp. 209–238). Hove, E. Sussex: Psychology Press.

Pettigrew, T. F. (1986). The contact hypothesis revisited. In M. Hewstone & R. Brown (Eds.), *Contact and conflict in intergroup encounters* (pp. 169–195). Oxford: Blackwell.

Pettigrew, T. F. (1991). Normative theory in intergroup relations: Explaining both harmony and conflict. *Psychology and Developing Societies, 3*, 3–26.

Pettigrew, T. F. (1997). Generalized intergroup contact effects on prejudice. *Personality and Social Psychological Bulletin, 23*, 173–185.

Pettigrew, T. F. (1998). Intergroup contact theory. *Annual Review of Psychology, 49*, 65–85.

Pettigrew, T. F., Christ, O., Wagner, U., & Stellmacher, J. (2007). Direct and indirect intergroup contact effects on prejudice: A normative interpretation. *International Journal of Intercultural Relations, 31*, 411–425.

Pettigrew, T. F., & Tropp, L. (2006). A meta-analytic test of intergroup contact theory. *Journal of Personality and Social Psychology, 90*, 751–783.

Reis, H. T., & Shaver, P. (1988). Intimacy as an interpersonal process. In S. Duck (Ed.), *Handbook of personal relationships* (pp. 367–389). New York: Wiley.

Rotenberg, K. J. (1986). Same-sex patterns and sex differences in the trust-value basis of children's friendship. *Sex Roles, 15*, 613–626.

Rubin, L. (1985). *Just friends*. New York: Harper & Row.

Sedikides, C., Olsen, N., & Reis, H. T. (1993). Relationships as natural categories. *Journal of Personality and Social Psychology, 64*, 71–82.

Sharp, M., Voci, A., & Hewstone, M. (2011). Individual difference variables as moderators of the effect of extended cross-group friendship on prejudice: Testing the effects of public self-consciousness and social comparison. *Group Processes & Intergroup Relations, 14*(2), 207–221.

Shelton, J. N., & Richeson, J. A. (2005). Intergroup contact and pluralistic ignorance. *Journal of Personality and Social Psychology, 88*, 91–107.

Shelton, J. N., & Richeson, J. A. (2006). Interracial interactions: A relational approach. In M. P. Zanna (Ed.), *Advances in experimental social psychology* (Vol. 38, pp. 121–181). San Diego, CA: Academic Press.

Shelton, J. N., Richeson, J. A., & Vorauer, J. D. (2006). Threatened identities and interethnic interactions. *European Review of Social Psychology, 17*, 321–358.

Shelton, J. N., Trail, T. E., West, T. V., & Bergsieker, H. B. (2010). From strangers to friends: The interpersonal process model of intimacy in developing interracial friendships, *Journal of Social and Personal Relationships, 27*, 71–90.

Sherif, M., Harvey, O. J., White, B. J., Hood, W. R., & Sherif, C. W. (1961). *Intergroup conflict and cooperation: The Robbers Cave experiment.* Norman, OK: University of Oklahoma Book Exchange.

Smith, E. R., Coats, S., & Walling, D. (1999). Overlapping mental representations of self, in-group, and partner: Further response time evidence and a connectionist model. *Personality and Social Psychology Bulletin, 25*, 873–882.

Stangor, C., Sechrist, G. B., & Jost, J. T. (2001). Changing racial beliefs by providing consensus information. *Personality and Social Psychological Bulletin, 27*, 484–494.

Stephan, W. G., & Stephan, C. W. (1985). Intergroup anxiety. *Journal of Social Issues, 41*, 157–175.

Tajfel, H., & Turner, J. C. (1979). An integrative theory of intergroup conflict. In W. G. Austin, & S. Worchel (Eds.), *The social psychology of intergroup relations* (pp. 33–48). Monterey, CA: Brooks/Cole.

Terry, D. J., & Hogg, M. A. (1996). Group norms and the attitude–behavior relationship: A role for group identification. *Personality And Social Psychology Bulletin, 22*(8), 776–793.

Terry, D. J., & Hogg, M. A. (2000). *Attitudes, behavior, and social context: The role of norms and group membership.* Mahwah, NJ: Erlbaum.

Tesch, S. A., & Martin, R. R. (1983). Friendship concepts of young adults in two age groups. *Journal of Psychology: Interdisciplinary and Applied, 115*, 7–12.

Tropp, L. R., & Bianchi, R. A. (2006). Valuing Diversity and Interest in Intergroup Contact. *Journal of Social Issues, 62*, 533–551.

Tropp, L. R., & Pettigrew, T. F. (2005). Differential relationships between intergroup contact and affective and cognitive dimensions of prejudice. *Personality and Social Psychology Bulletin, 31*, 1145–1158.

Tropp, L. R., & Wright, S. C. (2001). Ingroup identification as the inclusion of ingroup in the self. *Personality and Social Psychology Bulletin, 27*, 585–600.

Turner, J. C., Hogg, M. A., Oakes, P. J., Reicher, S. D., & Wetherell, M. S. (1987). *Rediscovering the social group: A self-categorization theory.* Oxford, UK: Basil Blackwell.

Turner, J. C., & Oakes, P. J. (1989). Self-categorization theory and social influence. In P. B. Paulus (Ed.), *Psychology of group influence (2nd ed)* (pp. 233–275). Hillsdale, NJ: Erlbaum.

Turner, J. C., Wetherell, M., & Hogg, M. A. (1989). Referent informational influence and group polarization. *British Journal of Social Psychology, 28*, 135–147.

Turner, R. N., Hewstone, M., & Voci, A. (2007). Reducing explicit and implicit outgroup prejudice via direct and extended contact: The mediating role of self-disclosure and intergroup anxiety. *Journal of Personality and Social Psychology, 93*, 369–388.

Turner, R. N., Hewstone, M., Voci, A., & Vonofakou, C. (2008). A test of the extended intergroup contact hypothesis: The mediating role of intergroup anxiety, perceived ingroup and outgroup norms, and inclusion of the outgroup in the self. *Journal of Personality and Social Psychology, 95*, 843–860.

van Dick, R., Wagner, U., Pettigrew, T. F., Christ, O., Wolf, C., Petzel, T., & Jackson, J. S. (2004). Role of perceived importance in intergroup contact. *Journal of Personality and Social Psychology, 87*, 211–227.

Vorauer, J. D., & Kumhyr, S. M. (2001). Is this about you or me? Self versus other-directed judgments and feelings in response to intergroup interaction. *Personality and Social Psychology Bulletin, 27*, 706–709.

Vorauer, J. D., & Turpie, C. A. (2004). Disruptive effects of vigilance on dominant group members' treatment of outgroup members: Choking versus shining under pressure. *Journal of Personality and Social Psychology, 87*, 384–399.

West, T. V., Shelton, J., & Trail, T. E. (2009). Relational anxiety in interracial interactions. *Psychological Science, 20*, 289–292.

Williams, R. M., Jr. (1947). *The reduction of intergroup tension*s. New York: Social Science Research Council.

Wright, S. C. (1997). *Friendship and intergroup contact: Connecting the interpersonal and the intergroup.* Paper presented at the Small Groups Preconference – Society for Experimental Social Psychology, Toronto, ON, Canada.

Wright, S. C. (2009). Cross-group contact effects. In S. Otten, T. Kessler, & K. Sassenberg (Eds.), *Intergroup relations: The role of emotion and motivation* (pp. 262–283). New York: Psychology Press.

Wright, S. C., Aron, A., & Brody, S. M. (2008). Extended contact and including others in the self: Building on the Allport/Pettigrew legacy. In U. Wagner, L. R. Tropp, G. Finchilescu, & C. Tredoux (Eds.), *Improving intergroup relations: Building on the legacy of Thomas F. Pettigrew* (pp. 143–159). Malden, MA: Blackwell.

Wright, S. C., Aron, A., McLaughlin-Volpe, T., & Ropp, S. A. (1997). The extended contact effect: Knowledge of cross-group friendships and prejudice. *Journal of Personality and Social Psychology, 73*, 73–90.

Wright, S. C., Aron, A., & Tropp, L. R. (2002). Including others (and groups) in the self: Self-expansion and intergroup relations. In J. P. Forgas, & K. D. Williams (Eds.), *The social self: Cognitive, interpersonal and intergroup perspectives* (pp. 343–363). Philadelphia: Psychology Press.

Wright, S. C., Brody, S. M., & Aron, A. (2005). Intergroup contact: Still our best hope for improving intergroup relations. In C. S. Crandall, & M. Schaller (Eds.), *Social psychology of prejudice: Historical and contemporary issues.* (pp. 115–142). Seattle, WA: Lewinian Press.

Wright, S. C., Davies, K., & Sanders, L. (2011). *Direct and extended contact effects on attitudes towards lesbians and gay men: Testing mechanisms.* Unpublished manuscript.

Wright, S. C., & Tropp, L. R. (2005). Language and intergroup contact: Investigating the impact of bilingual instruction on children's intergroup attitudes, *Group Processes and Intergroup Relation, 8*, 309–328.

Wright, S. C., & van der Zande, C. (1999, Oct.). *Bicultural friends: When cross-group friendships cause improved intergroup attitudes.* Paper presented at the annual convention of the Society for Experimental Social Psychology, St. Louis, MO.

Zhou, S., & Wright, S. C. (2011). *Expanding self-expansion: Role of the ideal self in self-expansion motives.* Manuscript currently under editorial review.

Part IV

Methodological concerns and future considerations

10 Methodological issues in the study of intergroup contact

Towards a new wave of research

Oliver Christ and Ulrich Wagner

Empirical research on intergroup contact has a long history, dating back to the 1940s (e.g., Williams, 1947). Since the seminal chapter on intergroup contact by Gordon Allport (1954), in his famous book *The Nature of Prejudice*, hundreds of research papers and book chapters have been published. The meta-analytic summary of 515 studies by Pettigrew and Tropp (2006) provided ample evidence that intergroup contact is capable of reducing prejudice, particularly when certain facilitating factors (i.e., common goals, cooperation, equal status, and institutional support) are present. While "there is little need to demonstrate further contact's general ability to lessen prejudice" (Pettigrew & Tropp, 2006, p. 768), intergroup contact theory is still advancing in new directions, as documented by the chapters of this volume. Research on intergroup contact has, however, not been without its critics. Most of the critiques relate to methodological issues, such as measurement problems, the question of causality, and the disregard of the social context. Our aim in this chapter is, first, to consider some of these critiques in more detail. Following that, we will outline, from a methodological point of view, the ways in which we think the next generation of intergroup contact research can face these challenges.

Methodological challenges for research on intergroup contact

Measurement issues

One important methodological challenge concerns the measurement of intergroup contact. Many studies on intergroup contact have used self-report measures. Pettigrew and Tropp's (2006) meta-analytic review of intergroup contact research is based largely on studies using self-reports (81 percent). In most cases, standardized questionnaires are used with discrete response categories. For example, Wagner, Christ, Pettigrew, Stellmacher, and Wolf (2006) used indicators measuring the quantity of contact to assess German respondents' experience with foreigners living in Germany (e.g., "How often do you have personal contact with foreigners in your neighborhood?"; Response options: 1 = never to 4 = often). The use of such self-reports for assessing intergroup contact is itself not beyond critique. For instance, researchers have argued that self-reports do not offer participants the opportunity to express their own construction of the meaning of intergroup encounters (J. Dixon, Durrheim, & Tredoux, 2005). Thus, it is proposed that these measures "reflect how social psychologists have classified and thought about contact" (J. Dixon et al., 2005, p. 697), instead of capturing people's own ways of making sense of intergroup interactions.

Two possible alternatives to standardized questionnaires, also used in previous research, are *observational approaches* and *experimental* studies (Hewstone, Judd, & Sharp, 2011). Observational approaches can be separated into two categories. In the first, intergroup contact can be assessed by examining the percentage of non-ingroup members (e.g., Cummings & Lambert, 1997; Fossett & Kiecolt, 1989) or the percentage of members of various minority groups (e.g., Hood & Morris, 1997; Oliver & Wong, 2003) in the respondents' area of residence, as objective indicators of the quantity of intergroup contact. However, as Hewstone et al. (2011; see also Pettigrew & Tropp, 2011) rightly pointed out, these kinds of observational studies measure only the *opportunity* for contact and do not reflect actual intergroup contact. Members of different groups can live close together without really coming into contact with each other (Festinger & Kelley, 1951; see also Wagner et al., 2006; Welch, Sigelman, Bledsoe, & Combs, 2001).This is also the reason why Pettigrew and Tropp (2006) chose to exclude these studies from their meta-analysis, since proximity is a necessary but not sufficient condition for intergroup contact.

A second kind of observational study involves recording actual contact in specific situations (e.g., Clack, J. Dixon, & Tredoux, 2005; Schofield, 1979; Schofield & Sagar, 1977). For example, Schofield and Sagar (1977) studied the interaction of Black and White students in a desegregated school by recording the seating patterns in a cafeteria over a period of a little more than four months. Racial clustering was measured using an index based upon the difference between the actual frequency with which Black and White students sit together and the expected frequency, given random distribution (for a critique of this index and an alternative measure, see McCauley, Plummer, Moskalenko, & Mordkoff, 2001). Results showed that there was indeed racial segregation, but that interracial interaction increased over time. This example, however, demonstrates that observational studies are mainly useful when it is of interest to examine the amount of contact in a specific location or organization (Hewstone et al., 2011), to track changes in intergroup relations over time, or to assess the effectiveness of interventions aiming to improve intergroup relations (McCauley et al., 2001). Observational studies have, so far, not been used as a between-subject measure of intergroup contact, and it would be extremely time-consuming to use an observational level as a measure of each individual's level of contact or as an index of the quality of contact (Hewstone et al., 2011).

An important alternative to studies using self-reports and observational approaches are experimental paradigms, in which aspects of intergroup contact are manipulated (e.g., Cook, 1984; Ensari & Miller, 2002; Shook & Fazio, 2008; Towles-Schwen & Fazio, 2006; Wilder, 1984; Wilder & Thompson, 1980; Wright et al., 1997). Wilder (1984, Study 1), for instance, varied the typicality (atypical vs. typical) and behavior (unpleasant vs. pleasant) of an outgroup member with whom participants interacted and completed a set of problem solving tasks. The outgroup member was a confederate. Moreover, a control group was included in which participants had no interaction with an outgroup member, but completed the same tasks. Results of this experiment showed that participants in the typical-pleasant condition evaluated the outgroup more positively after the interaction period, compared to the participants in the other experimental conditions. Thus, the experimental manipulation of contact allows the researcher to disentangle the effects of various facets of contact, including specific aspects of contact such as positive and negative intergroup contact, contact quantity, and so on, and to assess their effects on prejudice. Another advantage of experimental approaches is that they provide the opportunity to examine causal effects of intergroup contact on prejudice. We return to this point in the next section. In general, results of laboratory experiments confirm the positive effects of (positive) intergroup contact on intergroup relations (Brewer & Gaertner, 2001).

The question remains whether self-reports of intergroup contact are a valid and therefore viable method to examine intergroup contact effects. Although this is an important question, research has only recently considered this issue. In two studies, Hewstone et al. (2011) examined the validity of self-reports of intergroup contact using a round-robin design (Kashy & Kenny, 2000). A group of four close acquaintances were asked to rate themselves and each other on judgmental dimensions of prejudice, degree of intergroup contact, quality of intergroup contact, and a variety of other measures (e.g., extraversion). The authors examined whether observers made consensual judgments of the targets' degree and quality of intergroup contact, and whether these consensual judgments were correlated with the targets' own self ratings. Indeed, the results of both studies showed that there was a significant consensus between self-reports of participants and observers' ratings of the target's degree and quality of direct intergroup contact. Moreover, these researchers ruled out an explanation of their findings in terms of judges making inferences about other people's contact based on either the targets' perceived level of extraversion or their perceived prejudices, and generalized the findings across two different outgroups. Thus, the two studies by Hewstone and colleagues provided the first evidence that self-reports of intergroup contact are a valid measure of actual intergroup contact (see also Dhont, van Hiel, De Bolle, & Roets, 2012).

In many instances, self-reports are used for pragmatic reasons. They can be easily administered among a large sample of respondents and are thus an inexpensive and efficient way to measure various aspects of intergroup contact. It is not the aim of the present chapter to discuss inherent problems of self-reports in general (for an overview, see Schwarz, 1999). Nor do we argue against observing intergroup encounters (which is truly important, see Baumeister, Vohs, & Funder, 2007), or using qualitative methods to capture more directly the subjective experience of individuals of intergroup situations. For example, J. Dixon and Reicher (1997) interviewed white residents of a town in South Africa. Based on discourse analysis of the interview data, the authors aimed to identify how their respondents constructed their intergroup encounters, in order to get a deeper insight into the meaning of contact for individuals. We contend that self-reports should be used in conjunction with other methodologies, such as observational and experimental approaches, and that they should, when possible, be combined with qualitative methods. In the social sciences this strategy is known as *triangulation* (e.g., Jick, 1979). Our review indicates, however, that self-reports have been, are, and will continue to be an important and valid method to measure intergroup contact.

Since self-reports will also figure strongly in future research on intergroup contact, it is important to use state-of-the-art methods to get the most out of these data. We will return to this point later in this chapter, when introducing statistical techniques for the analysis of longitudinal and multilevel data.

The causal sequence problem

Just as most research on intergroup contact is based on self-reports, most research is cross-sectional. Fully 71 percent of the studies included in the meta-analysis by Pettigrew and Tropp (2006) were classified as survey or field research, and only a minority of these studies used a longitudinal design. This leads to the second major challenge in research on intergroup contact, the causal sequence problem (Pettigrew, 1998). The contact hypothesis proposes that contact is the *cause* of reduced prejudice. That is, the causal direction is from intergroup contact to attitude change. Cross-sectional designs, however, limit the causal interpretability of the relation between intergroup contact and intergroup attitudes. Thus, one cannot exclude the possibility that the negative correlations between contact and prejudice found in most cross-sectional research are due to a selection bias: highly prejudiced individuals avoid intergroup contact, and unprejudiced individuals seek out contact (for commentary, see Hodson, 2011; Hodson, Costello, & MacInnis, this volume). From this alternative perspective, prejudice could be the predictor of contact (avoidance).

Pettigrew (1998) identified three methods that overcome the limitation of simple correlational analyses of cross-sectional data: (1) examining intergroup situations in which the choice for intergroup contact is limited or even foreclosed; (2) using methods that allow the simultaneous testing of both paths, from intergroup contact to intergroup attitudes, and vice versa; (3) using longitudinal designs to identify causal processes. In the following, we will shortly describe each of these three methods in more detail. We will also discuss limitations of these approaches.

The strictest way to realize Pettigrew's (1998) first option, to study the contact-prejudice relation under conditions where participants have no choice of coming into contact with outgroup members, is the experimental approach. If, as in Wilder's (1984) experiment, participants in the experimental conditions have no choice about intergroup contact as a result of being randomly *assigned* to come into contact with an outgroup member (vs. a no-contact control condition), any observed positive evaluation of the outgroup (compared to the no-contact control condition) can be assumed to be causally driven by the contact experience.

Studying the effects of intergroup contact on prejudice experimentally has a number of clear advantages. Beyond a heightened construct validity of the inter-group contact indicator, experimental designs have high internal validity, yielding a clear answer to the question of whether contact has a causal impact on prejudice. Indeed, experimental evidence clearly indicates that contact not only reduces prejudice, but that these effect sizes are even larger than those generated with other research methods (Pettigrew & Tropp, 2006, Table 3). However, experiments typically share the limitation that they cannot simulate the cumulative effects of intergroup contact over diverse situations and qualities of experiences with different out-group members. For example, optimal intergroup contact requires *time* for the development of cross-group friendships. Here again self-reports come into play, especially those used in combination with longitudinal studies. They allow researchers to test the effects of contact on prejudice over longer periods of time, as well as the effects of the causal relation between contact and prejudice. We return to this issue in the next section.

Pettigrew's (1998) first solution to the causal sequence question, that is, examining effects of intergroup contact in no-choice situations, is also relevant for understanding and interpreting correlational data. If the causal sequence is from prejudice to intergroup contact, meaning that prejudiced individuals avoid intergroup contact, one would expect no correlation between intergroup contact and prejudice in no-choice situations where the contact is forced by the situation. If, however, the causal sequence is from intergroup contact to prejudice, as proposed by the intergroup contact hypothesis, the correlation should be reliable, irrespective of whether the contact is voluntary or involuntary.

In a cross-sectional study, Link and Cullen (1986) compared the correlation between two types of contact with people with mental illness and the perception of how dangerous mentally ill people are. One form of contact was rated as being under individual control (e.g., "Have you ever worked for pay or done volunteer work with people who have been hospitalized for a mental illness?"), whereas the other form was rated to be determined more or less by external circumstances ("Have you ever known a person who was hospitalized in a mental institution?"). Results showed that the correlations of these two types of intergroup contact with the perceived dangerousness measure were both significantly negative and almost identical in magnitude. Thus, these results are consistent with the claim that intergroup contact leads to more favorable intergroup attitudes.

Another approach to this question would be to examine contact in settings that severely limit the opportunities for highly prejudiced people to avoid contact. In several studies, Hodson (2008) found not only that interracial contact in prisons was associated with reduced prejudice (and increased empathy), but that these effects were *larger* (not smaller) than those found in typical high-choice contexts. Considering that it was the highly prejudiced inmates who benefitted most from prison contact, such results, despite being correlational, bolster the argument that contact indeed reduces prejudice. Furthermore, in their meta-analysis Pettigrew and Tropp (2006) directly compared sub-samples of participants who were either able to choose to engage in intergroup contact or who had no (or only limited) choice to engage in contact. Again, the meta-analytic results speak for the contact hypothesis: The effect size even for no-choice samples was negative and significant, again supporting the assumption of a causal influence from contact to reduced prejudice.

Pettigrew's (1998) second suggestion for overcoming the problem of determining the causal relation between contact and prejudice was to use methods that allow the simultaneous testing of both causal paths. The methods subsumed here can be divided further into methods that: (a) directly estimate both the contact-to-prejudice path and the prejudice-to-contact path, based on non-recursive models applied to cross-sectional data that allow for the estimation of feedback loops (Kline, 2010); or (b) try to account for a possible selection bias. The basic idea behind non-recursive models is to estimate the relative amount of variance explained when contact is assumed to predict prejudice, and when the effect of prejudice on contact is tested simultaneously (controlling for measurement error, i.e., using latent variables). An example of a non-recursive model can be found in Pettigrew (1998; see also van Dick et al., 2004; Wagner, van Dick, Pettigrew, & Christ, 2003).

As an example of this technique, Pettigrew (1998) used cross-sectional survey data from a large European survey and compared the path from intergroup contact to prejudice with the path from prejudice to intergroup contact, using a nonrecursive model. Results showed that prejudiced people avoid intergroup contact, but the path from intergroup contact to prejudice was significantly stronger. Kline (2010) provides a good overview on specification, identification, and estimation of nonrecursive models (see also Wong & Law, 1999). Nonrecursive models have, however, not escaped criticism. Hunter and Gerbing (1982, pp. 288–289) argued that "the problem that nonrecursive causations pose in cross-sectional models can be seen by considering the implication that a two-way arrow has for indirect effects." If contact and prejudice have an effect on each other, then contact has an impact on prejudice, which has an impact on contact, which has an impact on prejudice. "This cycling can go on [for] as many steps as can be imagined. In reality, there is no such instantaneous cycling process," they conclude (p. 289).

Another approach for estimating the causal effect of intergroup contact on prejudice is to use methods that account for possible selection bias. A key problem of cross-sectional data, including observational studies, is that the normally found negative relation between intergroup contact and prejudice is potentially the result of selection processes. For instance, it is possible that mainly individuals with positive intergroup attitudes engage in intergroup contact, whereas individuals with negative intergroup attitudes avoid intergroup contact (Jackman & Crane, 1986). Randomization in controlled experiments rules out this kind of selection bias (Shadish et al., 2002). Ideally, one would randomly assign participants to a contact condition (experimental group) and a no-contact condition (control group), as done, for example, by Wilder (1984). Random assignment reduces the plausibility of alternative explanations for observed effects since, among other things, the experimental and control groups are equated before treatment on observed and non-observed covariates (for an overview on the explanation of randomization, see Cox, 2009; Rosenbaum, 1995; Shadish et al., 2002).

In correlational and quasi-experimental studies, it is unknown whether individuals having intergroup contact and individuals having no contact are equal in all possible covariates. Thus, selection bias cannot be ruled out. In the past three decades, statisticians and econometricians have developed methods that enable researchers to account for selection bias in correlational studies (for an overview, see Rosenbaum, 1995; Winship & Mare, 1992). The first class of models matches treated and untreated respondents on observed covariates. The assumption is that those respondents, who look comparable on the observed covariates, are indeed comparable (i.e., also with respect to other, unobserved covariates). If this assumption holds, it would suffice to match treated and control respondents for the observed covariates (for an example, see Lewis, 2007). In this case, matching would lead to a reproduction of the distribution of treatment assignments in a randomized experiment.

One important development in this field is the propensity score (Rosenbaum & Rubin, 1983). The propensity score is the predicted probability of being in the treatment group (having intergroup contact) versus the control group (having no intergroup contact) given observed covariates from a logistic regression equation. In the logistic regression equation, those observed variables are included that possibly play a role in the selection process. Based on the propensity score, participants can be matched in order to balance the covariates in the two groups, and therefore reduce selection bias (for different matching options, see Harder, Stuart, & Anthony, 2010). One advantage of the propensity score is that it is possible to match participants on multiple variables simultaneously, since the logistic regression reduces each participant's set of covariates to a single propensity score. While propensity scores offer the possibility to control for selection bias in correlational studies, and intergroup contact research is mainly based on such correlational studies, this method is, in fact, rarely used in intergroup contact research or in psychological research more generally. One likely reason for the neglect of propensity scores in intergroup contact research is because work on propensity scores has mostly been published in journals on statistics and other fields and only rarely in psychology (Shadish, 2010). Moreover, there are not many accessible guidelines to aid applied researchers (but see Harder et al., 2010). It is, however, a powerful method to control for selection bias, and therefore should be used more frequently in intergroup contact research, not least because the typical future study on intergroup contact will, as in the past, be a correlational study (e.g., self-report surveys).

We know of only one study in the intergroup contact literature in which propensity scores were used to test for reciprocal causation. Lewis (2007) examined the relationship between knowing lesbian, gay, or bisexual persons (LGB) and support for gay rights based on data from 27 surveys of the national population in the U.S. conducted since 1983. He used propensity scores to test whether having positive attitudes towards homosexuality increases the probability of having contact with LGBs. First, he examined who knows LGBs. The pattern of results showed that especially younger, more educated, female, less religious, and more liberal respondents were more likely to know LGBs. So it seemed that this pattern supported the argument that people who know LGBs already had more accepting attitudes towards homosexuality. Lewis then calculated a logit regression with 'knowing LGBs' as the dependent variable, and the covariates as predictor variables. Based on the logit regression, he calculated for each respondent the probability of knowing LGBs (propensity score). In a next step, he matched respondents who knew someone gay with respondents who did not know someone gay based on similarity in the propensity score. In this way, he equated those who had contact with LGBs with those who did not have contact. Comparing the now-matched respondents showed that, even after controlling for the observed covariates, respondents who knew LGBs gave significantly more support to gay rights than did respondents who did not know LGBs. Thus, these results provided evidence consistent with a causal effect of contact on prejudice.

A good introduction to propensity score matching can be found in Guo and Fraser (2009) and West and Thoemmes (2008). Propensity score matching has, however, a number of shortcomings (Shadish et al., 2002). Large samples are needed and the group overlap (i.e., overlap in the distribution of the used covariates between the compared groups, e.g., contact versus no contact) must be substantial since otherwise not enough matches can be identified, with the consequence that any causal conclusion is necessarily restricted. More seriously, because matching only controls for *observed* covariates, hidden bias (i.e., differences on unobserved variables) between contact and non-contact respondents can remain.

The second class of models accounting for possible selection bias between people with and without contact additionally considers differences in unobserved variables. Sensitivity analysis (Rosenbaum, 1995) and selection models (Winship & Mare, 1992) belong to this class of models (for an overview on selection models, see Rosenbaum, 1995; Winship & Mare, 1992; Winship & Morgan, 1999; for a non-technical overview, see Shadish et al., 2002). Again, these methods are rarely used in intergroup contact research. We know of only one relevant study. Powers and Ellison (1995) used endogenous switching regression models (Mare & Winship, 1988; Winship & Mare, 1992), one example of a selection model, to account for the possibility that prejudiced individuals avoid intergroup contact. Based on cross-sectional survey data, Powers and Ellison (1995) analyzed the relation between the amount of contact of Black respondents, in the form of intergroup friendship with Whites, and their attitudes towards Whites. They compared four different models, of which the comparison between two of them is of most interest here. One of the models was the standard contact model in which it is assumed that intergroup contact is an exogenous determinant of prejudice. This implies that there is no selection process involved in having intergroup contact or not. Another model, the general model, included model parameters that provided information about whether respondents, net of observed covariates, were selected into their respective contact status category (having contact or not) on a non-random basis, thus allowing the researchers to test for selection bias caused by unobserved covariates. Results revealed no evidence that the observed association between intergroup contact and racial attitudes was caused by unobserved selection processes. The standard contact model fitted the data as well as the general model. Moreover, the general model provided no evidence for selection bias.

The last method identified by Pettigrew (1998) for estimating the causal effect of contact on prejudice is longitudinal research. One of the preconditions for inferring causality is that the assumed cause precedes the assumed effect (Shadish et al., 2002). This is exactly what longitudinal designs are able to take into account, namely that the cause (here intergroup contact) precedes the effect (here prejudice; Menard, 2002; see also Gollob & Reichardt, 1987, for a discussion of the need for time lags in causal models). Moreover, longitudinal designs allow the researcher to test simultaneously for reciprocal causation, that is, whether intergroup contact leads to more positive intergroup attitudes, and more positive intergroup attitudes lead to more intergroup contact. As pointed out by Finkel (1995, p. 2), ". . . panel [longitudinal] designs allow more rigorous tests of causal relations than are possible with cross-sections, and thus approximate more closely than other correlational research designs the controlled testing of causality possible with experimental methods." Thus, longitudinal designs should be attractive for intergroup contact researchers, because experimental tests are hard to implement, at least when long term effects of intergroup contact are of interest. Although the last few years have seen the publication of a number of longitudinal studies on effects of intergroup contact (e.g., Binder et al., 2009; Christ et al., 2010; Tropp, Hawi, Van Laar, & Levin, 2012), there is still a scarcity of such longitudinal designs within the intergroup contact literature (Christ, Hewstone, Tropp, & Wagner, 2012).

The common way to analyze longitudinal effects of intergroup contact is to use multiple regression in order to test a cross-lagged model (Finkel, 1995). In its simplest form, a two-variable, two-time model is used (see Figure 10.1) to estimate the causal effects of intergroup contact on prejudice and vice versa (Campbell & Kenny, 1999). In such models, both intergroup contact and prejudice can influence

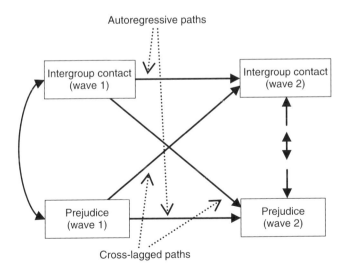

Figure 10.1 A simple two wave, two variables cross-lagged model

each other over a time lag. It is assumed that the cross-lagged paths (either from intergroup contact at time 1 to prejudice at time 2, or vice versa) provide estimates for the proposed causal effects. To make such a test more strict and convincing, the cross-lagged paths are calculated after controlling for, first, the autoregressive path (variables at time 2 being predicted by their corresponding value at time 1), and, second, the indirect effects from covariation of the two variables of interest, here contact and prejudice and the autoregressive path (Gollob & Reichardt, 1987).

To provide an example, Brown, Eller, Leeds, and Stace (2007) examined the longitudinal effects of intergroup contact on intergroup attitudes. Participants were students (n = 109) at a British state secondary school; their contact with and attitudes towards members of a private secondary school in the same town were assessed. At two waves, quantity and quality of intergroup contact, perceived typi-cality of the contacted member of the outgroup, and three measures of intergroup attitudes (desire for closeness, evaluation of the other school, and infrahumaniza-tion) were measured. Infrahumanization refers to the tendency of individuals to view out-groups as possessing a lesser degree of humanity than the in-group (Ley-ens et al., 2000). The time lag between the two waves was 14 weeks. To examine the causal effects of intergroup contact and intergroup attitudes, the authors used multiple regression. In a first step, the authors examined the longitudinal effects of intergroup contact on the different measures of intergroup attitudes. A series of multiple regression analyses were performed with contact quantity, contact qual-ity, and typicality at time 1 as predictor variables and the three different intergroup attitude measures at time 2 as outcome variables. In all regression models, the authors controlled for the intergroup attitude measures and their covariations with attitude indicators at time 1. In accordance with intergroup contact theory, higher quantity of contact at time 1 related to more desired closeness, less negative evalu-ation and less infrahumanisation at time 2. In a second set of analyses, the authors tested the reverse causal direction of variables. Here, quantity and quality of inter-group contact at time 2 were outcome variables, and the three intergroup attitude measures at time 1 were predictor variables. None of the intergroup attitude meas-ures had a significant relation with quantity or quality of intergroup contact over time (but see Binder et al., 2009).

As noted above, multiple regression is typically used in intergroup contact research to examine longitudinal effects of intergroup contact on intergroup atti-tudes. Few studies have used path analysis (e.g., Binder et al., 2009), allowing the researchers to test the causal paths from intergroup contact to intergroup attitudes and vice versa *simultaneously* (Finkel, 1995). We return to this point later in this chapter.

Cross-lagged models have, however, been the subject of some criticism (see Rogosa, 1980). Problems arise, for example, when measurement error is not taken into account (Finkel, 1995; Shadish et al., 2002). Both multiple regression analysis and path analysis are based on the precondition that variables are measured with-out error, an unrealistic assumption in the case of intergroup contact research (at least whenever self-reports are used). For instance, if there is measurement error in intergroup contact at time 1, both the autoregressive effect on intergroup contact at time 2 and the cross-lagged effect of intergroup contact on intergroup attitudes at time 2 would be underestimated. Thus, it is important to control for measurement error in cross-lagged models. This can be done using structural equation modeling, which we deal with below.

Specification bias is another serious problem in cross-lagged models. Any significant cross-lagged paths can be caused by indirect correlations between the variables of interests and omitted third variables. For example, an observed lagged effect of contact on prejudice could be due to the respondents' degree of formal education. Since formal education is in many cases positively related to intergroup contact and negatively associated with prejudice (Wagner & Zick, 1995), formal education can, as a third variable, result in significant cross-lagged paths between contact and prejudice. Avoiding spuriousness (i.e., the incorrect inference of a causal relationship between two variables) is not an easy task. One way to eliminate spuriousness in causal models is to include covariates in the model (in our example, formal education could serve as a covariate; see Little, Preacher, Selig, and Card, 2007, for different ways to control for covariates in these kinds of models). To test whether spuriousness is a potential problem, cross-lagged panel correlation can be used (Kenny, 1975; see also Campbell & Kenny, 1999). In its simplest form, two variables are measured at two times resulting in six correlations: two cross-sectional correlations (time 1 and time 2), two autocorrelations and two cross-lagged correlations. A spurious relation between the two variables results in equal cross-lagged correlations (assuming equal stabilities of the two variables). Thus, unequal cross-lagged correlations can be used to argue against spuriousness (Kenny, 1975).

Moreover, most longitudinal research on intergroup contact suffers from small sample sizes, having not tested for measurement invariance (e.g., Vandenberg & Lance, 2000), and having collected data from only two time points (see Swart, Hewstone, Christ, & Voci, 2011). Small samples restrict the type of statistical analyses that can be conducted on the data, and limit the complexity of the hypotheses that can be tested. Longitudinal studies also need to include an analysis of whether measurement invariance exists. The basic question here is whether the respective indicators represent the same underlying constructs over time (Little et al., 2007). This is of particular relevance to longitudinal survey research since measurement invariance is a prerequisite for making comparisons of responses to the same question(s) (and relations between different variables) over time possible. Longitudinal studies need to collect data over more than two time points if they are to explore full longitudinal mediation effects (Selig & Preacher, 2009). We will provide a more detailed example on these points later.

Neglect of context

According to Pettigrew (2008), the contact research literature suffers from the scarcity of multilevel studies (and longitudinal studies). He strongly advocates such studies since they ". . . are obviously necessary to place the intergroup contact phenomena in their full and evolving social context" (p. 193).

This relates to a major critique of research on intergroup contact, namely, that it has neglected the social context in which intergroup contact occurs. In their critical review J. Dixon et al. (2005) claim that ". . . the contact literature has become detached from (and sometimes irrelevant to) everyday life in divided societies" (p. 697). According to these authors, one problem of research on intergroup contact is that it has mainly focused on the prejudiced individual, thus ignoring the wider context (but see the examples provided below). Whereas J. Dixon et al. (2005) discuss the question of how far the prejudice-reducing contact effect observed in North America and Western Europe can be generalized to other contexts and cultures (see also Hewstone, Tausch, Voci, Kenworthy, Hughes, & Cairns, 2008; Wagner & Hewstone, in press), we will focus here on the problem of analyzing contact effects at different levels of analysis.

Forbes (1997, 2004) pointed to the fact that intergroup contact sometimes relates differently to intergroup attitudes when different levels of analysis are taken into account. Whereas on the situational (micro-)level the majority of studies show a negative relation between intergroup contact and intergroup attitudes (i.e., more contact is related to more positive intergroup attitudes), on a higher (macro-)level of analysis (e.g., comparing regions or nations), a positive relation is found (i.e., nation states with on average more intergroup contact show on average more negative intergroup attitudes; e.g., Coenders, Lubbers, & Scheepers, 2008). Such a seeming contradiction is a well-known statistical phenomenon: the relations between variables on different levels of analysis are mathematically independent from each other (see Hox, 2010, for a possible theoretical explanation of these differential effects of intergroup contact on prejudice).

If different levels of analysis are not taken into account, but inferences are made from one level to the other, the danger of the compositional fallacy (also known as the atomistic fallacy) and the ecological fallacy arises (Pettigrew, 1996). The compositional fallacy occurs when researchers analyze data on a micro level (e.g., individuals) and draw conclusions from these results on the macro-level (e.g., society). The ecological fallacy occurs when researchers analyze data on the macro-level and infer from that to the micro-level. One argument forwarded by critics, therefore, is that changes in intergroup attitudes on the micro-level are often unrelated to changes in intergroup conflict on the macro-level. Pettigrew and Tropp (2011, ch. 11) elegantly replied to these critiques by pointing out that future research on intergroup contact has to consider multiple levels of analysis simultaneously. They call for research to link the meso-level with the micro- and macro-levels of analysis (see also Pettigrew, 2006, 2008; Wagner et al., 2008). Intergroup contact occurs at the situational (meso-level) of analysis, but to fully understand intergroup contact effects and to make intergroup contact research more policy relevant, it has to be connected with the macro-institutional levels of analysis (e.g., Oliver & Wong, 2003; Schmid, Tausch, Hewstone, Cairns, & Hughes, 2008) as well as with the physiological and personality micro-levels (e.g., Blascovich, Mendes, Hunter, Lickel, & Kowai-Bell, 2001; Hodson, Harry, & Mitchell, 2009; see also Hodson, Costello et al., this volume). Multilevel analysis (Hox, 2010) allows researchers to combine different levels of analysis. But applications of multilevel analysis are seldom conducted in intergroup contact research (for exceptions, see J. C. Dixon, 2006; DeTezanos-Pintos, Bratt, & Brown, 2010; Wagner et al., 2006). We will provide a more detailed example after having first introduced multilevel analysis in more detail.

Promising statistical methods for the next generation of intergroup contact research

In the previous sections, we have reviewed challenges for intergroup contact research, namely measurement issues, the causal sequence problem, and the relative neglect of the social context in analyses. Our review of these challenges clearly shows the need for more longitudinal and multilevel studies in intergroup contact research.

In the following, we will introduce two promising statistical approaches for longitudinal designs based on structural equation modeling. These are latent cross-lagged models and latent growth curve models. Thereafter, we introduce multilevel analysis, a statistical technique that allows researchers to simultaneously analyze variables located on different levels of analysis.

The latent cross-lagged model

As previously discussed, cross-lagged models are attractive because they enable researchers to estimate causal effects on the basis of non-experimental data. The cross-lagged paths provide information about the structural relationships between constructs, such as contact and prejudice. Specifically, the magnitude of the cross-lagged coefficients indicates how much variation in one of the variables at time 1 predicts aggregate change in the other variable at time 2, or vice versa. Because the autocorrelation for each variable is statistically controlled by means of the autoregressive paths, the cross-lagged effects indicate the 'pure' influence of each construct of interest. Causal inference is, however, not unequivocal. Threats to the validity of causal inference, as mentioned before, are the presence of measurement error and selection bias. In addition, cross-lagged models assume stationarity (i.e., that the causal structure does not change over time; Kenny, 1975). Fortunately, measurement error can be easily handled by incorporating the measurement model into the cross-lagged model (Jöreskog, 1979) using structural equation modeling (SEM) instead of multiple regression. Traditionally, indicators of contact and prejudice are built on the basis of mean scores drawn from a number of relevant items, such as "How often do you have personal contact with foreigners in your neighborhood?" In SEM, these indicators are used to estimate latent variables. The estimates of the structural relations between latent variables are then considered free of any measurement error (Kline, 2010).

The handling of selection bias is far more problematic. Typically, potential covariates are considered (Little et al., 2007). Alternatively, although seldom done, common factor models can be used to test whether the covariation between variables can be explained by a common (unmeasured) third variable (Finkel,

1995; McArdle, 2009). Stationarity can only be tested when at least three waves of data are collected. In this case, all paths connecting wave 1 to wave 2 are assumed and tested to be identical to the paths connecting wave 2 and wave 3 (Cole & Maxwell, 2003; see also Little et al., 2007).

Swart et al. (2011) used a latent cross-lagged model to test the mediation of the effects of cross-group friendships on prejudice, perceived outgroup variability, and negative action tendencies via intergroup anxiety and affective empathy. They studied a sample of Colored (of mixed racial heritage) junior high school children (N = 465) in South Africa, who made ratings of their contact with and various measures of attitudes towards the White outgroup, in addition to key potential mediators. This study improves on previous longitudinal studies in three important ways: (1) The authors used latent variables in an SEM framework. Thus, in all analyses, constructs were controlled for measurement error. (2) Because the authors used latent variables, they were able to test whether the latent variables changed in their meaning (Vandenberge & Lance, 2000). This refers to the questions whether the indicators for the latent constructs represent the same underlying constructs at each time point (e.g., Little et al., 2007). Establishing longitudinal measurement invariance for each of the constructs is a necessary pre-condition for any meaningful comparisons of participants' responses (and the relationships between these responses) over time. (3) The analyses were based on three waves. This adequately captures the causal process since all variables – the predictor (intergroup contact), the mediators (anxiety and affective empathy), and the outcomes (outgroup variability and negative action tendencies) – were measured at all subsequent waves (Cole & Maxwell, 2003). Moreover, Swart et al. (2011) tested the stationarity assumption by comparing a model in which all autoregressive paths of one latent variable were constrained to be equal with a model without equality constraints. Results confirmed the assumption of stationarity since the model fit of the constrained model was comparable to the fit of the unconstrained model (i.e., the interrelations between latent variables did not vary between the different waves of data collection). Notably, the mediational analysis using a latent cross-lagged model supported the basic assumptions of the contact hypothesis: Full longitudinal mediation was only found in the direction from time 1 contact to time 3 prejudice (via time 2 mediators). Specifically, cross-group friendships at time 1 were positively associated with positive outgroup attitudes at time 3 (via affective empathy at time 2) and perceived outgroup variability at time 3 (via intergroup anxiety and affective empathy at time 2), and negatively associated with negative action tendencies at time 3 (via affective empathy at time 2).

One major drawback of cross-lagged models is that they do not account for absolute changes in individual scores for a construct of interest. That is, the autoregressive paths do not yield information about individual change in absolute scores across different points in time. For instance, although individuals may maintain their *relative* standing among group members, their individual scores might indeed be subject to an increase or decrease in the period under study (Rogosa, 1995; Stoolmiller & Bank, 1995). In addition, the fixed effects approach of the cross-lagged model assumes that the coefficients are the same for all individuals (for further critiques of the cross-lagged model, see Hertzog & Nesselroade, 2003). To account for such individual differences in processes of change researchers suggest the use of latent growth curve models.

Latent growth curve models

Meredith and Tisak (1990) first proposed the use of latent growth curve models (LGM). With LGM it is possible to analyze individual trajectories, that is, changes over time. Latent growth curve models are based on the assumption that a set of observed repeated measures taken on a given individual over time can be used to estimate an unobserved underlying trajectory. To describe this trajectory, two latent variables are estimated, the latent intercept factor and the latent slope factor. The latent intercept usually models the initial level in the measured variable (e.g., intergroup contact), whereas the latent slope expresses the linear growth rate (change) over time. Both the latent intercept as well as the latent slope variables are allowed to vary across individuals. A prerequisite of LGM is that the measurement model is the same at each time point (i.e., there is measurement invariance), otherwise growth cannot be modeled meaningfully.

Figure 10.2 presents a simple unconditional LGM, with three repeated measures of intergroup contact assessed at equal intervals. "Unconditional" here means that both latent factors are not affected by other variables. Factor loadings on the intercept factor are set to 1, and the three factor loadings on the slope factor equal $\lambda_t = t - 1$, where t is 1, 2, 3. Thereby, the slope-factor is constrained to a linear growth, in this case the mean change in intergroup contact over time. In this example, the intercept reflects the model-implied value of intergroup contact at the initial period of measurement because the factor loading on the slope-factor for the first measure was set to zero, and factor loadings on the intercept factor are constrained to one.

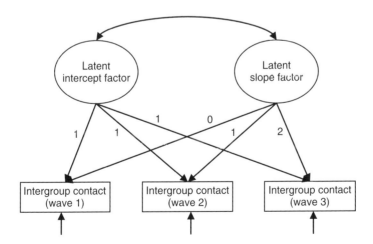

Figure 10.2 A latent growth curve model with manifest indicators and three waves

It is also possible to use alternative codings of time to define other meanings of the intercept term. In LGM, in addition to linear growth, nonlinear trajectories can also be modeled. Besides the question of the functional form of the trajectory, it is often of interest to identify variables which affect the change in constructs. The LGM can be easily extended by including exogenous predictor variables (Willett & Sayer, 1994). In these models the researcher can examine how the intercept and the slope of a repeated measure are affected by time invariant predictors (i.e., variables that do not change over time, such as sex or race). Good introductions to LGM are given by Bollen and Curran (2006) and Preacher, Wichman, MacCallum, and Briggs (2008).

We know of only one study which used an LGM in intergroup contact research based on an SEM approach. Titzmann and Silbereisen (2009) were interested in the mean level and rate of change in preference of intra-ethnic friends (friendship homophily) of newcomer and more experienced immigrant adolescents. Moreover, they examined predictors of interindividual differences in level and rate of change in friendship homophily, such as the ethnic composition of the school context, parents' objections to their children's adaptation, the use of new language, and perceived discrimination. A sample of 490 adolescent immigrants from the former Soviet Union to Germany (N = 218 newcomer and N = 272 experienced immigrants) were surveyed at four waves with 12 months time lag between the different waves. Friendship homophily was operationalized as the percentage of intra-ethnic friends out of all friends. In a first step, the authors estimated a multiple-group LGM comparing newcomer with experienced immigrants. Results showed that the intercept factor of the two groups differed significantly, with higher rates of intra-ethnic friends at wave 1 among newcomers compared to experienced immigrants. Only for newcomers was the latent slope significant with a negative estimate, meaning that over each wave there was a mean decrease in friendship homophily of 2 percent. Multiple-group comparison, however, showed no differences in the slope for the two groups. Thus, there was no significant difference in the rate of change in friendship homophily between both groups.

In a next step, Titzmann and Silbereisen (2009) included a number of predictor variables in the model to examine possible predictors of interindividual differences (variance) in the intercept and slope factor, such as age, ethnic composition of school, parental objections to their offspring's adaptation, language use, and perceived discrimination at wave 1. In addition, change scores for these indicators between waves 1 and 4 were included in the multiple-group LGM. School composition showed significant effects on the intercept in both groups: adolescent ethnic immigrants reported higher levels of friendship homophily if they attended schools with a high percentage of ethnic German immigrants than if they did not. There was no effect of this predictor on the slope in both groups. Language use at wave 1 significantly predicted the intercept in both groups and the slope in the newcomer group. Higher levels of new language use at the first wave (i.e., immigrants speaking German) predicted lower levels of initial (wave 1) friendship homophily and a more pronounced decrease in friendship homophily in the newcomer group (i.e., a decrease in homophily from wave 1 to wave 4).

Moreover, change in language use between wave 1 and wave 4 significantly predicted the slope in both groups, meaning that a higher increase in new language use was related to a higher decrease in friendship homophily.

Having now considered both latent cross-lagged models and latent growth curve models, the question arises, which model should be used for longitudinal data? The answer depends on the research question (see also Ferrer & McArdle, 2003; Hertzog & Nesselroade, 2003). For instance, if the aim is to test the direction of causation, cross-lagged models are the method of choice. When, however, absolute change and interindividual variability in absolute change is of interest, the LGM is more appropriate.

There are additional statistical methods for longitudinal data based on SEM, which we have not covered here. McArdle (2009) reviews different SEM techniques including cross-lagged models and LGM, but also latent change score models (for an application to intergroup contact research, see Dhont et al., 2012). Multilevel analysis can also be used to estimate growth models. To a great extent, the use of LGM and growth modeling based on multilevel analysis yields comparable results. The reader is referred to Chou, Bentler, and Pentz (1998) for further statistical details, and to Page-Gould, Mendoza-Denton, and Tropp (2008), and to Trail, Shelton, and West (2009) for applications to intergroup contact research. Again, which kinds of models researchers choose depends on their research question. Our aim here is to introduce different alternatives for modeling longitudinal data. It is our hope that future intergroup contact research will make more use of these more advanced longitudinal modeling techniques.

Multilevel analysis

As discussed above, one critique of intergroup contact research concerns the neglect of the wider social context. For example, Pettigrew and Tropp (2011; see also Pettigrew, 2008) have pointed out that future research on intergroup contact needs to place intergroup contact in its micro- and macro-contexts. This necessitates multilevel analysis (Pettigrew, 2006), a method so far rarely used in intergroup contact research. Multilevel analysis, as its name suggests, requires data located at multiple levels of analysis. For instance, data on the lower level (e.g., quantity and quality of intergroup contact, individual prejudice) is combined with the macro-level data (e.g., proportion of outgroup members in a certain geographical region). If in such a case contact and prejudice indicators of a number of individuals come from the same region, a hierarchical data structure is given, such that observations at one level of analysis (individual scores) are nested within observations at another, higher level (geographical region). The convention in multilevel research is that larger numbers indicate levels higher in the hierarchy, so individual contact would be level 1 of the analysis, and a proportion of outgroup members in the region constitute level 2 of the analysis.

In examining intergroup contact effects, Forbes (2004) has demonstrated that relationships between variables of interest at different levels of analysis are independent. He showed that intergroup contact can have a prejudice-reducing effect on level 1, but simultaneously a prejudice-enhancing effect at level 2. Any type of relationship at one level can theoretically coexist with any type of relationship at another level. Using a single-level analysis, performed on either the lower or higher level, can provide misleading results and inferences for another level (see earlier discussion of compositional and ecological fallacies). In multilevel modeling, variables from different levels of analysis are analyzed simultaneously. Relations between variables from different levels are analyzed at their appropriate level, thereby avoiding fallacies (for statistical problems caused by hierarchical data, see Hox, 2010).

We will introduce, as one type of multilevel analysis, the so-called Multilevel Random Coefficient Model (MRCM), which provides a highly reliable analysis suited to hierarchical data structures. There exists a number of excellent and detailed introductions to the statistics of MRCM (e.g., Hox, 2010; Kreft & de Leeuw, 1998; Raudenbush & Bryk, 2002; Snijders & Bosker, 1999). Moreover, there are several articles and chapters describing the application of MRCM to certain kinds of data, such as event- and interval-contingent data (e.g., Nezlek, 2001), as well as diary data (e.g., Nezlek, 2003), or to personality and social psychology in general (e.g., Christ, Sibley, & Wagner, 2012). Diary methods, collecting frequent reports on intergroup encounters and prejudice from individuals (Bolger, Davis, & Rafaeli, 2003; see Nezlek & Schaafsma, 2010, for a discussion on the application of diary data in intergroup contact research), in particular, have become a rich source for studies of intergroup contact (e.g., Schaafsma, Nezlek, Krejtz, & Safron, 2010; Shelton, Richeson, & Salvatore, 2005; Trail et al., 2009; West, Shelton, & Trail, 2009).

Central to MRCM is that coefficients describing phenomena at one level are analyzed at another level. Take, for example, the case in which researchers have measured both intergroup contact and prejudice at the individual level (level 1). Suppose also that they have indicators at a higher level of analysis, say the proportion of outgroup members in a given region (level 2). The researchers want to examine whether quantity of contact is related to prejudice. Moreover, they assume that higher proportions of outgroup members relate to more opportunities for intergroup contact. Therefore, it is likely that the proportion of outgroup members relates positively to both the amount of intergroup contact as well as to lower prejudice. Thus, the researchers assume that the amount of intergroup contact mediates the effect of the proportion of outgroup members on prejudice.

In MRCM, the relations of the variables at the different levels of analysis are estimated simultaneously. For example, a regression model is estimated at a lower-level (level 1). In this example, the amount of intergroup contact would be a predictor of the outcome variable, prejudice. In this simple regression at level 1, two regression coefficients are estimated: The intercept and the slope of the amount of intergroup contact. Since these data are nested (i.e., respondents are nested in neighborhoods), it is likely that these coefficients vary between regions, the level 2 units. Thus, for each coefficient, two parameters are estimated. The first parameter, the so called fixed-effect, is the central tendency of this parameter. In our example, this would be the mean intercept, averaged over all regions (prejudice score, when the predictor variable is zero) and the mean slope (the mean relation between the amount of intergroup contact and intergroup attitudes over all regions). The second parameter, the so called *random-effect*, is the random error. This is the estimate of the variance of the level 1 coefficients between the level 2 units, here regions. The coefficients of this lower-level analysis are then modeled as dependent variables at a higher-level of analysis. The random error indicates that coefficients from the lower-level analysis (intercept and slopes) vary between higher-levels of analysis. This variation can then be modeled at the higher-level using higher-level predictors to explain the variation. In our example, we would include the level 2 predictor variable 'proportion of outgroup members' (note that this variable varies only between regions) as well as the mean amount of inter-group contact (i.e., the group mean amount of intergroup contact) as predictor variables in these level 2 regressions. Regressing the random intercept on the pro-portion of outgroup members and the mean amount of intergroup contact would yield estimates for the relation between these variables on level 2. Regressing the random slope on the two predictor variables would test whether the level 1 rela-tion between the amount of intergroup contact and prejudice would depend on the values in the level 2 predictor variables. If a significant relation were found, a cross-level interaction would be present.

The example we have just used to illustrate the very basics of MRCM is derived from a study by Wagner et al. (2006; see also J. C. Dixon, 2006). Wagner and col-leagues used cross-sectional data from a recent German probability phone survey (N = 2,722) of the German adult population. They were interested in the relation between the proportion of ethnic minorities in a given region and prejudice within this region. Previous research had sometimes found a positive relation, sometimes a negative relation, or even no relation. Wagner and colleagues assumed, based on intergroup contact theory, that a proportion of ethnic minorities would be nega-tively related to prejudice. Moreover, they tested whether the mean quantity of intergroup contact within a given region mediated the effects of proportion of ethnic minorities on prejudice.

The survey data available to Wagner et al. (2006) included district codes that indicate the location of residence for each respondent. A "district" is an adminis-trative unit of about 50,000 inhabitants (and with a wide range of values). The dis-trict codes enabled the researchers to match objective statistical data, such as the proportion of ethnic minorities in the district, to the individual level data such as the quantity of intergroup contact and prejudice level. Results of MRCM showed that the proportion of ethnic minorities in the district and district respondents' prejudice were negatively correlated, meaning that a higher proportion of ethnic minorities within a district relates to lower prejudice scores of respondents liv-ing in this district on average. Moreover, a multilevel mediation analysis (Krull & MacKinnon, 2001) showed that the negative relation between ethnic minority proportion and prejudice was partly mediated (i.e., explained) by direct contact experiences (e.g., cross-group friendships), supporting the contact hypothesis.

In the case of multiple levels of analysis, two different kinds of mediation can be separated: upper level and lower-level mediation (Kenny, Kashy, & Bolger,

1998; Krull & MacKinnon, 2001). In upper level mediation, the effect of a level 2 or upper level variable is mediated by level 1 processes (see Wagner et al, 2006). In lower-level mediation, the effect of a level 1 or lower-level variable is mediated by level 1 processes. Both kinds of mediation can easily be tested using the standard single level procedures to establish mediational effects (Krull & MacKinnon, 2001; see Zhang, Zyphur, & Preacher, 2009, for a review of problems and solutions in testing multilevel mediational models). These standard procedures are, however, only appropriate for lower-level mediation as long as fixed-effect models are estimated. As Kenny, Korchmaros, and Bolger (2003) emphasize, lower-level mediation analysis becomes more complicated when effects are considered to be random. If the mediational links vary across the level 2 units, the random effects for the independent variable-mediator link and for the mediator-dependent variable link can be correlated. Bauer, Preacher, and Gil (2006) recently presented direct procedures to test random indirect effects in lower-level mediation models, but these procedures are not yet widely used in applied research.

One important recent extension of multilevel analysis is its use in combination with structural equation modeling. The advantage of multilevel structural equation modeling (ML-SEM) is that it combines the best of both worlds (Mehta & Neale, 2005). Specifically, it allows one to develop full SEMs at different levels of analysis (so far, this is restricted to two levels of analysis, except in formulating growth models). Thus, it is possible to model complex relationships between variables of interest. Moreover, measurement error can be taken into account by using multiple indicators for latent variables, satisfying the assumption in regular multilevel modeling that variables are measured without error. That is, more accurate estimates are provided in ML-SEM. An additional feature of ML-SEM is that a measurement model can be tested at different levels of analysis simultaneously (multilevel confirmatory factor analysis), which enables researchers to test for invariance of measurement model across levels.

Multilevel structural equation modeling is still a new area of methodological research (e.g., Bauer, 2003; Curran, 2003; du Toit & du Toit, 2003; Muthén, 1991, 1994; Rovine & Molenaar, 2000). In recent years, software advances in SEM have, however, made it easier to apply ML-SEM to the analysis of hierarchical data. For an excellent introduction to ML-SEM, presenting examples using the software package M*plus* (Muthén & Muthén, 1998–2007), the reader is referred to the book by Heck and Thomas (2008; see also Muthén & Asparouhov, 2010). There are already applications of ML-SEM in intergroup contact research (see De Tezanos-Pinto et al., 2010; Wagner et al., 2006).

The multilevel models described so far are restricted to cases where the dependent variable is measured at level 1, for example, in the form of individual prejudice. Although in many social psychological research questions level 1 dependent variables are of main concern, there are situations where level 2 outcomes are of interest, such as in upper level mediation (Krull & MacKinnon, 2001). An example would be to look for individual predictors for the aggregate level of prejudice in a geographical region. Snijders and Bosker (1999) differentiated between macro-micro situations and micro-macro situations. In macro-micro situations, the dependent variable is measured at level 1, and predictor variables are measured at level 1 and/or level 2. In micro-macro situations, the dependent variable is measured at level 2, and predictor variables are again measured either at level 1 or level 2. Croon and Veldhoven (2007) pointed out that the study of multilevel models has focused mainly on macro-micro situations; micro-macro situations have been virtually neglected. Most textbooks on multilevel modeling are also restricted to models that are appropriate to the macro-micro situation. Moreover, most software packages for multilevel modeling (e.g., MLwiN, HLM) are mainly designed exclusively for the macro-micro situation.

Croon and Veldhoven (2007) proposed a latent variable model for analyzing data from micro-macro situations. Their model applies to situations in which some or all predictor variables are measured at level 1. The authors showed that simply aggregating the lower-level predictor variables, as is often done in research that aggregates data to a higher-level, leads to biased estimates when using standard regression analysis. They proposed a two-stage latent variable approach in which the unobserved group mean for each higher-level unit is estimated using weights obtained by applying basic analysis of variance formulae. The adjusted group means are then used to run regression analyses at the higher-level to predict the higher-level outcome. The authors showed analytically and in a simulation study that the results based on the adjusted group means are unbiased.

More recently, Lüdtke, Marsh, Robitzsch, Trautwein, Asparouhov, and Muthén (2008) showed that using a multilevel latent covariate approach to estimate the unobserved group mean of level 1 predictor variables outperforms Croon and Veldhoven's (2007) two-stage approach, at least under certain circumstances. Thus, the multilevel latent covariate approach as implemented in Mplus (Muthén & Muthén, 1998–2007) can be easily used to estimate multilevel models capturing micro-macro situations.

Summary and conclusions: towards the next wave of intergroup contact research

We have reviewed major methodological challenges for intergroup contact research. These concern measurement issues, the causal order problem, and the neglect of the social context. We then introduced promising statistical methods that can help to develop the next generation of intergroup contact research. These were different methods for the analysis of longitudinal data (latent cross-lagged models and latent growth curve models) and methods for the simultaneous analysis of multiple levels of analysis. As Pettigrew (2008, p. 193) has pointed out, one of the key issues of future intergroup contact research is to "place the intergroup contact phenomena in their full and evolving social context." The presented methods can help to design future intergroup contact studies that fill this gap.

The majority of intergroup contact research relies on self-reports. Hewstone et al. (2011) have recently provided first evidence for the validity of self-reports in assessing quantity and quality of intergroup contact. This is important since it weakens critiques and supports the validity of results based on self-reports.

Nonetheless, future intergroup contact research should use a mix of different methods, such as correlational and experimental approaches (Pettigrew & Tropp, 2011). However, experimental research is primarily a viable option only for the analysis of short term effects of intergroup contact. In addition, social context variables are difficult to simulate experimentally (e.g., the proportion of outgroup members living in a neighborhood). Thus, correlational approaches using self-reports will still be needed and used in future intergroup contact research, based either on cross-sectional or, preferably, longitudinal designs.

A further major challenge concerns the causal order problem. Different approaches have been used in cross-sectional studies, such as methods to control and estimate selection bias, propensity scores or endogenous switching regression models. These techniques are not easy to apply. Therefore, applications are rare exceptions. Also promising are longitudinal studies and related methods to examine the causal relation between variables of interest. In recent years, an increase in longitudinal contact studies has been observed. However, our review of longitudinal studies published thus far showed that, in many cases, these studies have not used appropriate statistical methods. We have presented two important longitudinal methods, both based on an SEM framework: the latent cross-lagged model and LGM. Both methods account for specific forms of changes over time. The former method is appropriate if the causal relation between variables is of interest, whereas the latter method is optimal whenever absolute changes and interindividual differences in these changes of variables are of interest. There are many more longitudinal methods, either within the SEM framework (e.g., latent change models; McArdle, 2009) or variants of multilevel analysis (e.g., Nezlek, 2001). Due to space restrictions, we were not able to review all of these methods here. Our argument is that there are a variety of methods available that will help researchers to get more out of longitudinal data.

The social context is often neglected in intergroup contact research. Thus, future intergroup contact research has to combine the micro- with the macro-level of analysis. Multilevel analysis is a promising statistical method that enables researchers to simultaneously examine multiple levels of analysis. Of course, the ideal future intergroup contact study would combine experimental, longitudinal and multilevel studies. This would enable intergroup contact researchers to examine short term (experimental) and long term (longitudinal) consequences of intergroup contact in its social context (multilevel). This is a complex endeavor. However, to quote from the doyen of scholars of intergroup contact research, Thomas F. Pettigrew (2006, p. 616): "To be sure, multilevel approaches are complex; but 'the real world' *is* complex." In this chapter, we have shown that we now have powerful statistical methods at our disposal, for appropriate analysis of such complex data. We look forward with great confidence and optimism to the next wave of research on this important topic.

References

Allport, G. (1954). *The nature of prejudice*. Cambridge, MA: Perseus Books.

Bauer, D. J. (2003). Estimating multilevel linear models as structural models. *Journal of Educational and Behavioral Statistics, 28*, 135–167.

Bauer, D. J., Preacher, K. J., & Gil, K. M. (2006). Conceptualizing and testing random indirect effects and moderated mediation in multilevel models: New procedures and recommendations. *Psychological Methods, 11*, 142–163.

Baumeister, R. F., Vohs, K. D., & Funder, D. C. (2007). Psychology as the science of self-reports and finger movements. Whatever happened to actual behavior? *Perspectives on Psychological Science, 2*, 396–403.

Binder, J., Zagefka, H., Brown, R., Funke, F., Kessler, T., Mummendey, A., Maquil, A., Demoulin, S., & Leyens, J.-P. (2009). Does contact reduce prejudice or does prejudice reduce contact? A longitudinal test of the contact hypothesis amongst majority and minority groups in three European countries. *Journal of Personality and Social Psychology, 96*, 843–856.

Blascovich, J., Mendes, W. B., Hunter, S. B., Lickel, B., & Kowai–Bell, N. (2001). Perceiver threat in social interactions with stigmatized others. *Journal of Personality and Social Psychology, 80*, 253–267.

Bolger, N., Davis, A., & Rafaeli, E. (2003). Diary methods: Capturing life as it is lived. *Annual Review of Psychology, 54*, 579–616.

Bollen, K. A., & Curran, P. J. (2006). *Latent curve models: A structural equation perspective.* New York: Wiley.

Brewer, M. B., & Gaertner, S. L. (2001). Toward reduction of prejudice: Intergroup contact and social categorization. In R. Brown & S. L. Gaertner (Eds.), *Intergroup processes: Blackwell Handbook of Social Psychology* (pp. 451–472). Malden: Blackwell.

Brown, R., Eller, A., Leeds, S., & Stace, K. (2007). Intergroup contact and intergroup attitudes: A longitudinal study. *European Journal of Social Psychology, 37*, 692–703.

Campbell, D. T., & Kenny, D. A. (1999). *A primer on regression artifacts.* New York: Guilford.

Chou, C. P., Bentler, P., & Pentz, M. A. (1998). Comparisons of two statistical approaches to study growth curves: The multilevel model and the latent curve analysis. *Structural Equation Modeling, 5*, 247–266.

Christ, O., Hewstone, M., Tausch, N., Wagner, U., Voci, A., Hughes, J., & Cairns, E. (2010). Direct contact as a moderator of extended contact effects: Cross-sectional and longitudinal impact on outgroup attitudes, behavioral intentions, and attitude certainty. *Personality and Social Psychology Bulletin, 36*, 1662–1674.

Christ, O., Hewstone, M., Tropp, L., & Wagner, U. (2012). Dynamic processes in intergroup contact [Editorial]. *British Journal of Social Psychology, 51*, 219–220.

Christ, O., Sibley, C., & Wagner, U. (2012). Statistical approaches for multi-level analysis in personality and social psychology. In K. Deaux & M. Snyder (Eds.), *The Oxford Handbook of Personality and Social Psychology* (pp. 239–260). New York: Oxford University Press.

Clack, B., Dixon, J., & Tredoux, C. (2005). Eating together apart: Patterns of segregation in a multiethnic cafeteria. *Journal of Community and Applied Social Psychology, 15*, 1–16.

Coenders, M., Lubbers, M. & Scheepers, P. (2008). Support for repatriation policies of migrants: Comparisons across and explanations for European countries. *International Journal of Comparative Sociology, 49*, 175–194.

Cole, D. A., & Maxwell S. E., (2003). Testing mediational models with longitudinal data: questions and tips in using structural equation models. *Journal of Abnormal Psychology, 112*, 558–577.

Cook, S. W. (1984). Cooperative interaction in multiethnic contexts. In N. Miller & M. B. Brewer (Eds.), *Groups in contact: The psychology of desegregation* (pp. 155–185). Orlando, FL: Academic Press.

Cox, D. R. (2009). Randomization in the design of experiments. *International Statistical Review, 77,* 415–429.

Croon, M. A., van Veldhoven, J. P. M. (2007). Predicting group-level outcome variables from variables measured at the individual level: A latent variable multilevel model. *Psychological Methods, 12,* 45–57.

Cummings, S., & Lambert, T. (1997). Anti-Hispanic and anti-Asian sentiments among African Americans. *Social Science Quarterly, 78,* 338–353.

Curran, P. J. (2003). Have multilevel models been structural equation models all along? *Multivariate Behavioral Research, 38,* 529–569.

De Tezanos–Pinto, P., Bratt, C., & Brown, R. (2010). What will others think? In-group norms as a mediator of the effects of intergroup contact. *British Journal of Social Psychology, 49,* 507–523.

Dhont, K., Van Hiel, A., De Bolle, M., & Roets, A. (2012). Longitudinal intergroup contact effects on prejudice using self- and observer reports. *British Journal of Social Psychology.*

Dixon, J. C. (2006). The ties that bind and those that don't: Toward reconciling group threat and contact theories of prejudice. *Social Forces, 84,* 2179–2204.

Dixon, J., Durrheim, K., & Tredoux, C. (2005). Beyond the optimal strategy: A "reality check" for the contact hypothesis. *American Psychologist, 60,* 697–711.

Dixon, J., & Reicher, S. (1997). Intergroup contact and desegregation in the new South Africa. *British Journal of Social Psychology, 36,* 361–381.

du Toit, S., & du Toit, M. (2003). Multilevel structural equation modeling. In J. De Leeuw & I. G. G. Kreft (Eds.), *Handbook of quantitative multilevel analysis* (pp. 273–321). Boston: Kluwer.

Ensari, N., & Miller, N. (2002). The out-group must not be so bad after all: The effects of disclosure, typicality, and salience on intergroup bias. *Journal of Personality and Social Psychology, 83,* 313–329.

Ferrer, E., & McArdle, J. J. (2003). Alternative structural models for multivariate longitudinal data analysis. *Structural Equation Modeling, 10,* 493–524.

Festinger, L., & Kelley, H. (1951). *Changing attitudes through social contact.* Ann Arbor, MI: Institute for Social Research, University of Michigan.

Finkel, S. E. (1995). *Causal analysis with panel data.* Thousand Oaks, CA: Sage.

Forbes, H. D. (1997). *Ethnic conflict: Commerce, culture, and the contact hypothesis.* New Haven, CT: Yale University Press.

Forbes, H. D. (2004). Ethnic conflict and the contact hypothesis. In Y. T. Lee, C. McAuley, F. Moghaddam & S. Worchel (Eds.), *The psychology of ethnic and cultural conflict* (pp. 69–88). Westport, CT: Praeger.

Fossett, M. A., & Kiecolt, K. J. (1989). The relative size of minority populations and white racial attitudes. *Social Science Quarterly, 70,* 820–835.

Gollob, H. F., & Reichardt, C. S. (1987). Taking account of time lags in causal models. *Child Development, 58,* 80–92.

Guo, S., & Fraser, M. W. (2009). *Propensity score analysis: Statistical methods and applications.* Thousand Oaks, CA: Sage Press.

Harder, V. S., Stuart, E. A., & Anthony, J. C. (2010). Propensity score techniques and the assessment of measured covariate balance to test causal associations in psychological research. *Psychological Methods, 15,* 234–249.

Heck, R. H., & Thomas, S. L. (2008). *An introduction to multilevel modeling techniques* (2nd ed). New York: Routledge.

Hertzog, C., & Nesselroade, J. R. (2003). Assessing psychological change in adulthood: An overview of methodological issues. *Psychology and Aging, 18*, 639–657.

Hewstone, M., Judd, C. M., & Sharp, M. (2011). Do observer ratings validate self-reports of intergroup contact?: A round-robin analysis. *Journal of Experimental Social Psychology, 47*, 599–609.

Hewstone, M., Tausch, N., Voci, A., Kenworthy, J., Hughes, J., & Cairns, E. (2008). Why neighbours kill: Prior intergroup contact & killing of ethnic out-group neighbours. In V. Esses, & R. Vernon (Eds.), *Why neighbours kill* (pp. 61–92). Maldon, MA: Blackwell.

Hodson, G. (2008). Interracial prison contact: The pros for (socially dominant) cons. *British Journal of Social Psychology, 47*, 325–351.

Hodson, G. (2011). Do ideologically intolerant people benefit from intergroup contact? *Current Directions in Psychological Science, 20*, 154–159.

Hodson, G., Harry, H., & Mitchell, A. (2009). Independent benefits of contact and friendship on attitudes toward homosexuals among authoritarians and highly identified heterosexuals. *European Journal of Social Psychology, 35*, 509–525.

Hood, M. V., & Morris, I. L. (1997). Amigo o enemigo?: Context, attitudes, and Anglo public opinion toward immigration. *Social Science Quarterly, 78*, 309–323.

Hox, J. (2010). *Multilevel analysis. Techniques and applications* (2nd ed). New York: Routledge.

Hunter, J. E., & Gerbing, D. W. (1982). Unidimensional measurement, second-order factor analysis, and causal models. In B. M. Staw & L. L. Cummings (Eds.), *Research in organizational behavior* (Vol. 4, pp. 267–299). Greenwich, CA: JAI Press.

Jackman, M. R., & Crane, M. (1986). "Some of my best friends are black. . .": Interracial friendship and whites' racial attitudes. *Public Opinion Quarterly, 50*, 459–486.

Jick, T. D. (1979). Mixing qualitative and quantitative methods: Triangulation in action. *Administrative Science Quarterly, 24*, 602–611.

Jöreskog, K. G. (1979). Statistical estimation of structural models in longitudinal-developmental investigations. In J. R. Nesselroade & P. B. Baltes (Eds.), *Longitudinal research in the study of behavior and development* (pp. 303–352). New York: Academic Press.

Kashy, D. A., & Kenny, D. A. (2000). The analysis of data from dyads and groups. In H. T. Reis, & C. M. Judd (Eds), *Handbook of research methods in social psychology* (pp. 451–477). Cambridge, U.K.: Cambridge University Press.

Kenny, D. A. (1975). Cross-lagged panel correlation: A test for spuriousness. *Psychological Bulletin, 82*, 887–903.

Kenny, D. A., Kashy, D. A., & Bolger, N. (1998). Data analysis in social psychology. In D. Gilbert, S. T. Fiske & G. Lindzey (Eds.), *The handbook of social psychology* (4th ed, Vol. 1, pp. 223–265). New York: McGraw–Hill.

Kenny, D. A., Korchmaros, J. D., & Bolger, N. (2003). Lower-level mediation in multilevel models. *Psychological Methods, 8*, 115–128.

Kline, R. B. (2010). *Principles and practice of structural equation modeling* (3rd ed.). New York: Guilford Press.

Kreft, I. G. G., & de Leeuw, J. (1998). *Introducing Multilevel Modeling*. Newbury Park, CA: Sage Publications.

Krull, J. L., & MacKinnon, D. P. (2001). Multilevel modeling of individual and group level mediated effects. *Multivariate Behavioral Research, 36*, 249–277.

Lewis, G. B. (2007). *Personal Relationships and Support for Gay Rights*. Andrew Young School of Policy Studies Research Paper Series No. 07–10. Retrieved October 10, 2009 from http://papers.ssrn.com/sol3/papers.cfm?abstract_id=975975

Leyens, J. P., Paladino, P. M., Rodriguez, R. T., Vaes, J., Demoulin, S., Rodriguez, A. P., & Gaunt, R. (2000). The emotional side of prejudice: The role of secondary emotions. *Personality and Social Psychology Review, 4,* 186–197.

Link, B. G., & Cullen, F. T. (1986). Contact with the mentally ill and perceptions of how dangerous they are. *Journal of Health and Social Behavior, 27,* 289–303.

Little, T. D., Preacher, K. J., Selig, J. P., & Card, N. A. (2007). New developments in SEM panel analyses of longitudinal data. *International Journal of Behavioral Development, 31,* 357–365.

Lüdtke, O., Marsh, H. W., Robitzsch, A., Trautwein, U., Asparouhov, T., & Muthén, B. (2008). The multilevel latent covariate model: A new, more reliable approach to group-level effects in contextual studies. *Psychological Methods, 13,* 203–229.

Mare, R. D., & Winship, C. (1988). Endogenous switching regression models for the causes and effects of discrete variables. In J. Scott Long (Ed.), *Common problems in quantitative social research* (pp. 132–160). Beverly Hills, CA: Sage University Press.

McArdle, J. J. (2009). Latent variable modeling of differences and changes with longitudinal data. *Annual Review of Psychology, 60,* 577–605.

McCauley, C., Plummer, M., Moskalenko, S., & Mordkoff, J. T. (2001). The exposure index: A measure of intergroup contact. *Peace and Conflict: Journal of Peace Psychology, 7,* 321–336.

Mehta, P. D., & Neale, M. C. (2005). People are variables too: Multilevel structural equation modeling. *Psychological Methods, 10,* 259–284.

Menard, S. (2002). *Longitudinal research* (2nd ed). Thousand Oakes, CA: Sage.

Meredith, W., & Tisak, J. (1990). Latent curve analysis. *Psychometrika, 55,* 107–122.

Muthén, B. O. (1991). Multilevel factor analysis of class and student achievement components. *Journal of Educational Measurement, 28,* 338–354.

Muthén, B. O. (1994). Multilevel covariance structure analysis. *Sociological Methods and Research, 22,* 376–398.

Muthén, B. O., & Asparouhov, T. (2010). Beyond multilevel regression modeling: Multilevel analysis in a general latent variable framework. In J. Hox & J. K. Roberts (Eds.), *The handbook of advanced multilevel analysis* (pp. 15–40). New York: Taylor & Francis.

Muthén, L. K., & Muthén, B. O. (1998–2007). *Mplus User's Guide* (5th ed). Los Angeles, CA: Muthén & Muthén.

Nezlek, J. B. (2001). Multilevel random coefficient analyses of event- and interval-contingent data in social and personality psychology. *Personality and Social Psychology Bulletin, 27,* 771–785.

Nezlek, J. B. (2003). Using multilevel random coefficient modeling to analyze social interaction diary data. *Journal of Social and Personal Relationships, 20,* 437–469.

Nezlek, J. B., & Schaafsma, J. (2010). Understanding the complexity of everyday interethnic contact: Recommendations for researchers. *Social and Personality Psychology Compass, 4,* 795–806.

Oliver, E., & Wong, J. (2003). Intergroup prejudice in multiethnic settings. *American Journal of Political Science, 47,* 567–582.

Page–Gould, E., Mendoza–Denton, R., & Tropp, L.R. (2008). With a little help from my cross-group friend: Reducing anxiety in intergroup contexts through cross-group friendship. *Journal of Personality and Social Psychology, 95,* 1080–1094.

Pettigrew, T. F. (1996). *How to think like a social scientist*. New York: HarperCollins.

Pettigrew, T. F. (1998). Intergroup contact theory. *Annual Review of Psychology, 49,* 65–85.

Pettigrew, T. F. (2006). The advantages of multilevel approaches. *Journal of Social Issues, 62,* 615–620.

Pettigrew, T. F. (2008). Future directions for intergroup contact theory and research. *International Journal of Intercultural Relations, 32,* 187–199.

Pettigrew, T. F., & Tropp, L. R. (2006). A meta-analytic test of intergroup contact theory. *Journal of Personality and Social Psychology, 90,* 751–783.

Pettigrew, T. F., & Tropp, L. R. (2011). *When groups meet: The dynamics of intergroup contact.* New York: Psychology Press.

Powers, D. A., & Ellison, C. G. (1995). Interracial contact and Black racial attitudes: The contact hypothesis and selectivity bias. *Social Forces, 74,* 205–226.

Preacher, K. J., Wichman, A. L., MacCallum, R. C., & Briggs, N. E. (2008). *Latent growth curve modeling.* Thousand Oaks, CA: Sage.

Raudenbush, S. W., & Bryk, A. S. (2002). *Hierarchical Linear Models* (2nd ed). Newbury Park, CA: Sage Publications.

Rogosa, D. R. (1980). A critique of cross-lagged correlation. *Psychological Bulletin, 88,* 245–258.

Rogosa, D. R. (1995). Myths and methods: "Myths about longitudinal research" plus supplemental questions. In J. M. Gottman (Ed.), *The analysis of change* (pp. 4–66). Mahwah, NJ: Erlbaum.

Rosenbaum, P. R. (1995). *Observational studies.* New York: Springer.

Rosenbaum, P. R., & Rubin, D. (1983). The central role of the propensity score in observational studies for causal effects. *Biometrika, 70,* 41–55.

Rovine, M. J., & Molenaar, P.C. (2000). A structural equation modeling approach to multilevel random coefficients model. *Multivariate Behavioral Research, 35,* 51–88.

Schaafsma, J., Nezlek, J. B., Krejtz, I., & Safron, M. (2010). Ethnocultural identification and naturally occurring interethnic social interactions: Muslim minorities in Europe. *European Journal of Social Psychology, 40,* 1010–1028.

Schmid, K., Tausch, N., Hewstone, M., Hughes, J., & Cairns, E. (2008). The effects of living in segregated vs. mixed areas in Northern Ireland: A simultaneous analysis of contact and threat effects in the context of micro-level neighborhoods. *International Journal of Conflict and Violence, 2,* 56–71.

Schofield, J. W. (1979). The impact of positively structured contact on intergroup behavior. *Social Psychology Quarterly, 42,* 280–284.

Schofield, J. W., & Sagar, H. A. (1977). Peer interaction patterns in an integrated middle school. *Sociometry, 40,* 130–138.

Schwarz, N. (1999). Self-reports. How the questions shape the answers. *American Psychologist, 54,* 93–105.

Selig, J. P., & Preacher, K. J. (2009). Mediation models for longitudinal data in developmental research. *Research in Human Development, 6,* 144–164.

Shadish, W. R. (2010). Campbell and Rubin: A primer and comparison of their approaches to causal inference in field settings. *Psychological Methods, 15,* 3–17.

Shadish, W. R., Cook, T. D., & Campbell, D. T. (2002). *Experimental and quasi-experimental designs for generalized causal inference.* Boston: Houghton–Mifflin.

Shelton, J. N., Richeson, J. A., & Salvatore, J. (2005). Expecting to be the target of prejudice: Implications for interethnic interactions. *Personality and Social Psychology Bulletin, 31,* 1189–1202.

Shook, N. J., & Fazio, R. H. (2008). Interracial roommate relationships: An experimental field test of the contact hypothesis. *Psychological Science, 19,* 717–723.

Snijders, T., & Bosker, R. (1999). *Multilevel Analysis*. London: Sage Publications.

Stoolmiller, M., & Bank, L. (1995). Autoregressive effects in structural equation models: We see some problems. In J. M. Gottman (Ed.), *The analysis of change* (pp. 261–276). Mahwah, NJ: Erlbaum.

Swart, H., Hewstone, M., Christ, O., & Voci, A. (2011). Affective mediators of intergroup contact: A three-wave longitudinal analysis in South Africa. *Journal of Personality and Social Psychology, 101*, 1221–1238.

Titzmann, P. F., & Silbereisen, R. K. (2009). Friendship homophily among ethnic German immigrants: A longitudinal comparison between recent and more experienced immigrant adolescents. *Journal of Family Psychology, 23*, 301–310.

Towles–Schwen, T., & Fazio, R. H. (2006). Automatically activated racial attitudes as predictors of the success of interracial roommate relationships. *Journal of Experimental Social Psychology, 42*, 698–705.

Trail, T. E., Shelton, J. N., & West, T. (2009). Interracial roommate relationships: Negotiating daily interactions. *Personality and Social Psychology Bulletin, 6*, 671–684.

Tropp, L. R., Hawi, D., Van Laar, C., & Levin, S. (2012). Cross-ethnic friendships, perceived discrimination, and their effects on ethnic activism over time: A longitudinal investigation of three ethnic minority groups. *British Journal of Social Psychology, 51*, 257–272.

Vandenberg, R. J., & Lance, C. E. (2000). A review and synthesis of the measurement invariance literature: Suggestions, practices, and recommendations for organizational research. *Organizational Research Methods, 3*, 4–70.

Van Dick, R., Wagner, U., Pettigrew, T. F., Christ, O., Wolf, C., Petzel, T., Smith–Castro, V., & Jackson, J. S. (2004). Role of perceived importance in intergroup contact. *Journal of Personality and Social Psychology, 87*, 211–227.

Wagner, U., Christ, O., Pettigrew, T. F., Stellmacher, J., & Wolf, C. (2006). Prejudice and minority proportion: Contact instead of threat effects. *Social Psychology Quarterly, 69*, 380–390.

Wagner, U., Christ, O., Wolf, C., van Dick, R., Stellmacher, J., Schlüter, E., & Zick, A. (2008). Social and political context effects on intergroup contact and intergroup attitudes. In U. Wagner, L. Tropp, G. Finchilescu & C. Tredoux (Eds.), *Improving intergroup relations: Building on the legacy of Thomas F. Pettigrew* (pp. 195–209). Oxford, U.K.: Blackwell.

Wagner, U., & Hewstone, M. (in press). Intergroup contact. In L. R. Tropp (Ed.), *The Oxford handbook of intergroup conflict.* New York: Oxford University Press.

Wagner, U., Van Dick, R., Pettigrew, T. F., & Christ, O. (2003). Ethnic prejudice in East and West Germany: The explanatory power of intergroup contact. *Group Processes and Intergroup Relations, 6*, 22–36.

Wagner, U., & Zick, A. (1995). The relation of formal education to ethnic prejudice: Its reliability, validity and explanation. *European Journal of Social Psychology, 25*, 41–56.

Welch, S., Sigelman, L., Bledsoe, T., & Combs, M. (2001). *Race and place: Race relations in an American city.* New York: Cambridge University Press.

West, S. G., & Thoemmes, F. (2008). Equating groups. In P. Alasuutari, L. Bickman & J. Brannen (Eds.), *The SAGE handbook of social research methods* (pp. 414–430). London: SAGE.

West, T. V., Shelton, J. N., & Trail, T. E. (2009). Relational anxiety in interracial interactions. *Psychological Science, 20*, 289–292.

Wilder, D. A. (1984). Intergroup contact: The typical member and the exception to the rule. *Journal of Experimental Social Psychology, 20*, 177–194.

Wilder, D. A., & Thompson J. E. (1980). Intergroup contact with independent manipulations of in-group and out-group interaction. *Journal of Personality and Social Psychology, 38*, 589–603.

Willett, J. B., & Sayer, A. G. (1994). Using covariance structure analysis to detect correlates and predictors of individual change over time. *Psychological Bulletin, 116*, 363–381.

Williams, R. M., Jr. (1947). *The reduction of intergroup tensions*. New York: Social Science Research Council.

Winship, C., & Mare, R. D. (1992). Models for sample selection bias. *Annual Review of Sociology, 18*, 327–350.

Winship, C., & Morgan, S. L. (1999). The estimation of causal effects from observational data. *Annual Review of Sociology, 25*, 659–707.

Wong, C.-S., & Law, K. S. (1999). Testing reciprocal relations by nonrecursive structural equation models using cross-sectional data. *Organizational Research Methods, 2*, 69–87.

Wright, S. C., Aron, A., McLaughlin-Volpe, T., & Ropp, S. A. (1997). The extended contact effect: Knowledge of cross-group friendships and prejudice. *Journal of Personality and Social Psychology, 73*, 73–90.

Zhang, Z., Zyphur, M. J., & Preacher, K. J. (2009). Testing multilevel mediation using hierarchical linear models: Problems and solutions. *Organizational Research Methods, 12*, 695–719.

11 Advances in intergroup contact
Epilogue and future directions

*Gordon Hodson, Miles Hewstone,
and Hermann Swart*

The notion that intergroup contact can reduce prejudice is an appealing prospect, one that enjoys considerable support in meta-analytic reviews of both intergroup contact generally (Pettigrew & Tropp, 2006) and cross-group friendships specifically (Davies, Tropp, Aron, Pettigrew, & Wright, 2011). As the contributions in the present volume attest, our understanding of the contact phenomenon has grown substantially in recent years. The field has moved beyond merely demonstrating that contact "works," to exploring how (i.e., the processes by which) it works, in addition to mapping its boundary conditions. More recently, research has moved on from the basic principles involved in direct, face-to-face contact, to propose that more indirect forms of contact can also be effective. During this interval the field has taken advantage of statistical procedures that clarify underlying processes to address our most pressing questions. As noted by Hodson and Hewstone (this volume), this valuable information comes at a critical time in human history, as we experience unprecedented intergroup contact and migration while we deplete our finite resources at an escalating rate, irrevocably changing the planet and biosphere in ways that undoubtedly will put increased pressure on social relations and increase friction between groups. In this final chapter we review the central themes uncovered in this volume, and assess how far the research and theorizing has come, before discussing present unknowns and future directions for research.

Advances in intergroup contact: key themes in this volume

Each of the contributions to this book sheds light on unique aspects of intergroup contact. Yet throughout the book several key themes repeatedly emerged, providing fresh insights into the topics considered "essential" by the world's leading contact researchers. Our reflections should not to be considered exhaustive or all-inclusive, but rather reflect highlights of emerging conceptualizing in the contact field.

Theme 1: Intergroup anxiety and threat

Intergroup anxiety, the psychological experience of concern, worry, and embarrassment at the prospect of interacting with an outgroup, was initially proposed by

Stephan and Stephan (1985) as a proximal predictor of prejudice, explaining the effects of group contact (among other factors). Over the years this work developed into the Integrated Threat Theory of Prejudice (e.g., Stephan & Stephan, 2000), with the latest version emphasizing that intergroup contact can impact perceived threats to the individual and the ingroup (both realistic/material and symbolic in nature), which in turn influence group-relevant responses (e.g., prejudice, discrimination) (Stephan, Renfro, & Davis, 2008). In short, whereas negative contact can increase intergroup anxiety and subsequently prejudice, positive contact can decrease tensions and improve intergroup attitudes.

With intergroup anxiety playing such a critical role in predicting prejudice generally, what have we learned about the relation between contact, on the one hand, and intergroup anxiety and threat perceptions, on the other? Early research on this question reached a consensus that contact generally reduced prejudice by reducing intergroup anxiety. For instance, increased and more positive contact was found to predict prejudice and increased perceived variability among outgroup members (making "them" seem less homogeneous), an effect explained by decreased intergroup anxiety (Islam & Hewstone, 1993; Voci & Hewstone, 2003). Several contributors to this book, however, have emphasized the negative potential of contact on anxiety. Vorauer (this volume) concentrates on how intergroup contact between group representatives can be fraught with concerns over self-evaluation, most notably concerns that "they" think that "I" am prejudiced. As such, she argues, contact settings are rife with tension, meaning that problems often bubble just beneath the surface. Vorauer discusses our fears of being transparent to others, and how in particular the perception that the outgroup regards one's ingroup as prejudiced (called "meta-stereotypes") discourages intergroup contact from taking place. Indeed, experimental evidence confirms that this type of perception is among the most damaging to contact intentions (see MacInnis & Hodson, in press). As Voraeur demonstrates, concerns with being evaluated by an outgroup interaction partner are mentally draining. This generates not only an aversive state but can interfere with one's ability to notice that contact is actually running smoothly when it does. She concludes by pointing out the cyclical nature of contact relations: contact introduces evaluation concerns, particularly with regard to being seen as prejudiced, which in turn deter contact.

Others have highlighted related anxiety-relevant problems. For instance, West and Dovidio (this volume) have presented compelling evidence that, in interracial dyadic interactions over time, personal anxieties can impact contact relations, but so can the effect of one's partner's anxieties on one's own anxiety. Put simply, anxiety is contagious, which is exacerbated by the fact that humans are particularly adept at registering the awkwardness of interactions with representatives of other groups. Presumably such heightened sensitivities serve us well in our day-to-day lives, such as when navigating threatening contact with those intending to harm us personally, but can clearly lead to the deterioration of intergroup relations, even when interactants are relatively willing to engage in contact. Aboud and Spears Brown (this volume) echo similar concerns in their review of the contact literature among children. These authors note not only the strong potential for negative contact (exacerbated through bullying, etc.), but that children are particularly attuned to the nonverbal behaviours and implicit (i.e., indirect, or unconscious) intergroup attitudes expressed by ingroup authority figures (e.g., parents, teachers). As such, intergroup anxieties can be passed not only from outgroup member to the self (as West and Dovidio, this volume, demonstrate), but also between ingroup members (at a critical stage of attitude development).

Despite these sizeable anxiety-relevant obstacles, other contributors have underscored the power of contact to reduce bias. Davies, Wright, Aron, and Comeau (this volume) dig deeply into the benefits of cross-group friendships in forging positive intergroup attitudes, as discussed in more detail shortly. They note how others (e.g., Page-Gould, Mendoza-Denton, & Tropp, 2008) have adapted their "fast friends procedure," a methodology for developing intimacy in lab-settings, to examine repeated exposure to an outgroup member over time. Such research has revealed that although interactants find contact settings anxiety-provoking and threatening, such feelings dissipate over the course of friendship development. The literature reviewed by Davies and colleagues speaks clearly to the power of cross-group friendship in overcoming anxieties that can otherwise be evoked in contact settings.

In this vein, Hodson, Costello, and MacInnis (this volume) review recent evidence demonstrating that although highly prejudiced persons (e.g., authoritarians) dislike and avoid outgroups (e.g., homosexuals), viewing them as threatening, both contact and cross-group friendships predict less prejudice toward the outgroup as a whole (e.g., homosexuals) through the process of rendering the outgroup less threatening and thus less anxiety-relevant (e.g., Hodson, Harry, & Mitchell, 2009). Contact clearly has the potential to reduce threat reactions to outgroups, even among those normally predisposed to outgroup negativity, particularly (but not only) when such contact is positive or framed in terms of friendships. Crisp and Turner (this volume) push the boundaries of basic contact effects even further. As their review illustrates, simply imagining positive contact with an outgroup is sufficient to reduce intergroup anxiety, which has a knock-on effect that lowers prejudice against the group in question. Overall, the contributions of this volume consider the fluid relation between anxiety and contact: although intergroup contact can be fraught with awkwardness and unease, frequently deterring further contact, interactions with outgroup members by-and-large reduce our anxieties and apprehensions about "the other." Put simply, positive intergroup contact encounters have the power to undo our suspicions and hesitancy about interacting with other groups.

Theme 2: Empathy and perspective-taking

Generally speaking, prejudice researchers are quite optimistic about the power of empathy and perspective-taking in the reduction of prejudice and related biases (see Batson et al., 1997, 2002; Finlay & Stephan, 2000; Galinksy & Moskowitz, 2000). That is, forming an emotional connection with an outgroup member, and/ or experiencing the world from their point of view, goes a long way to boosting positive attitudes toward the group as a whole. For instance, having heterosexual students experience some of the situational pressures and discrimination faced by homosexuals in a mental simulation significantly increased empathy for homosexuals and decreased homophobia (see Hodson, Choma, & Costello, 2009). To what extent, however, does *contact* with outgroups induce empathy and perspective-taking in a manner that can similarly improve intergroup attitudes?

Recently, researchers have afforded these processes a prominent position in their theoretical models. In the contact literature, empathy and perspective-taking are frequently considered precursors to intimacy and overlap with the outgroup other (e.g., Aberson & Haag, 2007; Kenworthy, Turner, Hewstone, & Voci, 2005; Tausch & Hewstone, 2010). Yet West and Dovidio (this volume) have highlighted an important caveat: our tendency to be emotionally attuned to contact partners, particularly with respect to anxiety, can lead to a feedback loop escalating anxiety between partners. But it is important to note that our emotional interconnectedness can also enhance our inclination to engage in empathy and perspective-taking with "others" in the social context. As noted by Hodson and colleagues (this volume), contact has the ability to elevate empathy even in the most unlikely of places, and among the most unlikely of persons. That is, in a prison context interracial contact has improved racial attitudes among socially dominant inmates (i.e., those endorsing hierarchies and dominance between groups), an effect largely explained by increased empathy for the outgroup. This suggests that socially dominant people are not merely "enjoying" the contact situation because of the exploitation and dominance potential it presents, but that contact actually builds intimacy (a point elaborated by Davies et al., this volume, and Lolliot et al., this volume).

Contact, therefore, can improve intergroup relations through enhancing empathy and perspective-taking (see Lolliot et al., this volume, and discussion of Theme 6 below). However, the prejudice field has cooled somewhat in its initial enthusiasm for outgroup empathy as a means to improve intergroup attitudes. Some have suggested that we are often too detached from outgroups, meaning that outgroup empathy can be difficult to induce (for review, see Cikara, Bruneau, & Saxe, 2011). There is evidence of such cooling among some of the contact researchers in this book. For instance, Aboud and Spears Brown (this volume) point out that, among young children, the ability to adopt the perspective of others and develop empathy are linked to (often limited) cognitive skills. As such, we cannot expect success in the early stages of cognitive development, and we must be ready and willing to train children to compensate for such deficits. The authors argue that empathy on its own is often insufficient. Rather, children require specific and concrete examples of discrimination faced by outgroups if contact settings are to set the stage for positive attitude development. In many ways, however, this message itself is encouraging – with appropriate incentive and training, contact settings can become powerful conduits for harnessing empathy at critical developmental stages when biases are forming. Encouragingly, concrete intergroup interaction skills can be effectively communicated by role models represented in children's literature (Cameron, Rutland, Brown, & Douch, 2006).

Perhaps some of strongest caution is expressed by Vorauer (this volume). Somewhat counter-intuitively, her research suggests that people may experience negative outcomes when engaging in attempts to empathize with an outgroup interaction partner. This problem, she argues, centers around our evaluative concerns in intergroup contexts, where we worry that outgroup members see us personally as prejudiced. As Vorauer notes, "One of the very first things that individuals are apt to see when they try to look through the eyes of an outgroup member who is an interaction partner is *themselves*" (italics in original). The result, she argues, is behavior disruption, which can interfere with the positive flow of the interaction, or allow interactants to misread the signals given off during interactions. Paradoxically, empathy and perspective-taking inducements can worsen intergroup attitudes among those initially lower in prejudice, shifting them from their normally positive orientation toward negativity as a direct result of evaluation concerns during the interaction. Such findings provide a clear warning that contact settings differentially impact interactants as a function of individual differences, meaning that broad-strokes approaches risk missing the nuances necessary for ensuring positive contact outcomes.

Theme 3: Contact norms

Social psychologists have long recognized the importance of group norms (e.g., Asch, 1956; Sherif, 1935), particularly in forming and sustaining prejudice (e.g., Hogg & Abrams, 1988; Pettigrew, 1958). It is not surprising, therefore, that contact researchers have become increasingly interested in contact norms, particularly with regard to having ingroup friends with outgroup friends, where norms of acceptance are both implicitly and explicitly communicated (Pettigrew, Christ, Wagner, & Stellmacher, 2007; Wright, Aron, McLaughlin-Volpe, & Ropp, 1997). As highly social creatures with the means to control and shape our peers, norms may prove to be *the* critical factor in explaining prejudice reduction as a function of contact.

Being so valuable and influential, norms can of course be impediments to contact and reduced prejudice when negative. Aboud and Spears Brown (this volume) note that children typically *believe* that their ingroup peers would disapprove of outgroup contact and friendships, despite the fact that outgroup friendships are often of high calibre. The authors suggest that much of this resistance represents *pluralistic ignorance*, whereby children assume that outgroup contact would be seen more negatively by ingroup members than is actually the case. This is consistent with evidence of pluralistic ignorance among adults, whereby adults generally assume that outgroups are disinterested in and distrust contact, which has the negative consequence of reducing the desire for contact in the social perceiver (Shelton & Richeson, 2005). Aboud and Spears Brown point out a worrying extension of this basic finding – children actually *prefer* ingroup members who visibly exclude the outgroup. It is not difficult to see how group-level and personal prejudice emerge from proclivities to engage with the ingroup over the outgroup, such that prejudice-prone persons, when left to their own devices, move in "tight circles" (see Hodson, in press). Encouragingly, the authors point out that children turn to their authorities (e.g., parents, teachers) to support category-based preferences and behavior, meaning that positive role-modeling is not only possible but critical. Vorauer's (this volume) research echoes this message. As she demonstrates, explicitly dictated norms of anti-racism and color-blindness can backfire in adults (see also Wolsko, Park, Judd, & Wittenbrink, 2000). Consistent with her focus on self-evaluation concerns, presentation of such norms evokes high demands on self-control, which can be disruptive to positive contact goals and behaviors.

Fortunately, in their critical chapter Davies and colleagues (this volume) bring to the fore the positive influence of *contact norms*. As the authors note, in keeping with Self-Categorization Theory (Turner, Hogg, Oakes, Reicher, & Wetherell, 1987), when we identify strongly with our ingroups we self-stereotype. As a consequence we come to see the self as relatively interchangeable with other ingroup members, resulting in the strong activation and influence of group-level norms on the group member. With intergroup contact making group identities salient, therefore, ingroup norms will become particularly powerful. Davies and colleagues stress how norms predict whether contact will occur or not, but also moderate (i.e., qualify) whether contact will generate positive outcomes. This latter point harkens back to Allport's (1954) emphasis on institutional support for positive contact, a point supported in the literature (e.g., Hodson, 2008). But Davies et al. also stress the important mediational role of norms in contact settings. That is, contact can *change* norms, which can in turn decrease prejudice. Intriguingly, the authors also argue that contact can change perceptions of outgroup norms too. This idea is consistent with the notion that contact can weaken pluralistic ignorance about the outgroup, an idea with exciting potential that clearly warrants further attention.

Finally, there is reason to believe that, although prejudiced people generally form tight networks of closely-related others who share their negative orientations toward the outgroup and/or intergroup contact (Altemeyer, 1994, 1996; Hodson, in press; Poteat & Spanierman, 2010; Poteat, Espelage, & Green, 2007), they can nonetheless exhibit decreased prejudice to the extent that they perceive that higher-level authorities encourage positive contact. As discussed by Hodson and colleagues (this volume), White prison inmates scoring high in social dominance orientation (and thus endorsing group hierarchies) nonetheless expressed more favorable attitudes toward Black inmates when perceiving the social milieu of the prison as pro-contact (see Hodson, 2008, Study 1). Such findings highlight the powerful influence of contact norms, even among prejudice-prone individuals, in high-conflict contexts. As these authors note, manipulation of such norms provides fertile ground for researchers wishing to alter perceived support for contact among one's ingroup and institutional authorities.

Theme 4: Cross-group friendships

Since Pettigrew's (1998) reformulation of the original Contact Hypothesis, the field has become particularly drawn to the power of cross-group friendships as a powerful conduit for maximizing contact effects on attitudes. As many scholars have noted, friendship encapsulates many of the hallmarks of positive contact, with interactants often being of relatively equal status within the friendship, bearing similar friendship goals, and the relationship characterized by intimacy and trust. Friendships with outgroup members not only lower anxiety but improve intergroup attitudes, with lasting effects that include seeking out *additional* outgroup contact (e.g., Page-Gould et al., 2008). It is no surprise that the contributors to the present volume have drawn such sharp focus on both direct cross-group friendships (i.e., being friends with an outgroup member) and so-called indirect cross-group friendships or extended contact (i.e., having an ingroup friend with an outgroup friendship).

Davies and colleagues (this volume) make cross-group friendships a central focus of their chapter. Not only do friendships communicate positive norms about intergroup contact and friendship (see earlier discussion), but friendships bring about a sense of intimacy that is critical to positive intergroup relations. As the authors note, close contact of this nature brings about trust and self-disclosure, constructs that are currently emerging as important factors in ameliorating prejudice (e.g., Dhont & Van Hiel, 2011; Tam, Hewstone, Kenworthy, & Cairns, 2009; Turner, Hewstone, & Voci, 2007). In perhaps their most critical and novel contribution, Davies and colleagues explore *self-expansion*, the notion that "others", including outgroup members, can become integral to one's sense of self. Their notion of "inclusion of other in the self" has proven critical in understanding the pull of intimate intergroup connections. At its core this position proposes that we view the self positively; when others become integrated into our sense of self we extend positivity toward not only that other person, but this effect generalizes to the outgroup as a whole. Such a notion might seem unlikely to lay people or those personally involved in intractable conflict, yet the research record bears support for this idea. It is also worth recalling that during some of the twentieth century's most appalling moments, such as the Holocaust, there were still instances of helping hands being extended to outgroup members (see Oliner & Oliner, 1988). The human potential for empathy and caring should not be underestimated, even in protracted conflict zones.

West and Dovidio (this volume) examine how intimate relationships develop in less intractable, more day-to-day contexts – namely the relationships between different-race university roommates. As the authors note, such contexts are fruitful for researchers, because roommates are largely randomly assigned, are of relatively equal status on campus, and are able to equally access most campus resources. As their review reveals, cross-group friendships are difficult to forge in these contexts, often hampered by concerns with not appearing prejudiced and avoiding the appearance of anxiety. Despite these efforts, a cross-race partner may accurately read the signals of high anxiety. Even when attempting not to appear prejudiced, therefore, our partners are often not convinced, sensing instead our anxieties. Clearly, intergroup friendships can sometimes pose difficulties. As noted by Aboud and Spears Brown (this volume), cross-group relationships are significantly less stable than ingroup relationships, despite being high in quality. But we see evidence of considerable promise. West and Dovidio note that people who enter a relationship with an inclusive mindset (seeing similarities rather than differences between people) are better able to overcome any difficulties encountered in the course of the friendships, managing to sustain these intimate bridging relationships for longer. Such findings are encouraging, given the ease with which such inclusive mindsets can be manipulated (Gaertner & Dovidio, 2000; see also Costello & Hodson, 2010).

Particularly impressive are the findings that cross-group friendships can even be forged among highly prejudiced people and in extreme conflict settings. As reviewed by Hodson and colleagues (this volume), prejudice-prone persons exhibit significantly less outgroup bias as a linear function of the number of direct and indirect friendships with the outgroup. In keeping with Davies et al. (this volume), friendship operates on prejudice-prone persons by expanding the sense of self-other overlap (i.e., intimacy). Protracted conflict appears not to be a necessary barrier to positive intergroup relations and attitudes. Hewstone, Cairns, Voci, Hamberger, and Niens (2006) have found that those with deep personal losses (i.e., deaths as the result of intergroup conflict) were particularly likely to benefit from cross-group friendships, resulting in less outgroup prejudice. Together such findings indicate that contact and friendship can work well, often better, among those most in need of contact's benefits and perhaps least expected to benefit (see also Hodson, 2011).

Theme 5: Differential group status

From the early days of contact research, theorists recognized the importance of group status, advocating that contact between interaction partners should ideally be founded on a relatively equal status basis (e.g., Allport, 1954). As lamented by several experts (Cook, 1979; Stephan, 2008), this condition is rarely met in reality, presumably explaining much of why contact can sometimes fail. Recently the focus on group status has largely concerned the differential strength of contact effects as a function of group status: belonging to the dominant and advantaged (majority) group or the disadvantaged (minority) group. Meta-analytic evidence reveals that contact improves intergroup attitudes more effectively among majority than minority groups (although it is effective in each), and that the optimal conditions facilitating contact (see Hodson & Hewstone, this volume) are more influential among members of majority than minority groups (Tropp & Pettigrew, 2005). Recent research reveals another set of interesting findings: among the minority group, contact can improve attitudes toward the majority group, but counter-productively make the minority group less likely to enact social change (e.g., Dixon, Durrheim, Tredoux, Tropp, Clack, & Eaton, 2010). A better understanding of this paradox is needed to understand the effects of contact among minorities.

The authors in the present volume seek answers to a new set of status-relevant questions. Vorauer (this volume) notes that whether we consider the outgroup an important source of information in answering our self-evaluation concerns varies systematically as a function of group status. In particular she suggests that low-status groups look to high-status groups as valid sources of information, but only when the structural features of the intergroup context indicate that the power differential is relatively legitimate (and generally stable). However, Vorauer suggests that majority groups may turn to minority groups (as victims) as sources of "morality," particularly if the former is concerned that its actions have harmed the latter. In fact, consistent with majorities (vs. minorities) being more influenced by contact, Vorauer demonstrates that majorities also hold meta-stereotypes (perceptions that the outgroup considers the ingroup prejudiced) that are particularly malleable and unstable. It may be no coincidence that both intergroup attitudes and meta-stereotypes among majority members are more affected by contact than is the case for minority members.

Future research can further explore the association between these variables to provide insights into mediating processes. For instance, is contact particularly effective among the dominant group *because* contact changes their meta-stereotypes? In support of this intuition, recent evidence suggests that meta-stereotypes may be more important in predicting contact outcomes than even personal attitudes toward the outgroup (Finchilescu, 2010; MacInnis & Hodson, in press). At present very little evidence directly links contact effects with meta-stereotyping, making this topic ripe for future research. In a recent investigation of post-Apartheid intergroup contact, Tredoux and Finchilescu (2010) found that meta-stereotypes mediated (i.e., explained) the effects between increased contact and decreased affective prejudice, but not between contact and measures of social distance. The authors issue a call for additional research on meta-stereotyping in contact settings, a point that resonates with us.

Saguy, Tropp, and Hawi (this volume) center their discussion directly on power differentials between groups in contact. In keeping with our psychological emphasis on contact, the authors argue that minorities and majorities face and interpret different realities in the contact setting, including differences in how the status quo is interpreted and reacted to. In line with contemporary approaches of intergroup relations (e.g., Sidanius & Pratto, 1999), Saguy and colleagues argue that majority groups have a vested interest in maintaining their advantage over the minority group. In a novel twist for the contact literature, these researchers have explored the *content* of intergroup interactions. They find that, in general, majorities tend to minimize group differences and favor discussion of common identity and fate, in an effort to circumvent social change. In experimental tests, Saguy et al. (this volume) manipulated the stability present in the system, introducing factors that challenge the status quo. With this instability minorities bring forward the topic of their disadvantage and unfair treatment, attempting to effect social change. The advances proposed in this chapter are novel and informative because the actual content of intergroup interactions has historically been largely ignored by psychologists. Recognizing not only that contact differentially influences attitudes for high and low status groups, but that a contact setting will be approached, interpreted, and managed differently by groups differing in power, again highlights the highly psychological nature of intergroup contact (Hodson & Hewstone, this volume).

Theme 6: Attitude generalization

One of the most important issues concerning intergroup contact deals with attitude generalization. Pettigrew (1998) specified three types of generalization of improved attitudes via contact: (a) from an outgroup individual to the outgroup as a whole; (b) from the contact group to an uninvolved group; and (c) across situations (e.g., from workplace to recreational setting). In their meta-analysis, Pettigrew and Tropp (2006, Table 2) found evidence supporting all three types of generalization, leaving little doubt that contact with an outgroup representative leads to a host of positive intergroup outcomes (for an in-depth review, see Pettigrew & Tropp, 2011).

In this book, several authors have reached beyond whether generalization occurs to address *why* it occurs. Davies and colleagues (this volume) focus largely on generalization from one's contact partner to the outgroup as a collective. They provide compelling evidence that *intimacy* plays a key role. As discussed previously, these authors argue that contact heightens the sense of overlap between self and other, which draws in a host of related processes relevant to prejudice reduction, including increased trust and self-disclosure. In other words, we come to like the outgroup through a myriad of processes that also characterize intragroup relations, namely warmth and connectedness. The rationale is that objects associated with the self are viewed positively (Beggan, 1992), which is also the case with our ingroups (Smith & Henry, 1996). From the work of Davies and collaborators, we argue that associating the self with the outgroup engages similar processes that draw others into the sphere of self and imbue "the other" with the kind of positivity generally reserved for the ingroup.

Lolliot and colleagues (this volume), in contrast, tackle the type of generalization whereby contact with one group generalizes to positive attitudes toward an uninvolved outgroup, the so-called *secondary transfer effect* (Pettigrew, 2009; Tausch et al., 2010). Lolliot and colleagues consider the evidence for various processes involved in secondary transfer effects, including attitude generalization, deprovincialization, and empathy (see Pettigrew, 1997). With regard to deprovincialization there has been little research to date, and results have been mixed. Thus this chapter is especially useful, showing that contact with an outgroup makes one less inward focused and less ethnocentric. This, in turn, may make people more disposed to positive contact with and favorable evaluations toward uninvolved outgroups. For instance, experiencing increased contact with homosexuals might make a heterosexual man more favorable toward other minority groups, such as immigrants. Recent evidence suggests that contact does lead to deprovincialization (Verkuyten, Thijs, & Bekhuis, 2010). Needed at this point, we argue, are studies that control for dispositional levels of openness to experience, a construct with a negative effect on prejudice (Flynn, 2005; Sibley & Duckitt, 2008), even above and beyond contact (e.g., Jackson & Poulsen, 2005). At present this area of research looks very promising, particularly in light of findings that multicultural experiences generally generate greater creativity and openness (Leung, Maddux, Galinsky, & Chiu, 2008).

Lolliot and colleagues (this volume) propose a bold new direction for the role of empathy in contact settings. Specifically, the authors suggest that the empathy process might be critical in understanding why contact with one outgroup can generalize to attitudes toward another, unrelated outgroup. On the one hand they suggest that empathy can improve attitudes toward the contact group (as the above review suggests), where the empathy-to-attitude effect toward the first group generalizes (or extends to) the secondary outgroup (see Figure 4.2, this volume). Intriguingly, they also propose that empathy might play an even more central role, with contact boosting empathy toward the contact group, *which itself spreads to empathy toward the secondary group*, with positive knock-on effects regarding attitudes (see Figure 4.3, this volume). Put simply, outgroup empathy might promote positive attitudes that then generalize, or outgroup empathy might promote empathy toward other outgroups, which then promotes positive attitudes. These ideas are in the early stages, but they already provide rich theoretical ground for further elaborating the importance of empathy in contact settings.

Several other chapters in the present volume also touch on the issue of contact-based attitude generalization. For instance, Vorauer (this volume) reviews new evidence that those low in prejudice might not generalize from their immediate contact experience. Low-prejudice individuals are more likely to interact with an outgroup member, for example, but this experience may not generalize to the group as a whole. High-prejudice individuals, in contrast, apply what they learn from contact with an outgroup representative to the outgroup generally (of course, this would create a negative effect if the prior contact were negative). Vorauer interprets this finding as being consistent with low-prejudice individuals treating others as individuals rather than group members. We find these results very much in keeping with the considerable literature demonstrating that group categories must be salient for contact effects on attitudes to emerge (see, e.g., Van Ouden-hoven, Groenewoud, & Hewstone, 1996; for a comprehensive review, see Brown & Hewstone, 2005). Group membership categories are presumably more salient for those with negative contact dispositions (e.g., authoritarians) than for more egalitarian individuals; this suggestion warrants further examination. If established, it may explain why contact works well among prejudice-prone individuals (see Hodson et al., this volume), placing generalization processes at the very heart of the contact phenomenon.

Theme 7: Individual differences

A theme that has remained largely absent from the discussion of contact effects until recently is the role of individual differences. Hodson and colleagues (this volume) review this literature and consider why individual differences have been relatively neglected as relevant to the contact question. Most importantly, these authors review recent advances in the field, demonstrating that early pessimism about contact among prejudiced persons may have been largely unwarranted. As their review demonstrates, increased and more positive contact among prejudice-prone persons is generally associated with less prejudicial expressions of bias.

In many cases contact effects are even stronger among prejudiced (than non-prejudiced) persons, suggesting that contact effects may have historically been underestimated by collapsing across individual differences (see Hodson et al., this volume). Regardless of whether contact is more effective among low- or high-prejudice persons, the central point is that contact is generally effective among those most in need of intervention. As noted by Hodson (2011, p. 155), "contact works well, if not best, among those higher on prejudice-prone individual-difference variables. Failure to find contact benefits among such individuals is the exception, not the norm." Contact, it appears, is not simply effective among those naturally predisposed toward friendly relations with the outgroup.

A remaining issue, however, concerns bringing prejudice-prone people to the contact setting. Left to their own devices, such people tend to avoid the outgroup. Crisp and Turner (this volume) present a novel idea that encourages mental simulations of contact. The authors do not envision imagined contact as a substitute for actual contact, but rather suggest that imagined contact is ideal for preparing the way, reducing anxiety in advance of face-to-face contact. As they report, imagined contact reduces prejudice through many of the same mechanisms as actual contact, including anxiety reduction and stereotyping. Importantly, imagined contact also boosts willingness for future contact. Although the potential for implementation among highly prejudiced persons, particularly in field settings, is presently untested, this method shows considerable promise for reducing prejudice among dispositionally contact-averse persons.

Aboud and Spears Brown (this volume) present evidence that contact with one's *ingroup* peers might be an effective prejudice-reduction strategy among children. As noted by the authors, by the age of approximately 4 years some children exhibit lower prejudice whereas others continue to develop prejudice, setting the early path for individual differences in prejudice expression. However, the authors observe that pairing highly-prejudiced children with low-prejudice peers for conversations about outgroups leads to a reduction of prejudice among the former. These findings are consistent with recent evidence that, among young adolescents, contact with ingroup members reduces outgroup prejudice through perceptions of positive ingroup norms about the outgroup, and through reducing anxiety (De Tezanos-Pinto, Bratt, & Brown, 2010).

Such strategies that encourage positive role models and contact norms seem better suited to dealing with contact among prejudiced persons than do explicit instructions to avoid being prejudiced. Both Vorauer (this volume) and West and Dovidio (this volume) have eloquently demonstrated that attempts to control biases from fear of evaluation by one's partner can backfire and increase bias. Vorauer's research suggests instead that perspective-taking is beneficial among highly-prejudiced people in contact settings (consistent with other recent findings, e.g., Hodson, Choma et al., 2009; see Hodson et al., this volume). West and Dovidio highlight another mechanism: those who tend, dispositionally, to see the similarities rather than differences between groups of people are better able to ensure that contact relations do not deteriorate over time. Combined with the observations of Aboud and Spears Brown (this volume), this suggests that interventions emphasizing the importance of inclusivity in early developmental stages may play an important role in buffering negative effects of contact in adulthood.

Theme 8: Methodological and statistical innovations

One theme that will be especially useful to those interested in conducting research on intergroup contact concerns the methodological and statistical innovations reported in this volume. In terms of pure methodology, Davies and colleagues discuss the success that they and others (e.g., Page-Gould et al., 2008) have experienced with their so-called "Fast Friends Procedure." This technique allows researchers to examine the early stages of friendship formation immediately and in real time in the lab. This obviously facilitates experimental control over the situation, and allows observations to be collected immediately. In their particular adaptation, Page-Gould and colleagues successfully used the Fast Friends Procedure across repeated sessions, while collecting physiological measures of anxiety and arousal. This novel investigation provides some of the first insights into the negative effects of arousal that may be present early in friendship development that then deteriorate over repeated contact experiences. Such methodologies show considerable promise for export to classroom and work settings alike. This line of thinking is in keeping with Aboud and Spears Brown's (this volume) recommendation that children be taught practical skills and be given practice in navigating smooth intergroup interactions. Of particular value, these authors recommend that children's contact-relevant interventions be concrete and direct in order to enhance the likelihood of success in light of their developmental cognitive constraints. Combining these strategies, providing young children with "fast friends" opportunities and skill-based training and guidance at a young age represents a promising angle for future research.

In their chapter, West and Dovidio (this volume) provide new insights into intimate contact as it unfolds over time. Specifically, the authors employ relatively new methods of examining data from two interaction partners that consider the effects of each partner on the other (i.e., APIM; Actor-Partner Interdependence Model). The statistical procedures available for analyzing data, and the computing power to make them more powerful and more widely available, have truly revolutionized the contemporary contact field. Such methods not only provide the answers we seek but shape the questions we ask. Another methodological innovation discussed by West and Dovidio concerns the clever use of "delayed" electronic communication, such as what happens when audio tracks become delayed when discussants interact often across great distances. With our social lives becoming increasingly electronic and virtual, and with business and political leaders relying increasingly on new modes of communication (e.g., Skype), such methods are extremely relevant to communication and interaction in the "real world." But even more importantly, these methods allow researchers to examine key *contact* questions in the modern world. As the authors note, even slight and imperceptible delays in audio signals on video-based communications can convey the sense that contact is not running smoothly, increasing anxiety in the self and perceived anxiety in one's partner (which feed off each other). These effects emerged even in studies where participants spoke the same mother tongue; one can easily imagine the detriment of degraded digital contact when one participant has to speak a non-preferred language or the participants have markedly different contact goals.

In discussing methodological advances in contact research, Christ and Wagner (this volume) provide an up-to-date synthesis of modern research methods available. Early in their discussion, they demonstrate how modern methodological approaches (e.g., self- and peer-rated contact); (see Hewstone, Judd, & Sharp, 2011) have clarified the validity of self-reported contact effects, an issue that has dogged the field for decades. Support for self-reported contact measures has recently been corroborated in an independent study (see Dhont, Van Hiel, De Bolle, & Roets, 2012). Christ and Wagner also discuss important methods to limit self-selection, and how to use an interactant's choice in engaging in contact to the researcher's advantage. Following this advice the field can appropriately answer questions about selection effects, instead of considering selection effects as inherent problems per se. They also review and promote the advantages of the latest longitudinal analyses of contact, which have been long overdue and are overwhelmingly supporting for contact theory. Consider, for example, recent findings by Swart, Hewstone, Christ, and Voci (2011). Across three time waves, the authors measured contact variables, multiple proposed mediators, and multiple contact outcome variables. Swart and colleagues establish the clearest evidence of the temporal layout of cross-group friendship effects, in a South African context. They found that intergroup contact at Time 1 predicts lower anxiety and increased empathy at Time 2, which predicts outcomes such as more positive outgroup attitudes, reduced negative action tendencies, and greater perceived outgroup variability at Time 3 (all controlling for influence of variables at earlier waves). Still needed at this point, we argue, are studies utilizing experimental manipulations and control at Time 1, with the effects studied at multiple time-points later (e.g., Van Laar, Levin, Sinclair, & Sidanius, 2005).

One of Christ and Wager's (this volume) most critical distinctions concerns the *level* of contact's effect. Whereas most social psychologists study contact effects at the level of the individual (e.g., friendship, anxiety), there are many group-level and even societal-level factors that can now be incorporated in our models and analyses. The need for such integration has been stressed most fervently by Thomas Pettigrew and his colleagues (e.g., Pettigrew, 2008; Pettigrew & Tropp, 2011). This particular point has become very salient and important to social psychologists after Forbes (2004) argued and demonstrated that, although contact and prejudice are negatively correlated at the level of the individual, at the group level these constructs can be positively correlated. Thus, although individuals experiencing more contact with an ethnic outgroup might come to positively evaluate those members, neighborhoods or nations with relatively higher (vs. lower) contact often exhibit more prejudice toward the outgroup in question. As noted by Christ and Wagner, this can occur because effects at different levels of an analysis can be relatively independent from one another, be they micro-level (personality, physiology), meso-level (situational), or macro-level (nation-state). They advocate following Pettigrew's advice: analyze the effects of different levels *simultaneously*. Such methods were clearly beyond our reach decades ago but recent advances in software and statistical sophistication have opened up exciting new avenues for research. In this light, we completely agree with Pettigrew and Tropp's (2011, p. 212) sentiment that ". . . multi-level approaches are complex, but the 'real world' *is* complex" (emphasis in original). With statistical methods now available (see Christ & Wagner's summary), the onus truly is on the field to grasp this complexity with both hands. Of course, this will necessitate elaborations of our modelling of contact theory, but the field is clearly up to this challenge and cannot afford to bypass these exciting methodological advances.

Theme 9: Alternatives to direct contact

Actual or direct contact between group members has been the historical and empirical focus of contact researchers, and for good reason. The ultimate question, after all, concerns whether contact with members of other groups reduces prejudice. Our most comprehensive analyses have dealt at length with this particular question (see the meta-analysis by Pettigrew & Tropp, 2006). Even a casual perusal of this volume quickly reveals the degree to which researchers have made considerable gains in examining alternatives to direct contact of a general nature. Most notably, the contact literature has now more thoroughly researched the study of contact *and friendship*, including the effects of one's friend's friend, negating the need for personal contact altogether. Indeed, many of the contributors to this volume have explored both direct cross-group friendships (i.e., having an outgroup friend) and indirect or extended cross-group friendships (i.e., having an ingroup friend with an outgroup friend), delivering many promising results (Aboud & Spears Brown; Davies et al.; Hodson et al.; Lolliot et al.; but see challenges presented by West & Dovidio, all this volume). The benefits of cross-group friendships are now well-supported meta-analytically (Davies et al., 2011).

Reflecting modern social lives, several contributors have also focused on the effects of social media, literature, and television (e.g., Aboud & Spears Brown, this volume). According to the US Department of Labor, in 2010 Americans over the age of 15 averaged almost 3 hours of television per day, making it the top leisure activity (American Time Use Survey Summary, 2011). American TV-viewing tracker Nielsen puts this value closer to 5 hours per day, with Americans spending more time viewing TV than ever in their history (Gandossy, 2009). With social media and internet activity on the climb, multimedia will become more (not less) important in our social lives. The potential for prejudice reduction is clear, not only allowing consumers to learn about the outgroup and contemplate them in non-threatening ways, but to become accustomed to different mannerisms, customs, and beliefs (i.e., deprovincialization). A recent year-long field study utilizing radio programming in Rwanda confirmed this potential. Paluck (2009) exposed some communities to storylines concerning the day-to-day lives of two fictitious groups. Relative to a health-discussion control, those exposed to intergroup relevant radio-plays increased endorsement of pro-social norms (e.g., empathy). Unfortunately the effects on their personal beliefs were less malleable.

In many ways, therefore, it appears that contact need not be direct and face-to-face, so long as the experience captures key principles of contact theory. Crisp and Turner (this volume) have pursued this idea and investigated the impact of encouraging participants simply to imagine positive contact, allowing participants to learn to relax and see outgroups in more individuated ways. Hodson and colleagues (this volume) also discuss how group contact-relevant mental simulations can effectively increase empathy and reduce prejudice, with participants using the opportunity to play out "interactions" and reactions in safe contexts. In many ways, these forms of indirect contact share features with extended contact (i.e., having an ingroup friend with an outgroup friend). In each, personal outgroup contact is not needed. Rather, the understanding that contact *can* unfold without tension or conflict is made evident. As recommended by Aboud and Spears Brown (this volume), building skills and knowledge are central for laying down tracks for positive intergroup contact. Finally, in describing how contact with one group generalizes positive attitudes toward a non-contact group, Lolliot and colleagues (this volume) similarly expose the psychological nature of contact, such that personal contact with a specific outgroup is not absolutely essential for contact-effects to operate.

Theme 10: Contact is no panacea

To be clear, this book reveals a consensus that contact is not a panacea for prejudice. Although this point has been made previously (e.g., Hewstone, 2003), some have suggested that contact researchers are overly optimistic, accusing contact researchers of considering contact under idealized contexts (e.g., Dixon, Durrheim, & Tredoux, 2005). Replies to such concerns have been elaborated elsewhere (e.g., Pettigrew & Tropp, 2011, Chapter 11) and do not represent our focus. Rather, we wish to reiterate the position of the field generally: intergroup contact can be a very high-tension activity, fraught with suspicion, mistrust, and anxiety, with tremendous potential to worsen intergroup relations. By no means do we suggest that contact is comfortable, simple, or easy to control. Like most of human psychology, intergroup contact represents an extremely complex experience. This volume highlights many of the factors that can derail positive contact effects.

For instance, Vorauer's chapter (this volume) focuses on how contact generates self-evaluative concerns, with a host of negative outcomes for contact interactions. As she illustrates, contact attempts can "backfire" given failures to notice that contact is actually going well or that the outgroup holds positive beliefs about one's ingroup. Attempts to take the perspective and/or empathize with the outgroup can divert a critical eye to the self, which increases tensions. Even attempts to suppress biases or follow norms of color-blindness can increase prejudice by invoking a prevention focus on errors (rather than an approach focus on success). West and Dovidio (this volume) clearly back up Vorauer's argument: contact is difficult, strained, and fragile, disrupted even by relatively imperceptible factors associated with the contact partner or communication means. As noted by Hodson and colleagues (this volume), these types of concerns have troubled contact researchers right from the start, making them a cautious bunch, not idealistic cheerleaders.

For good reason, concerns persist. Aboud and Spears Brown (this volume) reflect considerably on how contact can easily be characterized as negative in nature (for a contrasting analysis, see Pettigrew & Tropp, 2011, Chapter 12). In particular the authors report how children can notice intergroup bullying yet stand on the side-lines, failing to intervene. It is worth noting, however, that failing to intervene need not necessarily indicate support for exclusion but rather fear of personal exclusion and other social ramifications. Indeed, Aboud and Spears Brown offer promise even in the context of bullying: negative contact provides children with concrete and salient examples of the damaging effects of exclusion, which can itself subsequently form the basis of interventions. That is, because children are hyper-aware of social exclusion and sensitive to its effects, teaching them the mindset and skills to challenge negative contact can provide a solid foundation of prejudice interventions.

Pettigrew's "problems": how far has the field come?

In 1998, Pettigrew published a highly-cited and influential review of the contact literature. Without doubt, his paper did more than simply summarize the field – it exposed several "holes" in our understanding about contact. The contact field arguably approached these problems as challenges, consistent with the marked surge of interest in contact over the last decade (see Hodson & Hewstone, Figure 1.1, this volume). What advances have been made in addressing Pettigrew's Problems?

Causal sequence (does contact affect prejudice or vice-versa)?

Pettigrew's (1998) first problem concerned whether contact reduces prejudice or whether prejudiced people simply avoid contact. This is indeed an important question, one that speaks to the heart of the contact hypothesis. He proposed three specific solutions to this question. First, examine contact settings where interactants have little choice about whether they have contact with the outgroup. Meta-analytic analyses demonstrate reliable contact effects in no-choice conditions that are significantly stronger than under high-choice contexts (Pettigrew & Tropp, 2006, Table 2). As noted by Christ and Wagner (this volume), "If the causal sequence is from prejudice to intergroup contact, meaning that prejudiced individuals avoid intergroup contact, one would expect no correlation between intergroup contact and prejudice in no-choice situations where the contact is forced by the situation." Recent evidence of interracial contact in extreme no-choice settings – prisons – reveals contact-prejudice associations that are approximately twice the magnitude of the meta-analytic average (see Hodson, 2008), clearly inconsistent with simple selection bias as an explanation of contact effects.

Pettigrew's (1998) second proposed solution was to examine cross-sectional data using sophisticated procedures that control for the influence of one variable on the other. Pettigrew (1997) himself used such procedures to establish stronger (negative) links between cross-group friendships and prejudice than the reverse path. Similar procedures have also proven useful in clarifying causal links between parental prejudice and child prejudice (see Rodriguez-Garcia & Wagner, 2009). In their chapter, Christ and Wagner (this volume) outline a range of sophisticated techniques for controlling the influence of variables on each other, some that involve matching on relevant covariates. Overall, the results of these new methods continue to confirm contact theory.

Pettigrew's (1998) third proposed solution was clearly his preferred one: longitudinal research, measuring contact and attitudes at multiple time-points. If contact genuinely causes reductions in prejudice and not simply the reverse, then cross-lagged (and more sophisticated) analyses ought to be capable of assessing the validity of contact's proposed effects. This question has been assessed now multiple times, in multiple contexts, examining a variety of outgroup types. Overall, the majority of longitudinal studies support the prediction that, with appropriate statistical controls in place, Time 1 contact predicts more favorable outgroup attitudes at Time 2 (e.g., Brown, Eller, Leeds, & Stace, 2007; Dhont et al., 2012; Van Laar et al., 2005; Vezzali, Giovannini, & Capozza, 2010). Several additional studies support a bidirectional relationship (Anderssen, 2002; Binder et al., 2009; Eller & Abrams, 2003, 2004; Levin, Van Laar, & Sidanius, 2003; Swart et al., 2011). At present, a solid accumulation of evidence has accrued, testifying to the power of contact effects to reduce prejudice over time, consistent with the underlying causal direction central to contact theory. The frequently obtained bidirectional relation between contact and prejudice fits with a dynamic understanding of contact and attitudes. In the real world, positive contact fuels positive attitudes, which encourage more contact (and, unfortunately, negative contact fuels negative attitudes, which discourages additional contact). Future researchers are encouraged to integrate these longitudinal findings into process-change models that also incorporate personality and ideology (to examine potential change in these variables, but, more likely, the moderating influence of person-factors on contact effects over time).

Specification of independent variables

Pettigrew's (1998) second concern involved the often lamented "laundry list" of conditions accrued by early researchers, which grew so quickly as to, by some accounts, render contact an impractical intervention. In his words, "this growing list of limiting conditions threatens to remove all interest from the [contact] hypothesis" (p. 69). Whether or not this long list deterred researchers at some point, researchers were not put off indefinitely, returning to contact research with great fervour (see Hodson & Hewstone, Figure 1.1, this volume). Intriguingly, Pettigrew cleverly intuited that many of the supposed conditions thought to be essential precursors for prejudice reduction were in fact *mediators* of contact effects, not moderators. With the benefit of hindsight we can judge the critical nature of his insight. For instance, whereas researchers may have once considered outgroup trust a precondition for contact effects to work, recent work corroborates trust as a mediating (or explaining) variable (e.g., Dhont & Van Hiel, 2011; Tam et al., 2009). That is, rather than trust being a precondition of contact, contact increases trust in the outgroup, which subsequently reduces prejudice. Finally, Pettigrew (1998, p. 70) also suggested that the field evidenced confusion over the specification of predictors because "writers often confuse *facilitating* with *essential* conditions" (italics in original). In a major advance for the field, the comprehensive meta-analysis by Pettigrew and Tropp (2006) substantially addressed this issue: contact under the so-called "optimal" conditions resulted in significantly stronger contact-prejudice effects ($r = -.29$), but contact was effective even in contexts not characterized by optimal contact ($r = -.20$). Contact, therefore, is facilitated by factors such as institutional support and cooperation, but these conditions are not essential, testifying to the power inherent in the contact concept.

In summary, many of Pettigrew's (1998) initial concerns with independent variable specification have been largely resolved. We have a clearer sense of which variables are essential to the contact effect and which are mere facilitators. In addition, many variables previously conceptualized as moderators (i.e., variables that qualify effects) are now considered mediating variables that explain *why* contact works (rather than under which conditions). In addition, several novel and critical moderators emerged during this interval. For one, contact works best (and often only) when group membership salience is relatively high (for a review, see Brown & Hewstone, 2005). In other words, contact with an outgroup member produces positive attitudes toward the outgroup as a whole, but only when one's interaction partner is psychologically construed *as* a member of the outgroup (and not merely an individual). This again speaks to the importance of generalization – for positive effects to spread from one's interaction partner to the whole outgroup, their group membership must be evident and prominent. At its core, the interaction needs to be an *intergroup* interaction, not an interpersonal one, for contact effects to be realized. As elaborated below, contact effects are also moderated by group status, working best among members of the dominant majority group rather than the disadvantaged group (Tropp & Pettigrew, 2005; for insights into dynamics, see Saguy and colleagues, this volume).

Lack of mediating (explaining) mechanisms

Over the long history of contact research scholars have demonstrated a host of benefits of contact, not only in terms of explicit attitudes toward the outgroup, but also a variety of other beneficial outcomes, including improvements in implicit (i.e., relatively inaccessible) attitudes, attitude strength, outgroup forgiveness, and generalization across individuals and groups (for a non-exhaustive summary, see Table 11.1). At this point in history there is little remaining doubt that intergroup contact has wide-ranging positive effects. But what about the essential psychological question – *why* does contact exert positive effects on intergroup attitudes?

Table 11.1 Examples of the broad range of beneficial outcomes achieved by direct, extended, and imagined contact

Citation	Target group	Outcomes						
		Explicit outgroup attitudes	Attitude strength	Implicit associations	Physiological reactions to outgroup members	Outgroup trust	Outgroup forgiveness	Attitude generalization
Direct contact (quantity)								
Blascovich et al. (2001), Experiment 3	African-Americans				✓			
Dhont et al. (2011), Studies 1–4	Immigrants	✓						
Page-Gould et al. (2010)	White- & African Americans				✓			
Tausch et al. (2010), Study 1	Greeks & Turks/Greek & Turkish Cypriots	✓						✓
Tausch et al. (2010), Study 2	Catholics & Protestants/racial minorities	✓						✓
Tausch et al. (2010), Study 4	Catholics & Protestants/racial minorities	✓						✓
Van Laar et al. (2005)	Latino & White-Asian, & African-American	✓						✓
Walker et al. (2008)	Blacks				✓			
Direct contact (quality)								
Mähönen et al. (2011)	Immigrants	✓						
Tausch et al. (2007), Study 2	Catholics & Protestants	✓		✓		✓		

Table 11.1 Continued

Citation	Target group	Outcomes Explicit outgroup attitudes	Attitude strength	Implicit associations	Physiological reactions to outgroup members	Outgroup trust	Outgroup forgiveness	Attitude generalization
Direct contact (quantity and quality)								
Aberson & Haag (2007)	African-Americans	✓						
Pettigrew (2009)	Foreigners/Muslims, Homeless, & homosexual men and women	✓		✓				✓
Prestwich et al. (2008)	Asian	✓		✓				
Tam et al. (2006)	Elderly	✓		✓				
Direct contact (quantity × Quality Index)								
Cehajic et al. (2008)	Serbs	✓				✓	✓	
Tam et al. (2007)	Catholics & Protestants					✓	✓	
Direct contact (cross-group friendships)								
Christ et al. (2010), Study 1	Foreigners	✓	✓					
Christ et al. (2010), Study 2	Catholics & Protestants		✓					
González et al. (2008)	Muslims	✓						
Hewstone et al. (2006)	Catholics & Protestants	✓				✓		
Page-Gould et al. (2008)	Latinos & White-Americans	✓			✓	✓	✓	

Study	Group					
Pettigrew (1997)	Western European outgroups/multiple non-Western European outgroups	✓				✓
Tausch et al. (2010), Study 3	White- & African-American/Hispanics, Vietnamese, & Indians	✓				✓
Turner et al. (2007b), Study 1	Asian	✓		✓		
Turner et al. (2007b), Study 4	Asian	✓			✓	
Vonofakou et al. (2007)	Homosexuals	✓	✓			

Extended contact						
Cameron & Rutland (2006)	Disabled	✓				
Cameron et al. (2007), Study 1	Disabled	✓				
Cameron et al. (2007), Study 2	Refugees	✓				
Christ et al. (2010), Study 2	Catholics & Protestants immigrants		✓			
Dhont et al. (2011), Study 2	immigrants	✓				
Eller et al. (2011)	British	✓				
Liebkind & McAlister (1999)	immigrants	✓				
Tausch et al. (2011)	Catholics & Protestants			✓		

Table 11.1 Continued

Citation	Target group	Outcomes						
		Explicit outgroup attitudes	Attitude strength	Implicit associations	Physiological reactions to outgroup members	Outgroup trust	Outgroup forgiveness	Attitude generalization
Imagined contact								
Harwood et al. (2011)	Immigrants							✓
Stathi et al. (2011)	British Muslims							✓
Turner & Crisp (2010), Study 1	Elderly			✓				
Turner & Crisp (2010), Study 2	Muslims			✓				
Turner et al. (2007a), Experiment 1	Elderly	✓						

Blascovich, Mendes, Hunter, Lickel, & Kowai-Bell (2001); Cameron & Rutland (2006); Cameron, Rutland, & Brown (2007); Cehajic, Brown, & Castano (2008); Christ, Hewstone, Tausch, Wagner, Voci, Hughes, & Cairns (2010); Dhont, Roets, & Van Hiel (2011); Eller, Abrams, & Zimmermann (2011); González, Verkuyten, Weesie, & Poppe (2008); Harwood, Paolini, Joyce, Rubin, & Arroyo (2011); Liebkind & McAlister (1999); Mähönen, Jasinskaja-Lahti, & Liebkind (2011); Moaz & McCauley (2011); Page-Gould, Mendes, & Major (2010); Tam, Hewstone, Cairns, Tausch, Maio, & Kenworthy (2007); Tam, Hewstone, Harwood Voci, & Kenworthy (2006); Tausch, Hewstone, Schmid, Hughes, & Cairns (2011); Turner & Crisp (2010); Vonofakou, Hewstone, & Voci (2007); Walker, Silvert, Hewstone, & Nobre (2008).

Note: Some of the outcomes provided here have also been shown to be mediators of the contact-prejudice relationship (e.g., Trust; see Dhont & Van Hiel, 2011; Moaz & McCauley, 2011).

At the time of writing, Pettigrew (1998) understandably lamented our lack of understanding concerning the reasons that contact reduces prejudice. Although intergroup anxiety was theoretically proposed (Stephan & Stephan, 1985), the field had not fully proposed and tested mediating mechanisms in the 1980s. The state of affairs has improved dramatically. In Table 11.2 we have compiled a lengthy, but non-exhaustive, list of recent contact studies considering direct, extended (indirect), and imagined contact effects as a function of their empirically supported mediating mechanisms. In particular, various types of contact have exerted beneficial effects on intergroup attitudes (and a variety of other outcome measures) through reducing intergroup anxiety, reducing perceptions of threat, and reducing concerns with rejection. But contact does not simply eliminate negative states and perceptions. Critically, contact augments positive emotions and encourages participants to reach out to others. In particular, contact effectively lowers prejudice by increasing empathy and perspective-taking, self-disclosure, and a sense of intimacy (overlap) with others. Contact also works because it encourages positive behaviors toward the outgroup, increases knowledge of the outgroup, promotes positive contact norms, and heightens trust in the outgroup. Other recent studies (not included in the table for simplicity) reveal that contact improves intergroup attitudes through the reduction of stereotyping (Gaunt, 2011; Vezzali & Giovannini, 2011). It is small wonder that contact has proven such a consistent and effective attenuator of negative outgroup biases. Intergroup contact operates on many levels, decreasing negativity while promoting positivity, and operating on emotional, cognitive, and behavioral factors. Few other means of reducing prejudice show such deep and diverse effects.

In answer to the question *how far have we come*, the answer is abundantly clear. The field now has solid evidence that contact benefits intergroup relations, with considerable insights into boundary conditions, and even more with regard to why contact works. Contact has clearly moved from being a mere "hypothesis" to being a full-fledged theory with clear predictions and implications (Hewstone, 2009; Hewstone & Swart, 2011).

Generalization of effects question

The fourth "problem" Pettigrew (1998) listed was not so much a problem as an unanswered question: how do contact-based attitude effects generalize across situations, from individual to group, and across groups? This issue remains somewhat unresolved, although researchers are making serious inroads (see Lolliot et al., this volume; Tausch et al., 2010). Considerable comfort can be drawn from the fact that generalization effects from contact are reliable (see Pettigrew & Tropp, 2006, Table 2). What is clear, however, is that the field has focused overwhelmingly on generalization from the individual to the group as a whole, relatively neglecting generalization across situations or to other groups. Recent progress on generalization to other groups (or *secondary transfer*) is promising (e.g., Pettigrew, 2009; Tausch et al., 2010; see also Lolliot et al., this volume), but contact generalization across situations remains a pressing issue for the field.

Table 11.2 Examples of the most common positive and negative mediators of direct, extended, and imagined contact effects

Citation	Target group	Outcome measure	Negative mediators reduced via contact			Positive mediators augmented via contact						
			Intergroup anxiety	Threat	Cognitions of rejection	Empathy	Self disclosure	Self–other overlap	Behavior change	Outgroup knowledge	In-/ outgroup positive contact norms	Outgroup trust
Direct contact (quantity)												
Dhont et al. (2011), Study 4	Immigrants	Modern racism	✓									
Dhont et al. (2011), Study 5	Immigrants	Modern racism	✓									
		Blatant racism	✓									
		Behavioral tendencies	✓									
Eller & Abrams (2004), Study 2	Mexicans	Outgroup evaluation								✓		
		Social distance								✓		
Hodson, Harry et al. (2009)	Homosexuals	Outgroup attitudes		✓				✓				
Hutchison & Rosenthal (2010), Study 1	Muslims	Outgroup attitudes	✓									
		Perceived outgroup variability	✓									
		Behavioral intentions	✓									

Study	Group	Outcome measure	Direct contact (quality)
Islam & Hewstone (1993)	Hindus & Muslims	Outgroup attitudes	✓
		Perceived variability	✓
Moaz & McCauley (2011)	Palestinians	Support for violating general principles of human rights	✓
Pagotto et al. (2010)	Immigrants	Outgroup attitudes	✓
		Crime estimation	✓
Prestwich et al. (2008)	Asians	Implicit attitudes	✓
Stephan & Stephan (1984)	Mexican-Americans	Outgroup attitudes	✓
Direct contact (quality)			
Aberson & Gaffney (2008)	African-Americans	Implicit attitudes	✓
		Explicit attitudes	✓
Eller et al. (2011)	British	Outgroup evaluation	✓
Harwood et al. (2005), Study 2	Elderly	Outgroup attitude	✓
		Perceived variability	✓
Hodson, Harry et al. (2009)	Homosexuals	Outgroup attitudes	✓

Table 11.2 Continued

Citation	Target group	Outcome measure	Negative mediators reduced via contact			Positive mediators augmented via contact						
			Intergroup anxiety	Threat	Cognitions of rejection	Empathy	Self disclosure	Self–other overlap	Behavior change	Outgroup knowledge	In-/outgroup positive contact norms	Outgroup trust
Islam & Hewstone (1993)	Hindus & Muslims	Outgroup attitudes	✓									
		Perceived variability	✓									
Mähönen et al. (2011)	Immigrants	Explicit attitudes	✓									
		Implicit attitudes	✓									
Prestwich et al. (2008)	Asians	Explicit attitudes	✓									
Tausch et al. (2007), Study 1	Catholics & Protestants	Outgroup attitudes	✓	✓								
Tausch et al. (2007), Study 2	Catholics & Protestants	Outgroup trust	✓	✓								
		Perceived variability					✓					
Viki et al. (2006)	Police	Willingness to cooperate									✓	
Direct contact (quantity and quality)												
Aberson & Haag (2007)	African-Americans	Intergroup anxiety				✓						

Study	Target group	Measure	Direct contact (quantity × quality index)
Eller & Abrams (2004), Study 1	French nationals	Outgroup evaluation	✓
		Social distance	✓
Hodson (2008), Study 2	Black inmates	Ingroup bias	✓
Tam et al. (2006)	Elderly	Interpersonal anxiety	✓
		Interpersonal empathy	✓
Stathi & Crisp (2010), Study 1	Foreigners and Britons	Outgroup evaluation	✓
Tam et al. (2009), Study 1	Catholics & Protestants	Positive behavioral action tendencies	✓
		Negative behavioral action tendencies	✓
Tam et al. (2009), Study 2	Catholics & Protestants	Positive behavioral action tendencies	✓
Voci & Hewstone (2003)	Immigrants	Outgroup attitudes	✓
		Subtle prejudice	✓
		Outgroup attitudes	✓

Table 11.2 Continued

Citation	Target group	Outcome measure	Negative mediators reduced via contact			Positive mediators augmented via contact						
			Intergroup anxiety	Threat	Cognitions of rejection	Empathy	Self disclosure	Self–other overlap	Behavior change	Outgroup knowledge	In-/outgroup positive contact norms	Outgroup trust
Direct contact (cross-group friendships)												
Barlow et al. (2009)	Australian Aborigines	Old-fashioned racism	✓									
		Issue avoidance			✓							
		Active avoidance			✓							
Binder et al. (2009)	European outgroups	Social distance	✓									
De Tezanos-Pinto et al. (2010)	Ethnic minorities	Outgroup attitudes	✓									
Eller & Abrams (2004), Study 2	Mexicans	Social distance							✓			
Feddes et al. (2009)	Turks & Germans	Outgroup evaluation		✓							✓	
Hodson, Harry et al. (2009)	Homosexuals	Outgroup attitudes						✓				
Swart et al. (2010),	White & Colored	Outgroup attitudes	✓			✓						

Study	Target group	Measure	
Study 2	South Africans	Action tendencies	✓
		Perceived variability	✓
Swart et al. (2011)	White South Africans	Perceived variability	✓
		Outgroup attitudes	✓
		Action tendencies	✓
Turner et al. (2007b), Study 1	Asians	Outgroup attitudes	✓
Turner et al. (2007b), Study 2	Asians & White British	Outgroup attitudes	✓

Direct contact (cross-group friendships)

Study	Target group	Measure	
Turner et al. (2007), Study 4	Asians	Empathy	✓
		Perceived importance of contact	✓
		Intergroup trust	✓
		Outgroup attitudes	✓
Turner et al. (2008)	Asians	Outgroup attitudes	✓

Extended contact

Study	Target group	Measure	
Cameron et al. (2006)	Refugees	Outgroup attitudes	✓
Cameron et al. (2011)	Indian-English	Explicit attitudes	✓
De Tezanos-Pinto et al. (2010)	Ethnic minorities	Outgroup attitudes	✓

Table 11.2 Continued

Citation	Target group	Outcome measure	Negative mediators reduced via contact			Positive mediators augmented via contact						
			Intergroup anxiety	Threat	Cognitions of rejection	Empathy	Self disclosure	Self–other overlap	Behavior change	Outgroup knowledge	In-/outgroup positive contact norms	Outgroup trust
Dhont & Van Hiel (2011)	Immigrants	Outgroup attitudes		✓								✓
Gómez et al. (2011)	Spaniards & immigrants	Outgroup attitudes	✓					✓			✓	
Hodson, Harry et al. (2009)	Homosexuals	Outgroup attitudes		✓								
Hutchison & Rosenthal (2010), Study 2	Muslims	Outgroup attitudes	✓									
		Perceived outgroup variability	✓									
		Behavioral intensions	✓									
Extended contact												
Mazziotta et al. (2011), Experiment 1 & 2	Chinese	Outgroup attitudes	✓									
		Willingness to engage in intergroup contact	✓									
Paolini et al. (2004), Study 1	Catholics & Protestants	Prejudice	✓				✓					
		Perceived variability	✓									

Study	Group	Measure		
Tam et al. (2009), Study 2	Catholics & Protestants	Positive behavioral action tendencies		✓
Turner et al. (2007b), Study 2	Asians & White British	Outgroup attitudes	✓	
Turner et al. (2007b), Study 3	Asians	Outgroup attitudes	✓	
Turner et al. (2008)	Asians	Outgroup attitudes	✓	

Imagined contact

Study	Group	Measure	
Husnu & Crisp (2010), Experiment 2	Muslims	Outgroup attitudes	✓
Turner et al. (2007a), Experiment 3	Homosexuals	Outgroup attitudes	✓
West et al. (2011), Experiments 3 & 4	People with schizophrenia	Outgroup attitudes	✓

Barlow, Louis, & Hewstone (2009); Binder. Zagefka, Brown, Funke, Kessler, Mummendey, Maquil, Demoulin, & Leyens (2009); Cameron, Rutland, Brown, & Douch (2006); Cameron, Rutland, Hossain, & Petley (2011); De Tezanos-Pinto, Bratt, & Brown (2010); Dhont, Roets, & Van Hiel (2011); Eller, Abrams, & Zimmerman (2011); Feddes, Noack, & Rutland (2009); Gómez, Tropp, & Fernández (2011); Harwood, Hewstone, Paolini, & Voci (2005); Hodson, Choma & Costello (2009); Hodson, Harry, & Mitchell (2009); Hutchison & Rosenthal (2010); Mahonen, Jsinskaja-Lahti, & Liebkind (2011); Mazziotta, Mummendey, & Wright (2011); Pagotto, Voci, & Maculan (2010); Paolini, Hewstone, Cairns, & Voci (2004); Prestwich, Kenworthy, Wilson, & Kwan-Tat (2008); Swart, Hewstone, Christ, & Voci (2010); Swart, Hewstone, Christ, & Voci (2011); Tam, Hewstone, Harwood, Voci, & Kenworthy (2006); Tam, Hewstone, Kenworthy, & Ca rns (2009); Tausch, Tam, Hewstone, & Kenworthy (2007); Turner, Crisp, & Lambert (2007a); Turner, Hewstone, & Voci (2007b) Turner, Hewstone, Voci, & Vonofakou (2008); Viki, Culmer, Eller, & Abrams (2006); West, Holmes, & Hewstone (2011).

In closing, the generalization question may very well prove to be the next big challenge in the contact literature. The field can now be confident that contact reduces prejudice and that the effects generalize. Yet, we have made more progress in our understanding of contact mediators than of the generalization processes involved. We still need to sharpen our focus in order to understand exactly why each type of generalization occurs, and their boundary conditions.

Outstanding issues and future directions

One promising avenue for future research concerns the distinction between contact effects on attitudes (i.e., liking an outgroup) and contact effects on policy support (i.e., favoring changes in laws or society that enhance the outgroup's position or access to rights and resources). The well-known paper by Jackman and Crane (1986) demonstrated that among White Americans, contact with Blacks was associated with more positive attitudes but not with support for policies (e.g., employment legislation) that would improve their lot in life. This interpretation has, perhaps appropriately, ushered caution among scholars (e.g., Dixon et al., 2005; Wright & Lubensky, 2008). The Jackman and Crane study has been very influential, and it certainly makes a fair point about the distinction between evaluations and reparations or policy change. However, a reanalysis of their findings demonstrates that Whites with close ties to Blacks actually do endorse public policies favoring Blacks relative to those without such ties (see Pettigrew & Tropp, 2011, p. 171). In keeping with this reanalysis, recent research among White South Africans reveals that in addition to improving attitudes toward Blacks, contact predicted policy support in multiple forms for Blacks (those dealing with compensatory measures and those granting preferential treatment; see Dixon, Durrheim, Tredoux, Tropp, Clack, Eaton, & Quayle, 2010). Given the wide-ranging effects of contact generally (see Tables 11.1 and 11.2), it is not surprising that contact effects benefit both evaluations and attitudes toward group treatment. Moreover, although potentially distinct constructs, policy support is considered by some theorists *as* a measure of racial attitudes. For instance, the Modern Racism Scale (McConahay, Hardee, & Batts, 1981), widely considered a measure of anti-Black prejudice, taps whether Blacks are given unfair advantages and influence while griping unduly. Note also that support for immigrants (as people) and immigration (as a policy) can be highly correlated (e.g., $r = .80$; Esses, Hodson, & Dovidio, 2003). In light of these considerations, it is understandable that outgroup evaluations and outgroup-relevant policy support can each be impacted by contact. Clearly this domain is a fertile ground for contact researchers.

Despite the recent advances in intergroup contact theory, the field would benefit from taking stock of what we still do not know or understand sufficiently. As mentioned previously, methodological and statistical advances have made it possible to examine the effects of contact at multiple levels, including the personal, group, neighborhood, and country (Christ & Wagner, this volume; Pettigrew, 2008). It is incumbent upon the field to utilize these methods in ways that facilitate the integration of psychological, sociological, and political models.

Many of the advances in intergroup contact have borne fruit from considering contact longitudinally. This, perhaps more than any other procedure, including experimental, has proven the strongest and most critical test of contact theory in the real world. These longitudinal tests have strengthened (not weakened) the case for contact. Future researchers are encouraged to follow up samples over prolonged periods rather than short periods. Several recent papers serve as excellent examples. Van Laar and colleagues (2005), for instance, randomly assigned participants to interracial contact partners, ruling out selection effects and many potential confounds, and subsequently followed contact effects over time. Future research can follow this procedure of random assignment followed by a longitudinal observation, going beyond random assignment to contact by additionally manipulating features of the contact situation (e.g., status; skills-training). Another example of modern progress is presented by Swart and colleagues (2011), where measures of cross-group friendship, anxiety, empathy, and prejudice were measured at multiple waves in a large sample. This approach not only allows examination of change in constructs (controlling statistically for competing predictors at different waves), but allows for the consideration of multiple mediators simultaneously to parse out which effects are unique to specific mediators of contact. Such strong interest in these cross-group friendships opens up opportunities to study changes in interpersonal closeness and empathy over time in conjunction with attitudes toward the group as a whole. Another fruitful avenue would be to examine even deeper and more intimate relationships, characterized through cross-ethnic dating or marriage.

With increased focus on longitudinal contact effects, the field can also address critical questions about *change* in contextual factors, such as alterations in the demographic make-up of neighborhoods, as when homosexuals or immigrants "move into" an area or host members drift out to the suburbs. These are effects we might try to simulate in our labs, but we also need to study these effects in neighborhoods, where the issues and implications impact group and personal life. Likewise, we can better focus on key transition points, such as moving from high school to university, or between university and work. At present many of our approaches wash over these critical influences, treating such variance as noise in the system that often weakens our effect sizes. We also encourage workers in the field to increasingly push contact research from the hallowed halls of academia to examine contact more in real world contexts. We are particularly impressed by the efforts of Dixon and colleagues to map *behavior*, such as changes in cafeteria seating choices or staking out places on beaches, research which involves observing and tracking behavioral changes systematically and unobtrusively (e.g., Clack, Dixon, & Tredoux, 2005; Dixon & Durrheim, 2003). In discussions with our colleagues we realize that the field pines for a return to the basic social psychology of the sort we love to teach in our classes – conducted by some of the pioneers of this field (Deutsch & Collins, 1951; Harding & Hogrefe, 1952; Minard, 1952; Wilner, Walkley, & Cook, 1952) – where real life intergroup processes, as experienced at work or in housing estates, transpired and was systematically observed. Our recent progress has uncovered much about mediating and moderating processes, which to some extent necessitated bringing contact back to the lab or other tightly controlled settings. With our present understanding now much improved, we can be encouraged to return to the field armed with this knowledge. The challenge, of course, will be to maintain the rigour of modern practice and an emphasis on inner processes (i.e., mediators) while balancing needs for realism.

Finally, a point raised by Aboud and Spears Brown (this volume) merits additional attention. As the authors note, limited cognitive abilities contribute to prejudice in children, so contact interventions need to teach children the *skills* for positive contact. With regard to the first component (ability), the implications for contact interventions have become increasingly clear. Intergroup contact, relative to ingroup contact, is mentally demanding and draining (Richeson & Shelton, 2003). This mental exertion explanation might account for why some people avoid contact and why contact can sometimes worsen over time. In keeping with this suggestion, recent research suggests that lower ability for abstract reasoning predicts heightened prejudice toward homosexuals through increased right-wing authoritarianism and decreased contact with homosexuals (Hodson & Busseri, 2012). Thus, adults with lower cognitive ability avoid contact, and this lower contact is associated with more prejudice. Cognitive ability, therefore, may pose a serious constraint or boundary imposed on contact interventions. However, with reference to Aboud and Spears Brown's second component, teaching skills for successful group interaction could make such encounters less mentally taxing in addition to less anxiety-provoking. The Fast Friends Procedure discussed by Davies et al. (this volume) provides a baseline framework for prompting and guiding interactants through the early stages of initial contact. Future research can explore the benefits of new contact interventions that provide the structure designed to keep the course of contact running smoothly, capitalizing on positive contact opportunities, and making successes salient. Low-threat versions of skill learning could be easily incorporated, for instance, into imagined contact paradigms (Crisp & Turner, this volume).

Concluding remarks

As is evident from this book, the field is employing a broader range of measures than was common decades ago (see Tables 11.1 and 11.2), a trend we hope to see continue. In addition to standard explicit (self-reported) measures, the field needs more implicit measures, physiological and neurological measures, and behavioral measures and outcomes, measured as unobtrusively as possible. The next stage of our model-building will undoubtedly incorporate many of the themes stressed throughout this volume, including individual differences, multiple-level effects, and the larger political and historical context framing contact. These models will need to incorporate many of the well-established *moderating effects*, such as contact improving attitudes: (a) more strongly when group memberships are salient (Brown & Hewstone, 2005); (b) well (if not better) among prejudice-prone persons (Hodson and colleagues, this volume; Hodson, 2011); (c) more strongly for majority (vs. minority) groups (Tropp & Pettigrew, 2005); and (d) more effectively through affective than cognitive or knowledge-based mechanisms (Pettigrew & Tropp, 2008). In terms of *mediating effects*, future models will likely continue to emphasize intergroup anxiety and empathy (Pettigrew & Tropp, 2008), but also more recently established mediators, such as trust and self-disclosure (see Table 11.2). With the addition of so many factors, contact theory runs the risk of becoming "too complex" once again, and thereby discouraging future researchers, and possibly policymakers too. We do not share this concern however. These recommendations are solidly grounded in the empirical record, meaning that more complex models are warranted and not mere expressions of scholars with active imaginations. Besides, contact researchers have shown an uncanny propensity to rise to existing challenges with considerable tenacity. At the end of the day, the stakes are simply too high not to model contact effects based on the empirical record, which necessitates a certain degree of complexity.

As noted in the Introduction to this book (Hodson & Hewstone, this volume), humanity is facing new challenges that will test us as never before. The world is becoming increasingly populated and increasingly migratory at the same time that finite essential resources are either plundered (e.g., oil) or polluted (e.g., water). The confluence of these trends will push the pressure points between groups. Full appreciation of the advances in intergroup contact has never been so imperative, but also never so possible. To the extent that wars are indeed fought in the "minds of men [sic]", we remain optimistic. As a species we have tremendous capacity not only for insight and flexibility, but for compassion and adaptation. Intergroup contact will undoubtedly have a prominent role in shaping the twenty-first century, not only among academics and educators, but also among policymakers.

Acknowledgments

Gordon Hodson was supported by Social Sciences and Humanities Research Council of Canada grant (410–2007–2133).

Miles Hewstone's contribution to this chapter was funded, in part, by a grant on 'Ethnoreligious diversity and trust in residential and educational settings' from the Leverhulme Trust, UK.

References

Aberson, C. L., & Gaffney, A. M. (2008). An integrated threat model of explicit and implicit attitudes. *European Journal of Social Psychology, 39*, 808–830.

Aberson, C. L., & Haag, S. C. (2007). Contact, perspective taking, and anxiety as predictors of stereotype endorsement, explicit attitudes, and implicit attitudes. *Group Processes and Intergroup Relations, 10*, 179–201.

Allport G. W. (1954). *The nature of prejudice*. Reading, MA: Addison-Wesley.

Altemeyer, B. (1994). Reducing prejudice in right-wing authoritarians. In M. P. Zanna, & J. M. Olson (Eds.), *The Psychology of Prejudice: The Ontario Symposium* (Vol. 7, pp. 131–148). Hillsdale, NJ: Lawrence Erlbaum.

Altemeyer, B. (1996). *The authoritarian specter*. Cambridge, MA: Harvard University Press.

American Time Use Survey Summary (2011). Bureau of Labour Statistics, United States

Department of Labor (Report USDL-11–0919). Retrieved from http://www.bls.gov/news.release/atus.nr0.htm

Anderssen, N. (2002). Does contact with lesbians and gays lead to friendlier attitudes? A two year longitudinal study. *Journal of Community and Applied Social Psychology, 12,* 124–136.

Asch, S. E. (1956). Studies of independence and conformity: I. A minority of one against a unanimous majority. *Psychological Monographs: General and Applied, 70,* 1–70.

Barlow, F. K., Louis, W. R., & Hewstone, M. (2009). Rejected! Cognitions of rejection and intergroup anxiety as mediators of the impact of cross-group friendships on prejudice. *British Journal of Social Psychology, 48,* 389–405.

Batson, C. D., Chang, J., Orr, R., & Rowland, J. (2002). Empathy, feelings, and action: Can feeling for a member of a stigmatized group motivate one to help the group? *Personality and Social Psychology Bulletin, 28,* 1656–1666.

Batson, C. D., Polycarpou, M. P., Harmon-Jones, E., Imhoff, H. J., Mitchener, E. C., Bednar, L. L., Klein, T. R., & Highberger, L. (1997). Empathy and attitudes: Can feeling for a member of a stigmatized group improve feelings toward the group? *Journal of Personality and Social Psychology, 72,* 105–118.

Beggan, J. K. (1992). On the social nature of nonsocial perception: The mere ownership effect. *Journal of Personality and Social Psychology, 62,* 229–237.

Binder, J., Zagefka, H., Brown, R., Funke, F., Kessler, T., Mummendey, A., Maquil, A., Demoulin, S., & Leyens, J-P. (2009). Does contact reduce prejudice or does prejudice reduce contact? A longitudinal test of the contact hypothesis among majority and minority groups in three European countries. *Journal of Personality and Social Psychology, 96,* 843–856.

Blascovich, J., Mendes, W. B., Hunter, S. B., Lickel, B., & Kowai-Bell, N. (2001). Perceiver threat in social interactions with stigmatized others. *Journal of Personality and Social Psychology, 80,* 253–267.

Brown, R., Eller, A., Leeds, S., & Stace, K. (2007). Intergroup contact and intergroup attitudes: A longitudinal study. *European Journal of Social Psychology, 37,* 692–703.

Brown, R., & Hewstone, M. (2005). An integrative theory of intergroup contact. In M. Zanna (Ed.), *Advances in Experimental Social Psychology* (Vol. 37, pp. 255–343). San Diego, CA: Academic Press.

Cameron, L., & Rutland, A. (2006). Extended contact through story reading in school: Reducing children's prejudice toward the disabled. *Journal of Social Issues, 62,* 469–488.

Cameron, L., Rutland, A., & Brown, R. (2007). Promoting children's positive intergroup attitudes towards stigmatized groups: Extended contact and multiple classification skills training. *International Journal of Behavioral Development, 31,* 454–466.

Cameron, L., Rutland, A., Brown, R., & Douch, R. (2006). Changing children's intergroup attitudes toward refugees: Testing different models of extended contact. *Child Development, 77,* 1208–1219.

Cameron, L., Rutland, A., Hossain, R., & Petley, R. (2011). When and why does extended contact work? The role of high quality direct contact and group norms in the development of positive ethnic intergroup attitudes amongst children. *Group Processes and Intergroup Relations, 14,* 193–206.

Cehajic, S., Brown, R., & Castano, E. (2008). Forgive and forget? Antecedents and consequences of intergroup forgiveness in Bosnia and Herzegovina. *Political Psychology, 29,* 351–367.

Christ, O., Hewstone, M., Tausch, N., Wagner, U., Voci, A., Hughes, J., & Cairns, E. (2010). Direct contact as a moderator of extended contact effects: Cross-sectional and longitudinal impact on outgroup attitudes, behavioral intentions, and attitude certainty. *Personality and Social Psychology Bulletin, 36*, 1662–1674.

Cikara, M., Bruneau, E. G., & Saxe, R. R. (2011). Us and them: Intergroup failures of empathy. *Current Directions in Psychological Science, 20*, 149–153.

Clack, B., Dixon, J., & Tredoux, C. (2005). Eating together apart: Patterns of segregation in a multi-ethnic cafeteria. *Journal of Community and Applied Social Psychology, 15*, 1–16.

Cook, S. W. (1979). Social science and school desegregation: Did we mislead the Supreme Court? *Personality and Social Psychology Bulletin, 5*, 420–437.

Costello, K., & Hodson, G. (2010). Exploring the roots of dehumanization: The role of animal-human similarity in promoting immigrant humanization. *Group Processes and Intergroup Relations, 13*, 3–22.

Davies, K., Tropp, L. R., Aron, A., Pettigrew, T. F., & Wright, S. C. (2011). Cross-group friendships and intergroup attitudes: A meta-analytic review. *Personality and Social Psychology Review, 15*, 322–351.

De Tezanos-Pinto, P., Bratt, C., & Brown, R. (2010). What will the others think? Ingroup norms as a mediator of the effects of intergroup contact. *British Journal of Social Psychology, 49*, 507–523.

Deutsch, M., & Collins, M. (1951). *Interracial housing: A psychological evaluation of a social experiment.* Minneapolis, MI: University of Minnesota Press.

Dhont, K., Roets, A., & Van Hiel, A. (2011). Opening closed minds: The combined effects of intergroup contact and need for closure on prejudice. *Personality and Social Psychology Bulletin, 37*, 514–528.

Dhont, K., & Van Hiel, A. (2011). Direct contact and authoritarianism as moderators between extended contact and reduced prejudice: Lower threat and greater trust as mediators. *Group Processes and Intergroup Relations, 14*, 223–237.

Dhont, K., Van Hiel, A., De Bolle, M., & Roets, A. (2012). Longitudinal intergroup contact effects on prejudice using self- and observer-reports. *British Journal of Social Psychology, 51*, 221–238.

Dixon, J., & Durrheim, K. (2003). Contact and the ecology of racial division: Some varieties of informal segregation. *British Journal of Social Psychology, 42*, 1–23.

Dixon, J., Durrheim, K., & Tredoux, C. (2005). Beyond the optimal contact strategy: A reality check for the contact hypothesis. *American Psychologist, 60*, 697–711.

Dixon, J., Durrheim, K., Tredoux, C., Tropp, L., Clack, B., & Eaton, L. (2010). A paradox of integration? Interracial contact, prejudice reduction, and perceptions of racial discrimination. *Journal of Social Issues, 66*, 401–416.

Dixon, J., Durrheim, K., Tredoux, C., Tropp, L., Clack, B., Eaton, L., & Quayle, M. (2010). Challenging the stubborn core of opposition to equality. Racial contact and policy attitudes. *Political Psychology, 31*, 831–855.

Eller, A., & Abrams, D. (2003). "Gringos" in Mexico: Cross-sectional and longitudinal effects of language school-promoted contact on intergroup bias. *Group Processes and Intergroup Relations, 6*, 55–75.

Eller, A., & Abrams, D. (2004). Come together: Longitudinal comparisons of Pettigrew's reformulated intergroup contact model and the Common Ingroup Identity Model in Anglo–French and Mexican–American contexts. *European Journal of Social Psychology, 34*, 229–256.

Eller, A., Abrams, D., & Zimmermann, A. (2011). Two degrees of separation: A longitudinal study of actual and perceived extended international contact. *Group Processes and Intergroup Relations, 14*, 175–191.

Esses, V. M., Hodson, G., & Dovidio, J. F. (2003). Public attitudes toward immigrants and immigration: Determinants and policy implications. In C. M. Beach, A. G. Green, & G. R. Jeffrey (Eds.), *Canadian Immigration Policy for the 21st Century* (pp. 507–535). Kingston: John Deutsch Institute, Queen's University.

Feddes, A. R., Noack, P., & Rutland, A. (2009). Direct and extended friendship effects on minority and majority children's interethnic attitudes: A longitudinal study. *Child Development, 80*, 377–390.

Finchilescu, G. (2010). Intergroup anxiety in interracial interaction: The role of prejudice and metastereotypes. *Journal of Social Issues, 66*, 334–351.

Finlay, K. A., & Stephan, W. G. (2000). Improving intergroup relations: The effects of empathy on racial attitudes. *Journal of Applied Social Psychology, 30*, 1720–1737.

Flynn, F. J. (2005). Having an open mind: The impact of openness to experience on inter-racial attitudes and impression formation. *Journal of Personality and Social Psychology, 88*, 816–26.

Forbes, H. (2004). Ethnic conflict and the contact hypothesis. In Y. T. Lee, C. McCauley, F. Moghaddam, & S. Worschel (Eds.), *The psychology of ethnic and cultural conflict* (pp. 69–88). New York, NY: Praeger.

Gaertner, S. L., & Dovidio, J. F. (2000). *Reducing intergroup bias: The common ingroup identity model.* Philadelphia, PA: Psychology Press.

Galinsky, A. D., & Moscowitz, G. B. (2000). Perspective-taking: Decreasing stereotype expression, stereotype accessibility, and in-group favoritism. *Journal of Personality and Social Psychology, 78*, 708–724.

Gandossy, T. (2009, February 24). *TV viewing at "all-time high", Nielsen says.* Retrieved from http://articles.cnn.com/2009-02-24/entertainment/us.video.nielsen_1_nielsen-company-nielsen-spokesman-gary-holmes-watching?_s=PM:SHOWBIZ

Gaunt, R. (2011). Effects of intergroup conflict and social contact on prejudice: The mediating role of stereotypes and evaluations. *Journal of Applied Social Psychology, 41*, 1340–1355.

Gómez, A., Tropp, L. R., & Fernández, S. (2011). When extended contact opens the door to future contact: Testing the effects of extended contact on attitudes and intergroup expectancies in majority and minority groups. *Group Processes and Intergroup Relations, 14*, 161–173.

González, K. V., Verkuyten, M., Weesie, J., & Poppe, E. (2008). Prejudice towards Muslims in the Netherlands: Testing integrated threat theory. *British Journal of Social Psychology, 47*, 667–685.

Harding, J., & Hogrefe, R. (1952). Attitudes of white department store employees toward negro co-workers. *Journal of Social Issues, 8*, 18–28.

Harwood, J., Hewstone, M., Paolini, S., & Voci, A. (2005). Grandparent-grandchild contact and attitudes toward older adults: Moderator and mediator effects. *Personality and Social Psychology Bulletin, 31*, 393–406.

Harwood, J., Paolini, S., Joyce, N., Rubin, M., & Arroyo, A. (2011). Secondary transfer effects from imagined contact: Group similarity affects the generalization gradient. *British Journal of Social Psychology, 50*, 180–189.

Hewstone, M. (2003). Intergroup contact: Panacea for prejudice? *The Psychologist, 16*, 352–355.

Hewstone, M. (2009). Living apart, living together? The role of intergroup contact in social integration. *Proceedings of the British Academy, 162*, 243–300.

Hewstone, M., Cairns, E., Voci, A., Hamberger, J., & Niens, U. (2006). Intergroup contact, forgiveness, and experience of "the troubles" in Northern Ireland. *Journal of Social Issues, 62*, 99–120.

Hewstone, M., Judd, C. M., & Sharp, M. (2011). Do observer ratings validate self-reports of intergroup contact? A round-robin analysis. *Journal of Experimental Social Psychology, 47*, 599–609.

Hewstone, M., & Swart, H. (2011). Fifty-odd years of inter-group contact: From hypothesis to integrated theory. *British Journal of Social Psychology, 50*, 374–386.

Hodson, G. (2008). Interracial prison contact: The pros for (socially dominant) cons. *British Journal of Social Psychology, 47*, 325–351.

Hodson, G. (2011). Do ideologically intolerant people benefit from intergroup contact? *Current Directions in Psychological Science, 20*, 154–159.

Hodson, G. (in press). Authoritarian contact: From "tight circles" to cross-group friendships. In F. Funke, T. Petzel, J. C. Cohrs, & J. Duckitt (Eds.), *Perspectives on authoritarianism*. Weisbaden, Germany: VS-Verlag.

Hodson, G., & Busseri, M. A. (2012). Bright minds and dark attitudes: Lower cognitive ability predicts greater prejudice through right-wing ideology and low intergroup contact. *Psychological Science, 23*, 187–195.

Hodson, G., Choma, B. L., & Costello, K. (2009). Experiencing Alien-Nation: Effects of a simulation intervention on attitudes toward homosexuals. *Journal of Experimental Social Psychology, 45*, 974–978.

Hodson, G., Harry, H., & Mitchell, A. (2009). Independent benefits of contact and friendship on attitudes toward homosexuals among authoritarians and highly identified heterosexuals. *European Journal of Social Psychology, 39*, 509–525.

Hogg, M. A., & Abrams, D. (1988). *Social identifications: A social psychology of intergroup relations and group processes*. London, UK: Routledge.

Husnu, S., & Crisp, R. J. (2010). Elaboration enhances the imagined contact effect. *Journal of Experimental Social Psychology, 46*, 943–950.

Hutchison, P., & Rosenthal, H. E. S. (2010). Prejudice against Muslims: Anxiety as a mediator between intergroup contact and attitudes, perceived outgroup variability and behavioural intentions. *Ethnic and Racial Studies, 34*, 40–60.

Islam, M. R., & Hewstone, M. (1993). Dimensions of contact as predictors of intergroup anxiety, perceived out-group variability, and out-group attitude: An integrative model. *Personality and Social Psychology Bulletin, 19*, 700–710.

Jackman, M. R., & Crane, M. (1986). "Some of my best friends are black . . .": Interracial friendship and whites' racial attitudes. *Public Opinion Quarterly, 50*, 459–486.

Jackson, J. W., & Poulsen, J. R. (2005). Contact experiences mediate the relationship between Five-Factor Model of personality traits and ethnic prejudice. *Journal of Applied Social Psychology, 35*, 667–685.

Kenworthy, J. K., Turner, R. N., Hewstone, M., & Voci, A. (2005). Intergroup contact: When does it work and why? In J. Dovidio, P. Glick, & L. Rudman (Eds.), *Reflecting on the Nature of Prejudice* (pp. 278–292). Malden, MA: Blackwell.

Leung, A. K., Maddux, W. W., Galinsky, A. D., & Chiu, C. (2008). Multicultural experience enhances creativity: The when and how. *American Psychologist, 63*, 169–181.

Levin, S., van Laar, C., & Sidanius, J. (2003). The effects of ingroup and outgroup friendships on ethnic attitudes in college: A longitudinal study. *Group Processes and Intergroup Relations, 6*, 76–92.

Liebkind, K., & McAlister, A. L. (1999). Extended contact through peer modelling to promote tolerance in Finland. *European Journal of Social Psychology, 29*, 765–780.

MacInnis, C. C., & Hodson, G. (in press). "Where the rubber hits the road" en route to intergroup harmony: Examining contact intentions and contact behavior under meta-stereotype threat. *British Journal of Social Psychology*.

Mähönen, T. A., Jasinskaja-Lahti, I., & Liebkind, K. (2011). The impact of perceived social norms, gender, and intergroup anxiety on the relationship between intergroup contact and ethnic attitudes of adolescents. *Journal of Applied Social Psychology, 41*, 1877–1899.

Mazziotta, A., Mummendey, A., & Wright, S. C. (2011). Vicarious intergroup contact effects: Applying social-cognitive theory to intergroup contact research. *Group Processes and Intergroup Relations, 14*, 255–274.

McConahay, J., Hardee, B., & Batts, V. (1981). Has racism declined? It depends on who's asking and what is being asked. *Journal of Conflict Resolution, 25*, 563– 579.

Minard, R. D. (1952). Race relations in the Pocahuntas coal field. *Journal of Social Issues, 8*, 29–44.

Moaz, I., & McCauley, C. (2011). Explaining support for violating out-group human rights in conflict: Attitudes towards principles of human rights, trust in the out-group, and intergroup contact. *Journal of Applied Social Psychology, 41*, 891–905.

Oliner, S. P., & Oliner, P. M. (1988). *The altruistic personality: Rescuers of Jews in Nazi Europe*. New York, NY: Free Press.

Page-Gould, E., Mendes, W. B., & Major, B. (2010). Intergroup contact facilitates physiological recovery following stressful intergroup interactions. *Journal of Experimental Social Psychology, 46*, 854–858.

Page-Gould, E., Mendoza-Denton, R., & Tropp, L. R. (2008). With a little help from my cross-group friend: Reducing anxiety in intergroup contexts through cross-group friendships. *Journal of Personality and Social Psychology, 95*, 1080–1094.

Pagotto, L., Voci, A., & Maculan, V. (2010). The effectiveness of intergroup contact at work: Mediators and moderators of hospital workers' prejudice towards immigrants. *Journal of Community and Applied Social Psychology, 20*, 317–330.

Paluck, E. L. (2009). Reducing intergroup prejudice and conflict using the media: A field experiment in Rwanda. *Journal of Personality and Social Psychology, 96*, 574–587.

Paolini, S., Hewstone, M., Cairns, E., & Voci, A. (2004). Effects of direct and indirect cross-group friendships on judgments of Catholics and Protestants in Northern Ireland: The mediating role of an anxiety-reduction mechanism. *Personality and Social Psychology Bulletin, 30*, 770–786.

Pettigrew, T. F. (1958). Personality and sociocultural factors in intergroup attitudes: A cross-national comparison. *Journal of Conflict Resolution, 2*, 29–42.

Pettigrew, T. F. (1997). Generalized intergroup contact effects on prejudice. *Personality and Social Psychology Bulletin, 23*, 173–185.

Pettigrew, T. F. (1998). Intergroup contact theory. *Annual Review of Psychology, 49*, 65–85.

Pettigrew, T. F. (2008). Future directions for intergroup contact theory and research. *International Journal of Intercultural Relations, 32*, 187–199.

Pettigrew, T. F. (2009). Secondary transfer effect of contact: Do intergroup contact effects spread to noncontacted outgroups? *Social Psychology, 40*, 55–65.

Pettigrew, T. F., Christ, O., Wagner, U., & Stellmacher, J. (2007). Direct and indirect intergroup contact effects on prejudice: A normative interpretation. *International Journal of Intercultural Relations, 31*, 411–425.

Pettigrew, T. F., & Tropp, L. R. (2006). A meta-analytic test of intergroup contact theory. *Journal of Personality and Social Psychology, 90*, 751–783.

Pettigrew, T. F., & Tropp, L. R. (2008). How does intergroup contact reduce prejudice? Meta-analytic tests of three mediators. *European Journal of Social Psychology, 38*, 922–934.

Pettigrew, T. F., & Tropp, L. R. (2011). *When groups meet: The dynamics of intergroup contact*. Philadelphia, PA: Psychology Press.

Poteat, V. P., Espelage, D. L., & Green, H. D. (2007). The socialization of dominance: Peer group contextual effects on homophobic and dominance attitudes. *Journal of Personality and Social Psychology, 92*, 1040–1050.

Poteat, V. P., & Spanierman, L. B. (2010). Do the ideological beliefs of peers predict the prejudiced attitudes of other individuals in the group? *Group Processes and Intergroup Relations, 13*, 495–514.

Prestwich, A., Kenworthy, J., Wilson, M., & Kwan–Tat, N. (2008). Differential relations between two types of contact and implicit and explicit racial attitudes. *British Journal of Social Psychology, 47*, 575–588.

Richeson, J. A., & Shelton, J. N. (2003). When prejudice does not pay: Effects of interracial contact on executive function. *Psychological Science, 14*, 287–290.

Rodriguez–Garcia, J. M., & Wagner, U. (2009). Learning to be prejudiced: A test of unidirectional and bidirectional models of parent-offspring socialization. *International Journal of Intercultural Relations, 33*, 516–523.

Shelton, J. N., & Richeson, J. A. (2005). Intergroup contact and pluralistic ignorance. *Journal of Personality and Social Psychology, 88*, 91–107.

Sherif, M. (1935). A study of some social factors in perception. *Archives of Psychology, 27*, 1–60.

Sibley, C. G., & Duckitt, J. (2008). Personality and prejudice: A meta-analysis and theoretical review. *Personality and Social Psychology Review, 12*, 248–279.

Sidanius, J., & Pratto, F. (1999). *Social dominance: An intergroup theory of social hierarchy and oppression*. Cambridge, UK: Cambridge University Press.

Smith, E. R., & Henry, S. (1996). An in-group becomes part of the self: Response time evidence. *Personality and Social Psychology Bulletin, 22*, 635–642.

Stathi, S., & Crisp, R. J. (2010). Intergroup contact and the projection of positivity. *International Journal of Intercultural Relations, 34*, 580–591.

Stathi, S., Crisp, R., & Hogg, M. (2011). Imagining intergroup contact enables member-to-group generalization. *Group Dynamics: Theory, Research, and Practice, 15*, 275–284.

Stephan, W. G. (2008). Brown and intergroup relations: Reclaiming a lost opportunity. In G. Adams, M. Biernat, N. R. Branscombe, C. S. Crandall, & L. Wrightsman (Eds.), *Commemorating Brown: The social psychology of racism and discrimination* (pp. 63–78). Washington, DC: American Psychological Association.

Stephan, W. G., Renfro, C. L., & Davis, M. D. (2008). The role of group threat in intergroup relations. In U. Wagner, L. R. Tropp, G. Finchilescu, & C. Tredoux (Eds.), *Improving intergroup relations: Building on the legacy of Thomas F. Pettigrew* (pp. 55–72). Malden, MA: Blackwell.

Stephan, W. G., & Stephan, C. W. (1984). The role of ignorance in intergroup relations. In N. Miller, & M. B. Brewer (Eds.), *Groups in Contact: The Psychology of Desegregation* (pp. 229–255). New York, NY: Academic Press.

Stephan, W. G., & Stephan, C. W. (1985). Intergroup anxiety. *Journal of Social Issues, 41*, 157–175.

Stephan, W. G., & Stephan, C. W. (2000). An integrated threat theory of prejudice. In S. Oskamp (Ed.), *Reducing prejudice and discrimination. "The Claremont Symposium on Applied Social Psychology"* (pp. 23–45). Mahwah, NJ: Lawrence Erlbaum Associates, Inc.

Swart, H., Hewstone, M., Christ, O., & Voci, A. (2010). The impact of crossgroup friendships in South Africa: Affective mediators and multigroup comparisons. *Journal of Social Issues, 66*, 309–333.

Swart, H., Hewstone, M., Christ, O., & Voci, A. (2011). Affective mediators of intergroup contact: A three-wave longitudinal study in South Africa. *Journal of Personality and Social Psychology, 101*, 1221–1238.

Tam, T., Hewstone, M., Cairns, E., Tausch, N., Maio, G., & Kenworthy, J. (2007). The impact of intergroup emotions on forgiveness in Northern Ireland. *Group Processes and Intergroup Relations, 10*, 119–136.

Tam, T., Hewstone, M., Harwood, J., Voci, A., & Kenworthy, J. (2006). Intergroup contact and grandparent-grandchild communication: The effects of self-disclosure on implicit and explicit biases against older people. *Group Processes and Intergroup Relations, 9*, 413–429.

Tam, T., Hewstone, M., Kenworthy, J., & Cairns, E. (2009). Intergroup trust in Northern Ireland. *Personality and Social Psychology Bulletin, 35*, 45–59.

Tausch, N., & Hewstone, M. (2010). Intergroup contact. In J. F. Dovidio, M. Hewstone, P. Glick, & V. M. Esses (Eds.), *Handbook of Prejudice, Stereotyping, and Discrimination* (pp. 544–560), London, UK: Sage.

Tausch, N., Hewstone, M., Kenworthy, J. B., Psaltis, C., Schmid, K., Popan, J. R., Cairns, E., & Hughes, J. (2010). Secondary transfer effects of intergroup contact: Alternative accounts and underlying processes. *Journal of Personality and Social Psychology, 99*, 282–302.

Tausch, N., Hewstone, M., Schmid, K., Hughes, J., & Cairns, E. (2011). Extended contact effects as a function of closeness of relationship with ingroup contacts. *Group Processes and Intergroup Relations, 14*, 239–254.

Tausch, N., Tam, T., Hewstone, M., & Kenworthy, J. (2007). Individual-level and group-level mediators of contact effects in Northern Ireland: The moderating role of social identification. *British Journal of Social Psychology, 46*, 541–556.

Tredoux, C., & Finchilescu, G. (2010). Mediators of the contact-prejudice relation among South African students on four university campuses. *Journal of Social Issues, 66*, 289–308.

Tropp, L. R., & Pettigrew, T. F. (2005). Relationships between intergroup contact and prejudice among minority and majority status groups. *Psychological Science, 16*, 951–957.

Turner, J. C., Hogg, M. A., Oakes, P. J., Reicher, S. D., & Wetherell, M. S. (1987). *Rediscovering the social group: A self-categorization theory*. Oxford: Basil Blackwell.

Turner, R. N., & Crisp, R. J. (2010). Imagining intergroup contact reduces implicit prejudice. *British Journal of Social Psychology, 49*, 129–142.

Turner, R. N., Crisp, R. J., & Lambert, E. (2007a). Imagining intergroup contact can improve intergroup attitudes. *Group Processes and Intergroup Relations, 10*, 427–441.

Turner, R. N., Hewstone, M., & Voci, A. (2007b). Reducing explicit and implicit outgroup prejudice via direct and extended contact: The mediating role of self-disclosure and intergroup anxiety. *Journal of Personality and Social Psychology, 93*, 369–388.

Turner, R. N., Hewstone, M., Voci, A., & Vonofakou, C. (2008). A test of the extended intergroup contact hypothesis: The mediating role of intergroup anxiety, perceived ingroup and outgroup norms, and inclusion of the outgroup in the self. *Journal of Personality and Social Psychology, 95*, 843–860.

Van Laar, C., Levin, S., Sinclair, S., & Sidanius, J. (2005). The effect of university roommate contact on ethnic attitudes and behavior. *Journal of Experimental Social Psychology, 41*, 329–345.

Van Oudenhoven, J. P., Groenewoud, J. T., & Hewstone, M. (1996). Cooperation, ethnic salience and generalization of interethnic attitudes. *European Journal of Social Psychology, 26*, 649–661.

Verkuyten, M., Thijs, J., & Bekhuis, H. (2010). Intergroup contact and ingroup reappraisal: Examining the deprovincialization thesis. *Social Psychology, 73*, 398–416.

Vezzali, L., & Giovannini, D. (2011). Intergroup contact and reduction of explicit and implicit prejudice toward immigrants: A study with Italian businessmen owning small and medium businesses. *Quality and Quantity, 45*, 213–222.

Vezzali, L., Giovannini, D., & Capozza, D. (2010). Longitudinal effects of contact on intergroup relations: The role of majority and minority group membership and intergroup relations. *Journal of Community and Applied Social Psychology, 20*, 462–479.

Viki, G. T., Culmer, M. J., Eller, A., & Abrams, D. (2006). Race and willingness to cooperate with the police: The roles of quality of contact, attitudes towards the behaviour and subjective norms. *British Journal of Social Psychology, 45*, 285–302.

Voci, A., & Hewstone, M. (2003). Intergroup contact and prejudice toward immigrants in Italy: The meditational role of anxiety and the moderational role of group salience. *Group Processes and Intergroup Relations, 6*, 37–54.

Vonofakou, C., Hewstone, M., & Voci, A. (2007). Contact with out-group friends as a predictor of meta-attitudinal strength and accessibility of attitudes toward gay men. *Journal of Personality and Social Psychology, 92*, 804–820.

Walker, P. M., Silvert, L., Hewstone, M., & Nobre, A. C. (2008). Social contact and other-race face processing in the human brain. *Social Cognitive and Affective Neuroscience, 3*, 16–25.

West, K., Holmes, E., & Hewstone, M. (2011). Enhancing imagined contact to reduce prejudice against people with schizophrenia. *Group Processes and Intergroup Relations, 14*, 407–428.

Wilner, D. M., Walkley, R. P., & Cook, S. W. (1952). *Human relations in interracial housing: A study of the contact hypothesis.* Minneapolis, MN: University of Minnesota Press.

Wolsko, C., Park, B., Judd, C. M., & Wittenbrink, B. (2000). Framing interethnic ideology: Effects of multicultural and color-blind perspectives on judgments of groups and individuals. *Journal of Personality and Social Psychology, 78*, 635–634.

Wright, S. C., Aron, A., McLaughlin–Volpe, T., & Ropp, S. A. (1997). The extended contact effect: Knowledge of cross-group friendships and prejudice. *Journal of Personality and Social Psychology, 73*, 73–90.

Wright, S., & Lubensky, M. (2008). The struggle for social equality: Collective action vs. prejudice reduction. In S. Demoulin, J. P. Leyens, & J. F. Dovidio (Eds.), *Intergroup misunderstandings: Impact of divergent social realities* (pp. 21–38). New York, NY: Psychology Press.

Index